Staten Island's Elliottville

Staten Island's Elliottville
Abolitionist Enclave, Gilded Age Retreat, Ferry Suburb

JAMES A. KASER

Artist unknown, *Elliottsville, S.I.* (New York: F. S. Palmer, ca. 1850). *Source:* The Staten Island Historical Society.

Published by State University of New York Press, Albany

© 2025 James A. Kaser

All rights reserved

Printed in the United States of America

No part of this book may be used or reproduced in any manner whatsoever without written permission. No part of this book may be stored in a retrieval system or transmitted in any form or by any means including electronic, electrostatic, magnetic tape, mechanical, photocopying, recording, or otherwise without the prior permission in writing of the publisher.

Links to third-party websites are provided as a convenience and for informational purposes only. They do not constitute an endorsement or an approval of any of the products, services, or opinions of the organization, companies, or individuals. SUNY Press bears no responsibility for the accuracy, legality, or content of a URL, the external website, or for that of subsequent websites.

EU GPSR Authorised Representative:
Logos Europe, 9 rue Nicolas Poussin, 17000, La Rochelle, France
contact@logoseurope.eu

For information, contact State University of New York Press, Albany, NY
www.sunypress.edu

Library of Congress Cataloging-in-Publication Data

Name: Kaser, James A., 1960– author.
Title: Staten Island's Elliottville : abolitionist enclave, gilded age retreat, ferry suburb / James A. Kaser.
Description: Albany : State University of New York Press, [2025]. | Includes bibliographical references and index.
Identifiers: LCCN 2024044678 | ISBN 9798855802382 (hardcover : alk. paper) | ISBN 9798855802344 (ebook) | ISBN 9798855802399 (pbk. : alk. paper)
Subjects: LCSH: Elliottville (New York, N.Y.)—History—19th century. | Staten Island (New York, N.Y.)—History—19th century.
Classification: LCC F127.S7 K37 2025 | DDC 974.7/26—dc23/eng/20250123
LC record available at https://lccn.loc.gov/2024044678

To the memory of my father, Leslie A. Kaser, who inspired my interest in history early in life, and to my friend and author Jonathan Ned Katz, who has reinvigorated my history writing.

Contents

List of Illustrations	ix
Preface	xi
Acknowledgments	xiii
Residents Significant to Elliottville History	xv
Timeline History of Elliottville	xxi
Introduction	1
Chapter 1 Elliottville: A Suburb of Affiliation	13
Chapter 2 Boston People: Elliottville Takes Shape	51
Chapter 3 The Years of Crisis: Elliottville, 1850 through 1865	71
Chapter 4 A Difficult Peace	123
Chapter 5 The Gilded Age Yachtsman: The Disillusionments of Reconstruction	135
Chapter 6 The 1880s: The Ascendancy of the Middle Class	175
Chapter 7 Erastus Wiman and the Death of Elliottville	213

Conclusion	241
Source Abbreviations	247
Notes	249
Index	291
About the Author	301

Illustrations

Figure 1.1	Francis "Frank" George Shaw, ca. 1861.	15
Figure 1.2	Sarah (Sturgis) Shaw and Frank Curtis, ca. 1867.	17
Figure 1.3	Elizabeth (Neall) Gay, 1854.	20
Figure 1.4	Sydney Howard Gay, ca. 1863.	21
Figure 1.5	Queens, Kings, and Richmond Counties, New York, 1829.	23
Figure 1.6	Elliottville, 1853.	28
Figure 1.7	Elliottville built environment, 1853.	31
Figure 1.8	Dr. Samuel Mackenzie Elliott, ca. 1840.	35
Figure 1.9	Dr. Elliott's house at 69 Delafield Place, built ca. 1840.	36
Figure 2.1	Sydney and Elizabeth Gay house formerly at 99 Davis Avenue.	55
Figure 2.2	Site plan by William Ranlett for "Sweet Brier [sic] Cottage" on Staten Island.	57
Figure 2.3	Frank and Sarah Shaw house formerly on Bard Avenue.	60
Figure 2.4	Alexander Jackson Downing plan on which the George William Curtis house was based.	61
Figure 2.5	George Cabot Ward, ca. 1850.	65
Figure 3.1	Elliottville, 1859.	72
Figure 3.2	George William Curtis, 1850.	78

x | Illustrations

Figure 3.3	Hand press theater program.	94
Figure 3.4	Theodore Winthrop, January 1, 1850.	97
Figure 3.5	Robert Gould Shaw, ca. 1861.	111
Figure 3.6	Josephine and Charles Russell Lowell, 1863.	118
Figure 4.1	Frank and Sarah Shaw house formerly at 4 Davis Avenue.	133
Figure 5.1	Elliottville, 1874.	136
Figure 5.2	William Thorn Garner, ca. 1875.	139
Figure 5.3	William Thorn Garner Mansion, 355 Bard Avenue.	144
Figure 5.4	The *Mohawk* racing off Sandy Hook.	147
Figure 5.5	Recovery efforts at the sunken *Mohawk*.	151
Figure 5.6	The Garner funeral in Elliottville.	154
Figure 5.7	Kaywood, the de Kay house on the southwest corner of Bard and Forest Avenues.	167
Figure 5.8	Helena (de Kay) and Richard Watson Gilder, ca. 1874.	171
Figure 5.9	Anna (Shaw) Curtis and Sarah Shaw Curtis, ca. 1864.	173
Figure 6.1	Elliottville, 1887.	177
Figure 6.2	Charles de Kay, 1868.	190
Figure 6.3	The Janet de Kay house formerly at 435 Davis Avenue.	192
Figure 6.4	Maria "Midy" Morgan, ca. 1890.	200
Figure 6.5	Maria "Midy" Morgan house at 16 Dekay Street.	203
Figure 7.1	Erastus Wiman, ca. 1886.	223
Figure 7.2	Dr. Elliott house, built ca. 1840, 30 Bard Avenue.	229
Figure 7.3	Staten Island from Wiman's perspective, 1885.	231
Figure 7.4	George William Curtis in his study, 1886.	233
Figure 7.5	Staten Island Athletic Club Boathouse, 1894.	237
Figure 7.6	Wiman's Worlds' Fair proposal, 1889.	240
Figure C.1	Broadside advertising auction of part of the late Janet de Kay's South Elliottville land.	244

Preface

This book grew out of a personal connection. For more than a decade, commuting to my office at the College of Staten Island, I drove past the former house of George William Curtis on Bard Avenue. I had a general awareness of Curtis's importance as a nineteenth-century essayist and thought the survival of his house remarkable. Eventually, my mild interest in the Curtis house shifted to broader curiosity about the Bard Avenue neighborhood when I was buying a house on the street and needed to research property maps to clarify the construction dates of outbuildings on the property.

In consulting detailed fire insurance maps, I was surprised by the number of significant houses, now long gone, owned by national figures. Over the next several years I looked at census information for Bard Avenue and began making charts of residents. I soon realized that the neighborhood had previously been named Elliottville for the earliest developer, Dr. Samuel Mackenzie Elliott, a Scottish oculist. Elliott built a series of distinctive houses he rented or sold to New Englanders, including several prominent abolitionists, such as Sydney Howard Gay (1814–1888), the editor of the *National Anti-Slavery Standard*, and his friend Francis George Shaw (1809–1882), who used his significant wealth to underwrite Brook Farm and support abolitionism. When novelist, lecturer, and essayist George William Curtis (1824–1892) married Shaw's daughter Anna in 1856, Shaw built the newlyweds a house on his property that is the one that still stands. In the years leading up to the Civil War, the neighboring properties were occupied by other highly visible New Englanders who attracted scorn for Elliottville. On Staten Island, a locale just as hostile toward the antislavery movement as New York City, the neighborhood was deemed a stronghold of "Black Republican fanatics."

After the Civil War, wealthy yachtsmen infiltrated this enclave of high-minded New Englanders. Many of the men had fortunes tied to the antebellum Southern economy and a few had even fought as Confederates. All the men had significantly increased their fortunes during the war. One of the wealthiest of the interlopers was William Thorn Garner (1840–1876) a textile magnate and member of the New York Yacht Club, who commissioned and sailed the nation's largest yacht.

While the original Bard Avenue residents privately disdained the yachtsmen and Southern sympathizers who had become their neighbors, they welcomed other newcomers. Among these were the children of Commodore George Coleman de Kay (1801–1849) and Janet (Drake) de Kay (1819–1890), who arrived to live in a house they renamed Kaywood with which they had acquired a large tract of land constituting most of South Elliottville. Janet was the daughter of Joseph Rodman Drake (1795–1820), one of the first American poets, and her children were active in the world of arts and letters in Gilded Age America.

Two other postwar arrivals, Maria "Midy" Morgan (1828–1892) and Anna Leonowens (1831–1915), were also culturally influential—as writers. Morgan, a friend of the de Kays, was a livestock journalist and expert on horses. Leonowens, who befriended Elliottville residents, wrote books about the Court of Siam while living in the neighborhood, for which she became widely known.

Researching and writing about Elliottville has been an outgrowth of my emotional connection to the Bard Avenue neighborhood. This connection is one I shared with the people about whom I wrote. Many of them lived the most important years of their lives in Elliottville and expressed in writing the neighborhood's significance for them. While I was fascinated by the personal histories of the residents, I focused on the emotional ties that linked Elliottville neighbors to each other and to the locale and the reasons why Elliottville largely disappeared as a distinct neighborhood in the first decades of the twentieth century.

Acknowledgments

Although the number of people involved is too large to list each individually, I am thankful to the staff members of Boston Athenaeum, Houghton Library, Harvard University; Massachusetts Historical Society; New York Public Library Manuscripts Division; Schlesinger Library, Radcliffe Institute for Advanced Study; and Wellesley College. For help securing an image, I thank Rachel Jirka, college archivist, Amherst College Archives and Special Collections. I also extend my gratitude to my local colleagues at Staten Island archives, Gabriella Leone (Staten Island Museum) and Carli Defillo (Historic Richmondtown) who assisted me in identifying and accessing relevant materials in the collections for which they are responsible. In addition, I extend my thanks to local historian Kristin Choo for graciously sharing information about Dr. Samuel Mackenzie Elliott and connecting me with a descendant of Dr. Elliott, Stephen Livingston. Livingston gave permission for me to use an image of the painting he owns depicting Dr. Elliott, who was his maternal grandmother's great-grandfather. Livingston also read a draft of this book and made helpful suggestions and comments. Finally, I thank Jessica Murray for her help with reviewing and editing the image files for the illustrations.

 I am grateful for the research support I received through two City University of New York programs. Through the Professional Staff Congress–City University of New York Research Award Program, I was granted travel funds for research in 2022/2023 and 2023/2024. Through the reassignment leave program, I was granted research time in fall 2023.

Residents Significant to Elliottville History

Bard, William (1778–1853). Dr. Samuel Mackenzie Elliott seems to have rented his first property in the neighborhood from William Bard prior to purchasing land from him. William Bard's grandsons, the Delafields, substituted Bard Avenue signs for the Elliottville one Elliott had put up, and the name endured.

Bonner, Edward H. (1839–1911); George T. (1837–1924). The Bonners were wealthy Wall Street brokers who settled in the heart of Elliottville and maintained large properties there into the twentieth century, preserving the neighborhood. George purchased Frank Shaw's house in 1882 and named it Stadacona. Edward purchased a neighboring property and named it Inchegeelah. They were active in Staten Island charitable and social organizations.

Curtis, George William [hereafter George Curtis] (1824–1892). A well-known novelist, essayist, and public speaker before marrying Anna Shaw (1836–1923) in 1855 and moving to Staten Island, Curtis was a founder of the Republican Party, had a long career in Republican politics, was the political editor for *Harper's Weekly*, and wrote the widely read Easy Chair column for *Harper's Magazine*. He lived all his married life on Bard Avenue and the neighborhood was closely identified with him.

de Kay Family. Janet (Drake) de Kay [hereafter Janet de Kay] (1819–1890), the only child of Manhattan poet and author Joseph Rodman Drake (1795–1820) and widow of Commodore George Coleman de Kay (1802–1849), moved onto a large tract of land with four of her children in 1867, keeping the property intact until her death, and helped maintain the character of Elliottville. The sale of the land, laid out in house lots, by her heirs after 1893, transformed the neighborhood. Janet's son Sidney Brooks (1845–1890) and his wife Minna (Craven) de Kay (1843–1927) lived in Haywood, near the corner of Bard Avenue and Castleton Street for almost twenty years, raised a family there, and were active in social life in the neighborhood. Two of Janet's other children, Helena (de Kay) Gilder (1847–1916) and Charles de Kay (1848–1935), came of age in the neighborhood, had a significant impact on local social life, and maintained lifelong friendships with residents. Helena was the wife of Richard Watson Gilder (1844–1909), poet and editor of *The Century*, and the Gilders were at the center of a social circle that included some of the most accomplished writers and artists of their day. Helena was a co-founder of the Art Students League and the Society of American Artists. Charles was a respected poet and art critic for *The New York Times*. In addition to serving as US consul general in Berlin, he was a founder of the National Arts Club, and a renowned fencer who founded the Fencers Club.

Dewing, Maria (Oakey) (1845–1927). Artist and wife of painter Thomas Dewing (1851–1938), Dewing grew up in Elliottville and was Helena (de Kay) Gilder's closest friend there. The two supported each other's artistic ambitions, shared a studio, and helped found the Art Students League.

Elliott, Dr. Samuel Mackenzie (1807[?]–1875).[1] A Scottish immigrant, he was a widely consulted oculist who treated Henry Wadsworth Longfellow and other men who later became well-known writers, like James Russell Lowell and Francis Parkman. He bought land on Staten Island in 1839 and built at least twenty-two houses, many designed by architect William Ranlett. Although he moved out of the neighborhood, he retained property in the neighborhood, where a number of his children lived. He returned in 1870 to live out the last years of his life in Elliottville. At the outbreak of the Civil War, he helped recruit men for the Seventy-Ninth New York Infantry Regiment and was for a time in command.

Garner, William Thorn [hereafter William Garner] (1840–1876). Garner and his wife, Mary Marcellite (Thorn) Garner (1842–1876), treated their mansion at 355 Bard Avenue as a summer residence. When they drowned on Garner's *Mohawk*, the world's largest private yacht, national newspaper coverage brought notoriety to Bard Avenue as the "Fifth Avenue of Staten Island," where a number of yachtsmen owned mansions.

Gay, Elizabeth (Neall) (1819–1907). The granddaughter of Quaker abolitionist Warner Mifflin and daughter of abolitionist Daniel Neal Sr., she attended the 1840 World Anti-Slavery Convention in London with Lucretia Mott, Sarah Pugh, and other women. Their experience of being excluded and confined to the spectators' gallery was an impetus for the American women's suffrage movement in the United States. Elizabeth married Sydney Gay in 1845. She became a treasured friend of Elliottville residents. It is due to her efforts to preserve her own correspondence and that of family members that we know so much about life in Elliottville. Two of her children, Sarah Mifflin Gay (1852–1901) and Martin Gay (1854–1935), were socially active among Elliottville young people in the 1860s and 1880s.

Gay, Sydney Howard [hereafter Sydney Gay] (1814–1888). An abolitionist, Gay edited the *National Anti-Slavery Standard* for fourteen years. With the help of Louis Napoleon and other Blacks, Gay aided hundreds of fugitives from slavery to pass through New York to freedom. During the Civil War, he was the influential managing editor of the *New-York Tribune*. He settled with his wife Elizabeth (Neall) Gay in one of Dr. Elliott's houses in 1847 and lived on the property, almost continuously, until his death. As the close friend of George Curtis and Frank Shaw, Gay was a key figure in social life in Elliottville.

Henderson, John C. (1809–1884). Henderson had made a fortune as a merchant and property developer. His large estate was across Bard Avenue from the Curtis, Shaw, and Gay properties. Over the course of two marriages, he had twelve children. He and his second wife, Jane Louisa Rapallo (1821–1880), and their family were significant for decades in Elliottville.

Johnson, Laura (Winthrop) [hereafter Laura Johnson] (1825–1889). Johnson, wife of William Templeton Johnson (1811–1868) moved with him to Elliottville in 1851, and they were neighbors and close friends of the Curtises, Gays, and Shaws. Johnson took seriously her role as a social organizer, hosting frequent events. Her twenty-seven-year correspondence with Annie Adams Fields (1834–1915), the wife of publisher James Fields, is an important resource for information about life in Elliottville. She edited for posthumous publication the novels and travel writings of her brother Theodore Winthrop, as well as publishing her own poetry and travel writings.

Leonowens, Anna (1831–1915). She opened a school attended by Elliottville children in 1868 (mostly taught by her daughter Avis Anna [Leonowens] Fyshe [1854–1902]) and became a lifelong friend of many people in the neighborhood (Avis was friends with young people in the neighborhood). Leonowens wrote the books on Siam for which she is known today in Elliottville, where she had her primary residence until 1874. George Curtis and Frank Shaw were crucial in establishing her as a writer and lecturer.

Livingston, Anson (1807–1873). Owner of the mansion that would give the surrounding area, including Elliottville, the name "Livingston" after his widow Ann (née Greenleaf) Livingston (1809–1887) sold the house to the Staten Island Rapid Transit Co. to be used as a station.

Morgan, Maria "Midy" [also sometimes "Middy"; hereafter Midy Morgan] (1828–1892). Nationally known as one of the first female journalists, she was respected for her knowledge of livestock, and particularly horses. She was a colleague of Charles de Kay at *The New York Times* and a friend of Jeannette Gilder (another female journalist), who was Helena (de Kay) Gilder's sister-in-law. For years, the detailed descriptions of the house she built on Bard Avenue attracted new interest in the neighborhood.

Rokeby, Ralph Thomas [hereafter Ralph Rokeby] (1863–1924). Owner of the Bard Avenue house named Willowbrook, Rokeby was an English immigrant who was a principal in international business corporations. His attachment to his property helped maintain the character of the neighborhood into the twentieth century.

Shaw, Francis "Frank" George [hereafter Frank Shaw] (1809–1882). Shaw moved his family to Elliottville while his wife, Sarah Blake (Sturgis) Shaw [hereafter Sarah Shaw] (1815–1902), was being treated by Dr. Elliott. The Shaw house, between George Curtis's and Sydney Gay's, was a focus of neighborhood social life. The Shaws were abolitionists and Frank Shaw helped fund Brook Farm, a social experiment to which many Elliottville residents were connected. Shaw held positions in national organizations focused on freedmen's education during and after the Civil War. Shaw's son, Robert Gould Shaw (1837–1863), died heroically in the Civil War while leading the first all-Black regiment formed in the Northeast. Shaw's daughter Josephine (Shaw) Lowell [hereafter Josephine Lowell] (1843–1905) was a Progressive reform leader after the Civil War active in many social justice causes, who is best known as the founder of the New York Consumers' League in 1890.

Willcox, Mary Otis (Gay) [hereafter Mary Willcox] (1861–1933). The youngest daughter of Sydney and Elizabeth Gay, she married William Goodenow Willcox (1859–1923) and the two of them lived on the Gay family property until each of them died. Willcox was a longtime board member of the Tuskegee Institute and Mary was a leader in the New York suffragist movement, and later in the League of Women Voters.

Winthrop, Theodore Woolsey (1828–1861). During the 1850s, Winthrop lived in the household of his sister, Laura Johnson, and wrote novels. After his heroic battlefield death at Big Bethel, the first pitched land battle of the Civil War, he quickly became the Union's first martyr. While living on Staten Island, he became friends with Elliottville neighbors, particularly Robert Gould Shaw and George Curtis. Curtis wrote a biographical essay for the first of his posthumously published novels.

Timeline History of Elliottville

1834   Dr. Samuel Mackenzie Elliott arrives in New York and first visits Staten Island.

1836   Dr. Elliott opens a Manhattan office.

1839   Dr. Elliott buys his first Staten Island property.

1840   Between 1840 and 1846, Dr. Elliott treats New Englanders who are either friends or relatives of the people who later settle in Elliottville. His patients include James Russell Lowell, Charles Eliot Norton, Henry Wadsworth Longfellow, and Francis Parkman.

1847   Sydney Gay and his wife Elizabeth begin living in one of Dr. Elliott's houses.

1847   Dr. Elliott treats Sarah Shaw, and, later, her husband and their children move to Elliottville and rent a house from Dr. Elliott for four years.

1847   Brook Farm, the utopian community supported by Frank, comes to an end. A number of former Brook Farm residents are treated by Dr. Elliott for eye disorders.

1848   John Bethune Staples (1807–1884) and his wife Elizabeth Douglass (Young) move to Elliottville.

1849   Birth of John Bethune Staples's son Markham (1849–1901).

1850   William Templeton and Laura Johnson move to Elliottville.

1851   The Shaws leave on an extended European trip.

1852   Birth of Sydney and Elizabeth Gay's daughter, Sarah Mifflin Gay.

1852   Birth of William and Laura Johnson's son, Oliver Templeton Johnson (1852–1891).

1853   Map of Staten Island published by James Butler includes an inset "View of Elliottville," whose properties are still mostly owned by Dr. Elliott.

1854   Frank Shaw purchases fifteen acres of land from Dr. Elliott and begins having a house designed and constructed.

1854   Laura's mother, Elizabeth Woolsey Winthrop (1794–1863), moves in with the Johnsons.

1854   Theodore Winthrop moves in with the Johnsons.

1854   Birth of Sydney and Elizabeth Gay's son Martin.

1855   Dr. Elliott moves to Grymes Hill.

1855   The Shaws return from Europe before their house is ready and they summer in Newport.

1855   George Curtis courts Anna Shaw in Newport; in December, they are betrothed.

1856   The Shaws move into their new house in Elliottville.

1856   Elliottville becomes a campaign base for presidential candidate John C. Frémont and Curtis is a key orator on his behalf.

1856   Curtis and Anna Shaw marry at the Unitarian Universalist Church of the Redeemer on Staten Island.

1857   George Cabot Ward (1824–1887) and his wife Anna move to Elliottville.

1857   Birth of George and Anna Curtis's son Francis "Frank" George (1857–1936).

1858   Dr. Elliott is one of the founders of the Highland Guard, or Seventy-Ninth New York Militia.

1859   The Curtises move into a new house, paid for by Frank Shaw and located next door to him (the address will become 234 Bard Avenue).

1860   Laura Johnson's brother William Winthrop (1831–1899) moves into the Johnson household.

1861	The Curtises' daughter Elizabeth Burrill (1861–1914) is born a few days after Ft. Sumter is fired upon.
1861	Robert Gould Shaw and Theodore and William Winthrop enlist in the Seventh New York Militia to defend Washington, DC.
1861	The Seventy-Ninth New York Militia is called into service; Dr. Elliott recruits men and takes command as lieutenant colonel on May 29, 1861.
1861	Theodore Winthrop, a recently commissioned Major, is killed at the Battle of Big Bethel on June 10.
1861	Dr. Elliott is seriously wounded on July 21 in the First Battle of Bull Run.
1861	Curtis helps Laura Johnson edit Theodore Winthrop's novel *Cecil Dreeme* and writes a biographical preface for the book that Curtis's friend James Field publishes in October.
1861	Anson Livingston and his family move to Bard Avenue.
1861	Sydney and Elizabeth Gay's daughter, Mary Otis (1861–1933), is born on December 20.
1862	Susie Shaw marries Robert Bowne Minturn Jr. in Elliottville in October.
1863	Robert Gould Shaw, Frank Shaw, George Curtis, and Frederick Law Olmsted are among the founders of the Union League Club, dedicated to supporting the Union and raising money for the United States Sanitary Commission. Other Elliottville men are early members.
1863	Robert Gould Shaw takes command of the Fifty-Fourth Massachusetts Volunteer Infantry.
1863	Draft riots spread to Staten Island and bands of youths make periodic violent attacks from July 14 through 20.
1863	Robert Gould Shaw is killed at Ft. Wagner on July 18.
1863	Susie and Robert Minturn's son, Robert Shaw Minturn (1863–1918), is born August 21.
1863	Josephine Shaw marries Charles Russell Lowell on October 31.

1863	George and Anna Curtis's daughter Sarah "Sally" Susannah Shaw (1863–1874) is born May 17.
1863	William and Laura Johnson's daughter Laura Winthrop (1863–1917) is born May 24.
1863	Elizabeth Woolsey Winthrop dies.
1864	Charles Russell Lowell dies from battlefield injuries October 20.
1864	Josephine Lowell gives birth to Carlotta Russell Lowell November 30.
1865	Robert and Susie Minturn's daughter Sarah (1865–1914) is born.
1866	The American Freedmen's and Union Commission is formed and Frank Shaw becomes a vice president and executive committee member; George Cabot Ward also serves as vice president and sometimes chairman of the finance committee.
1867	Ellen Shaw (1845–1936) marries Francis Channing Barlow (1834–1896).
1867	Susie and Robert Minturn's daughter Edith (1867–1937) is born.
1867	Janet de Kay and three of her children move to Bard Avenue.
1868	Anna Leonowens opens a school in Elliottville and lives nearby until 1874, becoming a close friend of many Elliottville residents.
1868	George Curtis addresses the Women's Suffrage Association and vigorously supports women's suffrage at the New York State Constitutional Convention.
1868	William Templeton Johnson dies.
1869	Ellen and Frank Barlow's son Robert Shaw Barlow (1869–1913) is born.
1869	Susie and Robert Bowne Minturn Jr. move into the Shaw house and Frank and Sarah Shaw move in December to a house on Richmond Terrace at 4 Davis Avenue.
1870	William Garner moves to Bard Avenue.
1871	George Curtis is appointed chair of the Civil Service Reform Commission by President Ulysses. S. Grant.

1871	Susie and Robert Minturn's son Francis (1871–1878) is born.
1872	Susie and Robert Minturn's daughter Gertrude (1872–1939) is born.
1873	Anson Livingston dies.
1875	William Garner launches his yacht *Mohawk* on June 9.
1875	Dr. Elliott dies.
1875	Susie and Robert Minturn's daughter Mildred (1875–1922) is born.
1876	Garner, his wife, and his brother-in-law die when the *Mohawk* capsizes on July 20.
1876	Josephine Lowell is the first woman appointed commissioner of the New York State Board of Charities.
1878	Susie and Robert Minturn's son Frank dies of diphtheria.
1881	George Curtis is founding president of the National Civil Service Reform League.
1882	Josephine Lowell founds the New York Charity Organization.
1882	Susie and Robert Minturn's son Hugh (1882–1915) is born.
1882	Frank Shaw dies.
1882	The Shaw/Minturn house is sold to George T. Bonner, who renames it Stadacona (he owns and lives in it for forty years).
1883	Midy Morgan begins building her house just off Bard Avenue.
1884	John Bethune Staples dies.
1884	John C. Henderson dies.
1885	Erastus Wiman (1834–1904), as an investor and president of the Staten Island Rapid Transit Co., formalizes an agreement with the Baltimore and Ohio Railroad that includes a freight line on the North Shore that separates Bard Avenue from the waterfront.
1886	The Anson Livingston mansion is sold and becomes a station for the Staten Island Rapid Transit Co.
1886	Josephine Lowell founds the House of Refuge for Women (later known as the New York Training Schools for Girls).

1887	George Cabot Ward dies.
1888	Sydney Gay dies.
1888	Josephine Lowell founds the New Brighton Village Improvement Association to address quality of life issues brought by the railroad line along the shore.
1889	Laura Johnson dies.
1889	Robert Bowne Minturn Jr. dies.
1889	George Curtis publishes his threnody of grief for the loss of Elliottville to "progress."
1889	Mary Otis Gay marries William Goodenow Willcox.
1890	Josephine Lowell founds the New York Consumers' League.
1891	Oliver Templeton Johnson dies.
1892	George Curtis dies.
1892	Midy Morgan dies.
1894	Josephine Lowell founds the Women's Municipal League.
1895	Josephine Lowell founds the Civil Service Reform Association of New York.
1899	Jane Morgan, Midy's sister, dies, and the house interiors are subsequently sold.
1901	Sarah Gay dies.
1902	Sarah Shaw dies.
1905	Josephine Lowell dies.
1907	Elizabeth Winthrop dies.
1907	Elizabeth Gay dies.
1914	Elizabeth Curtis dies.
1923	Anna Curtis dies.
1933	Mary Willcox dies.

Introduction

This book traces a Staten Island neighborhood's nineteenth-century history. While changes in the built and physical environment are of interest, the focus is on the friendships of residents, friendships that spanned decades and generations of families and established a sense of belonging and connection to a very specific place. The neighborhood was known as Elliottville[2] from, roughly, the 1850s through the mid-1870s, although the name never had any jurisdictional significance. The area was a district within the town of Castleton in Richmond County, New York. While the locality's name changed, the neighborhood remained a distinctive community from approximately 1840 to 1890 (and, therefore, "Elliottville" is used as a place designation throughout the book). In area, Elliottville was quite compact, covering approximately twelve blocks on either side of Bard Avenue. Dr. Samuel Mackenzie Elliott, a Scottish immigrant and eye surgeon, originally owned most of the land and built twenty-two houses. He preferred the name Elliottville, and the designation appears on a map from 1853. Nevertheless, the Bard family, from whom Elliott had purchased land, rejected the name. The Bard surname became attached to the central avenue, and over time the neighborhood was referred to as the Bard Avenue section of West Brighton and, finally, as the Bard Avenue neighborhood of Livingston. Most of these changes had to do with infrastructure developments (a post office in West Brighton and a streetcar depot in the former Livingston mansion). Elliottville residents tried to resist but eventually resigned themselves to their neighborhood being blended into larger geographic designations by government bodies, in part because their mail got misdirected when they did not conform. For them, no matter the name changes or postal jurisdictions, they had only one name for the quarter, "Our Neighborhood."[3]

Not only Elliottville residents but also the people of Staten Island, Manhattan, and to some extent the nation regarded the neighborhood as an enclave quite distinct from the rest of Staten Island. Initially, Elliottville residents shared New England origins and a commitment to the abolition of slavery. By the 1870s, although the neighborhood was still considered an enclave, the qualities the residents shared were more amorphous and had more to do with social distinction based on achievement or wealth rather than shared origins or a devotion to social reform (although reformers and New Englanders were still in the majority). Although references to the neighborhood in the local and national press changed over time from an enclave of abolitionists to the "Fifth Avenue of Staten Island" to "the intellectual part of Staten Island," from the 1840s to the 1890s there was general agreement that the residents were distinctive, and the neighborhood stood apart from the rest of Staten Island.

Using Elliottville as a frame for historical research is useful for exploring the series of topics with which this book is concerned. First, although biographies have been written about several residents (George Curtis, Sydney Gay, Anna Leonowens, Josephine Shaw, Robert Gould Shaw, and Frank Shaw), none of these accounts emphasize the importance of neighborhood friendships for their subjects—friendships that were often the most significant in their lives. Focusing on these friendships, as this book does, deepens our understanding of individual biographies.

Second, any history of Elliottville contributes to women's history since women were at the center of the community. Most residents moved to Elliottville to establish family life. The nineteenth-century cult of domesticity considered supremely important the role of women in maintaining a home, caring for her husband and children, providing a moral compass for her husband, and teaching morality to her children. Women were considered crucial to the maintenance of civilization. Elliottville women were at the center of social life, provided support for national and local charities and social reform organizations (dedicated to abolishing slavery, educating Blacks, aiding the poor, and securing women's rights), and maintained the friendship circles from which their husbands and children benefited. In general, neighborhood women were in companionate marriages and respected by their spouses. George Curtis wrote one of the most important nineteenth-century essays in defense of women's rights, and Sydney Gay contributed to women's rights publications. However, many of the women in Elliottville were deeply frustrated, mostly due to the social conventions that prevented women from having meaningful work outside the home. Not only were they barred from professions, even in the realm of social reform they were limited to women's auxiliary organizations. The neighborhood women born after the Civil War, like Maria (Oakey) Dewing and Helena (de Kay) Gilder, who had opportunities closed to earlier generations, were still relegated to supporting roles to their famous husbands. Even though Elliottville women loved their husbands, families, and friends, they spoke of feeling trapped in their households and limited in their opportunities.

Third, study of the neighborhood provides insights into a very specific type of suburban development that was distinctive in two ways, as a suburb of affiliation and as a ferry suburb. The earliest residents, who were also the most influential during the neighborhood's development, had a set of shared values. They were New Englanders, most of whom had a connection to Brook Farm and the transcendental movement in general. Their love of nature and conviction that self-cultivation was best achieved in a rural environment forced them out of rapidly urbanizing Manhattan. Furthermore, while Elliottville was a rural refuge across the water from the city, it was also a moral and intellectual refuge. In the decades before and during the Civil War, neighborhood residents were abolitionists, and several were movement leaders. Sharing their convictions in many settings, particularly New York City, could attract hostility.[4] At home Elliottville residents could openly share their convictions, their trials, and their breakthroughs, and benefit from the social support of their community. Regarding Elliottville as a suburb whose residents chose to live there, not exclusively due to real estate considerations but due to shared values, contributes to the history of suburbs in the United States. Although popular perception associates suburbs with the 1950s, in fact the 1840s and 1850s saw the growth of communities that today we would call suburbs, in areas adjacent to urban developments. Elliottville should be considered one of these early suburbs.

Elliottville is an example of a ferry suburb, and this work adds to the existing historiography on this very particular type of suburban development. The neighborhood would not have existed were it not for the fact that a ferry on the waterfront near the foot of Bard Avenue linked the community with lower Manhattan. While a few residents had independent means, most of them worked within walking distance of the Dey Street ferry dock in Manhattan in a neighborhood of law offices and brokerage houses. The dock was also near Park Row, or Newspaper Row, where George Curtis and Sydney Gay (and later Midy Morgan and Charles de Kay) worked. The ferry also linked residents to social life in

Manhattan and Brooklyn. Elliottville residents visited family members, attended school, participated in private clubs and social reform organizations, visited Central Park, and attended art exhibitions, concerts, lectures, and church in the greater metropolitan area. While many aspects of New York City suburban development have been explored, no one has looked at the ferry suburb of Elliottville.

Fourth, the story of Elliottville ends with environmental degradation that began as early as 1877. Pursuing this topic contributes to the environmental history of the United States. Thus far, Staten Island environmental history has focused on the twentieth century, due to Fresh Kills Landfill, a waste disposal facility established in 1948 that within seven years was the largest landfill in the world, and for the last decade it existed, was the only facility receiving New York City's residential waste. From 1840 to 1880, Elliottville was known for rural beauty and easy access to a scenic waterfront where people swam and boated. Starting in the 1880s a railroad freight line separated the community from the waterfront. By this time, New Jersey oil refineries across the Kill van Kull were polluting the water and destroying the air quality. The decline in quality of life in Elliottville was rapid and altered the community dramatically; over a few decades, the estate properties that had characterized the area were torn down, the land subdivided, and the built environment became more consistent with other early twentieth-century suburban development on Staten Island.

Chapter Overview

Chapter 1 looks at the founding of Elliottville in the context of suburban development on the North Shore of Staten Island, detailing what set Elliottville apart from other suburbs: the influx of people with New England ancestry who were attracted to rural beauty and the opportunity to live in a community with neighbors who shared their values. Of course, at the center of the story is Dr. Elliott, and an account of his medical career is used to uncover those qualities that attracted some of his patients to settle near him. Chapter 2 details the people who lived in Elliottville in the 1840s and 1850s, when the community was distinctive on Staten Island, and in the larger metropolitan area, for its abolitionist inhabitants, several of whom were nationally prominent, including orator and essayist George Curtis and Sydney Gay, who after his editorship of the *National Anti-Slavery Standard* went on to become managing editor of the *New-York*

Tribune, one of the country's most widely read pro-Union newspapers. Chapter 3 looks at Elliottville in the 1850s through the Civil War, when George Curtis and Sydney Gay played influential roles in shaping national opinion and two men from the neighborhood, Theodore Winthrop and Robert Gould Shaw, became national heroes after their battlefield deaths. Chapter 4 looks at the challenges of the postwar years, as old-time residents had to adapt to life without the cause of abolitionism to provide meaning, mostly through embracing Progressive reform, and examines the impact of Anna Leonowens on the neighborhood and the neighborhood on Leonowens's books. Chapter 5 presents the loss of homogeneity in the neighborhood as Gilded Age figures with vastly different values, some of whom had been Confederates, moved in. Chapter 6 looks at members of a newly emerging social class of managers and information professionals who settled in a rapidly changing Elliottville impacted by environmental degradation. Chapter 7 presents Erastus Wiman's successful plan to establish a freight railroad line along the waterfront at the foot of Bard Avenue. His populist campaign, mounted on behalf of progress and the public good, while mendacious, quashed effective opposition from Elliottville residents, who, despite their philanthropies and social activism, could easily be dismissed as "villa dwellers." The book ends with a description of the environmental degradation Elliottville suffered and the subsequent change in the built environment as houses were torn down, to be replaced with tract housing, and Elliottville lost its distinctive character, becoming indistinguishable from the rest of Staten Island.

A Note on Sources

What sources are available for such a project, particularly since most interactions among neighbors were direct? While people in the nineteenth century were inveterate writers of letters, there was usually no need to write letters to neighbors. A series of accidents resulted in historical documentation for the interpersonal connections among Elliottville residents, and neighborhood women preserved a significant amount of that documentation.

The Sydney Gay family was central to the life of the neighborhood, and Elizabeth Gay conscientiously preserved the family correspondence. Elizabeth was filled with energy and commitment to social reform but had few socially acceptable outlets for either. During her married life, she had to cope with Sydney's vocational crises and emotional and physical challenges. She also survived the death of her first child, the disability of one of her daughters, and anxieties over the illnesses of those close to her. Commencing when she was a young married woman and throughout the rest of her life, she wrote letters to friends, family members, and her own children. In her letters, she articulated her thoughts and feelings and communicated news of family and friends. Since many of her friends were Elliottville residents, the letters convey a sense of neighborhood life and her emotional connection to her neighbors. She had occasion to write to Sydney, her children, and her neighbors when she, or they, were away from home. She mostly traveled to Philadelphia to visit family and friends, but for several years she was forced to relocate to Illinois when Sydney worked as the managing editor for the *Chicago Tribune*.

We know that Elizabeth Gay accorded great importance to correspondence, since we have the letters in which she instructed her children on letter writing. Her most substantive instructions concerned what to include in letters. Most importantly, letters should contain information and observations that would be of interest to the recipient, but gossip was to be avoided. Letters should also be frequent. While one was to write to friends regularly, she encouraged her husband and children to write every day during periods of separation. Finally, letters were to have good handwriting. This was often difficult to achieve with a first try. Typically, the letters that got mailed were second drafts. Elizabeth Gay often retained her own drafts, which is why we have so many letters that would otherwise have been lost.

Elizabeth Gay also collected letters from their recipients, assembling an impressive archive. She had the longest correspondence of her life with a childhood friend, Sarah Pugh (1800–1884). Pugh was the leader of the Philadelphia Female Anti-Slavery Society and had also attended the World Anti-Slavery Convention in London in 1840 with Elizabeth. She returned to live in Philadelphia for the rest of her life. While Pugh and Gay periodically visited, correspondence was the most important way they maintained their friendship. When Pugh died, her family discovered Gay's letters and returned them. Gay was surprised and moved. The bundles of letters must have confirmed her long conviction as to the importance of correspondence, but they also prompted thoughts about other surviving letters and what would happen to them upon the deaths of their recipients. She contacted correspondents to ask for letters back. Since she also mentioned occasional efforts to find specific letters or copies of letters in the family attic; she seems to have organized her own and family member's letters to some extent.

Considering all her efforts to collect and organize the letters, it is surprising that either she made no definite plans for the archive upon her death or her family members failed to carry out her wishes. For decades, the bundled letters were forgotten and endangered, stored in the loft of a barn on the Gay family property on Staten Island until they were rediscovered in the 1950s and subsequently sold to Columbia University.

Although the Gay family papers constitute the most comprehensive body of material documenting life in Elliottville, other smaller collections also survived. Although Sarah Shaw, perhaps disturbed by Elizabeth Gay's attempts to gather private correspondence, instructed her correspondents to destroy her letters, she made certain that the letters of her son, Robert Gould Shaw, who died heroically during the Civil War, were preserved and shared. Frank and Sarah Shaw also kept and treasured the letters they received from Lydia Maria Child, the famous writer and abolitionist thinker who was one of their closest friends for decades. Although only Child's side of the correspondence survives, her letters often refer to, or comment on, news the Shaws conveyed about Elliottville. Child also visited the Shaws on Staten Island and wrote evocative descriptions of what she remembered from her visits.

While George Curtis's correspondence must have been vast, a modest number of his letters still exist as portions of the archives of historic figures. Interviewed in 1949, a Curtis family relative said that the Curtis archives had remained intact until they descended to his grandchildren, who sold autographed letters through the auction house Goodspeed and destroyed personal letters.[5] Most of the surviving letters are in the papers of the men to whom they were written: artist Christopher Pearse Cranch (1813–1892), scholar Charles Eliot Norton (1827–1908), and poet James Russell Lowell (1819–1891). Although few in number, the letters are useful since Curtis loved Elliottville and often wrote to his friends with news and observations about the neighborhood.

Like Curtis, Sydney Gay corresponded with James Russell Lowell. His surviving letters to Lowell are much more numerous and cover a much longer period than those of Curtis. One reason for the number of letters was Lowell's role as a contributor to the *National Anti-Slavery Standard*. Furthermore, Lowell and Gay, as young married men whose wives were acquainted, were experiencing major life events around the same time. Gay described his search for a family home and shared his excitement over Staten Island. In visiting New York, Lowell sometimes stayed with the Gays and became acquainted with residents of Elliottville, about whom Gay later shared news. Gay also corresponded with Edmund Quincy (1808–1887) in connection with the *Standard* and described his Staten Island life.

The other major body of surviving correspondence is that of Laura Johnson. Like Elizabeth Gay, Johnson was an active correspondent and shared her frustrations, news of her family and neighborhood, and the satisfaction she found in Elliottville. Although scattered letters exist in several collections, her twenty-seven-year correspondence with writer Annie Adams Fields (1834–1915) is seemingly intact. Johnson loved Elliottville but often felt isolated within her household. She admired and may have envied Annie Fields's life. Fields, the wife of publisher James Fields, was well known as a hostess for gatherings of authors, intellectuals, and Boston notables held in the parlor of the Fields' Beacon Hill house. Fields was also a published author of poetry, essays, memoirs, and biographies of her literary acquaintances. Johnson strove to write interesting letters, commenting on her reading to demonstrate her intellectual engagement. Occasionally she included her own poems, one of which James Fields published in *The Atlantic* ("On Picket Duty," April 1863). While she tried to carve out time for writing, Johnson was preoccupied with maintaining a large household that included her husband, three children, sister, mother, and occasionally her two brothers, as well as servants. Her husband was ill for many years, her elderly mother went into a prolonged depression after the death of Theodore Winthrop, and one of her daughters was developmentally disabled. Perhaps for these reasons she made much of the social and intellectual excitements of Elliottville, noting conversations with George Curtis and Anna Leonowens, as well as the musical evenings, dances, and book clubs in the neighborhood, making her letters excellent sources on neighborhood life.

Other writings of neighborhood residents Helena Gilder and Louis Pope Gratacap that ended up in archival collections have more fragmentary information about Elliottville. Some of Helena's correspondence survives in the Gilder Manuscripts Collection. Helena de Kay married Richard Watson Gilder, a prominent poet and editor for almost fifty years, and his renown meant that family correspondence was preserved. Helena and most of her siblings had come of age on Staten Island. She had lifelong friendships with other women who had grown up in Elliottville, like Maria (Oakey) Dewing, Sarah Gay, and Josephine Lowell, as well as maintaining an emotionally close friendship with Sarah Shaw (who referred to her as her adopted daughter). The letters that Helena wrote to friends while living on Staten Island, while few, illustrate the friendships among the young people in the neighborhood, and her letters to Shaw, written decades after each of them had moved away from Staten Island, demonstrate the enduring intimacy of their friendship.

Louis Pope Gratacap (1851[?]–1917) was a neighbor of Laura Johnson. Several of his diaries survive. One from 1863 records childhood life in Elliottville. Those from the 1870s detail the social life of young adults in Elliottville. In addition to describing group hikes, dances, parties, and concerts, he included accounts of amateur theatricals, sometimes pasting in the printed programs.

Although the discovery of archival documentation for Elliottville social life was heartening at the outset of the project, the limitations, in terms of detail, quantity, and chronological representation, have proved frustrating. Over the years, others have taken an interest in Elliottville.

Even though they were written almost one hundred years ago, the two standard published sources for information about Elliottville remain Charles G. Hine and William T. Davis's *Legends, Stories, and Folklore of Old Staten Island*, part 1, *The North Shore* (Staten Island, NY: Staten Island Historical Society, 1925) and the multivolume work by Charles W. Leng and William T. Davis, *Staten Island and Its People: A History, 1609–1929* (New York: Lewis, 1930). Although local historians treat these works as canonical, both have serious limitations, including their White, upper-class perspectives and their neglect in documenting sources. On this last point, *Legends* is more satisfying, since sections of the book consist of direct reminiscences by named informants. On the whole, however, the title of the book accurately describes the contents: legends, stories, and folklore. The named informants include Mary Willcox, Martin Gay, and Louis Gratacap, all of whom grew up in the neighborhood but whose childhood awareness would have been heavily influenced by their parents' perspectives and selective accounts of events before they were born. The 1870s and 1880s, when their direct experience would have been most informative, was not the main focus of Hine and Davis, who mostly wrote about Elliottville prior to and during the Civil War.

More recent interest in Elliottville has focused on the place as an abolitionist community, and internet searches yield tantalizing content. For instance, claims have been made that houses in Elliottville were on the Underground Railroad. Furthermore, any online presentation of the abolitionist movement on Staten Island usually focuses on the free Black communities at Sandy Ground and in the McKee Street neighborhood, leading to the conflation of the abolitionist activities of free Blacks on Staten Island with those of Elliottville Whites.

I have not found documentation for the claims that Elliottville houses were on the Underground Railroad nor that the White residents of Elliottville worked alongside Staten Island Blacks in the cause of abolitionism. I am aware that Mary Willcox refers to the Gay house "sometimes" being used to hide fugitives. However, she really seems to have one specific instance in mind, and since she was born in 1861, she would not have had direct experience of what she describes. She says that when a Southern lady brought an enslaved girl with her to New York, the child was taken from her hotel room to be liberated from bondage and brought to the Gay house. Willcox goes on to say that the child's stay was brief because Mrs. Gay was afraid of the effect of her behavior (she lied and had no manners) on her own children. Willcox also describes an instance in which Mrs. Gay witnessed fugitives hidden in her husband's Manhattan office.[6]

Sydney Gay's own notebook (*The Record of Fugitives*, in which he detailed the movement of people he aided) does not mention Elliottville or even Staten Island. In fact, scholar Eric Foner emphasizes that Gay was insistent that the *National Anti-Slavery Standard* office be the setting for his interactions with fugitives, even to the extent of requiring that office hours be observed. Furthermore, my research yielded no evidence of White and Black abolitionists on Staten Island working together. In the hundreds of Gay family letters, neighborhoods and people outside Elliottville are mentioned, but there is no mention of Black neighborhoods, churches, or individuals. Furthermore, the census records do not show that the Shaws, Curtises, Johnsons, or Gays employed Black people as live-in servants, which would have been a customary way of providing support to individuals (although *Legends* says that Frank Shaw employed, at some point before the Civil War, a butler named Green, who was Black and later owned a catering firm in New Brighton).[7]

If Elliottville's White abolitionists and Staten Island's Black communities did not have significant interactions, this would not have been surprising. Near-contemporary accounts of the abolitionist movement describe the division that existed between Black and White activism. In part, this was due to most White abolitionists' stances on aiding fugitives. While Sydney Gay made significant sacrifices to help fugitives, many White abolitionists considered such activities impolitic and a dangerous threat to the larger goal of abolitionism. Another source of frustration for Blacks was the hesitation of White abolitionists to vigorously combat racial prejudice. Unfortunately, even though Gay's aid to fugitives was so dependent on the risks taken by Blacks like Louis Napoleon and William Leonard and the anonymous Blacks who helped them by providing shelter for fugitives, in his account of abolitionism he characterized the movement as a "White humanitarian enterprise in aid of helpless Blacks."[8]

The one Black person treated at any length in *Legends* is Nicholas "Old Claus" De Hart (1800–1885). Born into slavery on the Crocheron family farm in the area of what would become Elliottville, De Hart remained in the vicinity after he was emancipated as a child. De Hart is presented as the stereotypical kindly, servile Black man hired as a laborer. James Parker, and later the Gays, employed him as a gardener. When he became too old for such work, he started a small oyster business, selling the bivalves cooked by his wife in his dockside shack or delivering them raw. Reading the account of De Hart in *Legends* highlights the skewed and unsatisfying nature of the documentary record for Elliottville.

Chapter 1

Elliottville

A Suburb of Affiliation

The Shaws and Gays

The Shaws and Gays were friends before living on adjacent properties in Elliottville. They were at the center of neighborhood social life through the Civil War. Members of the families were among the last of the early Elliottville residents to abandon the neighborhood.

The Shaws were probably the first to learn of Staten Island. Their friend Ralph Waldo Emerson had a brother, William Emerson, who was a judge living on Staten Island. Furthermore, another friend, Henry David Thoreau, had tutored one of William Emerson's sons in 1843. Thoreau wrote about the island, recording his appreciation for the beauty of the island's tulip poplars and the picturesque views of the ocean from amidst tilled fields.[1] Another friend, Lydia Maria Child, had moved to New York City in 1841 to become editor of the *National Anti-Slavery Standard* and wrote the Shaws about her visits to the artist William Page on Staten Island, referring to "the beautiful island."[2] In 1843, yet another friend, Sarah Margaret Fuller (May 23, 1810–July 19, 1850), moved to New York City to become a literary critic for the *New-York Tribune*. She wrote poetically to the Shaws in July 1845 of her first visit to Staten Island, "there are quite long wood-walks, and, as you go up and down them, for they are on hills, you catch glimpses of the sea and of the Narrows with the processions of ships gliding through and Coney Island with its long strip of silvery sand that cleaves the waters with such beautiful effect."[3]

In 1845, the Shaws were already living in a rural setting. Frank had purchased a farm outside Boston, in West Roxbury, and moved his family there so that they could have more direct contact with nature. The move was out of step with social expectations, due to the Shaws' high socioeconomic status in Boston. Frank Shaw was the oldest son of Robert Gould Shaw (1776–1853), who had leveraged ancestral wealth, built on the import/export trade with China and West India, to create a great fortune. The elder Shaw had diversified the family enterprises, establishing an auction and commission house and a dry goods store and building significant real estate holdings. Upon reaching maturity, Frank worked in the family firms. While adept at business, from early on he was more focused on using his wealth to improve society.

Frank married his half cousin Sarah Blake Sturgis in 1835. Frank was following the custom of the Shaws and Sturgises to marry within extended family networks with the effect of consolidating wealth. As a couple, Frank and Sarah were related to the most prominent families in Boston and New York, including the Cabotses, Forbeses, Hunnewells, Lodges, Parkmans, and Russells. While they may have wed, in part, due to family custom, there is no reason to doubt their romantic attachment.

In addition to their shared social network, they were both committed to social reform. Not long after their wedding, the Shaws joined the Boston Society of the New Jerusalem, an evangelical congregation of the Unitarian Church. The Shaws were devoted to American transcendental movement ideals and embraced self-culture to perfect the ability to intuit God's truth revealed in nature and be more completely in communication with the divine. The Shaws also integrated individualism and social conscience, embracing the ideal of service and using their wealth to improve the lot of others. They were particularly devoted to freeing enslaved African Americans and improving conditions for impoverished Northern laborers. When they joined the American Anti-Slavery Society in 1838, their friend Lydia Maria Child wrote them that although she sometimes doubted the sincerity of new members, with them she did not have "the slightest suspicion of their insincerity."[4]

Unlike many of his other philanthropic peers, Frank Shaw was also devoted to reforming society in the interest of social equality. He believed that the working class should share in society's wealth and that the social hierarchy that placed certain races higher than others and men above women was not divinely mandated, nor did it stem from some natural order, but was only an expression of a human, historically derived system of inequity that benefited the few at the expense of the many.[5]

When he was thirty-two, in 1841, Shaw withdrew from direct participation in his family enterprises out of distaste for accumulating wealth at the expense of, and through the oppression of, laborers. Throughout the rest of his life, he helped manage investments for his family members out of a sense of duty; although, he never again devoted himself to increasing his personal wealth.

Around the same time the Shaws were settling in West Roxbury, George and Sophia Ripley were forming the utopian community Brook Farm near Frank's land.[6] Ripley was a proponent of Association, an American version of Fourierism. The Ripleys wanted to build a society infused with the ideals of the transcendental movement that would free members from a life of labor and enable them to live a balanced existence of labor and leisure, permitting significant time for reflection, study, writing, and

Figure 1.1. Frank Shaw supported Brook Farm and Brook Farmers numbered conspicuously among Elliottville visitors and residents in the 1840s. *Source*: John A. Whipple, photographer. Courtesy of Staten Island Museum.

general self-cultivation. Material needs would be provided for through a financial structure that was based on a joint stock company in which profits were shared in return for an equal share in the work of the farm, which also included domestic work and the operation of a school, with all labor—menial, intellectual, and domestic—valued at the same rate. Members could choose their activities, rather than being assigned tasks.

Although the Shaws lived separately from Brook Farm, Frank thought the experiment a promising alternative to capitalism. He provided financial support and convinced his brothers-in-law George R. Russell (1800–1866) and Henry Parkman Sturgis (1806–1869) to do so as well. Russell and Sturgis had founded a trading firm in Manila and spent eleven years working as partners before leaving the business, having made their fortunes. Russell had married Frank's sister, Sarah Parkman Shaw (1811–1888) in 1835 and Sturgis was Sarah Shaw's brother.

Frank Shaw devoted himself to study and contributed articles to the Brook Farm publication, initially known as *The Phalanx* (later *The Harbinger*). In one of his essays, he challenged abolitionists to agitate for fundamental change in American society in addition to the legal abolishment of slavery. He also called upon women to work for their own liberation. He participated in intellectual discussions with Brook Farm residents and visitors, including Ralph Waldo Emerson, Nathaniel Hawthorne, Margaret Fuller, Horace Greeley, Bronson Alcott, and Orestes Brown, always seeking to cure the social ills of US society that he considered endemic to capitalism. When he found non-English-language books that could contribute to US social transformation, he translated them and had them published in the United States. One example was Francois Cantagrel's Fourier-inspired work *The Children of the Phalanstery: A Familiar Dialogue on Education* (New York: W. H. Graham, 1848). Shaw also translated some of George Sand's books (part of his lifelong commitment to the rights of women), and Heinrich and Emil Zschokke's instructive history of Switzerland, that emphasized participatory governance.[7]

The Shaws were Garrisonian abolitionists. They were personal friends of Garrison and embraced his call for uncompensated emancipation without expatriation and the use of moral suasion instead of political maneuvers to bring an immediate end to slavery, since he regarded the Constitution to be a proslavery document. Frank worked directly with the Boston Vigilance Committee, which aided runaway slaves on their flight to freedom. Sarah Shaw was involved in the women's auxiliary of the American Anti-Slavery Society, established by Maria Weston Chapman, and worked in the annual antislavery fairs. She also participated intellectually in the abolitionist movement.

The Shaws' gradual move to Staten Island began in the aftermath of Sarah's 1846 health crisis. She had never fully recovered after the birth of her last child, Ellen, in 1845. Margaret Fuller bluntly told her that she had started having children too soon, implying that her illness was partly emotional. In letters to her friends, Sarah made it clear that she found managing a household burdensome, even with the help of servants. When she began experiencing a respiratory illness compounded by an eye condition that made her almost blind, Frank sought out treatment.[8] Just as the Shaws had heard of the beauty of Staten Island from their friends, they had also heard of Dr. Elliott's skill in treating eye diseases. Many of his most prominent patients were Shaw friends or family members. Starting in 1842, Elliott treated James Russell Lowell (1819–1891), who was a

Figure 1.2. The Shaw family's eventual move to Elliottville was set in motion when Sarah Shaw was treated by Dr. Elliott in 1847. *Source*: Rockwood, photographer. Courtesy of Staten Island Museum.

cousin of both Sarah and Frank. Lowell resided in Elliottville in 1843 and returned a few years later so that Elliott could treat his wife Maria White Lowell, while living at 30 Bard Avenue. Elliott also treated Charles Eliot Norton (1827–1908) in 1843, another cousin of both the Shaws. Beginning in late 1843, Elliott treated Henry Wadsworth Longfellow, longtime friend of the Shaws, and in 1846 Elliott treated Francis Parkman (1823–1893), yet another Shaw cousin. In 1845, when Margaret Fuller was troubled by headaches, Sarah had written her a letter of reference to Dr. Elliott.

With the help of their friends and family in New York, Frank Shaw arranged for Dr. Elliott to treat Sarah in 1847, while he stayed with the children in West Roxbury. As with many of Elliott's patients, Sarah lived on Staten Island while she recovered, becoming part of the therapeutic residential community near Elliott's residence.

Lydia Maria Child visited Sarah Shaw frequently and wrote Frank Shaw to keep him apprised of Sarah's health. Child had become friends with the Shaws in 1833, prior to their marriage and in the same year as Child published *An Appeal in Favor of That Class of Americans Called Africans* (Boston: Allen and Ticknor). The work was the first book-length antislavery title to be published in the United States and argued for an immediate end to slavery. Child's decades-long correspondence with the Shaws reveals the intimacy of their friendship and the strength of their shared political views.[9] Child had moved to New York in 1841 to assume editorship of the *National Anti-Slavery Standard* (her husband took over the position in 1844 and the couple continued to live in the city through 1851).[10]

In her letters to Frank Shaw in February 1847, Child noted that Sarah Shaw responded well to treatment, and her general health and mood had improved on Staten Island.[11] Some of the evidence she presented included Sarah's renewed ability to walk without being led, to distinguish colors when items were brought near her eyes, and an improvement in the appearance of her eyes. Child helped Sarah get the open-air exercise Dr. Elliott prescribed and wrote Frank of the frequent visits Sarah received from attentive friends and the faithfulness of the servant Sarah had brought with her. She also reported that Sarah thought it best that Frank remain with the children in West Roxbury.

Eventually, Sarah Shaw's vision was restored, and she returned to West Roxbury in 1847, but later in the year she returned to Staten Island for further treatment. This time, Frank Shaw and the children came with her. Although the details are unclear, Frank seems to have rented a house for several years from Dr. Elliott that was near Sydney Gay's. Although Sarah's health was a determining factor in the relocation from West Roxbury, it is also likely that Frank wanted to get away from Brook Farm. The social experiment had begun to fail after an embrace of a more doctrinaire implementation of Fourier's principles in 1844, which drove some members away from the community. Frank was at the center of the controversy, since he was a strong advocate of Fourierism. Then, in 1846, the uninsured central building, which had taken several years to construct, burned to the ground, and the resulting financial challenges became a new source of divisiveness. In 1849, the Brook Farm property was sold to a farmer. While the Shaws lived on their own property, their farm had functioned as an adjunct of Brook Farm, and living in West Roxbury may have seemed less appealing without the community. In addition, Frank must have been frustrated and disappointed over the closure. Earlier, when Frank wanted to sell the West Roxbury farm, Sarah resisted. Now, when the Shaws returned there they missed Staten Island. Sarah, writing to Elizabeth Gay in June 1850, said, "If I had imagined half my regrets, I never would have stirred one step from Staten Island."[12] Frank, also writing Gay around the same time, said, "We are all regretting Staten Island as hard as possible, short of actual homesickness."[13]

They returned to Staten Island, but when Sarah's health worsened again, they decided European travel might improve her condition. The family left the United States in Spring 1851 and did not return until 1855. Even though they were living abroad, by 1854 Frank was in the process of buying Staten Island land on which to establish a primary residence for his family and become the Gays' neighbor. Frank bought almost fifteen acres of land from Dr. Elliott on March 9, 1854, for $15,000 (the equivalent of over $600,000 today).[14] He then contracted with an architect to design a mansion that took years to build and still was not ready when the Shaws returned from Europe in 1855.

The Shaws' decision to relocate to Staten Island clearly had an emotional dimension, connected as it was to Sarah's treatment by Dr. Elliott and the failure of Brook Farm. The Gays' earlier relocation also had an emotional component tied to distress over living in Manhattan.

Elizabeth Gay was the granddaughter of Pennsylvania Quaker Warner Mifflin, who had manumitted his slaves in 1774 and later petitioned the US Congress to abolish slavery.[15] Elizabeth's parents, Daniel and Sarah Neall, were also committed to the cause and in 1840 had underwritten Elizabeth's expenses so that she could represent the Philadelphia Female

Anti-Slavery Society at the World Anti-Slavery Convention in London. She and her fellow representatives, including Lucretia Mott and Elizabeth Cady Stanton, were refused admittance as representatives since they were women (an important formative experience for Mott and Stanton, who pledged to form a society for the rights of women). After meeting Elizabeth through antislavery meetings, Sydney courted her through an extended correspondence (her parents opposed the match).

In 1844, when Lydia Maria Child and her husband David stepped down as editors of the *National Anti-Slavery Standard*, Sydney Gay accepted the editorship, necessitating his relocation to New York City, which also afforded him greater opportunity to support vigilance committees and the work of the Underground Railroad in Manhattan.[16] The move also placed him geographically closer to Elizabeth in Philadelphia. However,

Figure 1.3. Elizabeth Gay placed a great deal of importance on correspondence, and it is due to her efforts that so much is known about Elliottville. *Source*: Uncredited photograph, Ida M. Tarbell, "The American Woman," *The American Magazine* 69, no. 3 (January 1910): 373. Public domain.

Elizabeth's parents still opposed the match. The couple eventually forced the matter by publicly announcing their engagement. The two married in November 1845 and Elizabeth separated from the Society of Quakers (to avoid being "read out" for marrying a non-Quaker).[17]

On his modest salary, the newlyweds had no option but boarding house life. The forced intimacy of the arrangement meant that everyone knew about Sydney Gay's job and the fact that he and Elizabeth were abolitionists. Like most New Yorkers, their landlady and the other boarders were hostile to the antislavery movement. The couple's only consolation lay in the fact that abolitionist Maria Weston Chapman's brother, Richard Warren Weston (1820–1873), and his new bride, Sarah Maria (Grant) Weston (1819–1902), boarded in the same establishment on Twelfth Street in Manhattan.[18] By early 1847 both couples were looking for other places to live.

Figure 1.4. Sydney Gay's distaste for city life drove the house search that took the Gays to Elliottville. *Source: The Twentieth Century Biographical Dictionary of Notable Americans*, vol. 4, 1906, under "Sydney Howard Gay." Public domain.

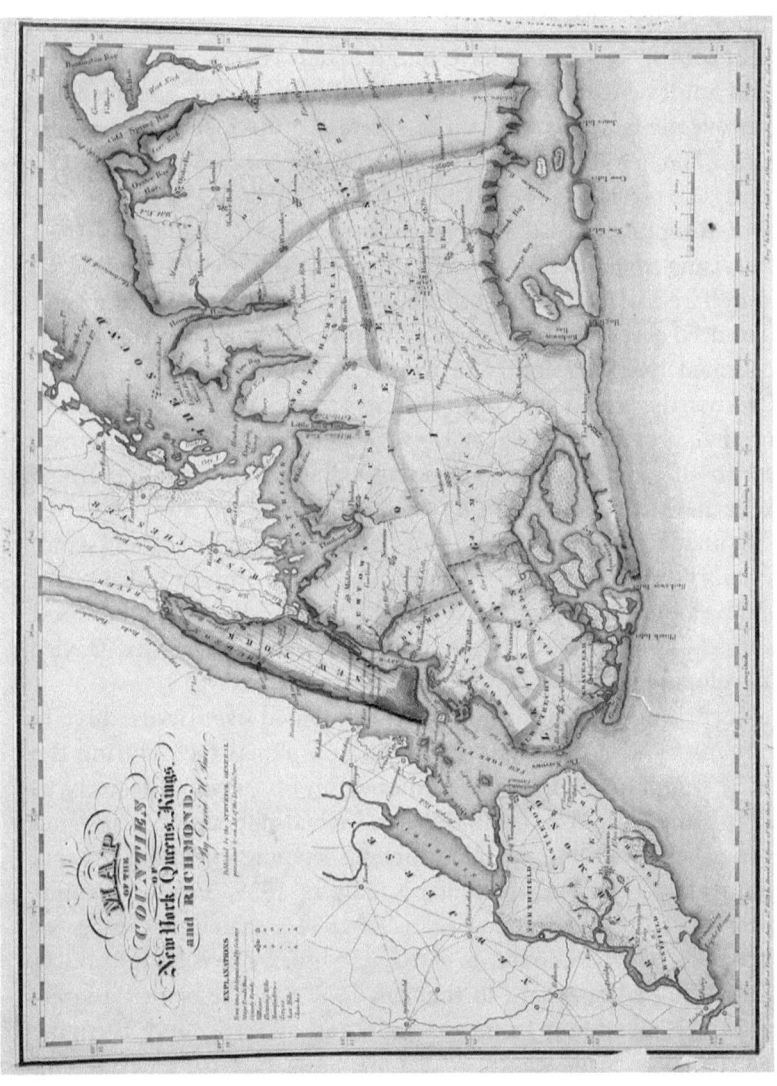

Figure 1.5. The surveys for this map were completed in 1829. In addition to showing Staten Island in regional context, the map shows that the island was relatively undeveloped. *Source*: David H. Burr and Simeon De Witt, Map of the Counties of New York, Queens, Kings, and Richmond (New York: Stone and Clark, 1839), New York Public Library Digital Collections, https://digitalcollections.nypl.org/items/510d47df-fb41-a3d9-e040-e00a18064a99.

development of a block of townhouses in partnership with the Stuyvesant family. That area was renamed St. Mark's Place, as it is still known today. Davis's bankers were American representatives of the Rothschild banking empire and provided him with access to significant credit, enabling his investment on Staten Island.[26]

Davis probably would not have found Staten Island, primarily agricultural and undeveloped, a promising investment had it not been for earlier improvements triggered by the interest of Daniel D. Tompkins (1774–1825) when he was serving as New York State governor (1807–1817), and, later, as vice president of the United States (1817–1825). During the War of 1812 Tompkins gained an appreciation of Staten Island's potential while supervising construction of defensive positions for the harbor. In 1814 he purchased several farms on the island's North Shore and a tract of seven hundred acres (about the area of Central Park in New York City). He incorporated the Richmond Turnpike Company in 1816 to build a toll road across the island, linking his land to the West Shore's Blazing Star Ferry that provided transportation to New Jersey. After acquiring an interest in the Fulton and Livingston steamboat monopoly, he also established a new ferry service in 1817 between his land and Whitehall Street in Manhattan, enabling travel from Manhattan, over Staten Island, into New Jersey, and onward to Philadelphia. These improvements, and the initial development of Tompkinsville (the Staten Island neighborhood directly across the water from Manhattan), were foundations for Davis's planned development.

In a surprising turn of events, Davis benefited even more directly from Tompkins by acquiring land from the Tompkins tract. During the War of 1812, Tompkins had borrowed money on his personal security to equip and arm the New York militia. When he had difficulties recovering the funds the state owed him, he had problems keeping up with payments on his obligations. Then he died unexpectedly in 1825, and the complicated matter of settling his estate began. In 1834 a major percentage of his land holdings were auctioned to satisfy creditors. Davis bought tracts at this sale and added farmland to them in 1835 until he owned a large, triangular parcel, extending from the terminus of Richmond Turnpike and the North Shore ferry station to Sailors' Snug Harbor, a developing charitable institution.[27]

Sailors' Snug Harbor had a major impact on the development of Staten Island's North Shore by attracting positive national press attention to the island's climate and location. The institution was founded through a bequest of Captain Robert Richard Randall (1750–1801), who had inherited a fortune from his father, Thomas Randall, a privateer during the French and Indian War. Thomas Randall had helped found the Marine Society of the City of New York for the aid of impoverished shipmasters, their orphans, and their widows. Robert Randall, who had remained unmarried, devised, with help from his lawyer Alexander Hamilton, a bequest-funded institution for the benefit of sailors no longer able to work as seamen that would provide housing, food, clothing, and recreation in an institutional setting. The Sailors' Snug Harbor was to be sited on Robert Randall's twenty-two-acre farm adjacent to what is now Washington Square, but a twenty-nine-year legal battle by his nieces and nephews (who, even though they had been handsomely provided for, nevertheless contested their uncle's philanthropic bequest) delayed the implementation. By the time the trustees of the new institution could begin work, the Randall land had become so valuable that leasing it made better financial sense than occupying it, and the trustees successfully petitioned for authorization to relocate Sailors' Snug Harbor to Staten Island. A 160-acre farm on the North Shore was purchased in 1831. The first building was completed in 1833, and the further development of the institution received national attention. Americans could take pride in the comfort in which the sailors lived, the appropriateness of the harbor-side setting, and the fact that the institution was nearly unique in the United States as a secular philanthropy.

Davis was aided in promoting his real estate endeavor by the fact that it was bookended by Sailors' Snug Harbor (with its developing campus of neoclassical buildings and extensive grounds) and Tompkinsville (with its transportation links). In naming his neighborhood "New Brighton," Davis referenced Brighton, England, and drew upon positive associations with the royal seaside retreat. Brighton had developed rapidly in the 1820s and 1830s, receiving international attention. The Prince of Wales, later George IV, had first visited there in 1783 to take the waters as a cure for his gout. He began construction of the Royal Pavilion in 1787 (although the John Nash design we know today was executed later, from 1815 to 1822). Davis's New Brighton would have called to mind a seaside community popular with royalty (after George IV's 1830 death, King William IV also visited frequently) and the affluent, before railways connected Brighton to London in 1840 and the town was available to the masses.

To establish the tone of his development, Davis constructed five substantial Greek Revival houses along the picturesque road that ran parallel to the shore from Tompkinsville to the North. Rather than continuing the venture on his own, in 1836 he sold his land to the New Brighton Association, a real estate corporation formed by five New York businessmen. Davis received $600,000, although he agreed to hold a $440,000 mortgage to be paid off as land sold. Promotional material for New Brighton trumpeted the community's "proximity to the great commercial mart of the western hemisphere . . . beauty of location, extent of prospect, and salubrity of climate . . . unrivaled in this country."[28] A picturesque street plan designed by surveyor James Lyons, responding to the shoreline and the rapidly rising land elevations in the area, was implemented as streets were graded and retaining walls constructed, giving New Brighton the physical characteristics that have caused researchers to claim it as one of the earliest and most fully realized suburban villa communities in the United States.[29] When J. L. & S. Josephs & Company failed during the 1837 financial crisis, the impact on the New Brighton Association was immediate. In 1842, creditors forced a foreclosure sale of unsold lots. By purchasing land at the sale, Davis was able to regain some of his original land at greatly reduced prices.

So, New Brighton moved ahead. While full-time residents occupied some houses, the neighborhood was mostly a summer resort in the 1840s and 1850s with bathing clubs, boathouses, fishing piers, and large hotels. Even the mansion Davis constructed for himself (near what is now the intersection of Richmond Terrace and St. Peter's Place) was transformed over time into the Pavilion Hotel (perhaps in reference to the Royal Pavilion at Brighton). Wings were added, as well as additional structures, until three hundred rooms were on offer, as well as public rooms for socializing. The Pavilion Hotel quickly became a center for the New Brighton summer community, serving as a gathering place for hotel guests and those who had constructed houses on the island, drawn by social events and musical evenings headlined by Jenny Lind, Nellie Melba, or Adelina Patti. National figures such as President Martin van Buren and Henry Clay stayed there, and the hotel remained popular with Southerners during the Civil War when Confederate officers sent their families to Staten Island as a place of refuge.[30] Other hotels in the area eventually included the Belmont House, Peteler's (later St. Mark's) Hotel, the Hotel Castleton (located on the top of the bluff rising above the waterfront and the largest of all), and the Planters' Hotel (seemingly named in recognition of Southerners who frequented the hotel).

Southern plantation owners left their homes in summer because death from disease, particularly from epidemics like yellow fever, was more common in the heat. Even Manhattanites had health concerns that prompted major population shifts beginning in the 1820s. In the eighteenth century there was usually no separation between residences and businesses in the city, both mostly confined to Lower Manhattan. As the population increased and manufacturing boomed, Lower Manhattan became an unpleasant place to live, with streets filled with dead animals, human and animal waste, noxious manufacturing byproducts, wastewater holding ponds, and rubbish piles. Efforts were made to separate residential from business districts, leading to the development of neighborhoods farther and farther uptown. Neighborhoods around Washington Square, in Chelsea, and in the West Village established the relatively new concept of the residential enclave. Such environs offered a measure of quiet and tended to insulate residents from contact with lower social classes, except tradespeople and servants. A parallel trend fueled gradual suburbanization, with developers touting one area and then another as healthful yet convenient. Even those who resisted relocating outside the city succumbed to the appeal of summering elsewhere, particularly after the cholera epidemics in the summers of 1832 and 1849.[31]

As New Brighton became established, other investors saw the potential for planned, suburban villa development on the North Shore. To the northwest of New Brighton, Hamilton Park took shape on thirty acres in the 1850s. Developed by Manhattan merchant Charles K. Hamilton and his wife Margaretta, Hamilton Park had the characteristics identified with the American romantic suburb, including ten-to-fourteen-room picturesque residences on park-like grounds and winding streets.[32] Already a resident of Staten Island for a few years, Hamilton was a commuter, traveling into his city office by ferry, and one imagines he promoted the advantages of his cottages to fellow businessmen.

William S. Pendleton (1795–1879) created a similar, albeit smaller, enclave on higher land above Hamilton Park along what became known as Pendleton Place. Pendleton and his brother were the first commercially successful lithographers in the United States.[33] By the late 1840s the Pendletons had become residents of Staten Island, and William invested in Staten Island real estate. He constructed houses on his land in the 1850s, of which he retained ownership, renting mostly to Manhattan businessmen who commuted by ferry and lived full-time on Staten Island.[34]

Dr. Elliott of Elliottville

Elliottville, then, was another of the North Shore Staten Island ferry suburbs inspired by the success of New Brighton. What made the development

Figure 1.6. Most of Elliottville was still owned by Dr. Elliott in 1853. *Source*: Section of James Butler, Map of Staten Island, or Richmond County (New York: James Butler, 1853), New York Public Library Digital Collections, https://digital collections.nypl.org/items/e7fbb6c0-1d5f-0131-6edb-58d385a7b928.

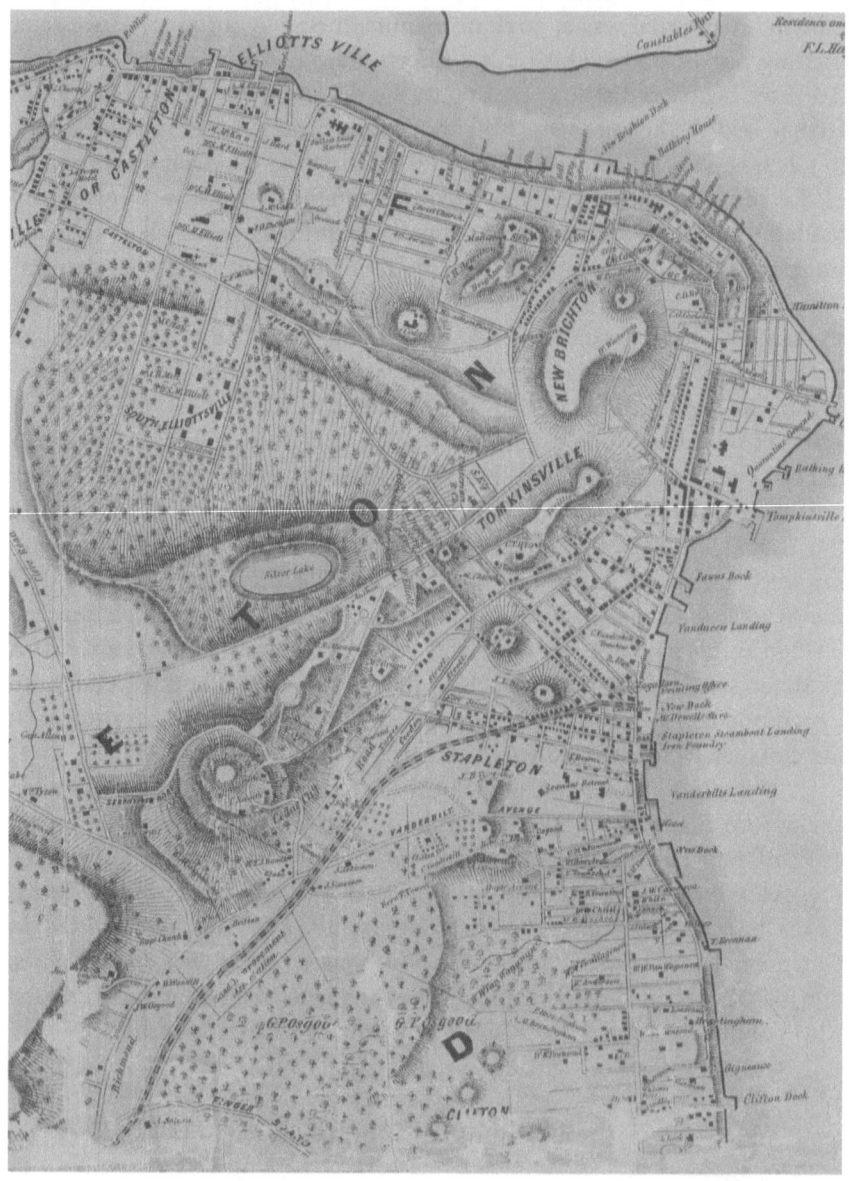

distinctive was the founder, Dr. Samuel Mackenzie Elliott. The New Brighton Association might tout a salubrious environment, but for a physician to do so was more convincing.

The physical setting of Elliott's land, on the opposite side of Sailors' Snug Harbor from New Brighton, was significant. If one were to drive a carriage in the late 1840s along the waterfront from the increasingly fashionable summer resort of New Brighton to Elliottville, one would take Shore Road (later Richmond Terrace) and enjoy notable scenery. Starting out, on the hills above the harbor one saw grand mansions set within substantial grounds with outbuildings, including elaborate carriage houses and greenhouses. Peteler's Hotel, also located on high ground, rose in the distance above the street, as did St. Peter's Roman Catholic Church with its dramatic bell tower. Elegant, temple-like Greek Revival houses built in the 1830s and 1840s bordered the road. One also passed the expansive Pavilion Hotel, with its colonnaded porches and bathing and boathouses on the shore. From the drive one also looked out at numerous sailing ships and Manhattan on the further side of the harbor. Further along, across the Kill van Kull, one could see picturesque oyster sloops, schools of dolphins, and the saltwater marshes of New Jersey. Just before reaching Elliottville, one passed Snug Harbor and its elegant neoclassical buildings designed by Minard Lafever, and then a bridge over a scenic marshy cove, extending inland. Over much of the drive, large elm trees cast shade. In the springtime, wild dogwoods covered the nearby hills in clouds of blossom. Upon reaching the foot of Bard Avenue, one saw the ferry landing serving Elliottville.[35] Soon after passing the ferry station, the shoreline curved, blocking areas devoted to small manufacturing and maritime industries in an area called Factoryville. The Barrett family had established a textile dying company there in 1819, and a manufacturing village with worker housing took shape. The firm's dying operations produced wastewater, collected in an aesthetically unpleasant drainage pond that must have been jarring after the scenic drive along the shore. Having arrived at Elliottville, one may not have been motivated to go further.[36]

Easy access to the shoreline was a major factor in Dr. Elliott's land purchases; we know the natural beauty of Staten Island impressed him when he first arrived in the United States.[37] Like other passengers arriving in New York harbor, Elliott was held on shipboard off Staten Island when he arrived in August of 1834.[38] However, as a ship's surgeon, he had a more privileged experience. He toured the New York Marine Hospital, commonly known as the Quarantine Hospital, with the chief medical officer. The facility, the largest of its kind in the United States, was where arriving passengers in ill health were held. The hospital was considered exemplary and was part of a walled complex that included thirty acres of grounds and multiple buildings, including the central Yellow Fever Hospital, later renamed St. Nicholas Hospital. The large neoclassical building with rooftop observatory was nicknamed the St. Nicholas Hotel for its appearance and because first-class passengers were quarantined there. An account of the quarantine grounds nearly contemporary with Elliott's arrival described the buildings as "lofty and spacious . . . whitewashed [walls and windows] with green Venetian blinds, g[a]ve the appearance of comfort and cleanliness."[39] One of the topics of Elliott's medical research was the health impact of environmental factors, and Elliott was soon convinced that Staten Island offered a uniquely healthy environment.[40] So it is no surprise that after studies and lectures in Cincinnati and Philadelphia he returned to establish a medical practice in Manhattan in 1836 and soon chose to live on Staten Island, eventually purchasing land adjacent to Sailors' Snug Harbor in 1839.[41]

Dr. Elliott purchased land from several individuals, including New Brighton developer Thomas E. Davis and William Bard. Bard was an insurance executive with family ties to Staten Island through his father, Dr. Samuel Bard, a famous colonial-era doctor.[42] Much of the rest of the land was obtained from physicians Alban Goldsmith and Granville Sharp Pattison, with whom Elliott was friends and colleagues. The fact that other physicians owned the land prior to Dr. Elliott may be a coincidence, stemming from attempts by many people in New York City to find a healthy environment outside the metropolis in the 1830s following repeated outbreaks of disease. However, the initial boost of Brighton, England, as a seaside resort came from English physician Richard Russell (1687–1759), who in addition to publishing an influential treatise on the health benefits of bathing in and drinking seawater, established a medical practice in Brighton, based in his residence, which included rooms for his patients. So it is tempting to speculate that other physicians besides Elliott may have contemplated a therapeutic community on Staten Island.

Dr. Elliott constructed as many as twenty-two houses in Elliottville between 1839 and 1850 in a cohesive style, referencing the English Romanticism of architect William Ranlett (1806–1865), from whom Elliott also purchased architectural plans.[43] Ranlett, who was living on Staten

Figure 1.7. Elliottville's distinctive built environment is evident in this 1853 depiction. *Source*: Inset from James Butler, Map of Staten Island, or Richmond County (New York: James Butler, 1853), New York Public Library Digital Collections, https://digitalcollections.nypl.org/items/e7fbb6c0-1d5f-0131-6edb-58d385a7b928.

In writing of the decision to Edmund Quincy, Sydney Gay made clear that he was under the care of a doctor and trying to live a healthier life. Writing to Elizabeth Gay in a letter missing its date, he extolled "the purity and freedom of the country life" and disdained "the city with all of its moral and physical impurity."[19] He considered New York "absolutely the wickedest place, the most destitute of souls, of any on the globe."[20] Referencing Emerson, he wrote Elizabeth, "We must go out into the open fields and forest to have a full communion with divinity."[21] His search was made challenging by the fact that the New York City region was experiencing a prolonged economic boom accompanied by rapid population growth. Sydney wrote Quincy, "The son of man has nowhere to lay his head. He has none here unless he is the son of a very rich man or is brought up to be nasty."[22] Then, in March 1847, Sydney delightedly announced, "The Lord has taken care of us after all. I have engaged a house to buy on Staten Island, one of Dr. Elliott's the Oculist."[23] In other letters he listed the advantages, which included the ease with which he could get to work (noting the four sailings of the ferry boat that enabled him to be in his office before nine o'clock in the morning and back home by four thirty) and the natural beauty of Staten Island, which he compared to the Isle of Wight and called "the gem of the ocean," while asserting there was no "more beautiful spot in the world."[24]

North Shore Staten Island in the 1840s

To place the new Gay residence geographically, Sydney told Quincy that the house was located in Elliottville near Sailors' Snug Harbor, between New Brighton and Factoryville. These references would have been meaningful to Quincy, because the North Shore of Staten Island was going through a period of development that had attracted widespread attention. In fact, Elliottville was one of three suburban developments underway on Staten Island in the 1840s, all inspired by the earlier planned community of New Brighton on the island's North Shore.[25]

New Brighton's origins dated back to 1834 and 1835 when Manhattan real estate developer Thomas E. Davis (ca. 1795–1878) assembled a tract, envisioning a residential community with expansive harbor views, healthy air, and easy access to Manhattan by ferry. Davis had already experienced success in Manhattan in the 1820s as a builder and real estate developer, having convinced banking firm J. L. & S. Josephs & Company to fund his

Island, was concerned about the way houses related to their grounds and to each other.[44] Many of his designs for Elliott were serially published, and several of them were featured in an 1853 map of Elliottville. In his designs, Ranlett included site plans for substantial landscaped grounds and dependent structures. Given Elliott's Scottish origins, it is not surprising that he favored Ranlett's Gothic Revival designs and often chose to build in locally quarried gray stone. The size, robust construction, and substantial grounds of Elliott's houses meant that his impact on the built environment persisted long after he left the neighborhood.

Elliott's community was in part a therapeutic community composed of patients. His family often used a house under construction as their primary residence. They would move on when another newly built house was nearing completion. After moving out, Elliott sometimes kept a house to rent out to his own patients. Although his office was in Manhattan, Elliott developed a nationwide reputation as an eye specialist, and some of his patients needed housing for the period of their treatment, which could be lengthy. In some cases, Elliott prescribed living on Staten Island as an important part of a patient's treatment. Eventually, Elliott sold most of the houses he built and even parcels of his original land purchase. By 1855 he had moved out of the neighborhood to build a house on Staten Island's Grymes Hill, about two miles from Elliottville, where he lived until 1870. He retained ownership of some Elliottville properties, and his son and other members of his family lived on Bard Avenue, some as late as the early twentieth century. When Dr. Elliott left Grymes Hill, he moved back to a house on the shore across from the foot of Bard Avenue, where he lived until his death in 1875.

Although the land that became Elliottville would have been developed anyway, it is due to Dr. Elliott that the area became a distinct neighborhood in the town of Castleton. We have already seen the impact he had on the built environment, but he also shaped the social climate by attracting New England intellectuals to his practice and to Staten Island, as is made apparent when one looks at the property owners prior to the late 1840s, almost all of whom were New Yorkers. One of the earliest of these was Daniel Pelton (1788–1897), a dealer in boots, shoes, and leather bindings. In 1835, he purchased the existing colonial-era Kreuzer (variously spelled Kruser and Cruser) house (begun in 1722) and retired there in 1836. He had a number of children who grew up on the property, and one of them married General Alfred Napoleon Alexander Duffie (1833–1880), who established a residence in Elliottville but lived mostly on military bases and then in Spain where he was consul to Cádiz.

Edward Bement (1795–1866) was also a New York businessman who retired to Staten Island. After service as a sailor in the War of 1812 he went into a business apprenticeship in New York, eventually becoming a partner in the banking house of Ketchum, Rogers, and Bement and helped develop the Great Western Railroad Company (later the Wabash Railroad Company) after the Civil War. He established his Staten Island residence in 1839 and owned several tracts of land in Elliottville

Businessman Lucius Tuckerman (1818–1890) also created a Staten Island residence before Elliottville existed. Tuckerman was a pioneer iron manufacturer, known for a refining process that made iron almost as strong as steel would later be. He never intended his Staten Island house to be more than a summer retreat. His New York house was at 22 Washington Place. Later he moved to 220 Madison Avenue and eventually spent the social season in Washington, DC, in a house set within gardens at 1600 I Street NW.

The other New Yorkers in Elliottville before that locale was on maps included Captain Fred Augustus DePeyster (1845–1867) and Charles M. Pine (1812–1897). Each of them moved to Staten Island for their careers. DePeyster's family was prominent in New York starting in the colonial era and was one of the wealthiest families in the city when DePeyster was born. He moved to Staten Island after retiring as a ship captain to become the commandant of Sailors' Snug Harbor. His successor as commandant, Captain Thomas Melville (1830–1884), also had a residence in Elliottville, also due to the proximity to Snug Harbor. Although Pine was not connected to Snug Harbor when he established a general store in 1848 at his residence on the shore (near the foot of what became Bard Avenue), he must have realized the advantages of the location's proximity to Snug Harbor and Factoryville. Eventually, his son Charles Theodore Pine (d. 1895), who fought in the Civil War with Company I of the 156th New York Infantry, joined the business.

Had the area that would become Elliottville continued to develop through people like Pelton, Bement, Tuckerman, DePeyster, and Pine, it would have been indistinguishable from other parts of Staten Island. Even in the earliest account of Elliotville from 1843, the distinctive character of the neighborhood, at that point a therapeutic community centered on Dr. Elliott, and primarily composed of New Englanders, had emerged.

Two of Louise Wigglesworth's family members were Dr. Elliott's patients in 1843, and Wigglesworth, a Bostonian, was living in Elliottville when she corresponded with relatives describing her experiences. The Wigglesworths rented a house from Elliott that Louise described as a dwarf castle that, at variance with her life elsewhere, was not on a street but set within fields. She was deeply impressed by the kindness of the Elliotts, saying Mrs. Elliott "does all in her power to make us comfortable" and Dr. Elliott "is always thinking of something to make people feel better" and placing their needs above his own.[45] Patients overwhelmed him, and even though many came from Boston (and were presumably affluent), he often refused cases in order to allow time to care for poor patients and to continue to study. As the Wigglesworths reached the end of treatment and anticipated their return to Boston, Dr. Elliott insisted that they stay with him and his wife as guests since "they are fond of a 'social fireside' and do not get many visitors in winter."[46] Wigglesworth stressed how at odds the family's experience was with the warnings they had received from physicians who insisted Dr. Elliott should not be consulted.[47] The Wigglesworths were so impressed with Elliott that when Sydney Gay began living in Elliottville in 1847, some Wigglesworths were still living nearby and he wrote about socializing with them since he and his correspondent, Edmund Quincy, were well acquainted with the family.

Given how central Elliott is to the history of the neighborhood, it is important to get a better understanding of him. There are no documented sources for his life; most of what is written about him derives from newspaper advertisements he placed, patient accounts, or obituaries.[48] His only biography in a reference work is in *Appleton's Cyclopaedia of American Biography*, a work deemed unreliable in the early twentieth century when it was realized that the encyclopedia included biographies for several hundred people who never existed. While the *Appleton's* entry for Dr. Elliott notes that he was sometimes described as a charlatan and criticized for not sharing his medical discoveries, the entry notes that Elliott successfully addressed these concerns by "obtaining a diploma, after an examination in the New York medical college" and by presenting a series of public lectures.[49]

In their excited letters to friends about their new home, the Gays conveyed their delight and amusement over Dr. Elliott and his wife. Their delight was partly based in the fact that Elliott was active in the New York abolitionist movement. Furthermore, he was an accomplished man, the physician to well-known cultural figures and writers the Gays admired.

Figure 1.8. Fanny Longfellow described the experience of meeting Elliott and seeing this portrait in a letter dated September 20, 1843: "The magical doors flew open, and as framed therein the stout doctor with shirt collar à la Byron and penetrating look as if he were enacting a tableau vivant of his portrait overhead." Qtd. in Edward Wagenknecht, *Mrs. Longfellow: Selected Letters and Journals of Fanny Appleton Longfellow, 1817–1861* (New York: Longmans, Green, 1956), 94. *Source*: Painting attributed to John James Audubon. Cindy Livingston, photographer. Collection of Elliott's descendant Stephen Livingston. Used with permission.

He was also an educated man, knowledgeable about astronomy with an observatory on the top of his house. Their amusement had several bases.

The first was "the Missus." While Dr. Elliott was Scottish, his wife, Letitia née Irvine, was born in Donegal County, Ireland, and spoke "with a great deal of Irish brogue."[50] Furthermore, she was "not particularly fair," at a time when ladies were expected to have fair complexions preserved by protecting themselves with bonnets and veils from the sun.[51] Reading between the lines, they were saying that no matter how educated the doctor was, his wife was somewhat common.

While her husband was Anglican and had constructed an Episcopal chapel topped with a cross and dedicated by priests, Mrs. Elliott, a Methodist, was outraged and considered the chapel further evidence of Elliott's lost soul. In a misguided attempt to assuage her, Elliott adorned

Figure 1.9. The only structure built by Elliott that is landmarked, the house is reputed to be the first he constructed and lived in on Staten Island. *Source*: Photo by the author.

the chapel with a marble statue of the biblical figure of Samuel at prayer. For her, this was a further outrage, since she considered the sculpture a graven image. According to the Gays, in retribution, she invited a "Rev. Hesekiah Howler" (a derogatory designation of the time for evangelical preachers) to conduct regular services at the Elliott residence and loudly pray for the soul of Dr. Elliott and all the other neighborhood sinners.[52]

Mrs. Elliott also amused the Gays by disdaining learning and science. She believed it sinful to read anything other than the Bible, except for biographies of John Wesley, and pled with her spouse to "leave his ogle scopes."[53]

A presentist assessment of the Gays' description of Mrs. Elliott might regard them badly. One should keep in mind that they were writing to their friends in the tone of popular writing of their era, which found humor in spousal conflicts and characters deemed to be of a lower social class. Perhaps of greater interest is Sydney Gay's assessment of Dr. Elliott's background. While riding the ferry with Dr. Elliott, Gay conceded that Elliott was able to point out constellations, the names of which Gay had forgotten or did not know. Nonetheless, Gay found Dr. Elliott's claim that he was educated at Oxford surprising considering several errors the doctor made in pronouncing Greek.[54]

Elliott's obituaries and the encyclopedia entry state that he was born in Inverness, the son of a British army officer, and that he was a graduate of the Glasgow Royal College of Surgeons (1828). Yet there is no trace of him in the registers of the University of Glasgow or the registers of the Royal College of Physicians and Surgeons of Glasgow. So this claim seems to be false. However, men often trained through apprenticeships, of which there may no longer be a formal record. Furthermore, Elliott first practiced in the United States as an oculist. Although this has the sound of a medical specialty, and in fact Elliott's practice focused on what we would today refer to as ophthalmology, in his own time in England "oculist" referred to a group of caregivers with no agreed upon required training, categorized with midwives and herbalists. While the medical profession in the United States would focus on certification at a later date, in England formal qualifications were already taking shape, and Elliott would not have been considered a doctor in his own country at the time he emigrated.

Elliott's obituary notes his study of eye diseases with Dr. Alban Goldsmith of Cincinnati.[55] Goldsmith (1788–1861) was chair of surgery at the Medical College of Ohio in Cincinnati in the 1830s.[56] He continued his association with that institution until 1837, when he became chair of surgery at the College of Physicians and Surgeons of New York.[57] Although Goldsmith remained there only until 1839, he did establish a practice in genitourinary surgery in New York. So Elliott may have apprenticed with Goldsmith, but in surgery, not ophthalmology (there is no record that Elliott studied at the Medical College of Ohio). Goldsmith and Elliott seem to have remained lifelong friends. While living in New York, Goldsmith was the witness on Elliott's naturalization papers in 1839.[58]

While Elliott's obituaries and the *Appleton's* biography attest that he gained a national reputation for innovative medical treatments, including pioneering surgical procedures such as cataract removal, they also note that his treatments were controversial and that he was accused of charlatanry. The fact that the accusations, and how Elliott addressed them, were still being rehearsed in his obituaries, even though he had retired from practice the previous year, may mean that his medical reputation was still under a cloud at the time of his death. Obituaries claim that doubts about Elliott stemmed from professional jealousy due to the fame of his patients and his financial success. Nonetheless, Elliott submitted to examinations. Based on when the examining physicians, from Bellevue and the University of New York, were active, he was examined twice, in the early 1850s and again in the 1860s (after he had practiced in New York for more than twenty-five years).[59]

Although Elliott's credentials upon arrival in the United States remain in doubt, after practicing in New York for nearly a decade, he took steps to regularize his qualifications. In the fall semester of 1845, he was listed as a student at Castleton Medical College in Montpelier, Vermont.[60] In 1849 he was examined by a panel of the University Medical College of New York (now New York University School of Medicine), who publicly attested he was qualified to "practice ophthalmic medicine and surgery."[61] Then, after the passage of six years, in 1851 he was awarded the doctor of medicine degree by New York Medical College; his thesis topic was amaurosis (a condition of partial or total blindness without any visible change in the eye).[62]

The degree was controversial in some circles. Dr. J. P. Batchelder brought a resolution before the New York Academy of Medicine seeking that body's admonishment of the college for awarding the degree.[63] Batchelder expressed doubts that Elliott had actually attended lectures or studied with any physician at the college, contesting that Elliott had simply paid his fees and been awarded the degree after a public examination by the board of censors appointed by the college. Speaking "vehemently against Dr. Elliott," he classified the incident as yet another medical school awarding a degree to an unqualified, irregular practitioner.[64] After a heated discussion, Batchelder's resolution was unanimously withdrawn. However, the motion to strike it from the record did not pass. A few months later, on February 5, 1852, a resolution was proposed at the New York State Medical Society meeting in Albany that the New York Medical College be censured for violating the state law requiring three years of study with a respectable practitioner and possess a good moral character by awarding a diploma to "a well-known Irregular Practitioner . . . at the close of its first courses of lectures."[65] Benjamin Fordyce Parker, a faculty member at the college, was prepared to respond and read character references by Valentine Mott, Samuel H. Dickson, J. W. Draper, and Granville Sharpe Pattison for Dr. Elliott, the irregular practitioner referenced, though unnamed, in the resolution. Parker received considerable back talk from the floor, asserting that it was common knowledge that Elliott was a "quack" and that he advertised widely in newspapers. When Parker presented church membership as further proof of Elliott's character, the response from the floor that it was a church he built himself must have garnered some laughs. The discussion soon moved away from assessments of Elliott to the larger issue of how the medical profession was to police itself, keeping practitioners from advertising untested ointments and services and publishing testimonials, as well as receiving degrees for merely paying fees and not actually attending lectures or being supervised by a physician. Although other, weaker iterations of the earlier resolution were proposed, none actually passed.

    The fact that Elliott advertised his complementary services for the poor, hair tonic samples, endorsements for other remedies, and patient testimonials might seem like evidence of a dubious character, but other physicians did the same sorts of thing. One important fact not openly presented in the meeting accounts is the nature of New York Medical College. It was a homeopathic college, and the New York Academy of Medicine was antipathetic to homeopaths. Nonetheless, the accounts of both meetings at which resolutions were proposed certainly demonstrate personal animus against Elliott.

    Despite his degree, Elliott submitted to reexamination in the 1860s when the medical profession was organizing. Credentialing in the United States was fluid until the 1870s, when state licensing became active. After the Civil War, physicians who had been in practice for decades but were not affiliated with a hospital or medical school often had to respond to detractors. So other physicians shared Elliott's experience, particularly when professional jealousy entered the equation.

Professional jealousy is believable in Elliott's case since he treated so many notable patients. Because many of these were, or became, authors and men of note, we have accounts of his treatment methods (although the equivocal, and sometimes hostile, nature of the accounts do not prove his medical skill with any finality). Furthermore, although the sample is skewed by its smallness and the patients' similarities, it is remarkable that each patient was undergoing some emotional crisis when they began having eye problems. One of the first conditions written about by the earliest generations of neurologists, like Jean-Martin Charcot, and psychoanalysts, like Sigmund Freud, was the condition of "hysterical blindness," which is today classified as conversion disorder or functional neurologic symptom disorder. Patients diagnosed with this psychiatric condition experience neurological symptoms (blindness, fits, numbness, or paralysis) that have no well-established organic cause and can be traced to a psychological trigger. Although a great deal of prudence must be exercised in diagnosing patients long dead, whose presenting conditions may be only cursorily described, nonetheless the connection between the onset of eye problems and emotional distress among Elliott's famous patients is striking.

One of the earliest treatment records we have is that of abolitionist and poet James Russell Lowell (1819–1891). Lowell graduated from Harvard College in 1838. Although he was from a wealthy and distinguished family when he became engaged to Maria White in 1840, her father insisted that the wedding be delayed until he was employed. With a good deal of hesitation, Lowell enrolled at Harvard Law School, but he contributed poetry and prose articles to magazines. His marriage continued to be postponed even after publication of his first book of poetry, *A Year's Life* (Boston: C. C. Little and J. Brown, 1841), perhaps because the book only sold three hundred copies. Lowell's eye troubles began in late 1842 after he commenced his law career. His eyes bothered him so much that he was prevented from legal work or continuing his editorship of *The Pioneer*, a literary magazine he was editing. In addition to distaste for the legal career he had been driven to choose and the stress of editorship and uncertainty over the reception of the first issue of his magazine, his mother had begun her descent into mental illness. When he sought treatment with Dr. Elliott in New York, one practical effect was a physical removal from his law office, from his future father-in-law, from the other men involved with *The Pioneer*, and from his faltering mother (with whom he had resided).[66]

In writing about his treatment, Lowell noted the long wait time involved in seeing Elliott, since "the Doctor is overrun with patients" (a theme with Elliott's patients).[67] Lowell's treatment necessitated daily office visits during which he was "made blind for the space of fifteen minutes."[68] How the blindness was induced is not clear. Lowell was also operated upon "with the knife," at least twice in January 1843.[69] In a letter, Lowell noted that he was "forbidden to write under pain of staying here forever or losing my eyes."[70] Unable to work, Lowell spent his time with literary friends, including his new acquaintance Nathaniel Parker Willis (1806–1867), the most highly paid magazine writer of his day, who was being treated by Elliott at the same time. Lowell concluded his course of treatment, returning home to find his mother's mind "completely disordered."[71] Nevertheless, he was able to finish editing his second book, *Conversations on Some of the Old Poets* (Cambridge, MA: John Owen, 1845).[72] Although the volume was not actually published until a few weeks after the wedding, he had convinced Maria White's father that the book would appear in December 1844, and on the strength of his assertion, the couple wed. Although Lowell continued to suffer ill health throughout his life, he lived until he was seventy-two years old with no further eye conditions.[73]

William Hickling Prescott (1796–1859), another of Elliott's well-known patients, sought treatment in 1842. Prescott's case is distinctive in this discussion since his condition began with a physical injury. While a junior at Harvard College in 1813, Prescott's left eye was struck by a crust of bread in a dining hall food fight, and he was nearly blinded in that eye. The sight in his right eye was weakened by infection. His challenges with his eyesight were compounded by what was described as acute rheumatism that struck shortly after his graduation from college. Devoting himself to historical study, he employed various strategies, including readers and the use of a noctograph (a combination writing grid and stylus system), and according to biographers his eyesight also swung between total blindness and good vision. By the time he consulted Dr. Elliott, Prescott had been married for twenty years and had published essays and reviews, a book on Charles Brockden Brown, and a widely read three-volume work on Spain's monarchs Ferdinand and Isabella that shaped his career focus on Spain's New World empire.

Prescott carefully analyzed both Elliott and his proposed treatment plan in a memorandum to himself dated April 28, 1842. As with so many of his patients, Elliott indicated that at least six months of direct treatment would be required for Prescott's left eye and five to six weeks for his right eye followed by a year of home remedies, including "unguents and internal medicines to put the body and spirits in a right state."[74] Prescott reviewed the costs in terms of time and the loss of reading time (since Elliott considered overuse a factor in the condition of Prescott's right eye). He concluded that the anticipated benefits of Elliott's treatment of his left eye were too uncertain and not worth the "tedium of the remedies."[75] About his right eye, Prescott said that he did not believe his vision in that eye to be dissimilar to that of Elliott's patients after treatment. Prescott conceded Elliott possessed knowledge of the eye's anatomy, would treat him with care, and had successfully treated many patients. However, Prescott also noted "nothing is easier than self-delusion with the eye" and that Elliott "overstates, and unwarrantably excites hopes by a sudden positive assertion . . . he has a quackish tone also, in his remarks on the phenomena of diseases."[76] In the end, Prescott decided not to pursue Elliott's treatment plan.[77]

Unlike Prescott, Charles Eliot Norton (1827–1908), another scion of a notable New England family, was undergoing an emotional crisis when treated by Elliott in 1843. Although Norton would go on to a significant career as one of the foremost men of American letters and a professor at Harvard, in 1843 he was a struggling Harvard freshman experiencing the distractions of campus life.[78] His father, the Rev. Andrews Norton, had high expectations for behavior and the effective use of time, and Harvard offered no opportunity to escape parental oversight since Norton's cousin was the institution's president. When Norton told his parents of eye problems, they sent him to Dr. Elliott, who prescribed a three-month course of treatment. The nature of Elliott's therapeutic intervention is not described, but Norton, living at a Manhattan boarding house, made the most of his freedom in the city. Using letters of introduction from Henry Wadsworth Longfellow (one of his professors), he gained entrée to the highest literary circles. When he returned home, his parents noted his strengthened eyes but were also pleased by his improved character. He was forming "habits of self-reliance, of trusting to one's own judgment, of being governed by one's own sense of right and wrong, of submitting patiently and cheerfully to disappointment and deprivation, and of controlling one's feelings."[79] He had gained some maturity by his New York experiences that enabled him to successfully return to his studies, in addition to whatever benefits his eyes gained from Elliott's ministrations.

When, in September 1843, Longfellow himself sought treatment from Dr. Elliott, the treatment focused on forming new habits. Longfellow's wife, Fanny, believed he was simply experiencing eyestrain, and she expected his speedy recovery from this minor condition under Elliott's care. Nevertheless, the doctor prescribed a month of thrice-per-week office visits that involved "dosings and blisterings."[80] Even when Longfellow returned to Cambridge, Elliott specified treatments to be administered by Fanny and adherence to a list of "admirable rules."[81] Fanny left the exact nature of the home treatments unspecified, but referenced Elliott's belief in the importance of exercise to redistribute the blood sent to the head by Longfellow's intellectual pursuits.[82] Fanny Longfellow wrote to a friend that Elliott said her husband's "frame demands a great deal of exercise" and that Longfellow responded by taking boxing lessons and long walks.[83] Two years later, Longfellow was still so troubled by his eyes that he underwent treatment with Dr. Wesselhoeft, a hydropath.[84] In 1849, he was still telling his friend Evert Duyckink that he was "half blind."[85] Having found no effective medical treatment, Longfellow seems to have continued to follow "admirable rules." He wrote and read only during the hours of the day with the best natural light, which meant that unlike scholars and authors whose writing was an isolating experience, drawing them away from family and friends, Longfellow kept the schedule of professionals who worked away from home and spent his evening hours enjoying the company of his family and friends. Whether necessitated by a physical condition or not, Longfellow's adaptation must have added years to the time that he was able to enjoy family and social life, while alleviating any feelings of guilt over unfinished reading and writing.

In 1846, when Francis Parkman (1823–1893) consulted Dr. Elliott, his treatment plan also focused on adaptation. Specifically, changes in the way he dealt with his emotions. Born into the highest ranks of Boston society, Parkman's father had hoped that Harvard would settle the young man in a respectable career. Instead, his father's insistence upon respectability had driven Parkman to explore his passion for scholarship. In 1846, after finishing the law degree his father had wanted for him, Parkman left to experience the frontier conditions that still existed in the West and live among the Oglala Sioux near Laramie, Wyoming. He hoped the experience would help him better understand the earlier frontier conditions that formed the backdrop for the contest between France and England for control of North America so that he could write about the era with more insight. Traveling over two thousand miles in six months, he returned exhausted. Almost blind, he consulted Dr. Elliott, who had successfully treated his sister.[86] The initial diagnosis was that two months of treatment would restore Parkman's eyes. Parkman's biographer, Howard

Doughty, described Dr. Elliott's system as a "rest cure" and the community of rental properties in Elliottville as "a forerunner of the modern sanitarium" where "a good many high-strung New Englanders" were patients.[87]

Two years later, Parkman was still living off and on in Manhattan (frequenting Delmonico's) and his eyes had grown worse. His sister said that Dr. Elliott had found "peculiarities of the system" not initially apparent and that Parkman's nervous system "was a good deal deranged," which impeded medical treatment.[88] Parkman's own description of his condition, as stemming from a "wild whirl" that uncontrollably took over his brain, seems to confirm Elliott telling Parkman's sister about the impact of Parkman's nervous state. The prescribed treatment was total rest from "brainwork," or what Doughty terms "sanative idleness."[89] In the end, though, Parkman concluded that brainwork was exactly what he needed.[90] To make it possible for him to write, he rigged up a board with guide wires, and he recorded accounts of his travels, published as installments for *Knickerbocker Magazine* (printed in 1849 as *The Oregon Trail*) and began work on the history that would be published in 1851 as *The Conspiracy of Pontiac and the Indian War After the Conquest of Canada*. He left Elliott's care to move back to Boston and marry in 1850.

Parkman's condition was never effectively diagnosed, and he remained partially sighted for the rest of his life (he lived to be seventy). However, during Elliott's treatment, Parkman seems to have resolved to be engaged despite physical disabilities (in addition to visual impairments, Parkman suffered from severe arthritis, digestive ailments, and insomnia). He had learned to be patient and to accept his physical challenges, rather than trying to vanquish them by forcing himself into the sort of physical activity that had been so deleterious on his trip West. Instead, he resolved to embrace a life of writing and research, despite his visual impairment, by utilizing enabling adaptations (in addition to his writing board, he hired readers and amanuenses). Accepting his physical condition as an unalterable fact seems to have overcome his father's objections to a life of scholarship and study, and Parkman went on to unabashedly draw upon significant inherited family resources to underwrite his life's work.

Fanny Longfellow had said that Dr. Elliott was "capable of inspiring much faith."[91] One can imagine how important this was at a time when much less was known about the cause of physical ailments. Then too, such qualities were even more important when the patient may have been suffering from conversion disorder. Even though Elliott was treating conditions of a specific organ, he also seems to have emphasized overall physical health, encouraging his patients to get exercise. His son, Dr. Samuel R. Elliott (1835–1909), who would eventually take over his father's practice, said, with an implicit wink, that Elliott told those patients who were staying on Staten Island about a therapeutic spring that could only be reached by a long walk.

Looking back from the present, when holistic approaches to health care have become common, Dr. Elliott may seem like a prematurely enlightened figure. However, he also drew upon a materia medica that included, in addition to the blistering mentioned in the treatment of Longfellow, bloodletting and a salve that he advertised in newspapers and sold through the mail (he also promoted a salve to remedy hair loss). Charles Sumner claimed to be relieved of inflammation of the eyelids by the salve in 1845.[92] Elliott also had a very sharp knife "whose infinitesimal blade was barely visible under a magnifying glass."[93] Elliott displayed the miraculous knife to patients before operating upon them and with much ceremony returned the blade to a locked safe in his office.

The lengthiest documented record of treatment in Elliott's career is that of the thirteen years that Edward Livingston Youmans (1821–1887) was a patient. After his treatment, Youmans helped found *Popular Science Monthly* and played a crucial role in publicizing evolutionary theory in the United States (he established and edited the International Scientific Series for D. Appleton, which published works by Charles Darwin, Herbert Spencer, and other key figures in the sciences, making certain they got paid royalties even though international copyright had yet to be established).

When he was thirteen, Youmans began to experience ophthalmia, an eye inflammation that is symptomatic of several underlying conditions. By seventeen he was only partially sighted, and after consulting several other physicians in Manhattan, he finally made his way to Dr. Elliott's office in 1840. Youmans's biographer, John Fiske (1842–1901), noted that "Dr. Samuel M. Elliott gave him most encouragement, and something in his manner inspired confidence."[94] Initially, Elliott said a cure was obtainable within six months.[95] No specifics are given as to Youmans's treatment, except that during the summers he spent time on Staten Island, where he was able to swim, ride horseback, and generally engage in outdoor activities.[96]

While the lack of a treatment plan does not further our understanding of Elliott as a physician, through Fiske's biography we do gain insight into Elliott's character. After Elliott revised his initial diagnosis, letting his patient know that years would be needed to effect a cure, the doctor announced he would take no additional fees. In Fiske's account,

Elliott also had a crucial role in launching Youmans on his career. Around that time, Youmans's sister, Eliza Ann, got a teaching job in Manhattan, enabling her to spend her leisure with Youmans, writing for him and reading to him. Elliott arranged for Youmans to lodge in the offices of his medical practice and permitted him to use the chemical apparatuses there, leading his sister in experiments. Within a short time, Elliott was allowing Youmans to offer a lecture series in the office, covering topics such as "the relations of organic life to the atmosphere," "the sources and nature of alcohol and its effect on the human system," "the relation of sun to life on our planet," "the chemistry of the sun and the stars," and "the links uniting the realms of matter and mind."[97] Youmans built a lyceum circuit career from this beginning that extended through 1868. After the success of a teaching tool that presented atomic structure in chart form, in 1851 Youmans published the textbook *Class-Book of Chemistry* with D. Appleton, which went through three editions in his lifetime and sold more than 144,000 copies.

According to Eliza Ann, after the textbook was published, Youmans's health improved dramatically. Not only did he lose "the introverted expression of the blind," but his "eyes became so much stronger that he could now say farewell to the doctor."[98] So this would seem to be another case in which one of Elliott's patients consulted him while undergoing a period of emotional turmoil (in Youmans's case the uncertainties of being able to support himself financially through intellectual endeavors). Once the emotional turmoil was resolved, the eye condition was relieved without additional intervention from Elliott. Youmans's case might also further our understanding of Elliott as a holistic practitioner. Eliza Ann wrote that "Youmans's constitution, originally robust, had been impaired by his sedentary habits," and she blamed his decline in the years before his death and even his early demise on a failure to follow medical advice to spend time in the country and engage in "open-air occupations."[99]

The only detailed account of Elliott's surgical interventions describes the cataract treatment of John B. Wood, night editor of *The Sun*.[100] When Wood was almost blind, *The Sun*'s publisher, Charles Dana, made an appointment for him with his own oculist, Dr. Elliott. Elliott showed his patient a minute knife, and after assuring him there would be no pain and no need for chloroform, cut his "dead lens" with "a few skillful whirls." In this treatment, the cornea was cut to release the aqueous humor from the eye, which dissolved the dead lens and allowed a new one to generate after repeated cuts and releases of aqueous humor. In between each operation, the patient was to "live high," eating nourishing food like beefsteak, cream, and oatmeal. After several months, the patient's eyesight was restored, but he ended his account with the peroration that it was not his night work under gaslight that caused the condition but a sedentary and unhealthy life, working "for three years from twelve to fourteen hours a day, taking no open-air exercise, and eating the innutritious, indigestible victuals that are served in the hotels and restaurants." Living in this manner, the blood flow to his eyes was reduced and his cornea died from lack of nutriment. "If, when dimness of sight first began to manifest itself, I had taken an hour a day from my desk and walked in open air, and at the same time eaten beefsteaks and that incomparable food, oatmeal and cream, I might have fortified myself against the insidious march of death."[101] So even in this account of surgical intervention, the focus is on holistic health care.

New Englanders who settled in his neighborhood would have welcomed Elliott's alternative approach to medical practice. Within the abolitionist movement, nontraditional approaches to medicine were part of the larger constellation of social reform commitments. William Lloyd Garrison, for instance, advocated homeopathy. Lydia Maria Child, in her decades-long correspondence with the Shaws, wrote favorably of a form of homeopathy that was linked to her Spiritualism and her embrace of phrenology. The Gays also mentioned homeopathic and other alternative medical practices in their correspondence, particularly with James Russell Lowell. As late as 1892, when George Curtis was enduring his final illness, his wife Anna wrote to Charles Eliot Norton that they had returned to homeopathic practice "after losing four weeks to please" their son Dr. Frank Curtis, who had become a physician.[102]

Beyond what can be garnered from Elliott's treatment plans for his famous patients, we know some other things about him: people thought him eccentric but knew him to be kind and charitable. In 1912, when Anna Curtis was interviewed about him, she spoke in some detail about the number of charity patients he treated on Staten Island. She said he would let them visit him early in the morning, until he would see the eight o'clock boat for New York pass the end of Bard Avenue from his window. At that point he would hurry to his buggy and race the boat to the second landing after Bard to begin his journey into the city.

Some of his reputation for eccentricity stemmed from his manner of conversation, mode of dress, and family life, all of which made him stand out among the New Englanders of Elliottville but were less remarkable in his native Scotland. For instance, it was commonly known that he had two wives and two families. The first marriage grew out of a youthful love affair in Scotland. The Scots had a term that had come into usage in the mid-1700s, "Scotch marriage," for such alliances, which were what we would refer to as common law marriages. Although in Scotland law these marriages are based on a consensual contract, no formal ceremony is involved. Even though Elliott married a second time, to Letitia Irvine (1802–1881), after he was settled on Staten Island, he sent for his first wife, Dianah Taylor Elliott (1801–1876) and their two daughters and settled them on a farm in New Jersey. The daughters visited Dr. Elliott's household, and after he died they were eventually treated as equals in the division of his property.[103]

We also know that Elliott had a great deal of pride in his native country and patriotism for his adopted country. In 1858 he was one of the founders of the Highland Guard, or Seventy-Ninth New York Militia, which functioned as a fraternity of men of Scottish ancestry. Although the militia's formation was aided by the Caledonian and St. Andrews societies of New York, financial backing came from Elliott, Sir Roderick Cameron (another Staten Island resident), and other affluent men. As with other such militia units, the Seventy-Ninth had colorful uniforms (Cameron tartan trousers and blue jackets with red collars, cuffs, and white piping) and conducted parade ground drills and heavy artillery training that appealed to audiences of women and boys. Official duties were ceremonious, like providing an honor guard in 1860 during the visits of Albert Edward, the Prince of Wales, and the New York visit of the first Japanese diplomatic mission to the United States.[104] Elliott was so closely identified with the Seventy-Ninth that "at the request of many country men and friends," he published an account of the history of the regiment's service in 1861 (dated November 1861, Elliottville, Staten Island).[105]

When the Civil War began in 1861, the Seventy-Ninth volunteered for active service. Dr. Elliott provided money to recruit additional men (since the militia was under strength). When the regiment was mustered in on May 29, 1861, for three years' service Elliott, with the rank of lieutenant colonel, was in command. Three of his sons, Quarter-Master Sergeant Alban W. Elliott, First Lieutenant Samuel R. Elliott, and First Lieutenant William St. George Elliott, also served with various companies in the regiment. The Seventy-Ninth, with a troop strength of 895 men, marched down Broadway on June 2, 1861, on their way to the defense of Washington.[106] One of the earliest regiments to arrive in the federal city, the regiment changed commanding officers, reputedly influenced by

Secretary of War Simon Cameron to select his brother, Colonel James Cameron, to lead.[107] Cameron was killed in action at the First Battle of Bull Run on July 21, 1861. Elliott was seriously wounded in the same battle when his horse was shot from under him and he suffered internal injuries that prevented further active duty. He continued to recruit troops as needed, and after the Seventy-Ninth term of service ended in 1864 he was authorized to form the "New Cameron Highlanders," a regiment whose volunteers served through the end of the war, before returning to New York State militia status.

The documentary record for Elliott becomes much sparser after the Civil War. Some of his obituaries claim that he never fully recovered from his wartime injury and was forced to limit his medical practice. He may also have been less active as a medical practitioner once his son, Dr. Samuel R. Elliott, joined his practice. Unlike his father, the younger Elliott had a broad range of medical training and experience abroad in Germany and Paris.

So far as Elliottville was concerned, Dr. Samuel Mackenzie Elliott seems to have been far less of a presence after his relocation to Grymes Hill. The few references to him in correspondence date from after the Civil War and concern his certification difficulties and his final illness and death.

Conclusion

During his lifetime, Elliott earned wide admiration for his medical skill, his charitableness, and his patriotism, but not necessarily for his real estate endeavors. If Dr. Elliott envisioned founding an enduring, eponymous village through his land transactions and residential construction, he was quickly disappointed. For a time in the 1850s, Elliottville did exist on maps of Staten Island. Legend has it that Dr. Elliott put up signs for Elliottville on the one road (later Bard Avenue) through the properties he was developing.[108] After he had moved out of the neighborhood in 1855 to build a house on Grymes Hill,[109] Elliottville came to be referred to in connection with Bard Avenue.

Dr. Elliott had purchased his first land in the neighborhood in 1839 from Thomas E. Davis and William Bard (1778–1853), between what is now Bard and Davis Avenues.[110] Bard was the son of a famous physician, Dr. Samuel Bard (1742–1821), who among his distinctions performed surgery on George Washington and was a founder of Columbia University's medical school. William Bard's grandfather, John Bard (1716–1799), also a physician, had rented the extensive Staten Island property known as Duxbury Glebe prior to the American Revolution. Through his wife Suzanne Valleau's inheritance, John Bard also became a major landholder in Hyde Park.[111] Dr. Samuel Bard inherited most of the estate of his father, John Bard. William married wealthy heiress Catherine Cruger (1781–1868) and, as Dr. Samuel Bard's only son to survive to adulthood, also inherited most of his father's fortune.[112] Some years after receiving his inheritance he founded the New York Life Insurance Company in 1830.[113] Perhaps William Bard found Dr. Elliott's pretensions irksome, particularly since he was the son of such a famous physician. It was Bard's Delafield grandsons in the neighborhood who supposedly replaced Elliottville signs with Bard Avenue signs.[114] The name persisted.[115] William's daughter Eliza (1813–1902) continued to live on the Bard Avenue property with her family until the 1880s (she married Rufus King Delafield, son of one of the wealthiest men in the country, and the couple raised their seven children on the Bard estate).[116] Although the name Elliottville lingered on due to the properties Elliott continued to own, it was entirely supplanted after the neighborhood came to be referred to as Livingston, the name of the local railway station in the 1880s.[117] Since Livingston referred to a larger area than the original Elliottville, Bard Avenue referred to the area that was originally Elliottville.

This chapter has traced the origins of Elliottville with a particular focus on founder Dr. Elliott. His construction of substantial houses in the neighborhood had a significant impact on later development. Through the accounts of authors he treated, we get a sense of his commitment to holistic health care. In addition, he seems to have had the ability to inspire a confidence in his patients that was therapeutic. Since several of his patients mention living in Elliottville during their treatment, the neighborhood functioned, in part, as a residential treatment community of the sort that was not uncommon when patients had to travel significant distances to consult a specialist. Although Elliott did not document his political convictions in writing, his crucial role in the formation of the Seventy-Ninth regiment and his heroic command of the regiment demonstrate his patriotism and commitment to the Union in the Civil War. In the next chapter, we will see how his medical practice attracted a group of residents to Elliottville that shaped the outside perception of the community and influenced its development.

Chapter 2

Boston People

Elliottville Takes Shape

Life on Staten Island had from the first been an exceptionally interesting one. By some fortuitous circumstance there had settled on the North Shore a group of unusual character, people largely of New England birth, of Abolitionist tendencies, and of Unitarian faith.

—Mary Willcox, "A Gay Life"[1]

Introduction

From the outset, the qualities that made Elliottville distinctive were the built environment and social cohesiveness. These elements endured throughout the history of the neighborhood, although they weakened in the 1870s and 1880s. By the time these elements were no longer notably present in the late 1890s, the neighborhood had lost its distinctiveness and blended in with the rest of Staten Island's North Shore.

When Dr. Elliott chose William Ranlett to design Elliottville houses, Ranlett was living on Staten Island, not far from Elliottville.[2] He is considered a successor of Andrew Jackson Downing, who is discussed later in this chapter. However, Ranlett's Staten Island houses and his serial publication *The Architect: A Series of Original Design*, vols. 1 and 2 (New York: Dewitt & Davenport, 1847–1849) appeared only somewhat after Downing's book on landscape design and around the same time as Downing's first pattern book. Unlike Downing, Ranlett, who had trained as a carpenter-builder, included extensive details in his building designs, as well as landscape renderings for each of his structures.

Ranlett pointed out that the Staten Island projects in which he was involved combined "to some extent the advantages and pleasures of city, and country life"[3] that later came to be associated with suburbs. These were the qualities that Frederick Law Olmsted referenced as well, praising New Brighton as "wholly untownlike . . . surrounded by grounds with a variety of trees, magnificent views; roads well lighted and bordered by sod."[4] Transportation was one crucial element that was making suburbs possible, and for residents of Elliottville that meant travel into the city by ferry. Although Downing did not comment specifically on Staten Island, he applauded the kind of residential development being enabled by improved transportation: "Hundreds and thousands formerly obliged to live in the crowded streets of cities, now find themselves able to enjoy a country cottage, several miles distant—the old notions of time and space being half annihilated."[5]

Although other suburbs were developing on Staten Island around the time of Elliottville, none of them had the same architectural cohesiveness. Ranlett designed in a Romantic Revival–style that usually combined Gothic and Tudor elements, often with cut stone construction. There were quarries on Staten Island, and of course, Elliott, who spent so much time in Edinburgh, would have considered stone construction customary, even though in the United States wood was much more common in residential construction.

Ranlett laid out settings for the houses he designed that included gardens, meadows, and outbuildings. Such designs were not intended to be merely decorative but evinced an underlying philosophy of how residents of Elliottville would live. Put most simply, if Jeffersonian democracy were to be expressed in landscape design, the result would have much in common with Ranlett's designs. These were not merely decorative landscapes of aristocrats; these were meant to be working landscapes, where residents could raise much of the produce for their table. Such landscapes were consistent with the yeoman farmer concept that Jefferson idealized. The landscape of industrializing Manhattan, a physical expression of Jacksonian democracy, contrasted dramatically with Ranlett's designs. So too did the landscapes common in the slaveholding states that Frederick Law Olmsted, a friend of many Elliottville residents, would later describe and attribute so much significance to in his *A Journey in the Seaboard Slave States: With Remarks on Their Economy* (New York: Dix and Edwards, 1856).

Ranlett termed the mode of living his designs enabled "living cottagely," a mode achievable in a modest cottage or a wealthy man's villa.[6] In an era when social philosophers decried the misery of isolated households and vaunted communal life (where raising food, caring for children, and earning a living could be shared in a Fourier-style phalanstery), Ranlett asserted that living cottagely was best suited to a Christian republic and conformed best to nature. The republic's political institutions enabled each man to have his own household, and such establishments best reflected political independence. Ranlett insisted that the independent, self-sustaining household did not entail a brutish descent into nature. Instead, living cottagely gave citizens the opportunity to cultivate their tastes and morals by residing in an aesthetically pleasing structure and engaging in landscape gardening, an art that, unlike the plastic arts, spread "its beauties before the public eye—allowing rich and poor alike to look upon them."[7] Living cottagely, then, for Ranlett ultimately had a social dimension, serving to cultivate the individual and through him the community.

While Elliottville residents did not directly express philosophies on the design of residences and the meaning of landscapes, they did write about what was important to them about the physical environment of their neighborhood. Firstly, they spoke of the beauty of the natural setting that combined shoreline, woodland, and high hills (some points on Staten Island have the highest elevations of any on the Eastern Seaboard south of Maine). Secondly, their letters are filled with details about the flowers, fruits, poultry, and vegetables they raised. Although they had household help, many residents, particularly women and children, gardened and took pride in their efforts. In the first years she lived in Elliottville, Elizabeth Gay had Nicholas De Hart, the Black laborer the Gays employed as a gardener, drive her into the woods to select native trees and plants for him to dig and replant at the cottage. During temperate months, she and her children detailed in correspondence the seedlings that were germinating and the yields they were getting from strawberries, blackberries, cherries, grapes, and apples, and their flocks of chickens and ducks. Neighborhood women also raised flowers that they turned into displays, sometimes quite elaborate, for social events in their houses and church. The Gays' neighbor, Laura Johnson, was especially known for extensive flower gardens and for generously providing cut flowers to neighbors. Finally, the surviving documents confirm the importance their houses had for Curtis, Shaw, the Gays, and Laura Johnson.

Three Elliottville Houses

Looking at the houses of Curtis, Gay, and Shaw furthers our understanding of why Elliottville was important to them. Sydney Gay, in recounting his housing search to Edmund Qunicy, expressed dismay over the high cost of Manhattan, but also related his disgust over the built environment, where residences were adjacent to businesses such as lumberyards, slaughterhouses, and distilleries. In the city, Gay observed that dairies fed their cows on grains that were byproducts of the distillation process and pointed out that the milk was tainted with alcohol.[8]

Unlike his friend, Frank Shaw, a Bostonian, and George Curtis, who was raised in Providence and moved with his family to Manhattan while still a young man, Sydney Gay grew up in Hingham, Massachusetts, where his family had lived for generations, and the experience was a lifelong influence. Gay was the son of lawyer Ebenezer Gay (1771–1842) and his wife Mary Allyne Otis (1779–1866).[9] One of Sydney Gay's paternal ancestors arrived with the fleet of Governor John Winthrop in 1630, the same year as one of his maternal ancestors was arriving elsewhere in the Bay Colony. Gay had a relatively affluent upbringing as a middle child with eleven siblings. Although he began classes at Harvard College, illness forced him home in his junior year, and between 1832 and 1836 he tried out various means of making a living as a businessman. He had Boston relatives in the China trade, but he had health crises while working in their Boston office. Sent by his parents to relatives in Charleston, South Carolina, to recover his health, he had his first exposure to slave culture, before returning to business. After another health crisis, his father arranged for Gay to establish an export business in Canton, China, and when that effort failed, in other cities in the United States, including St. Louis and New Orleans. He returned to Hingham, a failure at business and in poor health, to work as a tutor in 1838.[10]

Social life in Hingham revolved around public meetings. People gathered to exercise their rights as citizens in local government meetings and to hear preachers and lecturers. In many of these assemblies there was agitation over social reform, with various regional movements recruiting local adherents. Abolitionism was spotlighted in 1839 when a local newspaper opened the slave debate, and a new local minister began criticizing slavery from the pulpit and allowing abolitionist speakers to hold meetings in the church hall. Since Hingham was largely opposed to abolitionism, an uproar followed. Gay, newly convinced of the evils of slavery (he had previously been critical of abolitionists) participated in the public debate. After his father's death in 1842, the small legacy he received freed him to begin lecturing for the American Anti-Slavery Society with the likes of Frederick Douglass and Charles Redmond. The hardship of frontier travel and challenges of hostile audiences, angry mobs, and threats of violence fortified his commitment to abolitionism, and he abandoned teaching to devote himself to abolitionist organizations.[11]

Gay's increasing organizational commitments brought him into contact with Frank and Sarah Shaw, and a close personal friendship developed. Abolitionist circles fostered unusually close friendships since the people who devoted themselves to the cause sought emotional support in the face of society's hostility. Gay later said that abolitionists were generally perceived as "pestilent fanatics," but for him they were "the most charming circle of cultivated men and women it has ever been my lot to know."[12] For many years, being a part of the abolitionist movement was an all-encompassing experience for Gay, occupying the whole of his personal and professional life.

Figure 2.1. This view shows the size of the Gays' house and documents that it followed the Ranlett practice of not being orientated to a street. *Source*: Robert Mathewson, photographer, January 17, 1947. Courtesy of Staten Island Museum.

When Sydney and Elizabeth Gay decided to move to Staten Island, they chose one of Dr. Elliott's houses that was already under construction on an existing cart track called Hayley's Lane. Although the property extended to what would become Bard Avenue, the main access was from another street and the house would eventually have a mailing address of 99 Davis Avenue. The way the house was sited was in accord with Ranlett's practice of placing a dwelling within landscaped grounds. The Gays, who moved in as renters, had only minor input in the design of their house, unlike Frank Shaw, who worked directly with an architect, and George Curtis, who chose a design by his friend Alexander Jackson Downing. The Gays tried to influence some practical aspects of the design, but to no avail.[13] Nonetheless, the Gays took pride and comfort in their new property. In Sydney Gay's letters announcing their move, the first thing he mentioned was the beauty of Staten Island and the immediate setting of the house. Elliott had planted the property with ailanthus trees (*Ailanthus altissima*, commonly tree of heaven). Currently despised as invasive, at the time the trees might have been interpreted as symbols of reform-mindedness. Although they had first been introduced to the United States in Philadelphia in 1784, in New York they only became available in 1820 and were considered novel ornamentals. In writing about the trees, Gay says they provided excellent shade and repelled mosquitos.[14] In the first years of living in the house, the Gays referred to the property as Ailanthus Cottage.

In describing his house to Edmund Quincy, Gay adopted a somewhat derisory tone, claiming that the dwelling was no better than an impoverished editor could expect to live in. He even claimed that Elliott originally intended the structure as a barn and then had Ranlett add Gothic ornaments. However, reading between the lines, Gay clearly took pride in his new house. The Gothic-Tudor style was distinctive, and, according to Gay, Ranlett had published the design. The house, situated on four acres, had a "piazza"[15] and double parlors, with a study for Sydney off one of them. Because the walls were filled with brick, the structure was well insulated.[16]

Although the Gays decided on the house in March 1847, they had to wait to move in. Initially promised for June, which was already inconvenient, requiring them to board far longer than they wished, the house was not actually finished until July, and even then some important elements were left unfinished. When they first moved in, they had no kitchen range, no fence around the property, no well, and every rainstorm filled their basement with water. Despite some of the shortcomings, both of the

Figure 2.2. This plan shows the way Ranlett intended his cottages to be sited and the grounds to be utilized. *Source*: William Ranlett, *The Architect: A Series of Original Designs, for Domestic and Ornamental Cottages and Villas* [. . .], vol. 1 (New York: William H. Graham, 1847), design 1, plate 2. Courtesy of College of Staten Island Archives and Special Collections. Public domain.

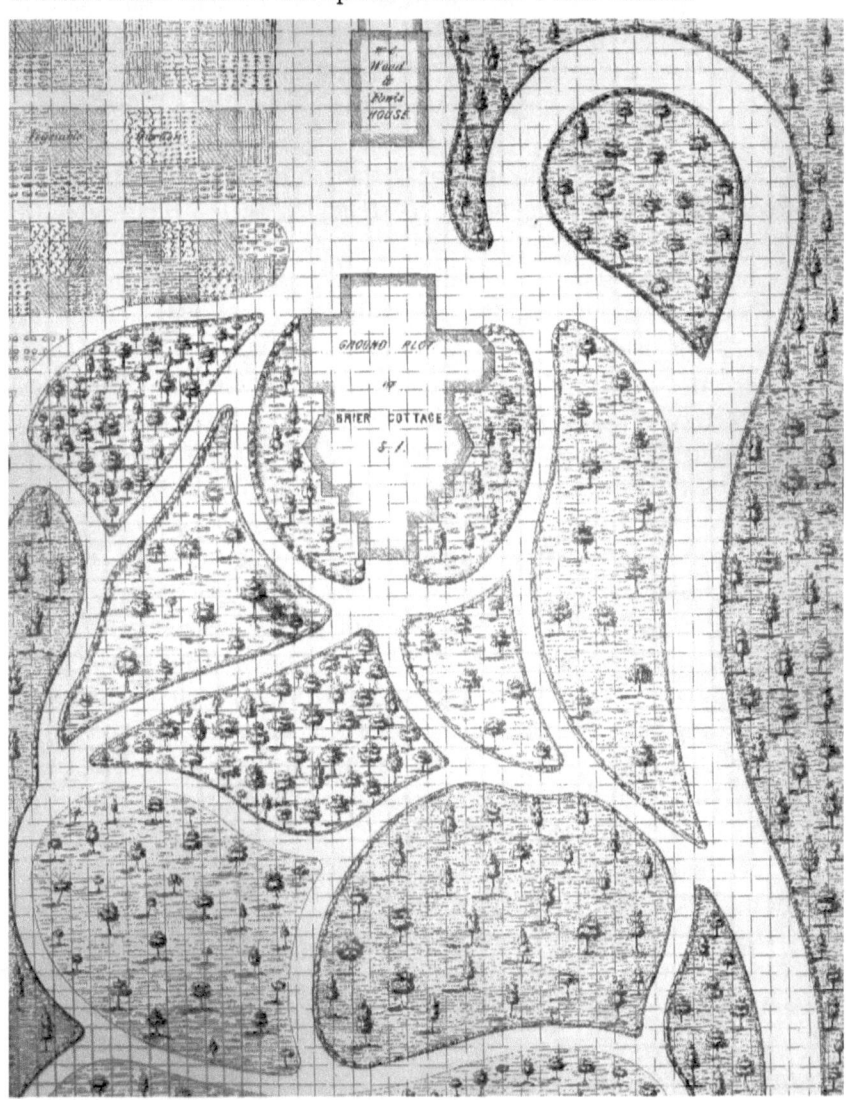

Gays were delighted with their house. In addition to the beautiful, rural setting, Sydney emphasized their interesting and compatible neighbors: in addition to Dr. and Mrs. Elliott, the Shaws, the family of Dr. Edward Wigglesworth (d. 1896), and some of Elliott's patients, there was a cousin of Edmund Quincy and a mutual friend from Hingham. Elizabeth, in anticipation of setting up house, in April 1847, said she felt very happy that "we have so delightful a property,"[17] and in August, after they had moved in, "I am very happy my dear, dear husband that I am writing thee from our own home."[18]

The Gays could finally purchase their house in 1850 for $4,500 (approximately $181,000 in today's currency).[19] Their delight, and Dr. Elliott's happiness for them, is reflected in the peculiar wording of the deed. No doubt Gay had shared with Elliott his distaste for living in the city where abattoirs, feed lots, houses, and distilleries were side by side, and his pleasure in the residential character of Elliottville. Therefore, in addition to the Ranlett-style proscription on building any structure within fifty feet of any street, Elliott incorporated a ridiculously long list of buildings that Gay could not erect. These twenty-five proscribed building types included slaughterhouse, forge, steam engine, iron factory, and distillery. The list no doubt prompted shared laughter at the property transfer.

When the Shaws followed the Gays in moving to Staten Island in 1847, they also lived in one of Dr. Elliott's houses, renting for approximately four years while settling into community life. Frank became a trustee of the Staten Island Hospital and of the Seaman's Retreat (later Bayley Seton Hospital), as well as an important figure in the local Unitarian church. In addition to the Gays, the Shaws saw other friends and acquaintances on Staten Island, including former Brook Farm members and relatives being treated by Dr. Elliott. Emotional distress over the closing of Brook Farm had affected the health of many former residents. Years later, Dr. Elliott's son remembered this period as one in which Brook Farmers formed a significant percentage of his father's practice.[20]

When the Shaws decided to settle permanently on Staten Island they did not choose a Ranlett house, but hired a young Boston architect, Benjamin Franklin Dwight (1824–1893), to design their residence.[21] Even while under construction, the house attracted considerable attention that was not entirely favorable. To describe the house as grand seems accurate since the final cost was $80,000 (approximately $3 million dollars today) and the size and neoclassical style of the house made the establishment far different from other Elliottville residences.[22] The structure was much larger, had a symmetrical design, and had an exterior of painted clapboard out of keeping with the English Romantic style of Ranlett. Ranlett advocated country "villas" that were asymmetrical and "natural-hued" (often built out of local cut stone).[23] The Shaw house had eleven bedrooms. The master bedroom was on the first floor; each of the five children had suites of rooms on the second floor, each consisting of two bedrooms and a sitting room.[24] In a letter to his parents, Robert Gould Shaw, then away at college, relayed the gist of a letter he had received from their neighbor Mrs. George Cabot Ward, who said neither the style nor the cost of the house matched the character of the neighborhood.[25] Elizabeth Gay, in writing to her friend Sarah Pugh, described the structure as "an immense pile" and claimed that Sarah Shaw was "frightened out of her wits at the thought of it."[26] James Russell Lowell, writing to Sarah Shaw, referred to the house as a "palace."[27] The Shaw house, like the houses Ranlett designed, was set on extensive grounds that Frank gave a great deal of thought to laying out. His interest in plants was that of the amateur botanist (he encouraged Robert Gould Shaw to share his interests by studying the subject at Harvard), rather than a hobbyist gardener. Frank employed eight servants to cook, clean, garden, and drive the family carriages and maintain the horses and equipage.[28]

Why would Frank Shaw have built such a house? Surely he did not intend the house as a display of his wealth. He and Sarah were self-conscious about their fortune. Over the decades of their friendship with Lydia Maria Child, an outspoken critic of people of wealth and fashion, they repeatedly asked for and got reassurance that she did not hold their wealth against them (Child was comfortable with the fact that Frank used his wealth for good).[29] So, if the house was not an expression of affluence, what was it? Frank advocated social reform. He would have been unlikely to build in the style of Ranlett, which looked to the past and used Gothic and Tudor vocabularies that referenced social orders controlled by the church and monarchy. Instead, he built in a style that referenced classical democracy. Furthermore, he did not build such a large house to be ostentatious. He appreciated Fourierism. In Fourierist communities, buildings were designed to enable communal life while maintaining equality and independence for individuals. A Fourierist phalanstery balanced large meeting rooms and gardens with private spaces. The Shaws' house had large spaces where friends and neighbors could gather with the Shaw family and private suites where family members and overnight guests could enjoy independence. Tutors could live with their students, friends could stay for months, and, as

Figure 2.3. In writing to Sarah Shaw, James Russell Lowell, somewhat jokingly, referred to the Shaws' new house as a palace. Sited close to Bard Avenue, like Ranlett-designed properties, the house was not orientated to the street, and the fifteen acres of grounds were extensively landscaped. *Source:* William Rhinelander Stewart, *The Philanthropic Work of Josephine Shaw Lowell* (New York: Macmillan, 1911), 6. Public domain.

would happen after Anna Shaw and George Curtis wed, married children could live with their spouses within the family household.

During most of the three years Anna and George were living in Frank's house, their own house was under construction next door, a gift from Frank, begun in 1857 and finished in 1860. Although the house was built on part of Frank's land, the structure was separated from the Shaw house by a brook and hedge, and from neighboring houses by meadows.[30] Although the residence is in keeping with the spirit of Ranlett, the design was Downing's.[31]

Downing and Curtis had become friends through Christopher Pearse Cranch. Cranch and Curtis had first known each other at Brook Farm. Cranch had married Elizabeth DeWint in 1843, daughter of John

Figure 2.4. When Frank Shaw offered the wedding present of a house, George William Curtis chose a design published by his friend Alexander Jackson Downing. *Source: Alexander Jackson Downing Cottage Residences: Or, a Series of Designs for Rural Cottages and Adapted to North America* (New York: Wiley & Putnam, 1842), 88. Public domain.

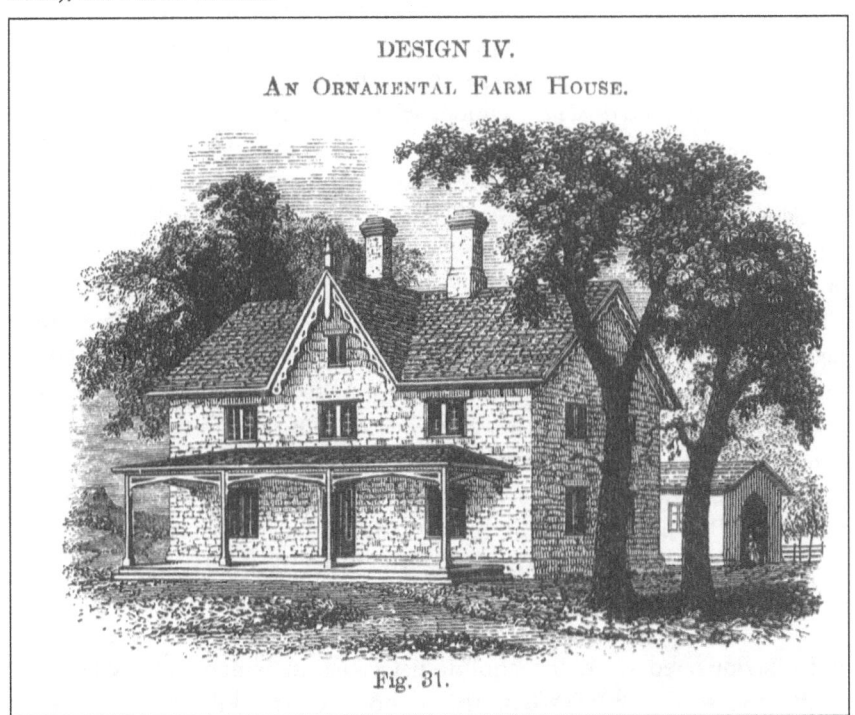

Peter DeWint (1787–1870), who owned thousands of acres of land and several businesses in Fishkill Landing and across the river in Newburgh, New York. DeWint was a devoted amateur horticulturalist, and in 1838 another of his daughters, Caroline DeWint, had wed Newburgh resident Andrew Jackson Downing (1815–1852), a prominent founder of landscape architecture in America and popularizer of the Gothic Revival. In 1845 Curtis visited the DeWints and called upon Downing at his residence, Highland Gardens and a friendship developed. Downing's understanding of domestic architecture, landscape architecture, and the way that domestic establishments related to each other in communities became major influences on Curtis (as they had been for Ranlett).[32]

Prior to meeting Downing, Curtis had read his *A Treatise on the Theory and Practice of Landscape Gardening, Adapted to North America* (New York: Wiley and Putnam, 1841) and *Cottage Residences: Or, a Series of Designs for Rural Cottages and Adapted to North America* (New York: Wiley and Putnam, 1842). So he was already familiar with Downing's celebration of the American continent—its landscape, trees, and plants—as well as Downing's attempts to dissuade his fellow citizens from building Greek Revival houses set in formal gardens merely to display social status. Instead, Downing encouraged his readers to educate and refine their tastes and then create domestic settings that reflected what was distinctive about the United States. Domestic settings that were the product of self-cultivation enabled people of any means to live in surroundings that were beautiful and adapted to their site and purpose. In 1845, Downing published *The Fruits and Fruit Trees of America* (New York: Wiley and Putnam) in which he emphasized that fruit trees in cultivation are cultural productions, the result of grafting, and that the fruits from any given tree are influenced by pruning, watering, fertilizing, sun exposure, and other aspects of cultivation. Downing's lyrical descriptions led transcendentalists to appreciate pomiculture as a metaphor for human culture and the project of self-cultivation.[33] Curtis was to become Downing's most influential biographer, and his visits to Highland Gardens that began in May 1846 and were repeated in succeeding years informed the prefatory essay he wrote for Downing's posthumously published *Rural Essays* (New York: G. P. Putnam, 1853).[34] Curtis chose Alexander Jackson Downing's plan entitled Design IV: "An Ornamental Farm House" for his own house.[35]

The design of houses, landscapes, and suburbs may seem trivial and disconnected from the abolitionist cause in which Elliottville residents were so deeply invested. This is not the case. Elliottville residents were committed to broad social reform that touched upon all aspects of social and political life. Ranlett's understanding of households featuring grounds that provided the means for raising food and that were integral to community life, found expression throughout Elliottville and, for our purposes, notably in the Gays' house. As we have seen, the socioeconomic theories of Fourier got translated into community formation and architecture and in a modest way found expression in the Shaws' house. Finally, Curtis thought a good deal about Downing's philosophy that landscape design and architecture could, and should, express what was distinctive about the American continent, and he chose to live in a Downing house.

Curtis, the Gays, and the Shaws were all friends of Frederick Law Olmsted. Although Olmsted's landscape design practice and writings did not come until later, in the 1840s, he was already fully engaged in thinking and talking about land use. His father had bought him a 125-acre farm in Staten Island in 1847. Called Tosomock Farm, the property was approximately ten miles to the South of Elliottville. Olmsted used his farm to experiment with agriculture and landscape design. He hybridized fruit and nut trees and developed drainage techniques, establishing a cylindrical drainage tile works that was one of the first in the United States. His work attracted local attention and he became secretary of Staten Island's Richmond County Agricultural Society.[36] His interest in agricultural innovation led to his travels in England, where he was first challenged to articulate his understanding of slavery. The experience prompted his later travels in the South and his writings about the slave economy and the way slavery transformed the landscape. These were matters that he certainly discussed with his friends, Curtis, the Gays, and the Shaws, in Elliottville and at the house of their mutual friend, publisher George Palmer Putnam, who lived in Stapleton, equidistant between Tosomock Farm and Elliottville.[37]

The landscape and built environment must be seen as an important aspect of why men like Curtis, Gay, and Shaw were so attached to their neighborhood. While the social transformation needed to abolish slavery was still years away, on their properties and in interactions with their neighbors they had already redeemed some small part of the United States.

"Boston People"

The shared characteristics of Elliottville residents made the neighborhood distinctive from other Staten Island suburbs of the 1850s and 1860s. Most

Elliottville residents were linked to their neighbors through ancestry and social ties. They were New England transplants with connections to the transcendental movement from which sprang their conviction that they should live close to nature in a way that Elliottville's location amid woods near the waterfront offered. Other suburbs and older communities on Staten Island were not so cohesive, and the other suburban developments, like New Brighton, were speculative projects of Manhattan businessmen.

Curtis repeatedly articulated the crucial importance of New England in the development of the United States. While other explorers and colonizers came to the American continent to establish an empire, search for gold, discover new trade routes, or even locate the fountain of youth, the Puritans, who established New England, risked everything for religious freedom. "Freedom to worship God is universal freedom, a free state as well as a free church," expressed in the signing of the Mayflower Compact before setting foot on the shores of New England.[38] Curtis celebrated the historicity of the Puritan heritage of the United States. He claimed England's Tudor era, the age of Puritan activity in England, should be regarded as that country's most heroic (because of the Reformation break with Roman dogma). However, for Curtis, historical origins were secondary. The universal principles embraced by the Puritans made them worthy of celebration. As in Athens and in the Roman forum, in the Puritan movement "the human heart . . . beat for liberty . . . the human consciousness . . . quickened with its divine birthright . . . and freedom challenge[d] authority."[39] These principles were the acorn from which New England grew, influenced colonial settlements, shaped the formation of the United States in the early days of the Republic, and were the touchstones for frontier communities in the Alleghenies and, later, the American West. New Englanders shaped the continent, bringing institutions through which "liberty ceases to be merely the aspiration of hope, and becomes an actual possession . . . the free church, free school, the town meeting."[40] Ultimately, it would be "the Puritan principle of liberty and equal rights" that would break the chains of the enslaved. In celebrating the Puritan founders of New England, Curtis contrasted them with the Cavaliers, with whom Southerners identified. The Cavaliers were followers of Charles I, the monarch who fought the English Civil War, maintaining the divine right of kings, turning his back on Protestant reformers, and attempting to suppress applications of the Magna Carta.

Curtis was sensitive to the ways in which Uncle Sam, the ultimate New England Yankee, had been caricatured as a sanctimonious zealot descended from Cromwell's parliament. Southerners employed satirical attacks on Yankees to dismiss the New England origins of the antislavery movement as yet another fanaticism. For that reason, Curtis was deeply appreciative of his friend James Russell Lowell's literary creation Hosea Biglow and Lowell's other attempts to use humor to reclaim the image of the Yankee, revealing the Yankee's "unbending principle, his supreme good-sense, his lofty patriotism, his unquailing courage."[41]

In addition to Brook Farmers and relatives who were temporarily in Elliottville, the Gays and Shaws made friends with neighborhood residents who shared their New England origins and social commitments. George Cabot Ward (1824–1887) was one neighbor with whom the Shaws developed a decades-long friendship. Ward descended from families that were early settlers of Salem, Massachusetts. Ward grew up at his family's substantial house at 3 Park Street in Boston, less than a block from the Massachusetts

Figure 2.5. George Cabot Ward grew up on Beacon Hill and had friends and relatives in common with Elliottville residents, as well as being a Unitarian and abolitionist. *Source*: Samuel Gray Ward, *Ward Family Papers* (Boston: Merrymount, 1900), image following page 204. Public domain.

State House. He knew Ralph Waldo Emerson and other transcendentalists and, later, was a Unitarian. His father had become an important Boston banker when he was appointed an agent of the London banking house, Baring Brothers. Like Sydney Gay, as a young man Ward had spent time in Asia at the beginning of his business career, in 1842, in Ward's case, in India. By 1845 he was living in New York City, working in the firm of Charles Goodhue and encouraged by his father to visit Staten Island, where Goodhue lived. After a while, like George Curtis, Ward rejected business. In 1845, he announced to his father that he had decided to become an author and insisted he needed to further his education abroad to be taken seriously. Unlike Curtis, however, after three years in Germany, France, and Italy, Ward returned to the United States to resume a business career. Determining that he would get his best start not in Boston but in New York, he opened a commission brokerage with significant underwriting from his father. In 1850 he traveled to Cincinnati, St. Louis, and New Orleans on behalf of his father to investigate cotton prospects and the impact of emigration to the West on grain production, which gave him an opportunity to make observations about slavery and the prospects for abolitionism. At that point, he thought that as impoverished poor Southern Whites moved West to take advantage of opportunities there, the labor shortage in the South would mean that slaves would be regarded as ever more valuable and therefore be educated, treated better, and eventually freed.[42] Although Ward had an active brokerage, Ward, Campbell & Company in Manhattan, in 1862 he went into partnership with his brother Samuel Gray Ward (1817–1907) under the name S. G. and G. C. Ward. Upon their father's retirement, Samuel had succeeded him as the US representative of Baring Brothers, London. In 1862 Samuel relocated the business and his residence to New York, since Manhattan had become the dominant business center of the US. He and his brother were committed abolitionists who gave money for the cause, and although Samuel lived in Manhattan, the Shaws and Gays knew him through their mutual friendship with Emerson and Margaret Fuller, as well as their friendship with his brother.[43]

The Shaws and Gays also befriended John Bethune and Elizabeth Douglass née Young Staples.[44] Staples had been educated at Yale (entered in 1822) and was admitted to the bar in 1829 after studying in the office of his father, Seth Perkins Staples (1776–1861). Seth Staples had relocated to New York after Yale absorbed the New Haven Law School (which Staples had founded) as Yale University Law School.[45] Seth Staples was one of the lawyers who had assisted in the defense of the *The Amistad* captives.[46]

A commitment to abolitionism probably formed the basis for the friendship with the Stapleses; however, Elizabeth Staples also taught local children and organized pastimes for them, as well as hosting memorable Christmas celebrations for the whole neighborhood, with elaborate trees featuring ornaments that she made throughout the year. The Stapleses' house on Shore Road, between what are now Bard and Davis Avenues, faced the water, and their imposing boathouse became the base from which neighborhood children learned to swim. Elizabeth Staples organized outings across the Kill van Kull to gather crabs in the meadows of New Jersey and then hosted crab feasts. During the winter, Mrs. Staples listened to local children recite their lessons (learned at home) while she sewed or engaged in handicrafts. For Elliottville women she hosted a book group to read and discuss French novels, to maintain their language skills. The Stapleses' barn also served as the theater of the Richmond Dramatic Club, in which the Gays and Shaws were active.[47]

Since the Gays and Shaws lived on adjacent properties, it is not surprising that their closest neighbors, William Templeton Johnson (1814–1868) and his wife Laura (Winthrop) Johnson (1825–1889), should be drawn into their circle, but the Johnsons also had New England ancestry. The Johnsons lived to the north of Bard Avenue, at the back of the Shaw property (once streets were laid out, the Johnsons' address would be 123 Bement Avenue). Johnson was the son of a New York court reporter.[48] However, he was also a direct descendant of Massachusetts Bay colonists who had arrived with Governor John Winthrop, from whom Laura was a direct descendant.[49] Johnson was a lawyer who had graduated from Columbia College in 1832. The Johnsons had begun married life in 1846 in one of the first houses to be constructed on Manhattan's Gramercy Square, a Greek Revival, red brick house at No. 23. Why the Johnsons relocated is not clearly documented, but Johnson's health was poor, and when they decided to move to Staten Island in winter 1850, relatives understood the move was for his health.[50] He may even have been under Dr. Elliott's care; Laura would later claim that her husband would have died at a far earlier age if he had not moved to the healthful environment of Staten Island.[51] The couple also had begun having children and may have wished to raise their family outside the city. Their first child, a daughter, Elizabeth "Bessie" Winthrop Johnson [hereafter Bessie Johnson] (1850–1929[?]) was born in Manhattan. The other two children, Oliver Templeton (1852–1891) and Laura Winthrop (1862–1917), were born on Staten Island.

Laura Johnson referred to the families along Bard Avenue as "Boston people." Johnson corresponded for twenty-seven years with Annie Adams Fields (1834–1915), the wife of publisher James Fields (a friend of Curtis), revealing in her letters, the close community that existed among Elliottville's "Boston people." Even if, like Johnson herself, they had never lived in Boston, or had lived most of their lives in New York and not New England, Boston people shared ideals and admiration for New England literary culture and thinkers. Johnson contrasted Boston people with other Staten Island neighbors, who she considered "nice" and with whom she might socialize, but as a form of missionary outreach, a form of social uplift for them.[52] Laura noted that her husband and Curtis were good citizens, involving themselves in Staten Island civic affairs, but that the work of shaping the opinions of Staten Islanders was an effort since they were not Boston people.

Samuel Ward articulated a view of New England culture in his writings that is particularly useful in understanding why people in Elliottville felt such affinity for each other. In later life, Ward wrote a privately printed book entitled *Ward Family Papers* (Boston: Merrymount Press, 1900), an account of the Ward family in America that begins in the Colonial era. The book is also Ward's autobiography, in which he relates his perspective on the United States of his youth in the 1830s and 1840s from the vantage point of the late nineteenth century. Like Elliottville residents, he was descended from colonists, and took pride in inheriting "a quite advanced civilization, which had been maturing for two hundred years, with great vicissitudes."[53] Like them, he celebrated ancestors who had brought civilization to the untamed wilderness, grandfathers who had been prepared to sacrifice everything for the principles of the American Revolution, and parents who had helped establish the institutions of the Republic. Like them, he entered adulthood as American civilization flowered in a New England–based literary movement that "played the largest part in the literary development of the country."[54] In the religious realm, the flower of New England civilization was Unitarianism, which attracted "the most intelligent and leading minds" and was above persecution, despite the heretical abandonment of the doctrine of the Trinity "due to the numbers, standing, intelligence, and wealth" of members.[55] At the center of the Unitarian movement was a group of extraordinary preachers, and the first among them was Ralph Waldo Emerson. Ward described hearing Emerson as receiving a compelling "vision of a higher life" that was extraordinarily personal: "Every man was to him a new Adam, with something in him differing from all other men, which was his individual genius, which if happily developed was a new thing under the sun, a revelation, which it was each man's duty to guard jealously and live up to."[56]

The transformative impact of direct contact with Emerson for Ward echoes throughout the documentary record left by Elliottville residents. Many neighborhood men maintained lifelong friendships with Emerson, including Curtis, Shaw, and George Cabot Ward.[57] Late in her life, Sarah Shaw wrote to Charles Eliot Norton that she was fourteen when she first heard Emerson preach and "he won my heart & *my soul!*"[58] Laura Johnson wrote of the excitement of hearing Emerson speak, and Annie Fields fed Johnson's enthusiasm over many years with an Emerson autograph, copied quotations, and a thirty-six-page summary of the series of lectures Emerson gave at Harvard titled "The Natural History of the Intellect." According to George Curtis's brother James Burrill Curtis, Emerson permanently shaped his and his brother's "ideals of character and culture and modes of living."[59]

Conclusion

In the years between 1845 and 1855, Elliottville evolved from a neighborhood primarily associated with Dr. Elliott and his patients to an enclave of idealistic social reformers. Although their main cause was the abolition of slavery, they were devoted to a constellation of social reform ideas that included wide-sweeping economic and political reform grounded in the philosophical and spiritual perspectives that we today refer to as American transcendentalism. Many of them were connected to Brook Farm and were friends and admirers of Ralph Waldo Emerson. The contemplation of beauty was as important to American transcendentalism as engagement in moral action. Elliottville offered natural beauty and the opportunity to live in harmony with nature, and one's neighbors, that the urban landscape could not offer. George Curtis was to write, "God might have made a more beautiful spot than Staten Island, but he never did."[60]

Chapter 3

The Years of Crisis
Elliottville, 1850 through 1865

Introduction

Elliottville residents created a haven for themselves, a neighborhood of like-minded people who supported one another. Their extended families, social connections, and involvement in national organizations meant that they were in frequent and direct contact with the prominent writers and thinkers of their day devoted to abolitionism. Nonetheless, Elliottville was located on Staten Island, a favorite summer resort of Southerners and proximate to Manhattan whose economy was intimately tied to slavery. Staten Island, a base for maritime industries, was also home for a number of ship's captains. Although specific documentation has not made its way into the archival record, a surviving firsthand account claims Staten Islanders were active in the slave trade and that slave ships sailed from Staten Island as late as 1860.[1]

In the decades before the Civil War, businessmen and politicians in the New York region advocated for compromise with the South. Opposition to abolitionism and animosity toward abolitionists was a corollary of their accommodationist stance. They eventually created the Union Safety Committee and distributed propaganda nationwide. Two of the leaders of the committee were prominent on Staten Island. The hostility of the social and political environment immediately beyond Elliottville was a dismaying aspect of life in the neighborhood through the 1850s and the Civil War.

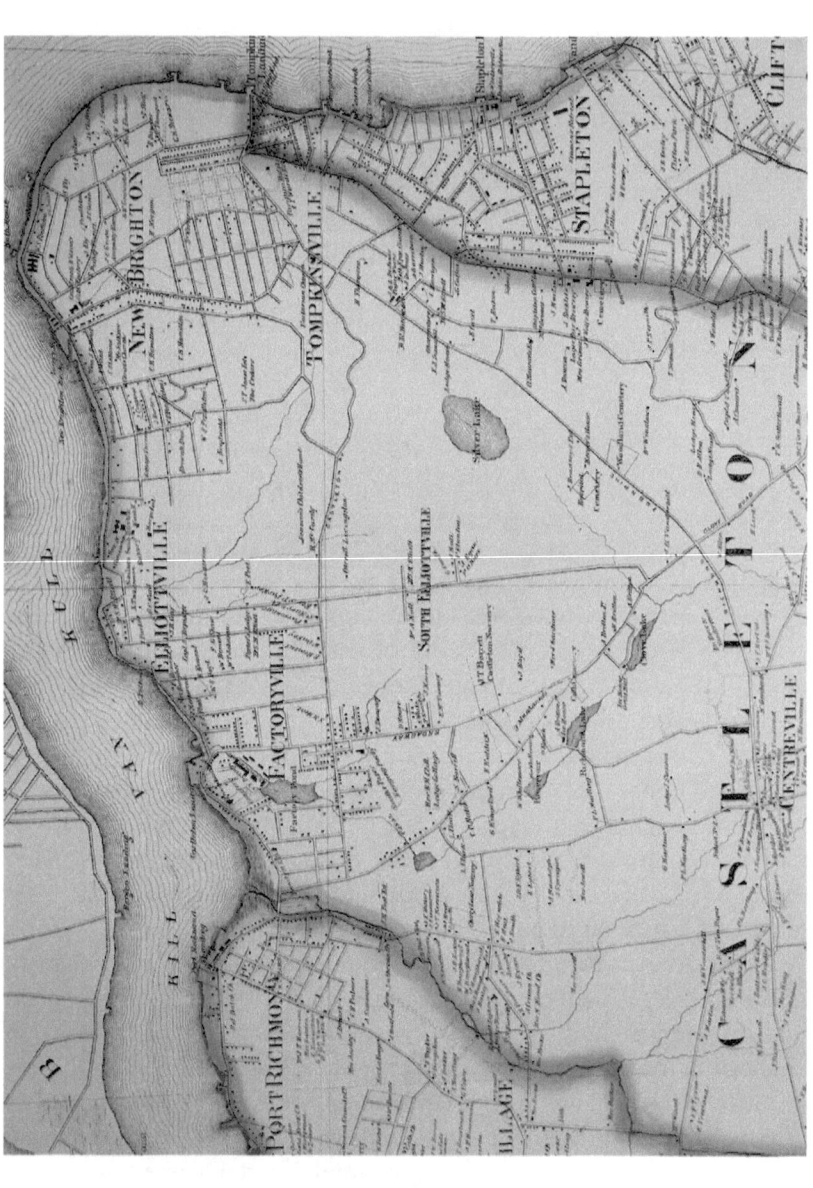

Figure 3.1. By 1859, Dr. Alexander B. Mott, the son of Dr. Elliott's friend and supporter Dr. Valentine Mott, owned much of South Elliottville. *Source:* Section of H. F. Walling, Map of Staten Island, Richmond County, New York (New York: D. Fox, 1859). Map Division, Library of Congress. Public domain.

George William Curtis

Although Curtis did not move to the neighborhood until 1857, he would become the most prominent national figure in the neighborhood and the man with whom Elliottville came to be identified. He shaped public opinion through speeches and essays. In 1859, he became the sole author of the monthly Easy Chair column in *Harper's Magazine*, a position he held for over thirty years, and in 1863 he became the political editor of *Harper's Weekly*, for which he wrote the Lounger column. He was active in the formation of the Republican Party and was one of the most prominent campaign orators on behalf of John Frémont. He became chairman of the Republicans on Staten Island, a position he held for decades. As county delegate to the second national Republican Party Convention in Chicago, he played a crucial role in constructing the platform and later campaigned prominently for Lincoln and represented the nominating committee in formally presenting Lincoln the National Union Party nomination in 1864.

Curtis had known the Shaws for more than a decade before moving to Elliottville. He shared their deep personal commitment to the ideals of the transcendental movement, ideals that he developed during his time at Brook Farm and cultivated through his friendships with prominent cultural figures who were also friends of the Shaws. An account of his young adulthood shows what he had in common with Elliottville residents, the surprising number of people in his social circle for whom Staten Island was important, and the numerous connections he had to the Shaws.

Curtis, the son of George (1796–1856) and Mary Elizabeth Burrill Curtis (1798–1826), had been born in Providence, Rhode Island, and spent his childhood there.[2] Like so many Elliottville residents, his family had deep roots in the Massachusetts Bay Colony, going back to the early settlement period. His grandfather, David Curtis, a blacksmith, was a leading citizen of Worcester, Massachusetts, and descended from an early settler of the Bay Colony. His mother and stepmother were each directly descended from Rhode Islanders prominent in government during the federal period and after. Curtis's father was a member of the Common Council of Providence and served in the Rhode Island legislature, including terms as presiding officer.

In 1839, when Curtis was fifteen, his family moved to Manhattan. Curtis's father had gotten a senior position with the Bank of Commerce of New York and the family settled into a house at 27 Washington Place.[3] For some young men, the move would have determined the rest of their lives, but although Curtis tentatively pursued entry-level business positions, he abandoned the world of commerce to join his brother, James Burrill Curtis, to live and study at Brook Farm. They arrived in May 1842, not as members of the "Association" but as boarders pursuing a college preparatory course devised by Brook Farm founder George Ripley and other "farmers," like George P. Bradford (1807–1890) and Charles A. Dana (1819–1897). Curtis established lifelong friendships with his Brook Farm teachers, residents (particularly Christopher Pearse Cranch [1813–1892]), neighbors (like the Shaws), and visitors (like Ralph Waldo Emerson, Margaret Fuller, Amos Bronson Alcott [1799–1888], William Henry Channing [1810–1884], and the Reverend Theodore Parker [1810–1860]). Likewise, the principles of the Brook Farm experiment, which emphasized respect for the individual, cooperation over competition, and spiritual and intellectual growth over the accumulation of wealth and possessions, became the touchstones for Curtis's understanding of society, current events, and his own priorities in life. He and his brother continued their intellectual and spiritual development by following George P. Bradford to Concord, Massachusetts, in 1844. While pursuing outdoor life and earning a living through agricultural labor, they engaged in guided reading and conversation with Bradford, as well as Amos Bronson Alcott, Ellery Channing, Ralph Waldo Emerson, Nathaniel Hawthorne, and Henry David Thoreau.

Curtis completed his education with a four-year European sojourn, begun in 1846, with his Brook Farm friend Christopher Pearse Cranch (and Cranch's new wife Elizabeth de Wint). While studying and touring in Italy, Germany, Switzerland, and France, he spent time with other former Brook Farm residents (some of whom had gone to Europe after the dissolution of Brook Farm), transcendentalists, and other New Englanders traveling and studying abroad. One of these was Dr. Elliott's former patient Charles Eliot Norton, who would become Curtis's lifelong friend. Curtis also became a published writer in 1848 through his friendship with former Brook Farm trustee Charles A. Dana, who was in Paris working for the *New-York Tribune*. The *New-York Tribune* published a series of Curtis's letters on the political situation in France and the formation of the Republic. Curtis also occasionally traveled with Shaw family relatives, including Sarah's brother Robert Shaw Sturgis (1824–1876) and Frank's brother Quincy Adams Shaw (1825–1908). Quincy Shaw persuaded Curtis to travel down the Nile and spend two months in Egypt before continuing by camel caravan to Jerusalem, Damascus, and Beirut.[4]

Curtis made a detailed record of his Middle Eastern trip with the idea of publishing a book and spent part of 1850 back in Manhattan writing *Nile Notes of a Howadji* (New York: Harper and Brothers, 1851). This book and the 1852 sequel, *The Howadji in Syria* (New York: Harper and Brothers) were immediately popular with an audience of general readers avid for travel reminiscences. However, Curtis also won sophisticated readers with his approach. Noting that "the highest value of travel is not the accumulation of facts, but the perception of their significance," he said it is not seeing great works of art or inspiring landscapes that is of permanent value, but "the breadth they give to experience, the more reasonable faith they inspire in the scope of human genius, the dreamy distance of thought with which they surround life."[5] The success of the books and the broad acclaim they garnered for Curtis earned him the enduring sobriquet "Howadji."

Curtis was soon writing again for the *New-York Tribune*; his cultural tourism had earned him credibility as an art and music critic. The newspaper also gave Curtis an extended assignment in 1851 to report on Eastern summer resorts. When he reached Nahant, Massachusetts, on his tour, he remained to spend time with the Christopher Pearse Cranches and the sometime patients of Dr. Elliott: Charles Sumner, Charles Eliot Norton, and Henry Wadsworth Longfellow. By spring of 1852, Curtis was editing his resort accounts for the *New-York Tribune* into another book, published that year as *Lotos-Eating* (New York: Harper and Brothers).

By summer 1852, Curtis had received an honorary master's degree from the University of Rochester, was securely launched on his literary career, and had established himself on the lecture circuit. He spent the rest of the summer in Newport. The Longfellows had rented a house in the resort and Curtis shared the place with them and Mrs. Longfellow's brother Thomas Gold Appleton (1812–1884).[6] By the end of the summer George was engaged to marry another Newport summer resident, Elizabeth Winthrop (1820–1907), the sister of Laura (Winthrop) Johnson, who would go on to spend more than forty years as Curtis's neighbor on Staten Island.

Since the Winthrops had many connections to New York, Curtis and Elizabeth Winthrop may have met prior to Newport. Although Elizabeth grew up in Connecticut, her father's business interests often took him to Manhattan (where her Winthrop uncles had established themselves). The trip between New Haven and Manhattan was relatively quick once the

New Haven Line was established and Winthrop family members visited back and forth during the social season and even in the summer, when the Winthrops summered on Staten Island.[7] Whether or not the two had become acquainted over a period of time, Curtis and Elizabeth's engagement was soon broken off, although the exact reasons are unknown. At the time, some speculated that the Winthrops were offended by the satirical pieces Curtis had begun publishing about New York society members that would later become *The Potiphar Papers* (first printed serially in *Putnam's Monthly Magazine of American Literature, Science, and Art* in 1853).

In Curtis's view, as he expressed it in *The Potiphar Papers*, there were three types of society figures in New York by the 1850s: the newly moneyed, who received his harshest assessment; the descendants of old families, who felt entitled to social precedence, no matter their own lack of accomplishments; and the lively, attractive, well-dressed young men who are tolerated in society as sycophants and suitable dancing partners at balls. The Winthrops certainly took pride in their ancestry, but they also built fortunes in Manhattan and, due to their numbers, were everywhere in society and business. Whether Curtis had any of them in mind as he wrote *The Potiphar Papers* is unclear. His writings certainly did not make him a social pariah. One of the marks of an established social figure was club membership, and the most prestigious club was the Union Club, founded in 1836 and modeled on English clubs for gentlemen. Curtis's father was an original member and Curtis was elected to membership in 1853, the same year *The Potiphar Papers* appeared in book form (New York: G. P. Putnam).

Again spending the summer in Newport in 1855 with the Longfellows, Curtis found his friends the Shaws in residence, returned from the European trip they had begun in 1851 for Sarah's health. Sarah Shaw was a woman who felt the losses and setbacks of her friends deeply and personalized public events. Her emotional state had a deep impact on her health. The poor health that she had suffered in 1850 was partly due to the death of the Gays' sons. In his 1848 letters Sydney Gay conveyed his excited anticipation of the birth of his first child.[8] Neighbors, and particularly friends like Sarah Shaw, would have formed a supportive community for the Gays as they navigated pregnancy and then childbirth. Walter Otis Gay was born in July 1848. In the following year, Gay mentioned his son in letters to Lowell with great tenderness and from descriptions by others in the neighborhood, he seems to have been a particularly attractive child with blond hair and flushed cheeks. Walter died of an illness at eighteen months old.⁹ The Gays were inconsolable for years over the death. Even James Russell Lowell and his wife Maria, who had also lost infant children, could provide no effective consolation. As late as spring of 1851, Lowell wrote compassionately to Sydney that he was "grieved to find that the cloud does not begin show a bright edge yet" for Sydney.¹⁰

The intimacy of their friendship meant that the Shaws were deeply affected by the Gays' bereavement. Sarah Shaw's health collapsed, and James Russell Lowell said her illness was the motivation for leaving for Europe in early 1851.¹¹ By the time they left, the Shaw children ranged in age from fifteen to six (Anna, 1836–1923; Robert Gould, 1837–1863; Sarah Susannah "Susie," [hereafter Susie] 1839–1926; Josephine, 1842–1905; and Ellen, 1845–1936), and the four-year sojourn afforded them educational opportunities as they traveled and lived in the same places Curtis had on his somewhat earlier trip—France, Germany, Italy, and Switzerland, and the Middle East.

When the Shaws returned to the United States in 1855, their Staten Island house still unfinished, they went directly to Newport for several months, where they found Curtis summering. Curtis began courting nineteen-year-old Anna Shaw. Twelve years younger than Curtis, she had been a child of seven when he first met the family. The courtship continued as the Shaws settled into their new house on Staten Island, and an engagement followed.¹²

The Shaws were delighted at the prospect of their daughter's marriage to someone who shared their values and was already accomplished. George Palmer Putnam, another Bostonian who had relocated to Staten Island and had published *The Potiphar Papers* as a book, had also gotten Curtis to write essays for Putnam's *Homes of American Authors* and contracted with him to edit Andrew Jackson Downing's essays for a posthumous publication. Curtis's literary productions had attracted a large reading public and given him name recognition. When Curtis embarked on the lecture circuit he drew enthusiastic audiences through his attractiveness, appealing personality, pleasing speaking voice, and skillful delivery. Even by his second year on the circuit, Curtis was already making a significant income.¹³

By the time Curtis was in Newport courting Anna in 1855, he was also an investor in *Putnam's Monthly Magazine*, the publication that was introducing the world to a generation of writers producing distinctively American work. George Palmer Putnam had begun publication of the literary magazine in 1852 and recruited Curtis as a member of the editorial

Figure 3.2. Curtis was a friend of the Shaws from the days of Brook Farm. By the time he married Anna Shaw and moved to Elliottville, he had published four books and become a popular lecturer. *Source*: Mathew Benjamin Brady, photographer, Library of Congress Prints and Photographs Division, Brady-Handy Photograph Collection, accessed August 12, 2024, http://hdl.loc.gov/loc.pnp/cwpbh.02947.

board. Putnam sold to Joshua Dix and Arthur Edwards in January 1855. To afford the purchase, they had recruited investors, including Curtis.[14] Dix and Edwards offered Curtis the editorship of the newly constituted magazine, but he preferred the shared editorship model already in place; he needed time for more lucrative undertakings, like lecturing and his new salaried position begun in 1853 with *Harper's Monthly*.

So, in spring 1855, Dix and Edwards recruited Frederick Law Olmsted to be *Putnam's* editor in exchange for a significant financial investment they claimed he would recover through his salary. The shared editorship of the magazine continued as before with Curtis, Charles A. Dana, and Parke Godwin participating in editorial decisions and providing articles, reviews, and editorial content for the magazine. This cooperative model enabled Curtis to travel on the lecture circuit and spend time away from New York, as he was doing in summer 1855 when he became reacquainted with the Shaws and courted Anna.[15]

Elliottville and the Compromise of 1850

When the Shaws returned to Elliottville in 1855, they were reentering an abolitionist community transformed by the Compromise of 1850. The compromise had delivered the abolitionist cause a major setback, heightened animosity against abolitionists (particularly in New York), and revealed just how unlike Elliottville was from the rest of Staten Island. In fact, Staten Islanders had become key figures in inciting new animosity toward abolitionism.

In the 1840s, most New Yorkers considered abolitionists a troublesome threat to a burgeoning regional economy heavily dependent upon maintaining good trade relations with the South. Then Congress enacted five measures that came to be collectively known as the Compromise of 1850. Four of the measures focused on keeping slave and free states balanced, but part of the compromise was an amendment to the Fugitive Slave Law that required the arrest and return of escaped slaves to their owners, even if they were in a free state. The law also said that abolitionists directly aiding escaped slaves would face federal prosecution.[16] Free Blacks, abolitionists, and citizens, in some parts of the country, were outraged.

Although the abolitionists of New York were incensed, their numbers were minuscule. Scholar Eric Foner has pointed out that even though the American Anti-Slavery Society and the American and Foreign Anti-Slavery Society established headquarters in New York, few abolitionists lived there. For instance, only 102 Manhattanites subscribed to the *National Anti-Slavery Standard* out of a population of over 500,000.[17]

Many historians have pointed out the economic factors that dissuaded New Yorkers from openly opposing slavery or doing anything to offend Southern trading partners. Instead, they embraced every form of compromise. For this reason, New Yorkers, who had always opposed abolitionists, became vicious as abolitionists attacked the Compromise of 1850.

Local newspapers provide clear evidence that the majority opinion on Staten Island followed New York. Even though New York State had adopted an act to gradually abolish slavery in 1799, and full emancipation was achieved in 1827, Staten Island newspapers were filled with hostility toward free Blacks and abolitionists.[18] In addition to claiming that "a free negro is a social monstrosity that all hate," that Blacks are "deficient of brain," and that freedom for Blacks had brought nothing but social problems for the North, newspaper editorials claimed that Blacks preferred to live in slavery rather than in freedom.[19] Abolitionists were referred to as "negro-worshippers," "woolly headed," "dusky voters," "disunionists," "sectionalists," and "fanatics." Once the Republican Party was founded, party members were invariably "Black Republicans." In addition to Staten Island newspaper editorials drawing upon Southern perspectives, the newspapers simply reprinted articles from Southern newspapers. Some of these stated that the Declaration of Independence could not be applied to Blacks since they are not mentioned in the document. Others claimed that the higher authority of the Bible teaches that slaves should obey their masters and that Blacks are the accursed descendants of Cain and the people of Canaan. Throughout the 1850s, even the less rabid Staten Island newspapers claimed that the country's founding fathers had embraced compromise in framing the Constitution. They repeatedly argued that the abolitionists' insistence on an end to slavery throughout the United States violated the concept of state's rights and the spirit of compromise underlying the Constitution.

In the intimate social setting of Staten Island, attacks on Elliottville abolitionists were direct. Years later, Mary (Gay) Willcox told a story to illustrate the personal animosity her mother experienced. She wrote that while Elizabeth Gay was riding the ferry back to Staten Island with Harriet (Forten) Purvis (ca. 1810–1875), her abolitionist friend from Philadelphia, the two heard persistent murmuring. Gay had been active as a young woman in the Philadelphia Female Anti-Slavery Society, founded by Purvis's mother, sisters, and Lucretia Mott. Gay's constant correspondent, Sarah Pugh, who continued to live in Philadelphia, was also prominent in the organization. Purvis, an affluent woman of distinguished appearance, was Black, and eventually one of the murmuring men on the ferry approached to look under the bonnet that partly covered her face. Confirming her skin color, he called back to his friends, "By God! She is a nigger." Willcox noted that the man knew her mother and knew that she knew him.

These personal affronts were fueled by the propaganda war funded by New York merchants and bankers. In 1850, ninety-one of New York City's most prominent businessmen created the Union Safety Committee with the goal of influencing public opinion throughout the country to support the Compromise of 1850 and, particularly, the Fugitive Slave Law. They sponsored large public rallies and began flooding the United States with sermons and essays of the sort that were published in Staten Island newspapers.[20]

While many abolitionists regarded the Fugitive Slave Law as the most egregious component of the Compromise of 1850, not everyone in the movement endorsed helping enslaved people escape. While in contemporary culture, abolitionism is treated as synonymous with the Underground Railroad, some abolitionists believed that gradualism was the only practical stance to adopt to end slavery. A corollary to this approach was the colonization of free Blacks in Liberia on the west coast of Africa. In fact, the few abolitionists on Staten Island prior to the founding of Elliottville were supporters of the American Colonization Society.[21] More moderate abolitionists thought that abolition could never practically be achieved without acknowledging the economic loss slave owners would suffer and coming up with a plan for financial compensation. Traditionally, the Garrisonian abolitionists' call for immediate emancipation was the most radical stance. Although many more abolitionists became radicalized during the Crisis of 1850 and embraced the views of Elliottville's Garrisonian abolitionists, not all did.

As late as 1857 Elizabeth Gay ran up against the divisiveness of aiding fugitives from slavery. Women had traditionally supported the abolitionist cause by organizing fairs at which goods were sold to raise money to fund antislavery organizations and their publications. Gay and New Yorker Abigail Hopper Gibbons formed a new Anti-Slavery Fair Association in 1857 and stated that the first $1,000 of fair proceeds would be used to aid fugitives passing through New York (with Sydney Gay as treasurer of the funds). Any money above the first thousand would go to support the *National Anti-Slavery Standard.* The fair was not a success because it got no support from the organizers of the Boston antislavery fairs who opposed aid to fugitives.[22]

Sydney Gay's direct aid to fugitives from slavery, based in the office of the *National Anti-Slavery Standard*, are unusually well documented due to a notebook found among his papers.[23] Because aiding fugitives was illegal and a federal offense after 1850, few people were brave enough to keep records of their activities. In analyzing Gay's records, Eric Foner has discovered that many of the fugitives who came through Gay's office were forwarded from Philadelphia by William Still and that they typically arrived on trains or ships and were sent as soon as possible to upstate New York or New England, although most often they were sent to Albany or Syracuse.[24] Since fugitives attracted least attention in the company of fellow Blacks, Gay's efforts were made possible by his employment of two Black men in his office, Louis Napoleon and William H. Leonard. Louis Napoleon is sometimes identified as a Staten Island figure,[25] but Foner's research shows that Napoleon lived in Lower Manhattan at 33 Spruce Street and 27 Leonard Street, convenient locations for helping fugitives.[26]

He later lived uptown at 97 West Thirty-Third Street,[27] and after his retirement was an honored Brooklyn resident.[28]

Present-day accounts of Elliottville claim that neighborhood houses were on the Underground Railroad.[29] In the decades after the Civil War, the network of individuals and organizations that provided direct aid to fugitives became a focus of the collective imagination. Throughout the intervening years, romanticized accounts of the Underground Railroad have multiplied, and efforts to document routes fugitives took and those who enabled their journeys have increased. In some ways, Elliottville would have been an unlikely place to take fugitives since it was a White community and so publicly identified with abolitionism. Mary Willcox's account of the treatment of Harriet Purvis illustrates how much Blacks were noticed. Furthermore, housing fugitives in Elliottville would have been out of keeping with Gay's insistence that his Underground Railroad activities be based out of his office and inconsistent with the goal of moving fugitives further north as quickly as possible, since they were in real danger in New York. While the Fugitive Slave Law became practically unenforceable in many locales due to public antipathy, New Yorkers cooperated with the law. While Elliottville residents may not have housed fugitives after 1850, it is likely that they aided Gay's efforts financially. He kept a careful record of his expenditures and Foner says he often needed to come up with more money.[30]

New Yorkers' obedience to the Fugitive Slave Law had a great deal to do with the activities of the Union Safety Committee. Enforcement of the law had gotten off to a rocky start. A mere eight days after its passage, the city became the site of the first arrest in the country. James Hamlet, a resident of Brooklyn for the previous two years, who lived there with his wife and three children, was arrested and speedily transported to Baltimore, even though his fugitive status was in some doubt. The arrest made it clear to New Yorkers that the Fugitive Slave Law amendment gave federal law precedence over state law. As in Hamlet's case, the decision to return accused escaped slaves was now made in special federal courts with federal administrators. The accused, deemed not to have legal rights, were not allowed to speak in their own defense. As in many localities, there was initial outrage since people suddenly felt that even non-slave states were not free states.

Public opinion in New York quickly shifted after large protests by some of the city's more than thirteen thousand Blacks. After Black churches quickly raised enough money to buy Hamlet's freedom and he was freed, thousands of New Yorkers turned out to welcome him. Frightened that the news coverage in the South would affect commercial relations, the Union Safety Committee sponsored large counterrallies in defense of the Fugitive Slave Law to reassure Southern merchants that most New Yorkers supported the law.[31]

Two of the most important leaders of the Union Safety Committee were prominent on Staten Island. William H. Aspinwall (1807–1875) was one of the organization's wealthiest and most powerful officers. He did not just live on Staten Island but lived in one of the landmark structures most associated with the island. His grand mansion, located approximately four miles from Elliottville, was on high ground overlooking the Narrows. Passengers on all ships into and out of the harbor could not help but notice the house, and the residence was also prominently featured in a Currier and Ives lithograph of New York Harbor. Aspinwall eventually commissioned his son-in-law, James Renwick, to design a separate dramatic tower near the house to display his internationally significant art collection to the public. Aspinwall was also prominent in the life of his neighborhood and was one of the founders of St. John's Episcopal Church there.

One of the other most influential committee leaders, George Law (1806–1881), was the owner of a Staten Island ferry line. In 1853, he increased his presence on Staten Island by becoming the primary investor in a consolidated ferry company, enabled by his purchase of Cornelius Vanderbilt's ferry (Vanderbilt threw in his recently completed mansion on Staten Island to sweeten the deal for Law).[32]

In addition to the Union Safety Committee, George Law was a leader of New York's Young America movement within the Democratic Party. Young Americans were anti-British and saw British plots to regain control of the United States everywhere. To Young Americans, the antislavery movement was a British plot, and they considered abolitionists to be traitors, intent on destroying the Union. With no patience for discussions of the morality of slavery, Young Americans focused only on state's rights and economic considerations. In fact, in a surprising number of instances Young American positions coincided with the financial interests of movement leaders. For instance, Law (and the New York Young Americans) advocated Cuban annexation after his shipping firm, the United States Mail Steamship Company, was awarded a government contract to deliver mail there. New York Young Americans also supported the Hungarian revolution once George Law's ships were to be used to transport weapons.[33] The positions Young Americans advocated in South America coincided with the interests of Aspinwall's Pacific Mail Steamship Company and Law's United States Mail Steamship Company, which had been granted monopolies for the Panama Isthmus route during the California gold rush (with Aspinwall controlling the route from Panama to San Francisco and Law operating on the Atlantic coast). Young American positions on Panama and Nicaragua also favored Aspinwall and Law over Cornelius Vanderbilt, whose Nicaragua route competed with the Panama Isthmus route.[34]

The contrast between men like Aspinwall and Law and Elliottville residents like Frank Shaw represents a deep divide in nineteenth-century American culture between rapacious entrepreneurs who valued those aspects of the US political system that enabled them to build vast personal fortunes and idealists who expended their wealth to perfect human society. As Elliottville abolitionists were dealing with the practical implications of the Compromise of 1850, they were also coping with the effects of Union Safety Committee propaganda efforts. In addition to pamphlets and newspaper and magazine articles, the committee sponsored huge rallies in Manhattan to demonstrate to the South that New York would never support any political action that would upset the national economy. The physical immediacy of the rallies and the large numbers of participants must have had a discouraging effect on Elliottville.

As the abolitionists experienced attacks and reversals in the 1850s, there was often a personal dimension for the residents of Elliottville, even when it came to national events. In 1856, when Senator Charles Sumner was left bleeding and unconscious on the floor of the US Senate after a beating by US representative Preston Brooks of South Carolina, the Shaws experienced the event as an assault on a friend who had been treated by Dr. Elliott and was known in Elliottville. As news of the violent guerrilla wars in Kansas filled newspapers, Elliottville was directly informed because Frederick Law Olmsted was actively supplying weapons to militias of free-soil settlers. After news came of John Brown's raid on Harper's Ferry, Elliottville felt connected through Thomas Wentworth Higginson, a friend of several Elliottville residents, who was one of the "secret six" abolitionists who financially supported the raid. When Brown was hanged, Elliottville residents mourned him with a sense of personal loss. Sydney wanted to rush to attend his burial in upstate New York and made a miniature coffin, representing Brown, to be sold at the annual Anti-Slavery Society Fair.[35] Sarah Shaw took to her room, saying the day of the hanging was akin to the day of Christ's crucifixion.[36] By contrast, the local Staten Island newspaper, *Richmond County Gazette*, published an editorial claiming that "Fanatics both at the North and in the South, have made a hero and martyr out of a misguided and hot-headed man."[37] Thirteen days after Brown's hanging, Curtis was in Philadelphia delivering his lecture "The Present Aspect of the Slavery Question." Six of his friends armed themselves with revolvers to protect him and six hundred police officers held off the mob outside the lecture hall, although they were unable to prevent them shattering the windows with bricks and stones.

While Elliottville residents often had a personal connection to national events related to the abolitionist movement, due to their friendships with movement leaders, it is more difficult to find examples of Elliottville residents interacting directly with free Blacks on Staten Island who were also working to end slavery. There were two free Black communities on Staten Island, one along McKeon Street in Tompkinsville and another near Rossville in an area known as Sandy Ground. Nevertheless, there is no evidence that the residents of Elliottville worked alongside these Blacks. Even though they did sometimes work with Blacks active in national organizations, as in so many of their reform activities, Elliottville residents were more accustomed to working on behalf of the people they helped, rather than side by side with them. In fact, it has been claimed that Gay initiated the distorted portrayal of abolitionism as an effort of White humanitarians working on behalf of impotent Blacks. In the 1850s, he had taken exception to some of Frederick Douglass's positions. Although attacks on Douglass soon appeared more widely than just in the *National Anti-Slavery Standard*, that is where the first attacks appeared. Much later, when Gay was writing his centennial history of the United States and describing aid to fugitives and the abolitionist movement, he focused on the activity of Whites.[38]

As the 1850s progressed, Elliottville was galvanized to engage in political action. The Compromise of 1850 shifted many abolitionists' views on political involvement and led them to abandon the Garrisonian view that even when abolition was the goal it was impossible to work within a political system based on the proslavery Constitution. In the political environment after the passage of the Fugitive Slave Law, Northerners saw what it meant for them and their legal institutions to be obligated to enforce slavery. When the Kansas-Nebraska Act was signed into law in 1854, opinion shifted further. Curtis had never supported the Garrisonian view, but the Shaws had. For years they had worked to end slavery through a process of moral suasion that would lead to conversion, personal sanctification, and eventual societal regeneration. For the Shaws and many like them, gentlemen were expected to influence society by example and through cultural and charitable organizations, not through active political involvement; Curtis advocated direct action. While Curtis tried and failed to raise the political commitments of friends like Henry Wadsworth Longfellow, he did convince the Shaws to engage in politics.[39]

Frank Shaw had been engaged in civic life in Massachusetts and Staten Island, after 1850 he became increasingly involved in politics. While living in West Roxbury, he held positions that were typically offered to affluent landowners: member of the school committee, overseer of the poor, justice of the peace, county jury foreman, president of the first common council of Roxbury. From the time he first settled on Staten Island in 1847, he held similar positions in local organizations, like the Seaman's Retreat and the Sailors' Fund. However, by June 1856 he was president of the Castleton Republican Club and accompanied Curtis as an official delegate to the first national convention of the newly formed Republican Party in Pittsburgh. He helped pass an antislavery platform (the first time a political party had done so). He also took increasingly public stances in opposition to the New York Marine Hospital's Quarantine station on Staten Island (commonly referred to as the Quarantine). For decades the location of the Quarantine had been controversial since it was linked to contagious disease outbreaks. Shaw helped organize direct action at the Quarantine in 1858. Having exhausted avenues of political influence and legal remedies, the secret committee of Staten Islanders of which he was a part carefully planned the destruction of the facility after a thorough evacuation of the station's tenants and removal of medical supplies.[40] In 1859, he spoke on the floor of the New York State Assembly to call for the ban of quarantine operations from any location on Staten Island. In 1860, he ran for the elected office of town supervisor of Castleton on a coalition ticket representing the Whig, Republican, and People's Parties. Even though he received the most tallied ballots, the election became so acrimonious when the ballot box was destroyed, after which there were demonstrations and counterdemonstrations, that he refused the position so that it could be offered to a nonpartisan appointee.

The determination of Staten Island Democrats to attack their Republican opponents, no matter the issue, is nowhere as apparent as in the Quarantine issue. Everyone on Staten Island knew that Republicans were leading the campaign against the Quarantine. Editorials in *The Staaten Islander* bizarrely asserted that Republicans were just pretending to support the Quarantine's removal. In that way, the editorialists claimed, Republicans could win votes and gain a majority in the New York State legislature. In 1858, when the Republican-controlled legislature appointed commissioners, the commissioners decided to relocate the Quarantine to a remote Staten Island location at Seguine's Point. Editorials claimed that by keeping the Quarantine on Staten Island the system of "despotic power of the Health Officer [to] give the Black Republicans here an influence at the polls and elsewhere disproportioned to their small numbers" would continue.[41]

Of course, the Republican Party's first era of widespread public attention was during the presidential campaign of 1856, when Curtis was the chief orator electioneering for the party's candidate, John C. Frémont, who as the first US senator representing California had been outspoken in his opposition to slavery. In July, Curtis began campaigning on Staten Island; then, teaming up with William Cullen Bryant, he spoke in Yonkers before heading on a circuit through upstate New York. Curtis's activities brought immediacy to the presidential campaign for Elliottville, as did the fact that due to him Frémont and his wife spent time on Staten Island. When Curtis took Elizabeth Gay to meet Frémont, she found him "frank, genial, attractive, honest and true in his speech."[42] The Shaws related approvingly that Mrs. Frémont had told them how much the candidate hated the taint of fame.[43]

Curtis, who declared to his friend Christopher Pearse Cranch that "we are in the midst of a revolution," made a speech during the campaign that inspired a whole generation of gentlemen to political action.[44] The speech, titled "The Duty of the American Scholar to Politics and the Times," was delivered for the first time to the assembled literary societies at Wesleyan University on August 6, 1856, and was to become one of Curtis's most requested orations, as well as his most widely published. Soon after its Wesleyan presentation, it was printed in its entirety in the *New-York Tribune*. In his address, Curtis called upon his audience to "recognize that the intelligent exercise of political rights, which is a privilege in a monarchy, is a duty in a republic . . . when the good deed is slighted the bad deed is done."[45] The duties of citizenship necessitated full participation in politics, which would elevate public discourse and was crucial to the preservation of liberty. He pointed to Kansas as the political crisis of the moment and called for action to prevent the spread of slavery. Through the rest of his campaign speeches, he openly denounced the position taken by the Democrats and their candidate, James Buchanan, that the status quo must be maintained to prevent sectionalism and anarchy. Lydia Maria Child wrote the Shaws to praise the oration and congratulate them on their future son-in-law's "lofty stature of manliness."⁴⁶ *The Staaten Islander*, on the other hand, attacked the speech, failing to acknowledge the point of the presentation. Following other Democrat publications, the newspaper's editorial forestalled any discussion of the content of the talk by simply claiming it was inappropriate for Curtis to introduce politics in the setting of a college literary society, which should be an arena free of politics.⁴⁷

No matter what good effects the Frémont campaign had in getting a new generation of men involved in politics, the Democrat's candidate, James Buchanan, won the election. Although Curtis found positives in the electoral returns, Staten Island Democrats were delighted that having "the orator of the Black Republican Party" in residence had not weakened the Democratic vote on the island.⁴⁸ They crowed that Richmond County had "given a Democratic majority to Buchanan larger in proportion to her number of votes than any county in the state and gave a larger majority for Buchanan than Frémont received in votes."⁴⁹

Curtis and Anna Shaw had delayed their wedding while Curtis was so actively involved in campaigning. A few weeks after Buchanan won the election, they wed on November 26, 1856, in Elliottville's Unitarian Universalist Church of the Redeemer. Jesse and John Frémont attended, along with Curtis and Anna's immediate family members and close friends.

The national political crises of the 1850s were not the only news events to have personal immediacy in Elliottville. The economic panic of 1857 also had a personal dimension that would have a long-lingering impact for Curtis and Shaw. *Putnam's Monthly* under Dix and Edwards's ownership had continued to be financially troubled, and by the end of 1856 their partnership was on the verge of financial collapse. In a legal agreement with creditors, Dix and Edwards were released, and the restructured firm was named Miller and Company, with the principals being printer J. W. Miller, Olmsted, and Curtis. The firm failed in August 1857 (Olmsted had withdrawn from the partnership before the collapse, after pledging to take responsibility for his share of the debts). Frank Shaw had invested money in the firm, and through inaccurate statements filed by Dix and Edwards, was listed as a general partner at the time of the collapse. As a result, creditors had a legal right to pursue Shaw for compensation. Olmsted lost $5,000 lent by his father, Curtis lost $8,000, and Shaw lost $70,000.⁵⁰ Curtis and Olmsted felt a moral obligation to repay Shaw, as well as the $24,000 in unrecovered losses of the creditors.⁵¹ The amounts of money must have seemed impossibly large, and Curtis began giving as many as one hundred lectures each year.⁵² After years of struggle, Olmsted and Curtis eventually repaid the debts.

One aspect of Curtis's debt repayment is not usually discussed. He did not moderate his antislavery stance to make getting speaking engagements and publications easier. Writing to Charles Eliot Norton in 1860 of his struggle over the previous three years to repay debts, he noted, "I suppose the H[arper]'s are troubled by my recent anti-slavery publicity. In the last advertisement of the weekly I see they drop my name and the announcement of my novel altogether. . . . It is laughable and melancholy to know that if I openly advocated the selling of negro babies, they would be perfectly satisfied to associate my name with their house!"⁵³

A Long Golden Summer: 1856 to 1861

Happy Island. The people are beautiful, the place is beautiful, the weather is beautiful, everything is beautiful.

—George Curtis to Charles Eliot Norton, January 3, 1860⁵⁴

Decades later, Louisa Schuyler, who had grown up on Staten Island and was a lifelong friend of Josephine Lowell, would say of the Shaw family, "I love to dwell upon those early days on Staten Island, and the home life there. They were all—all the family—deeply interested in public affairs, they held strong anti-slavery views. . . . The whole atmosphere of the home was of the purest and highest."⁵⁵ No matter how troubling the state of the nation was in the 1850s, Elliottville residents had the consolation of family life and neighborhood friendships to sustain them. For the people who lived in Elliottville for the last four years before the war, the period must have seemed the most wonderful in the neighborhood's history.

The intimacy of neighborhood life is obvious from letters Elliottville residents wrote to their nonresident friends. While they frequently called upon each other, they also had long-standing informal social engagements. Sundays they attended the neighborhood church, the Unitarian Universalist Church of the Redeemer. The church had gotten its start when Staten Island's two liberal Christian churches, the Congregational Church of the Evangelists and the United Independent Church of Stapleton, merged in 1852. Established as a Unitarian church in 1853, with few exceptions everyone in the neighborhood worshipped there in the 1850s and 1860s.[56] For many years, during which there was no paid preacher, Curtis gave inspirational readings and talks. Sunday afternoons and on into the evening, everyone called upon the Gays. The arrangement was so habitual that anyone not attending would send a note to say why. On pleasant evenings on other days of the week, neighbors would gather on the porches of the Curtises or Shaws to discuss the news of the day. Neighbors also liked to host each other at teas, luncheons, and dinners that often featured the best seasonal fruits and vegetables from their gardens. They enjoyed music, and neighbors would be invited to share their skills or come listen to musicians from elsewhere on Staten Island or Manhattan. Curtis and Mrs. Staples played the piano. Later, several neighborhood young men learned to play the guitar and would serenade. When someone was sick or bereaved, neighbors called, and Curtis might read comforting texts. Even when traveling into the city, the neighbors were often in each other's company since the ferry departed from the foot of Bard Avenue and most of the passengers were from Elliottville.

The men of the neighborhood sometimes gathered at the Shaws, since Mr. Shaw had a billiard room. Sydney Gay especially enjoyed relaxing over a game, and in the male space of the billiard room the men could more freely discuss matters without needing to maintain the politesse female company required. Curtis and William Johnson would accompany each other to political meetings on Staten Island. When Curtis and Gay were in the city on business they often lunched on Gay's favorite dish, oyster stew. Gay and Curtis also walked long miles over the hills and shores of Staten Island to counteract the effects of the hours they spent at their desks.

Women would visit each other during the day, bringing their mending and needlework along, and share news of mutual friends learned through their extensive correspondence. The women also gathered to maintain their language skills by reading and discussing books in French. Instead of walking for exercise, the women took rides to get fresh air. Both Sarah Shaw and Anna Curtis were particularly fond of inviting other women on carriage and sleigh rides.

Everyone in the neighborhood participated in a book club that Elizabeth Winthrop founded in 1856. In the club's seventeenth year, Winthrop wrote a letter to the editor of *The Literary World* recounting the history and success of the club as a model for others to follow.[57] Accustomed to the availability of libraries in New Haven, Winthrop devised the club to provide similar access to the latest books and a means for neighborhood families to build home libraries. Interestingly, even though she limited her recruitment efforts to a two-mile radius, she quickly had twenty families participating, paying an annual subscription fee of five dollars (having a value of around $200 today). The fee entitled each household to two books each fortnight. At the end of the loan period, the books were forwarded to the next household on the list. At the end of the year, all the books were auctioned and the proceeds used to purchase new volumes. The importance of the club to Bard Avenue residents can be appreciated through mentions in correspondence, from which one also learns that George Curtis was favored as the book auctioneer at year's end.

In his personal life, while Curtis had taken up the burden of debt repayment, he was also enjoying his role as, what we might today call, a public intellectual, with a national audience interested in his views. Furthermore, he was only in the first decade of his forty-year career. He had youth, an attractive young wife, and a home in a neighborhood he treasured. He and Anna had their first child, Francis George, in 1857, the start of a family life that would be so satisfying and important.

Frank and Sarah Shaw had been invigorated by their exposure to national politics. As they entered middle age, they had the satisfaction of seeing their children begin to enter young adulthood. In addition to Anna's marriage, Robert Gould Shaw began his studies at Harvard in 1856.

Sydney Gay ended his work at the *National Anti-Slavery Standard* in 1857, in order to recover his health at home and enjoy the company of his two children (Sarah Mifflin, 1852–1901; Martin, 1854–1935). He began work in 1858 at the *New-York Tribune*, where he was to have such an influential role between 1862 and 1864 as managing editor.

Surveying the neighborhood as a whole, Elliottville was filled with children and interesting young people. The married couples included the John Bethune Stapleses, who were similar in age to the Shaws and had three children (Cornelia F., b. approx. 1838; Markham, 1849–1901; and John, b. 1854); the George Cabot Wards, who were similar in age to Curtis and had two children (Samuel, b. 1855, and Marian, 1857–1928); the Rufus King Delafields, who were similar in age to the Shaws and had seven children (Edward, 1837–1884; William, 1838–1863; Rufus, 1840–1861; Henry Parish, 1842–1904; Bertram, 1844–1865; Catherine, 1847–1926; and Richard, 1853–1930); the Richard Warren Westons, who had followed the Gays from boarding house life to Elliottville and had three children (Rosamond, 1848–1928; Helen, 1851–1920; and Warren, 1854–1916); and the John Hendersons, who had twelve children, ranging in age from one to seventeen. Henderson (1809–1884) was similar in age to Frank Shaw, but after the death of his first wife he had married Jane Louisa Rapallo (1821–1880), who was of a much younger generation and had many family connections in New England, although she had been raised in New York.

A child in the neighborhood, Louis Pope Gratacap (ca. 1850–1917) kept a diary in 1863 that captured aspects of his experiences in Elliottville.[58] As a thirteen-year-old, Gratacap's life was focused on family, school, and the other children in the neighborhood. He attended school in Manhattan and taking the ferry and then horsecars in the city occupied a great deal of his weekdays. Ferry service was at the mercy of weather and Gratacap was not infrequently delayed by storms and fog. When the water was rough, he got seasick. Depending upon conditions, the ferry might not be able to land at the dock closest to Elliottville and Gratacap would have to make his way from an alternative landing. In the city he dreaded weather necessitating a landing at the Dey Street dock, with its mud and confusion. Fearing permanent changes to ferry services due to the monopolizing efforts of George Law, he signed a petition to the legislature. He traveled back and forth to the city at a time of day when many men were commuting to their jobs and he sometimes witnessed disorderliness on the boats (public drunkenness, men daring each other to jump from the boat to the dock). There were also other boys commuting to school and they sometimes got into fights with each other. The ferry commute to school took up so much of his energy that he avoided making weekend trips to the city for leisure activities, finding neighborhood social life more enticing.

In his own household he had a brother and both his parents, but his brother was ten years older, his father in his mid-fifties and retired, and his mother in her mid-forties. There were many livelier households in the neighborhood. The son of his mother's brother, Samuel Benton (1826–1879), and his wife Julia (Benjamin) Benton (1829–1884), lived nearby with their son Edward M. Benton (1855–1884). The Bentons and Gratacaps visited back and forth frequently, and Edward Benton was a lively playmate for Gratacap. The Johnson children next door, however, were his most constant companions. Bessie and Oliver were almost exactly the same age as Gratacap and most days he was at the Johnsons or they came to him. Furthermore, the Johnson household included the unmarried Elizabeth Winthrop. Winthrop seems to have been one of the most approachable adults in the neighborhood, happily spending time with the children, helping them with their art projects, and making handicraft items for them. Occasionally, Bessie, Oliver, and Gratacap were invited to play at the Gays by Sarah and Martin. While Sarah and Bessie were great friends, though, Elizabeth Gay considered Oliver a bad influence on Martin, and even Martin could get angered at Oliver's behavior. Occasionally, Gratacap got to play with Richard Delafield, whose parents were much more affluent than the Gratacaps. While Gratacap got a pair of slippers as a New Year's gift, Richard got a magic lantern and a sleigh. When Gratacap invited Richard to his house Mrs. Delafield sometimes prevented the visit, perhaps out of snobbery.

While the children spent much of their time with other children, for them, women dominated the neighborhood, more so than men. Gratacap references his father rarely, mostly in connection with his return from trips or his sharing of war news. Gratacap refers to the houses in the neighborhood by the names of women (i.e., "Mrs. Gay's house"), and when he called at houses, he interacted with the women of the house. He was fond of visiting Mrs. William (Catherine Cruger) Bard and expressed great respect for the widowed woman's charitableness. He entertained her by reading from his diary and she treated him to pieces of fruit.

In addition to school, Gratacap spent time on his own engaged in self-reflective activities and in playing games with other children. In addition to practicing his piano and writing his diary, Gratacap devoted each Saturday morning to composition. While some compositions were essays for school, he, like other children in the neighborhood, wrote stories to share. A few times he tried to reflect on the Civil War and what battlefield action must have been like, but on the whole his life was so far removed from the conflict that he spent little time thinking about it. He was much more likely to reflect on the beauty of the natural environment around him, including sunsets and sunrises, snow on the trees and fields, and the mist, fog, and qualities of light in the harbor. Some of his stories he acted out on his toy theater stage, and for a while he got neighbors to attend his performances on Friday evenings. Like his compatriots, he collected printed images, using them as the basis for stories, trading them for others he liked better, and keeping some in scrapbooks. As he got older, Gratacap was invited to participate in Richmond Dramatic Club Productions, as were other neighborhood children. The plays had elaborate sets, costumes, and printed programs but were presented in the John Bethune Staples's barn.

Figure 3.3. Laura Johnson and Louis Gratacap appeared as mother and son in this Elliottville production of *Hamlet*. The play was performed with original music several times in 1866 in the Richmond Dramatic Club's theater, which also served as the Staples family barn. *Source*: Laura Winthrop Johnson Papers, 1862–1889, MSS Col 1573, Manuscripts Division, New York Public Library. Public domain.

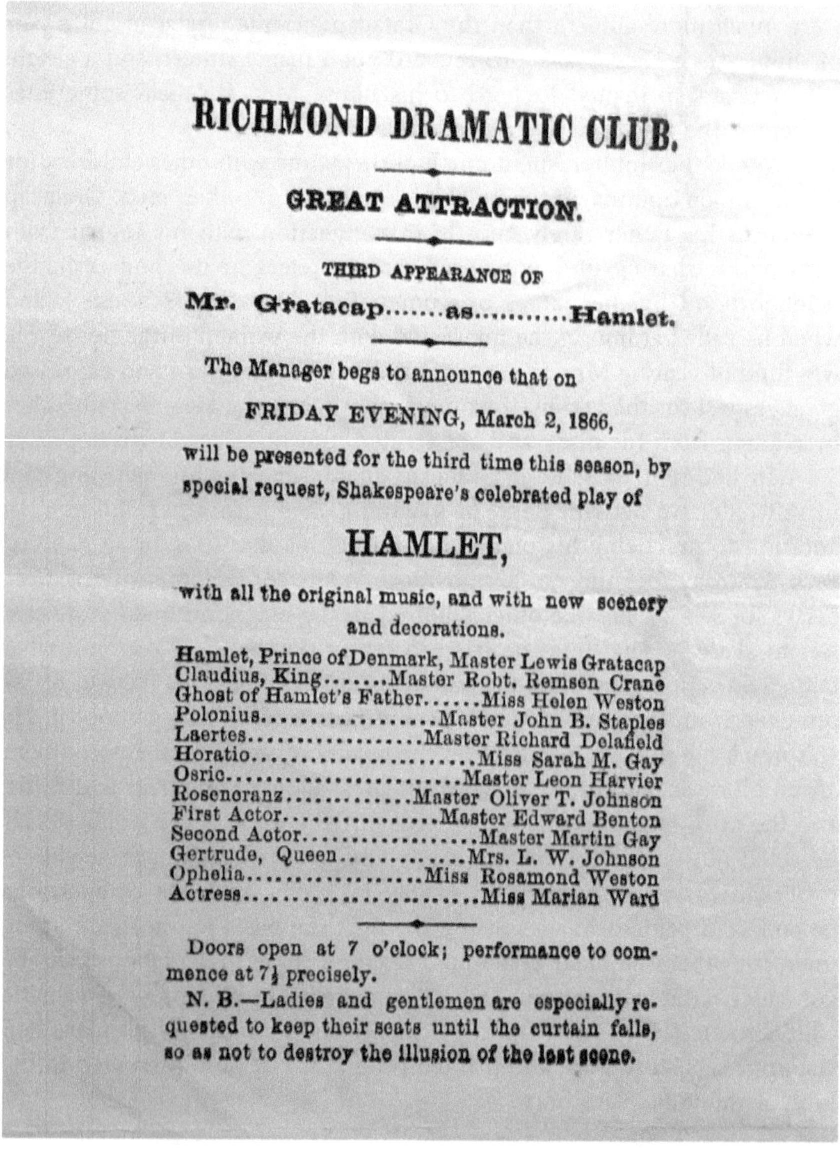

RICHMOND DRAMATIC CLUB.

GREAT ATTRACTION.

THIRD APPEARANCE OF

Mr. Gratacap........as..........Hamlet.

The Manager begs to announce that on

FRIDAY EVENING, March 2, 1866,

will be presented for the third time this season, by special request, Shakespeare's celebrated play of

HAMLET,

with all the original music, and with new scenery and decorations.

Hamlet, Prince of Denmark, Master Lewis Gratacap
Claudius, King.......Master Robt. Remsen Crane
Ghost of Hamlet's Father......Miss Helen Weston
Polonius....................Master John B. Staples
Laertes..................Master Richard Delafield
Horatio.......................Miss Sarah M. Gay
Osric........................Master Leon Harvier
Rosencranz..............Master Oliver T. Johnson
First Actor................Master Edward Benton
Second Actor..................Master Martin Gay
Gertrude, Queen............Mrs. L. W. Johnson
Ophelia..................Miss Rosamond Weston
Actress........................Miss Marian Ward

Doors open at 7 o'clock; performance to commence at 7½ precisely.

N. B.—Ladies and gentlemen are especially requested to keep their seats until the curtain falls, so as not to destroy the illusion of the last scene.

While these activities were the basis for interaction with other children and adults, Gratacap got most excited about active play. Although the children skated, walked in the woods and on the beach, and played marbles, most of their games were ones they made up themselves, like Hide the Handkerchief, Bear, Buffaloes, and Cut Up. The point of the first of these is clear, but the other games are more obscure. Cut Up involved a "butcher" pretending to skin and carve a "calf" (with both roles played by children) and sell the resulting cuts to other participants. Buffaloes was about hunting, with children pretending to be buffaloes. Each participant in Bear pretended to be a bear and established a den. A few times Gratacap played with toy soldiers in Sham Fight, but only once played Unionists and Secesh, imagining capturing Jefferson Davis and General Beauregard.

Laura Johnson left a record that captures some of what life was life in Elliottville for children in her pseudonymously published *Little Blossom's Reward: A Christmas Book for Children*.[59] Dedicated to Bessie and Oliver (Johnson's third child, Laura, had not yet been born), the book celebrated an extended Yuletide holiday in which nonresident family members visited and entertained the children with stories, always calculated to teach morals and featuring wild and domestic animals, as well as imaginary creatures like nymphs and fairies. The family setting, with uncles, aunts, and a grandmother spending days around the hearth, would certainly have been an important aspect of many Elliottville children's lives, since, as with the Johnsons, it was often the case that, in addition to households including extended family members, relatives stayed for long periods. Beyond conveying a sense of the social setting, the book described the natural environment and the delight that adults and children shared in their garden and woodland activities.

Laura described the Johnson house, nearby woods, brooks, ponds, and the seashore in some detail, capturing the delight with which her children viewed them. The house, sited on a sloping lawn and shaded by large trees, was on a property that included plantings of shrubbery inhabited by songbirds, and a large garden with flowers and fruit as well as vegetables. Mature chestnut, oak, and walnut trees formed woodland glades beyond the property, and from the piazza of the house one could see, a mile away in the distance, the harbor and waves breaking on rocky islands, on one of which was a lighthouse to which their father had once rowed the children.[60] Around the harbor were sandy beaches from which the children collected prized seashells and from which they bathed. In the woods surrounding the house they learned the names of plants (anemone, hepatica, pyrola, Solomon's seal, and wintergreen). They were taught to look closely at flowers and leaves to appreciate their beauty; to be aware of the sky and the light falling on tree bark, lichens, and the emerald grass; and to value the tranquility of lying "upon the soft green moss and look[ing] up into the trees among the interlacing boughs, and watch[ing] the light glancing upon the quivering leaves."[61] Leisure hours filled with intensively observing nature, playing in the nearby brook, and walking along the seashore alternated with lessons in the home schoolroom, working in the garden with child-sized tools, and harvesting food from the nearby woods and pastures, including blackberries, mushrooms, whortleberries, chestnuts, and hickory nuts.

As well as her husband and children, Laura Johnson's household included other members of her family. In addition to her sister Elizabeth, George Curtis's one-time fiancée who never married and lived in the Johnson house for the rest of her long life, Laura's mother Elizabeth Woolsey Winthrop lived with the Johnsons from 1854 until her death in 1863. In the years before the war, Laura's brothers Theodore and William Winthrop were residents for extended periods. Both young men were active in the social life of the Curtis, Shaw, and Gay households and the front porch political discussions of the neighborhood men.[62] For various reasons, including the fact that they were close to the same age, Theodore became a good friend of Curtis.

Theodore Winthrop

The earliest of Theodore Winthrop's surviving letters were written in 1847 and 1848, before and after graduating from Yale College. The summer after his graduation he wrote from the farm where he was helping a fellow graduate get established. As a whole, these letters illustrate his love of the outdoors, his energy and occasional high spirits, and his attitudes toward the abolitionist movement. In an early letter, he described a twenty-eight-mile hike, at the end of which, as darkness was falling, he amused himself by singing opera arias.[63] Music was important to him, and it is for the music that he seems to have taken Laura Johnson to Broadway Tabernacle in fall 1847. He approved of the music there but apologized to Johnson for an unpleasant evening due to the "uncomfortable feeling of rowdiness which a place like the Tabernacle and a very mixed audience gives."[64] Broadway Tabernacle had been organized by Lewis Tappan for Charles Grandison

Finney in 1832. Although Finney had left to become a theology professor at Oberlin College (he was later president), the Tabernacle, which could accommodate up to 2,400 people, continued as a center for abolitionist meetings. From the letter, one gets the sense that the social context of abolitionism was difficult for Winthrop to countenance.

Winthrop first met Curtis in Europe; Winthrop had sailed for England on July 27, 1849. Between then and January 1851, he traveled in France, Italy, Greece, Switzerland, Germany, and Holland with a cache of letters of introduction and frequently encountered family friends, relatives, and former classmates. Occasionally, his sojourns coincided with his uncle, Yale president Theodore Dwight Woolsey (1801–1889). Woolsey traveled with Staten Islander William Henry Aspinwall and Aspinwall family members. Woolsey and Aspinwall were related by marriage, since Aspinwall's sister Emily had married Edward John Woolsey. Theodore Winthrop spent several months with his uncle and the Aspinwalls in Rome in the winter of 1850. He considered them very good company and became friends with

Figure 3.4. George Curtis opened his biographical sketch of Theodore Winthrop by describing the emotional impact his death had in Elliottville. *Source*: Prints and Photographs Division, Library of Congress, https://www.loc.gov/item/2005683064/.

their daughter Anna. By the time Aspinwall met Winthrop he had made his most recent fortune through the Pacific Mail Steamship Company's pioneering steamship route to California. Aspinwall asked Winthrop to work in his office and prepare his son Lloyd (1834–1886) for Yale when he returned to the United States. When Winthrop began the job, he was fascinated by the scale and lucrativeness of Aspinwall's business. He eventually alternated between office work on days steamers were setting sail and staying at Aspinwall's Staten Island house to tutor Lloyd in 1851.[65]

Winthrop's appreciation for Staten Island was heightened by a distaste for the city that echoed that of Sydney Gay. Winthrop despised the air of the city as "gutter-reeking, Paddy-exhaled, tar impregnated, dead dog-cat-rat-horse-tainted, Deutschlander-pipe-smoked . . . eddying up from the foul cabins of fated emigrant prison ships."[66] Only in the country did his "soul revive" and he could declare: "I am an individual."[67] On Staten Island, he bathed in the sea with Lloyd Aspinwall, took carriage rides with Anna Aspinwall to admire the views from Todt Hill, and watched the ships in the harbor and the sunset near the telegraph pole above Aspinwall's house. Because he visited Elliottville often, he trekked across the hills between his sister's house and Aspinwall's, many times at night. While the views from Staten Island's high hills enchanted him, the character of the harbor pleased him most: "The Bay is like a quiet lake and the stretch of water from the Quarantine to Sandy Hook seems like a broad River."[68] William Templeton Johnson had gone into partnership with some neighbors, the Hoyts and Bements, to commission a large rowing boat named *The Trio* (it was rigged to accommodate two pairs of oars or three pairs of sculls). Theodore Winthrop liked to row his sisters in *The Trio* out against the tide, "right down the path of the sun to its setting," then float "homeward on the spontaneous tide" to the boat landing at the foot of Bard Avenue, "floating along in the moonlight."[69] While Winthrop was an Episcopalian and never a member of an abolitionist society, he spoke rhapsodically "of insects chattering, of leaves whispering, all things pouring forth their confidence to Nature their ever listening mother . . . who readily supplies the needs of each" sounding very much like the transcendentalists of Elliottville.

Winthrop did not settle in Elliottville until 1854. First, Aspinwall delegated him to take Lloyd Aspinwall to a Swiss school in 1851. Then, after another stint in Aspinwall's Manhattan office, Winthrop asked for a transfer to the shipping company's office in Panama City, where he worked from August 1852 to March 1853. Dissatisfied with the routine of business life, he resigned to make a seven-month trip through California and the Washington and Oregon territories. During his travels in the Northwest and West, Winthrop met a number of people who were, or would become, men of note, including fur trader and explorer Peter Skene Ogden (1790–1854), explorer Colonel Benjamin Louis Eulalie de Bonneville (1796–1878), George B. McClellan (1826–1885), and, as he was making his way back across the continent to New Haven, Brigham Young (1801–1877). In 1854 Winthrop was a volunteer in Lieutenant Isaac G. Strain's Darien Expedition to survey a canal route across the Isthmus of Panama. Finally, near the end of 1854 he was back in New York and living in the Johnson household on Staten Island.

During that time, Winthrop was studying law in the office of Charles Tracy (1810–1885). Tracy had graduated from Yale in 1832 and was a great supporter of his alma mater, eventually serving for more than a decade as president of the New York association of Yale alumni and publishing a memoir of his time at Yale. Whether Winthrop being a nephew of Yale's president had any bearing on how he came to know the decades-older Tracy is not clear. Tracy was known as a learned man with literary interests (he wrote poetry). Unlike Winthrop's earlier mentor, Aspinwall, Tracy was an abolitionist.[70] Tracy usually broke from work in the summer to spend time in the country. In 1855 he took a group of twenty-seven family members, friends, servants, and a piano to Mount Desert Island. Winthrop was a member of the party, as was artist Frederic Edwin Church (1826–1900), and the two became close friends.[71] In 1856 Winthrop and Church made a summer trip to Maine together and spent a good deal of their time in each other's company when they were in New York City.

Another man Winthrop would befriend, Robert Gould Shaw, had returned from his studies in Hanover, Germany, in April of 1856 and was living in his parents' Bard Avenue house while prepping for the Harvard College entrance examinations, hoping to enter as a junior.[72] His parents had hired Francis Channing Barlow (1834–1896) as his tutor. Barlow, although born in Brooklyn, was the son of a Unitarian minister and spent time as a student at Brook Farm before entering Harvard. He graduated at the top of his Harvard Law School class in 1855. He worked as a lawyer on the staff of the *New-York Tribune* and it would not be surprising if Curtis introduced him to the Shaws. Some years later he would marry Ellen Shaw. Robert Gould Shaw left for Harvard in August of 1856, although he visited his family on Staten Island fairly regularly.

Winthrop also spent some time away from Staten Island in 1857. While Church was on a landscape-painting trip in Ecuador, Winthrop made a journey that clarified his devotion to Staten Island and gave him an opportunity to declare in writing his dedication to abolitionism. In December of 1856, claiming that he was making no contribution to the office, he resigned from Tracy's law firm. In early spring of 1857, he decided to move to the West Coast, but when he arrived in St. Louis, Missouri, in March to attend the wedding of Yale friend Henry Hitchcock (1829–1902), he was drawn into St. Louis social life and accepted a partnership in Hitchcock's law office. In sending the news back to Elliottville, Winthrop carefully articulated his initial qualms about settling in a slave state but pointed out that all his St. Louis friends were antislavery, that "no one objects to my Black republicanism," and that he was close to another Yale alumnus B. Gratz Brown (1826–1885), who was nationally known as a leader of the Missouri Free Soil movement.[73] He urged his readers to "say to Mrs. Shaw that I am just as firm in the cause as ever."[74] However, by May he was writing, "Not until I was actually gone did I discover that Staten Island of late had begun to seem homelike to me and here in a land little picturesque your landscape returns and grows dearer."[75] By July, his partnership had dissolved, and after traveling with the Hitchcocks back East and spending time in Newport, he was back on Staten Island.

When Frederic Edwin Church returned to New York in 1858, he rented one of the twenty-three studios in the Tenth Street Studio Building and Winthrop rented one as well.[76] Winthrop devoted himself to writing fiction and accounts of his adventures in South America and the West. His mother had a number of investments and owned valuable land in Manhattan, about which Winthrop had aggressively advised her in letters over the previous years and she may have allowed him to manage some of her affairs. Still living with the Johnsons, Winthrop's studio would have offered a writing environment away from the distractions of family life.[77] The Studio Building was designed by Winthrop's friend Richard Morris Hunt for use by the most prominent artists of the day, and taking a studio there reveals Winthrop's confidence and investment in his writing. Located at 51 West Tenth Street, between Fifth and Sixth Avenues in Manhattan, in addition to camaraderie with other artists in the building, the location offered easy access to the neighborhood's student and bohemian life.[78]

Church had exhibited his *Niagara* to international acclaim in 1857 (at the Corcoran Gallery of Art in Washington, DC) and was at work on *The Heart of the Andes*. Curtis later recalled that Winthrop "haunted" Church's studio to watch the canvas progress.[79] On his part, Winthrop was working on a novel that would be published posthumously as *Cecil*

Dreeme. The book's gothic atmosphere and melodramatic plot has shaped much recent interpretation. David Peters Corbet has pointed out that at the center of the book is a dialogue on the nature of art.[80] Recent *Cecil Dreeme* criticism is more likely to use the novel as a platform from which to speculate on the author's personal life. The plot deals with an intense, emotional friendship between two males, a friendship the novel compares to Damon and Pythias and considers finer than any connection between man and woman. Nonetheless, the intensity of the friendship also troubles the protagonist, and with relief he discovers by the end of the book that his intense friendship was with a woman who had disguised herself as a man to avoid bad treatment. The exact nature of Winthrop's personal friendships with Frederic Edwin Church and other men, and the pleasure or suffering they may have caused, cannot be decisively known. We do know that Winthrop, with a workspace in the Studio Building, interacted with men at the center of artistic life in the 1850s, and by frequenting a nearby, European-style rathskeller, he was also at the center of bohemian society.

Winthrop patronized the Vault at Pfaff's, a beer cellar at 653 Broadway near Bleeker Street. Started by Swiss-German immigrant Charles Ignatius Pfaff in 1855, the dimly-lit basement establishment offered inexpensive food and drinks in wide variety and quickly became the center of American bohemian life due to the influence of Henry Clapp Jr., a Fourier translator from Massachusetts, who, on his return from Paris, longed for the café society he had known and attracted like-minded friends and acquaintances to the Vault. He also founded the *New York Saturday Press*, a newspaper that celebrated New York bohemia and published works by the counterculture writers of the day. In fact, actors, authors, poets, and journalists, like Walt Whitman, Edwin Booth, George Arnold, Thomas Nast, and William Dean Howells, were for a time known as Pfaffians. Pfaff's Vault had a thirty-chair table down the center of the room for the inner circle of the place, among whom Winthrop figured.[81] Pffaf's was another setting in which Curtis's and Winthrop's social circles overlapped, since Curtis also frequented the Vault and was friends with Pfaff regulars Bayard Taylor, Fitz Hugh Ludlow, Richard and Elizabeth Stoddard, Edmund Clarence Stedman, and Fitz-James O'Brien. Dr. Elliott's son, Samuel R. Elliott, who after graduating from New York Medical College in 1854 and getting medical experience in Germany and Paris had returned to enter his father's practice, also frequented Pfaff's. During this period, the Elliotts' office was only a few blocks away and was said to be an outpost of Pfaff's since so many Pfaffians frequented the place.

The contrast between Winthrop's bohemian social life in Manhattan and his domestic life in the family circle back on Staten Island must have been dramatic. In addition to William Johnson, who seems to have been a dour and frequently ill man, Winthrop's elderly mother was also in residence.[82] Around 1860, Winthrop's younger brother William Winthrop joined the household. Unlike Theodore Winthrop, William took his profession seriously. After graduating from Yale Law School in 1853, he had completed additional study at Harvard Law School and practiced law in Boston and St. Anthony's, Minnesota, before establishing a partnership in 1860 with former Yale classmate Robbins Little at 43 Wall Street in New York City.[83]

By the time William Winthrop moved into the neighborhood, Robert Gould Shaw was also back at home. Persuaded by his uncle George Russell to end his studies at Harvard, in March 1859 he had moved back to Staten Island to begin a career in the firm of another uncle, Henry P. Sturgis, whose import business was in New York. So the Winthrop brothers, Robert Gould Shaw, Curtis, and other Elliottville men were discussing the politics of the day in the presidential election year in the 1860s.

The Winthrop brothers were against slavery, but their position was different from other Elliottville abolitionists. They had been children in New Haven when the town was energized by the controversy over *The Amistad*. As Episcopalians, the Winthrops were accustomed to religious rhetoric that spoke of sin and were more swayed by the evangelical stance on slavery, in which society should be freed of all forms of sin. One of the great divides in the antislavery movement was over this very issue. While the Winthrops may have thought that the sin of slavery should be eradicated from society, they were also firm supporters of the Constitution (unlike the Garrisonians). They believed slavery should not spread but that the federal government had no power to eradicate the institution, since to do so was to overstep federal authority. However, they did believe that the federal government had the power to put down insurrection.[84]

From Laura Johnson's letters, one gets a sense of how Curtis's presence in the neighborhood gave immediacy to national politics for other residents. While newspapers often printed accounts of his lectures and he published many essays, Elliottville neighbors heard his firsthand accounts of what he witnessed and said at political meetings around the country. As the chair of Staten Island's Republican Party, he attended the 1860 Chicago nominating convention. He had supported the New York candidate William H. Seward, but as balloting progressed, he shifted his support to Lincoln and related the experience to his neighbors. As in the Frémont campaign, Curtis was one of the Republican Party's lead orators, and members of his Staten Island circle heard him speak there, as well as elsewhere in the metropolitan area. William Winthrop also addressed political meetings alongside Curtis, including rallies for the Lincoln/Hamlin ticket and gatherings of the Wide Awakes.

Staten Island and the Election of 1860

Having Curtis in their midst may have swayed some Staten Islanders, but Staten Island (and New York) still voted overwhelmingly for the Democratic ticket. Historians have explained the New York City vote by pointing to the city's economic ties to the South and the ways in which laborers influenced the results. However, specific attention has rarely been paid to Staten Island. Immigrants had been attracted to Staten Island in the 1850s to work in new breweries (Bachmann, Constanz, and Bechtel all opened during the decade) and factories (new firms producing bricks, dyed textiles, and paper commenced), and to construct a steam railroad that opened in 1860. While the Republican Party tried to show the harm that slavery did to free labor, most immigrant laborers found more convincing the Democratic scare claim that freed slaves would destroy the labor market by literally working for nothing. As in New York City, this tactic was likely influential on Staten Island. Like New York City, Staten Island also had strong links to the South due to the importance of maritime industries and the textile-finishing industry for the local economy.

While Staten Island may have been akin to Manhattan in the way that laborers, influenced by economic concerns, determined the vote, Staten Island was also under a peculiarly local influence: the fact that a significant number of Southern families summered on Staten Island. Southern families traveled to the North to escape the heat and disease of summers in the South. The fact that New York City had developed into a vast market of consumer goods meant that a summer visit could also serve as an extended shopping excursion. Some purchases met the practical needs of plantations. For instance, New York had become known for ready-made clothing. Made of the cheapest textiles (known as shoddy and fabricated from yarn produced by tearing up old woolen rags), much of this clothing was used for dressing slaves.[85] In addition, the city had also become a center for a wide range of luxury goods that appealed to plantation families. Although Manhattan may have been an attractive market, it was not an attractive summer residence. Heat made the crowds, dirt, and street refuse unbearable, and the threat of disease had been made all too apparent by the cholera epidemics of 1832 and 1849.

For these reasons, many Southerners summered on Staten Island. Most stayed in hotels in New Brighton, including the Planters' Hotel. There was also a resident Southern social circle to welcome visitors that was dominated by Madame Suzette Grymes (1796–1881). Grymes's first husband had been William C. C. Claiborne (d. 1817), the first governor of Louisiana. She was remarried to John R. Grymes (d.1854), noted as one of the leading orators and lawyers of the South. In 1836 when the couple decided to live apart, she purchased a Staten Island hilltop and built a mansion there that became a magnet for visiting Southerners. The Gardiner-Tyler house in West New Brighton, a short distance from Elliottville, also attracted Southerners. Juliana, the widow of David Gardiner, purchased the house, then named Castleton Hill, in 1852. Her daughter, Julia, had married President John Tyler in 1844 and become the mistress of Sherwood Forest Plantation in Virginia with its seventy slaves. An outspoken champion of her husband's political views on state's rights and the institution of slavery, she went so far as to author a newspaper article in 1853 that was widely republished and became notorious for claiming that slaves enjoyed comforts Northern industrial workers did not. The Tylers visited and socialized on Staten Island in the 1850s and 1860s. After John Tyler's death in 1862, Julia Tyler moved into Castleton Hill with her mother, managed her plantation from there, and worked on behalf of the Confederacy. While Southerners also visited Manhattan, the small population of Staten Island and the relative affluence of the visitors gave their presence much more of an impact on Staten Island and probably had a greater impact on local opinion.

The prominent businessmen and bankers of New York and Staten Island had done all they could to defeat Lincoln, playing upon fears of economic collapse and an accompanying collapse of the labor market. When Lincoln won the election, over two thousand New York merchants signed a pledge to support letting Southern states leave the Union in peace. An editorial in the *Richmond County Gazette* rued the fact that the rest of New York State had not heeded the newspaper's call for Union as Richmond County had and hoped that now that Lincoln had been elected the "compromises of the Constitution" would be upheld in order to destroy the "black demon" of sectionalism.[86] As the weeks progressed without compromise the newspaper's editorials claimed "party spirit" (i.e., political party animosities) had led to a wide range of crimes on Staten Island, including arson, assaults, burglary, and murder, that constituted a "public calamity."[87] Near the end of January 1861, the newspaper was still claiming that the institution of slavery was "beneficent to the African race" and "necessary to the social economy of countries whose climate is not genial to White labor," and that the Union was breaking up over an abstract notion that slavery was wrong, when, in fact, that was not "the common sentiment of mankind."[88]

From December through January, a series of states left the Union. New York political officials and business leaders agitated for Northern concessions. In a now notorious statement to the city council, Mayor Fernando Wood proposed that New York City should secede so that commerce with the South could continue without impediment. In January 1861 the most prominent of the city's capitalists traveled by special train to Washington, DC, to carry a petition to legislators signed by forty thousand business leaders specifying extensive concessions that should be offered to the South. William H. Aspinwall, representing the Union Safety Committee, was a member of the party.

The course of events soon justified the business leaders' fears. One early action by the Confederate States of America was a coordinated effort to renege on debts owed in the North. While the loss of approximately $478 million was felt across the North, the action was directed against New York City, and by early 1861 an economic panic had taken hold of the city.[89] Even influential Republicans across the North began calling for compromise with the South.

However, the tide of events eventually rallied even the most avaricious business leaders to the preservation of the Union. Near the end of February, when Jefferson Davis was elected the provisional president of the Confederacy, even Staten Island newspapers declared the act a revolution that required Lincoln to act, although they did not urge an armed response. On April 1, the Confederate States announced that its ports would have new tariffs that were half of those in the North, and panicked businessmen envisioned the collapse of the import business in New York. On April 12, Fort Sumter was fired upon and on April 15 Lincoln called for seventy-five thousand men to volunteer for ninety days in response to the South's insurrection.

The years of conciliation were at an end, and New York's businessmen rushed to support the Union. The businessmen organized a rally on

April 20 at Union Square that was attended by over one hundred thousand to demonstrate broad public confidence in the leadership of the business community. A Union defense committee was established, constituted of an even number of Democrats and Republicans. In response, the following day Lincoln secretly transferred $2 million to the committee to purchase war materiel and enlist troops. The business of the war (that would make so many New York merchants and bankers rich) had officially been set into motion.

After the evacuation of Fort Sumter, Major Robert Anderson and his command sailed for New York City. When the ship arrived in New York Harbor on April 18, 1861, it received a fifty gun salute, and Anderson and his troops were celebrated at public receptions. On Staten Island, the old Quarantine grounds in Tompkinsville was the venue for a public meeting on April 27, 1861, chaired by George Curtis, whose purpose was to plan Richmond County's response to outbreak of war. While Curtis's proposals, when written down, covered many pages, his oratorical presentation led to their enthusiastic passage. Curtis asserted that an armed response by the US government was legitimate and necessary because the US Constitution had been violated. He called for each town on Staten Island to organize militias to arm, drill, and train the men. He requested women in each town to form relief societies to prepare bandages and similar supplies for the men. In addition, he proposed that each town form a committee to raise money by direct appeals to citizens in order to accumulate funds to pay for military equipment for volunteers and for financial aid to the families of volunteers.[90]

"Goodbye the Drum Is Beating"—Robert Gould Shaw to Sarah Shaw, April 20, 1861[91]

As discussed earlier, Dr. Elliott's Seventy-Ninth Highlanders was one of the first regiments to appear in Washington after Lincoln's call for troops to defend the city. Theodore and William Winthrop and Robert Gould Shaw had all enlisted in the Seventh Regiment New York National Guard and begun drilling on Staten Island (where many Civil War regiments eventually formed and trained). Originally a battalion of the New York State Militia, the Seventh had existed since 1806 and had been stationed in the harbor forts of New York in the War of 1812. Known for the high percentage of socially elite members, the Seventh had often performed ceremonial functions (as it had during celebrations honoring the Marquis de Lafayette on his visit to the city). Occasionally, the Seventh was also mobilized during periods of social unrest. During these events, usually termed riots, the city was treated to the spectacle of the city's elite pitted against members of the underclasses. Oddly enough, before 1861, the most recent time the militia had been called into service was during the Quarantine "Riot" of 1858, when the Quarantine facility on Staten Island had been burned to the ground.

When the Seventh left for Washington on April 19, 1861, a crowd, reported to be nearly a million strong, turned out to cheer the regiment's march along Broadway as the men headed to board waiting trains. Although many men had their own uniforms tailored, Aspinwall paid for Brooks Brothers jackets for regiment members who needed them. Thereafter, the uniforms were known as Aspinwalls. The Shaw family missed the Seventh's departure since they were vacationing in the Bahamas when Shaw enlisted and subsequently departed.[92] However, Gay and Curtis saw him off.

Elliottville's women also responded to the war. By late April 1861, after three thousand women met at Cooper Union to strategize on how they could support the war effort, the New York City Women's Central Association for Relief of the Army and Navy of the United States was formed.[93] The organization was the precursor to the Sanitary Commission, which was established in June 1861. The Women's Central became the "main branch" of the Sanitary Commission. Louisa Schuyler, who lived near Elliottville in West New Brighton, was the manager of the Women's Central, and the women in the Curtis, Gay, Shaw, and Winthrop/Johnson families all participated. The women knitted mittens, inventoried donations, rolled bandages, collected money, repacked donations, distributed work assignments, and organized and worked at Sanitary Fairs. Sarah Shaw also hired women on Staten Island to sew items for the troops.[94]

The Elliottville neighbors had firsthand accounts of the Seventh's activities in Washington via Shaw's letters back to his family. Theodore Winthrop also wrote to his family, but he corresponded to the nation as well, writing accounts of the Seventh's experiences for *The Atlantic Monthly* (then under the editorship of Curtis and Laura Johnson's friend James Fields). Shaw and the Winthrops spent a good deal of time together in Washington. William Winthrop and Shaw, both serving in the infantry, were tent mates. When stationed in the Capitol Building, Theodore Winthrop used family connections to get the keys to the House of Representatives Post Office so that Shaw and the Winthrops could sleep in relative comfort and privacy.

Theodore Winthrop also called upon family friends to pursue a commission in the cavalry. He could drop the names of both Hamilton Fish and George Curtis with Secretary of State William Henry Seward (1801–1872), who had initially been Curtis's choice for president. When Theodore Winthrop met with Seward, he chose to call socially at the New Yorker's residence and met Lincoln, who was visiting at the same time. Although Seward supposedly urged Lincoln to make a lieutenant of "Mr. Winthrop, a scholar and a gentleman," his actual commission did not come until much later and through Benjamin Butler.[95]

Butler's account of Theodore Winthrop's commission, published long after the war, claimed that the young man had approached him, but Butler had told him to serve out his enlistment with the Seventh and then "come to me wherever I was, and I would give him a place on my staff."[96] William Winthrop's biographer, Kastenberg, speculates on the more likely scenario that Butler approached Theodore Winthrop, whose writing for *The Atlantic Monthly* could further Butler's political ambitions.[97] When Winthrop had exhausted all other routes to a commission and after his initial term of enlistment ended, he did approach Butler and was appointed a major and aide-de-camp. Supposedly frustrated with the slim possibilities for proving his heroism in such a role, Winthrop volunteered for General Ebenezer W. Pierce's staff.

When Butler called for an attack on Confederate troops near Big Bethel, falling for the enemy's stratagem to engage the Union prematurely, Winthrop proposed a night march and dawn attack on June 10, 1861, that was endorsed. Butler, though, remained absent from the battlefield and his staff was too inexperienced to successfully carry the day. Winthrop, while commanding an assault on four companies of the First Regiment North Carolina Infantry led by Colonel (later Lieutenant General) Daniel Harvey Hill, marshaled a charge, urging his men forward from atop a fallen tree and was shot down (later, three different men, including an African American slave of a Confederate officer, claimed to have made the kill, although it has generally been assumed that he fell in friendly fire).[98] William Winthrop had the sad duty of retrieving his brother's body from an unmarked grave and recovering some possessions. After lying in state at the Seventh Regiment Armory on Tompkins Square, a funeral was held on June 21 and Theodore Winthrop was subsequently buried in the Winthrop family plot in Grove Street Cemetery in his hometown of New Haven.

The emotional impact on Theodore Winthrop's family and Staten Island circle was intense. We know from his sister Laura Johnson's letters that his mother's decline into illness and death began with his demise. Johnson continued to mourn him for the rest of her life.[99] In writing to Johnson, Elizabeth Gay gave some indication of the impact on the neighborhood when she said, "His loss is a sad one to all, but to those in whose homes he had been so familiar a guest it is a gap that cannot be filled."[100] Robert Gould Shaw, in his letters home, revealed how deeply he felt the death of his friend.[101] The introductory essay Curtis wrote for Theodore Winthrop's novel, *Cecil Dreeme*, which Curtis aided in getting posthumously published, gives a good indication of Curtis's emotions and the intimacy of their friendship.

James Fields had accepted Winthrop's novel for publication by Ticknor and Fields before the war, but Winthrop had never finished preparing a final manuscript. Laura Johnson and William Winthrop recruited Curtis to finish editing the work. Curtis also supplied a biographical sketch as an introduction to the novel that became Theodore Winthrop's authoritative biography and had first appeared in shorter form in *The Atlantic Monthly*. Curtis wrote the magazine article shortly after Winthrop's death; however, it was not published until August, timed to appear after both of Winthrop's pieces for the magazine—"Our March to Washington" and "Washington as Camp"—had already been published.

Although Curtis conveyed some of the tenderness with which he regarded Theodore Winthrop, his essay can also be seen as part of an effort to shield Winthrop from criticism of his heterodox lifestyle and make him a heroic martyr.[102] Even though Winthrop was thirty-two years old at death, he had never married, never had a career, and had only published a few short stories and some poems. One assumes Curtis's explanation is so convoluted because he cannot frankly present Winthrop's bohemian social life centered on Pfaff's and the Tenth Street Studio Building. Theodore Winthrop's cousin George Templeton Strong (1820–1875) had observed Winthrop in traditional social settings and said Winthrop may have endured all sorts of hardship during his frontier adventures, "but skirmishing with Indians, shooting jaguars, and doing and suffering other things incident to journeying in desert places and among pagan savages . . . [had] not taken the stiffness out of his vertebral column, nor the solemnity out of his face."[103] When Winthrop was around ladies he behaved "as if he were at a funeral."[104] Curtis conceded that Winthrop was criticized for being aloof in society but attributed Winthrop's lack of social accomplishments to having modesty, "heroic sincerity," and a "pure, manly morality."[105] Winthrop, Curtis claimed, would never try to force attention. Then, in the outbreak of war "his day had at length dawned."[106] For Curtis, the outbreak of war had engendered in Winthrop an "electric vitality," and the meaning of his death lay in its power to enkindle in others the passion to quell the South and free the slaves.[107] Curtis quoted Winthrop: "We must conquer the South. Afterward we must be prepared to do its policing in its own behalf, and in behalf of its Black population, whom this war must, without precipitation, emancipate."[108]

Curtis wrote out of genuine sorrow over the death of his neighbor and friend, but his biographical sketch and the rushed publication of *Cecil Dreeme* must be viewed in the context of the war effort. Frequently, Curtis needed to make discouraging war news palatable and even inspiring in *Harper's Weekly* editorials and his essays for *Harper's Monthly*. He also needed to enkindle "electric vitality" for abolitionism in a reluctant general population. Through the publication of Theodore Winthrop's writings, Winthrop's heroic death was kept before the public and interest in him remained strong even in the decades after the war (his sister published his poems and an account of his life in 1884). The first edition of *Cecil Dreeme* appeared in October 1861 and was successful enough to be reprinted several times. Even though the novel has been claimed as a queer text in recent decades, the work was received quite differently by contemporary readers and got positive mainstream reviews upon publication. In January 1862, another of Theodore Winthrop's novels, *John Brent*, was published and was eventually reprinted sixteen times. With settings in the American West and London, most of the plot focuses on the rescue of a woman, but the novel also features the escape of a fugitive slave from the pursuit of men intent on recapturing him. Winthrop's other novel, *Edwin Brothertoft* (July 1862), portrays a family with a long history in America and a troubled relationship to the English monarchy and is set immediately before the American Revolution. Sections of the book foretell the birth of an American worldview after the Revolution and several African American characters are presented in a positive light. The other writings published in the years after Winthrop's death include a fictionalized account of his travel through the Pacific Northwest, *The Canoe and the Saddle* (Boston: Ticknor and Fields, 1862), which was influential in shaping perspectives on the territory, and *Life in the Open Air* (Boston: Ticknor and Fields, 1863), which presented a version of the notes Winthrop made about his travels in Maine with Frederic Edwin Church, along with short stories, Winthrop's accounts of the Seventh Regiment, and his essay on Church's *Heart of the Andes*. Laura Johnson capped the publications with *The Life and Poems of*

Theodore Winthrop (New York: Henry Holt, 1884). The wartime accounts of his death and posthumous publications firmly established Winthrop as a Union martyr. Decades after the war, when John Nicolay and John Hay wrote their comprehensive account of Abraham Lincoln, they maintained that Winthrop was a symbol of great importance for the North.

Theodore Winthrop's friend Robert Gould Shaw was to eclipse Winthrop's own fame as a war hero. In recent years, much has been written about Shaw, making it less necessary to give a complete account here. Shaw had served out his enlistment with the Seventh; subsequently, he was commissioned as second lieutenant in Company H of the Second Massachusetts Infantry and fought in the first Battle of Winchester and the battles of Cedar Mountain and Antietam before taking command of the Fifty-Fourth Massachusetts Volunteer Infantry, a Black regiment.

Figure 3.5. This image of Shaw was published as a carte de visite and widely distributed. *Source*: John Adams Whipple, photographer, Colonel Robert Gould Shaw of Seventh New York Infantry Regiment, Co. H, Second Massachusetts Infantry Regiment and Fifty-Fourth Massachusetts Infantry Regiment in uniform (Boston: Whipple, ca. 1861), https://www.loc.gov/item/2022630577/.

Formed by Massachusetts Governor John A. Andrew soon after the Emancipation Proclamation, the regiment was only the second Black unit in the country. Andrew chose Frank Shaw and George L. Stearns to recruit New York troops and officers (who Lincoln and Stanton had said must be White). Troops were also recruited from Massachusetts, New York, and Pennsylvania. One Staten Islander, a mixed-race farm laborer named Thomas P. Robinson (born ca. 1843), was recruited (receiving the fifty-dollar state bounty payment). Andrew dispatched Frank to personally ask his son to take charge of the regiment. After initial qualms, he agreed.

Shaw's parents considered their son's command of the regiment a great privilege. For abolitionists who had engaged in a decades-long struggle with few victories to celebrate, the Emancipation Proclamation, followed by the recruitment of Black troops, was deeply gratifying. After Robert Gould Shaw accepted his commission, his mother wrote, "I believe this time to be the fulfillment of the prophesies, and that we are beholding the Advent of Christ."[109] Shaw took command in Boston on February 15, 1863. The experience of seeing Shaw leading the Black regiment through the streets of Boston on their way to war was memorably emotional for a whole generation of Bostonians. The Shaws' great friend Lydia Maria Child was to write years later that "people were then impressed as by the presence of an angel."[110]

Shaw faced a number of challenges in getting fair treatment for the troops in his command. One of the most egregious challenges came on June 11, 1863, when Colonel James Montgomery ordered Shaw to burn Darien, Georgia, even though women and children would die. Montgomery told Shaw that the Black troops were "outlawed, and therefore not bound by the rules of regular warfare." Shaw vigorously protested an attack on "the innocent and defenseless" and Montgomery relented.[111]

Today, Shaw is mostly remembered for his death by enemy fire on July 18, 1863, while leading his troops on horseback in a hopeless attack on a Confederate battery at Fort Wagner. In an intended insult, he was buried in a mass grave along with members of his regiment. The Confederate commanding general, Johnson Hagood (1829–1898), had returned the bodies of Union officers in the command of White troops but publicly said he had buried Shaw "with his niggers."[112]

Incensed by Hagood's behavior, Shaw's fellow officers sought Frank Shaw's permission to recover the body on behalf of the family. Shaw movingly responded on behalf of the family, "We would not have his body removed from where it lies surrounded by his brave and devoted soldiers. . . . We can imagine no holier place than that in which he lies, among his brave and devoted followers, nor wish for him better company—what a body-guard he has."[113] Eventually, Shaw's letter was widely published.

George M. Frederickson has analyzed the ways in which Robert Gould Shaw was transformed into a symbol for the cause of abolitionism and points to the publicity that the ostensibly private letter by Frank Shaw got.[114] Those who understand the physical and social context in which the Shaws lived—Curtis was by then political editor of *Harper's Weekly* and Gay was the managing editor of the *New-York Tribune*—will see the public relations impact of the Elliottville social circle in the transfiguration of Winthrop. Robert Gould Shaw's death leading Black troops made an even more compelling image than Winthrop's death had.

Shaw's personal life contributed to the poignancy of his death in a way that Winthrop's could not. Shaw had married on May 2, 1863, to Anna Kneeland Haggerty (1835–1907). She remained in the United States for a time after Shaw's death before moving to France and was a notable, much-mentioned presence as she stood on Broadway in April 1864 as part of the crowd sending off New York's first Black volunteer regiment to war.[115]

Word of Shaw's death reached Elliottville at an anxious time on Staten Island. Support for the war had always been uneven. As early as June of 1862 the fervidness of the first weeks of the war had waned, and the local newspaper encouraged citizens to demonstrate their patriotism to refute references to Staten Island as "Secession County."[116] From the outset, Staten Island was the base for training camps for newly recruited regiments, like Wilson's Zouaves (Sixth New York Infantry Regiment). Staten Islanders living near the camps complained about the behavior of the new recruits, who were often young, hitherto undisciplined men who could drink too much and behave disrespectfully to local citizens, particularly young women.

While many Staten Island men had volunteered in the first months of the war, as the war continued and the demands for recruits increased, many communities on Staten Island felt burdened. At first, it was relatively easy to raise money in order to pay bounties for volunteer enlistments by direct appeals. To relieve volunteers' concerns about weakening the financial situation of their families, Richmond County Supervisors also issued bonds to pay financial support to families. After the passage of the 1862 Militia Act, which authorized state military drafts when said states could not meet their required troop numbers with volunteers, raising money for volunteer recruitment became even more consequential, since war supporters wanted to avoid the hostility conscription would arouse. Residents of Elliottville subscribed heavily to direct appeals. For instance, in September 1862, Frank Shaw pledged $300, as did George Cabot Ward; Mrs. William (Catherine Cruger) Bard, pledged $200.[117] Despite Richmond County's success at recruiting volunteers and avoiding a state-authorized draft in 1862, after the US Congress passed the Enrollment Act of 1863 the county was expected to supply an additional four hundred men and conscription was inevitable. The public outcry over conscription was further exacerbated by the fact that well-to-do men could pay to be exempted from the draft.

When the 1863 draft riots began in New York, Elliottville residents assumed that the neighborhood, so publicly identified with abolitionism, would be attacked. Curtis sent Anna and their two babies (Elizabeth and Sarah) to relative James Sturgis in Roxbury and his son Frank to Sarah Shaw, who was staying with Susie Minturn on her in-laws' property along the Hudson. However, thinking Staten Island safer than the city, Curtis brought Horace Greeley and Wendell Phillips to his house. George Cabot Ward, who at that time lived in a large Bard Avenue house, secretly sheltered Frank, Josephine, and Ellen Shaw, as well as Elizabeth Gay and her children. Sydney Gay had been warned that a mob would try to destroy his presses and stayed at his *New-York Tribune* office. He prepared by having his pressmen devise a defense, utilizing the steam pipes that powered the presses.[118]

The rioting on Staten Island turned out to be less widespread than had been feared. Between July 14 and 20 bands of Staten Island youths, identified at the time as Irish, attacked socially and politically powerless African Americans, focusing on the Black community along McKeon Street in Stapleton. Decades after the war, the story of the threats to Elliottville and the response was recorded as a firsthand account by Martin Gay, a nine-year-old child at the time. Even in his account, what kept the rioters from attacking remained a matter for speculation. Martin had heard that the rioters stopped to fuel their courage at a nearby saloon and the barman warned them not to pursue their intentions, falsely claiming that federal troops had been stationed on Bard Avenue.[119] Whether or not this is entirely accurate, one can easily imagine that the national stature of Curtis and Gay and Frank Shaw's affluence would have deterred the rioters due to the certainty of punishment. Across Staten Island, public meetings were held to distribute handbills claiming that Richmond County had raised enough volunteers to avoid the draft. In the following weeks, county supervisors issued more bonds, this time to raise money to pay exemption fees for drafted men.[120]

In the immediate aftermath of the events on Staten Island, *The Richmond County Gazette* presented a lengthy editorial analysis of what had happened. The article declared that the roads and properties around the McKeon Street settlement, where buildings had been vandalized and burned, were littered with pamphlets and handbills from the houses there. Here, the editorial claimed, was the key to the violence, citing handbill phrases like "Let us stop questioning whether the negro is a man. In many respects he is a superior man."[121] Describing the events in Staten Island and New York as a "war of the races," the editorial concluded, "Who but the fanatics who set this ball in motion must be held responsible for its crushing effects upon the objects of their insane worship."[122] Although there had been no attacks on Elliottville, in all likelihood if there had been, the editorialist would have considered them to be justified.

How painful it must have been for Frank Shaw, who had engaged in so much philanthropy on behalf of workers, that he would be threatened with violence by laborers. Then, amid the rioting, news came of Robert Gould Shaw's death. Laura Johnson described the bereaved Sarah Shaw to Annie Fields. Johnson felt deeply the way grief transformed her appearance: "I saw poor Mrs. Shaw day before yesterday. She is totally changed. All the light has gone out of her face and the blue from her eyes and the daughters are so pale and sad!"[123]

Johnson also witnessed Sarah Shaw's attempts to embrace Spiritualism. The longing for further contact with deceased loved ones, whose sudden battlefield deaths had prevented the deathbed scenes many considered part of a good demise, inspired a broad interest in Spiritualism during and after the Civil War. Spiritualism had first appeared in New York State's burned over district in the 1840s and attracted a following among social reformers, particularly abolitionists, who were dismayed by the slight efforts mainstream churches had made to fight slavery. For many years, Lydia Maria Child shared her conviction with Sarah Shaw that spiritual communication was possible. Johnson claimed Shaw wished Spiritualism was true but never got to the stage of assured belief; even though she longed for contact with her son, she could find no proof for Spiritualism. Her doubts were bolstered by the fact that spirits never seemed to appear during the day and often believers were women suffering from emotional or physical illness. Johnson wrote that Frank Shaw "rather laments" over his wife's interest [even though, or perhaps because, Frank's father had visited mediums].[124] In her letters to Frank Shaw, Child often chided him for his lack of belief.[125] Even though Sarah may never have gained assurance about spiritual contact in this life, she seems to have shared the conviction with Lydia Maria Child that after death she would experience a reunion with her son in his "spiritual body."[126]

The loss of their sons was a great bond between Elizabeth Gay and Sarah Shaw. Almost a year after Robert Gould Shaw's death, Shaw wrote Gay to thank her for thinking of him and let her know that she considered Gay the only one to truly understand her suffering over his loss. She confided that each day she longed to see Robert again and that "once in a while I see him in my sleep and that comforts me."[127]

Other battlefield traumas and deaths would add sorrows to the war years for Elliottville. The Rufus King Delafields lost their son Rufus, who had trained as a physician and was serving as a medical officer in Alexandria when he died of typhoid fever in 1861. Curtis lost his half brother, twenty-six-year-old Lt. Col. Joseph Curtis, in the battle of Fredericksburg in December 1862. The Shaws also lost a new son-in-law to the war.

Their daughters, Susie and Josephine, both married during the war. Susie wed first, on October 30, 1862, to Robert Bowne Minturn Jr. (1836–1889).[128] Robert's father and namesake, Robert Bowne Minturn (1805–1866), was one of the most successful merchants and shippers in the United States.[129] Descending from several families involved in the China trade, the firm in which Minturn was a partner, Grinnell, Minturn, & Co., expanded dramatically while transporting immigrants during the Great Irish Famine (1845–1849) and the California gold rush. Like Frank Shaw, he used his wealth to help others, supporting philanthropic organizations. He helped found the Association for the Improvement of the Condition of the Poor and used his influence to advance legislation establishing the New York Commissioners of Emigration in 1868 (he later served as a commissioner, becoming personally involved in protecting emigrants and ameliorating the poor physical conditions they endured). The descendant of a Quaker family long committed to abolitionism, Minturn directly purchased slaves to set them free and was a major financial supporter of the Freedmen's Association. He was also the first president of New York's Union League Club, founded in 1863 by men such as Frederick Law Olmsted and George Templeton Strong who had banded together to provide cash support to the US Sanitary Commission (Shaw, Curtis, Gay, and the Wards were all members). In addition to signaling their support for the Union, the name pointed to the fact that most members had broken away from the Union Club, the prestigious social club that had refused to expel Southerners after the declaration of war.

Although they would later live in Elliottville, the Minturns began married life in Manhattan in a house Frank Shaw had purchased for them at 16 West Seventeenth Street in Manhattan. Within a few months, Susie was pregnant. She gave birth while the Shaws were still in mourning. The Minturns honored Susie's brother by naming their firstborn son Robert Shaw Minturn.

Josephine Shaw's wartime marriage was to James Russell Lowell's nephew, Charles Russell Lowell (1835–1864).[130] James Russell Lowell was Josephine's godfather, and while he was living at Brook Farm, his nephew Charles Lowell would call upon the Shaws on visits to his uncle. Robert Gould Shaw had been Charles Lowell's friend at Harvard and Josephine had attended the school Charles Lowell's mother operated in Boston. When Charles Lowell began his business career, Sarah Shaw's cousin, John Murray Forbes, the railroad magnate and abolitionist, mentored Lowell, appointing him to positions to further his advancement. Letters within the extended Lowell and Shaw families reveal the delight with which everyone viewed the young couple's engagement in March 1862. Lowell had enlisted in the Union Army in June 1861 and was aide-de-camp to General George B. McClellan during the formation of the Army of the Potomac, continuing at his side through 1862 before organizing and recruiting the Second Massachusetts Calvary funded by Forbes. The Shaws were still formally in mourning when the couple married quietly on October 31, 1863, in Elliottville's Universal Church of the Redeemer, shortly after Lowell had taken command of the Second Massachusetts.

Not long after the wedding Josephine Lowell traveled with her husband to the winter encampment of the Second Massachusetts in Vienna, Virginia (officers were permitted to have their wives in camp). She nursed wounded soldiers and wrote letters for them (a task for which her command of several languages proved useful since there were native speakers of French, German, and Italian). She also tutored ex-slaves during her nine months in camp. When Charles Lowell was posted to duty in the Shenandoah Valley in July 1864, Josephine returned to her parents' house, bringing with her his favorite horse for safekeeping.

Word reached Josephine less than two weeks before her first wedding anniversary that Lowell had died October 20, 1864, from battlefield

Figure 3.6. Charles Lowell had a long friendship with the Shaws, who were delighted when he became engaged to Josephine in 1862. By the wedding day, the Shaws were mourning the death of Robert Gould Shaw. *Source*: William Rhinelander Stewart, *The Philanthropic Work of Josephine Shaw Lowell* (New York: Macmillan, 1911), 38. Public domain.

injuries received in the Battle of Cedar Creek. He had a reputation for battlefield heroism and in his final battle, even after receiving a bullet through a lung, demanded to be lifted onto a horse to lead a charge. Another bullet severed his spinal cord. Death was not immediate, and he composed a farewell message to his wife that fueled her commitment to a life of service. Josephine was too far along in her pregnancy to attend Lowell's funeral in Harvard College Chapel on October 28 or his burial in Mount Auburn Cemetery. She gave birth to Carlotta Russell Lowell on November 30, 1864. Josephine never came out of mourning, wearing black clothes until her own death. Her friend Louisa Schuyler said that "those years of the war were the abiding influences in her life, not of despair or bitterness, but of sweetness and strength."[131] Josephine devoted her life to helping others, becoming a prominent figure in charitable work in New York City.

The war years brought Curtis, Gay, and Shaw new opportunities to advocate for abolitionism. Curtis continued to lecture widely, but his editorial pieces in *Harper's Monthly* dramatically increased his influence. Prior to the war, the Harper brothers enforced a moderate editorial stance to retain Southern readers. However, editorials became pro-Lincoln once war broke out. In 1863, Curtis began his decades-long career as political editor of *Harper's Weekly*. Even with the loss of Southern readership, the weekly publication still had a circulation of more than 120,000. In his writings, Curtis utilized his skill of effectively presenting both sides of a question, while confidently persuading his readers to adopt his Republican, antislavery stance. His approach contrasted with the Thomas Nast cartoons that also appeared in *Harper's Weekly* during the Civil War. Nast declared: "I try to hit the enemy between the eyes and knock him down."[132] Curtis treated his enemies respectfully and reasoned with them to change their views. During the first years of the war, the rallying cry of "defense of the Union" was being used to ignore the controversial issue of slavery, and Curtis tried to win his fellow citizens over to the cause of abolitionism by emphasizing that everyone's freedoms were threatened by the denial of rights to Blacks.

The war years also brought great opportunities to Gay when he became managing editor of the *New-York Tribune*, whose influence extended far beyond circulation numbers of 200,000, since the newspaper's editorials were widely reprinted. The Shaw/Curtis circle had deep ties to the *Tribune*. Horace Greeley, a proponent of abolitionism and Fourierism, established the publication in 1841. Shared convictions brought Greeley and Frank Shaw together. Greeley chose Margaret Fuller, a friend of Curtis, the Shaws, and Gay, to be literary editor for the *Tribune* and Greeley promoted the works of Thoreau and Emerson. As noted earlier, Curtis published some of his earliest writings in the *Tribune*, and his friend Charles A. Dana, as managing editor from 1849 onward, eventually turned the newspaper into the country's most influential antislavery voice. Dana and Greeley recruited Gay in 1858, and over time he became a contributing editor, increasing his role during the 1860 presidential campaign. After Greeley asked Dana to step down over disagreements about the conduct of the war, Gay was named managing editor in April 1862.

Although the *Tribune*'s wartime influence has often been noted and attributed to Horace Greeley's convictions, Greeley had ceded control of editorial policy to Gay.[133] The *Tribune* was known for reliable war reporting because the newspaper sent correspondents, illustrators, and reporters into the field. Editorially, the *Tribune* advocated strong positions, including an end to slavery and a mandatory draft of soldiers (we have seen that the policy made the newspaper offices a target during the draft riots). Lincoln acknowledged Gay's power when he secretly invited him to a private White House meeting in August 1862 in the hope of getting the *Tribune*'s unquestioning loyalty. Gay went to the meeting but resisted a pledge of absolute loyalty, taking the position that newspapers should accurately report events. He took pride in forthrightly reporting bad war news, even when he was filled with personal sadness.[134] Gay did use the meeting with Lincoln as an opportunity to press Lincoln for abolition.[135] Greeley had been active in trying to get Lincoln to enforce the Confiscation Act and to free slaves in the Confederacy via proclamation, but Gay was in favor of waiting for the abolition of slavery, even though the delay was as excruciating for him as it was for other abolitionists.[136] Amid deep personal loss, many must have felt, as Laura Johnson did, that "we deserve all our defeats and miseries for our lack of earnestness. If this was meant for a holy and just cause . . . we should have made it so. We had the chance, but we lost it."[137]

Even if Gay's meeting with the president did not have obvious and direct outcomes, it was heartening for Elliottville. In a letter to his wife, Curtis relayed the news that Gay "has returned quite enamored of the President."[138] In one of her letters to Annie Field, Johnson also conveyed the neighborhood excitement over Gay's meeting with Lincoln.

While Curtis and Gay were influencing opinion, Frank Shaw was bettering the lives of formerly enslaved people. He served as president of the New England Freedmen's Aid Society. The privately funded organization, founded to get clothes, food, medicine, and other necessities to ex-slaves, was quickly overwhelmed, prompting Shaw, along with Levi Coffin and J. Miller McKim, to spend time in Washington during the Congressional session of 1863–64 to lobby for passage of a bill to authorize a federal freedmen's bureau. Although the bill did not pass until the following Congressional session, Shaw and his fellow lobbyists laid the groundwork for passage. After the agency's founding, the first head, General Oliver O. Howard, called for a unified approach between the federal agency and church-supported aid societies formed during the war. As a result, the American Freedmen's and Union Commission was formed in 1866. Shaw became a vice president and executive committee member, and George Cabot Ward served as a vice president.

Conclusion

Elliottville's abolitionism contrasted dramatically with Staten Island and the rest of the New York City area, which overwhelmingly supported accommodation with the South. In the years after the Compromise of 1850, George Curtis gained national political influence. He helped found the Republican Party, campaigned for Frémont and Lincoln, and lectured and wrote about politics. During the Civil War, Curtis's importance grew, while Sydney Gay, as managing editor of the *New-York Tribune*, shaped the way the war was reported to a large, national readership. Frank Shaw, through leading organizations formed to support freedmen, had a positive influence on thousands of lives. When Theodore Winthrop and Robert Gould Shaw died, they came to be recognized as national heroes, in part because Curtis and Gay wove the story of their sacrifice into a rhetorical stance on the war that reminded readers of the antislavery cause. During and after the war, the publication of a series of books by Winthrop written in Elliottville further expanded the neighborhood's reputation.

Chapter 4

A Difficult Peace

Introduction

For many in Elliottville, abolitionism was an invigorating cause that gave purpose to their lives, shaped their motivations, and defined their notions of service to others. The "calling" of abolitionism also bound generations of families together and tied them to national organizations and prominent individuals. In the aftermath of the war and the ratification of the Thirteenth Amendment, they combated the emptiness left by family and community members who had sacrificed their lives on the battlefield and the disillusionment attendant upon an imperfect victory. While the institution of slavery was no more, the former slaves faced a grim plight as many of the same men who had controlled Southern politics before the war returned to power, and, after Reconstruction, wielded economic suppression, legal chicanery, and violence to prevent African Americans from exercising the rights they had been accorded by federal legislation. The identification of Elliottville with abolitionist activism continued, but in the decades following the war, much of the emotional intensity aroused by that association waned.

As we have seen, calls for abolition were followed by demands for education. Three generations of Elliottville residents worked to advance educational opportunities for Blacks. Frank Shaw and his daughter Josephine Lowell were active in the freedmen's education movement quite early. After the war, even though Shaw was already seventy-three, he continued to hold leadership positions and served in the New York Branch of the American Freedmen's and Union Association until it disbanded, by which time he was eighty. Lowell carried on with the efforts she had begun during the war to teach freed slaves. In 1866, she joined a committee of the National Freedmen's Relief Association of New York, overseeing a network of schools the society had established in Virginia. Later, in 1866, she and another committee member visited the Virginia schools to write a report. She went on to become secretary of the New York society and served until 1871, even after the national association had disbanded and the New York branch struggled on for a few years more before finally closing.[1] In the twentieth century, a third generation of Elliottville residents would take leadership roles in Black education. Sydney and Elizabeth Gay's daughter, Mary Otis (1861–1933), married William Goodenow Willcox (1859–1923), who was born in Massachusetts and was from a Garrisonian abolitionist family. The two of them were major supporters of the Tuskegee Institute. Willcox served on the board of trustees for many years, including terms as chairman, and provided financial support during his lifetime and through a significant bequest. After his death, Mary Willcox continued his work. Several Tuskegee buildings were named to honor the Willcoxes' efforts.

Of course, Elliottville abolitionists had been committed to a range of social reforms and they continued their activities after the Civil War. The underprivileged of Staten Island received some of their attention. In the decades after the war the number of manufacturers on Staten Island increased and whole new industries took shape (including production of candy, dental supplies, gypsum products, paint, plaster of Paris, and terra cotta tile), increasing the island's population of working poor and recent immigrants. Laura Johnson detailed efforts in which she and other neighborhood women engaged to aid these Staten Islanders. They focused on health care, through the Samuel R. Smith Infirmary (founded 1869), and education, including sponsoring the Industrial School for Girls and the Baldwin Boys Union. The Industrial School, located at 96 Broadway in West New Brighton, was established in 1877, and from the outset Sarah Shaw was listed as "proprietor" (i.e., chief operating officer).

In all their efforts to aid the less fortunate, Elliottville residents found themselves needing to build support, even among those they helped. Johnson wrote, "Our work among the poor is discouraging here, because so few take an interest . . . fewer and fewer at present . . . and the poor children, though there are numbers of them, don't come to our Industrial School."[2] She realized that philanthropy was undergoing dramatic change after the war and contrasted the philanthropy of a woman like Sarah Shaw, whose efforts were based on "goodness and charm," with the "genius" for organization of members of the younger generation represented by

Josephine Lowell and her friend Louisa Schuyler.[3] After the Civil War, organizations with professional staffs, and, increasingly, government funding, had begun to predominate and take a scientific approach to poverty, which meant a much less direct and satisfying role for women like Shaw and Johnson. Johnson described the difficult interactions she and her fellow committeewomen had with "sheriffs," and "superintendents of the poor." She compared efforts of persuasion with such men with trying "to move rocks and soften stones."[4]

Although Lowell's focus was much broader than Elliottville, her achievements, advice, and connections bolstered neighborhood efforts. Lowell became widely known as a Progressive reformer who worked through institutions to improve the lives of the poor, particularly women and children. She had gotten her start through Louisa Schuyler, who recruited Lowell to volunteer with the State Charities Aid Association soon after its founding in 1872 as a member of the Richmond County Visiting Committee on Staten Island. Schuyler had founded the State Charities Aid Association to provide visiting committees for each county of New York State to inspect poor houses and report conditions to the state authorities. From this beginning, Lowell took larger and more influential roles in New York City and the state, while Frank and Sarah Shaw remained on the Richmond County Visiting Committee. As Lowell's time filled with meetings in Manhattan, Frank bought her a townhouse at 120 East Thirtieth Street. In 1876 she was the first woman appointed as commissioner of the New York State Board of Charities. In 1878, she was instrumental in establishing the New York Custodial Asylum for Feeble-Minded Women (as an outgrowth of her concern that such women were endangered when they were simply placed in almshouses).[5]

On Staten Island, George Curtis and his daughter Elizabeth Curtis created organizations to aid the poor. George Curtis was a charter member of the Richmond County Society for the Prevention of Cruelty to children, incorporated in December 1880. The social welfare agency was granted a significant degree of responsibility as the only body on Staten Island authorized by law to intercede on behalf of abused and neglected children (Mary Willcox also served on the agency's board). Elizabeth Curtis was a founder and president of the Charity Organization Society in 1884 established to coordinate relief efforts and encourage individuals to donate money to organizations rather than door-to-door indigent solicitors.

Of course, Frank Shaw had a lifelong commitment to a reformed social structure that would end poverty. In the final years of his life, he became the major supporter of Henry George in the United States. As Lorien Foote has pointed out, Shaw would have seen continuity in the writings of George, with the antebellum spirit of social redemption that had inspired both the strain of abolitionism he had supported and the Fourier notion of Association, whose implementation was attempted at Brook Farm.[6] George argued that the concentration of unearned wealth in the hands of landowners and monopolists leads to intractable poverty for a percentage of the population and that the situation could be partially redressed through a land value tax that would prevent private interests from passively profiting through simple possession and the assessment of rents or fees. Shaw's financial support made George's *Progress and Poverty* one of the bestselling books in American history; the book inspired the single tax movement (usually referred to as Georgism) that was influential in early twentieth-century politics in the United States and in Denmark and Britain.[7] Lowell also found George's understanding of the causes of poverty compelling, as did Gay's daughter, Sarah, who became a proponent of Georgism in women's suffrage circles, where she introduced economic analysis into the discussions of inequities women experienced.

In her women's suffrage activism, Sarah Gay carried forward another social reform cause long supported by Elliottville residents. The Curtises, Gays, and Shaws had advocated for the rights of women and participated in early rights conventions. Curtis had spoken at such events and published his views on the equality of women. He was one of the few male writers and thinkers with a national audience to speak in favor of women's rights. As early as 1858, he addressed a Women's Rights Convention in New York's Mozart Hall, sharing the platform with William Lloyd Garrison and Frederick Douglass. He was to repeat the address he gave there, "Fair Play for Women," many times as an invited speaker.

The women's suffrage movement became more insistent after the war and opportunities to publicly support women's rights increased. Starting in 1865, former Confederates could take the oath of amnesty and regain their rights of citizenship (appeals for universal amnesty would eventually bring passage of the Amnesty Act of 1872). Loyal Northern women who could not vote were outraged. In 1867 at the New York State Constitutional Convention, Curtis spoke vigorously in favor of women's suffrage, poignantly referencing New York mothers who had raised patriotic sons, surrendered them to army service, grieved their battlefield deaths, and then were asked to think it just or even commonsensical that "we give the ballot to the New York boy's murderers and refuse it to his mother."[8]

Curtis addressed the Women's Suffrage Association in 1868 and spoke repeatedly in favor of education for women (he was the dedication orator for Wells Seminary, a college for women, in 1868).[9]

Of course, Curtis was often accompanying his wife (and later his daughter) and other neighborhood women at suffrage conventions and women's meetings. His mother-in-law was one of these. Sarah Shaw said she had wanted the vote for women starting in the 1850s, presumably so that she could vote for Frémont.[10] Elizabeth Curtis carried on the campaign into the twentieth century, as did Mary Willcox, who was prominent in local and statewide organizations.[11]

Of all the causes that Elliottville residents of the 1850s pursued after the war, Curtis's civil service reform activism was the most widely noted and most closely identified with Elliottville. At the time, political parties controlled most civil service positions and granted them as rewards, requiring those holding the jobs to pay significant percentages of their salaries toward political party expenses. For Curtis, such compulsory assessments represented a theft of labor on a continuum with the slaveholders' theft of the labor of the enslaved.[12] President Grant appointed him to chair the Commission on Civil Service Reform in 1871, giving him authority to shape the Commission's December 1871 report that was intended to become a blueprint for ongoing reform. Curtis also played a crucial role in the subsequent preparation of detailed regulations as a member of the Civil Service Advisory Board. However, Curtis resigned from the board when the Grant administration did not act expeditiously on implementation, continuing his fight for reform through editorials and public speaking during the rest of the Grant presidency.

When Rutherford B. Hayes began his term, the Civil Service Commission was revived, and Hayes consulted Curtis for advice and guidance. Curtis had been the only New York delegate to support Hayes over Roscoe Conkling for the 1876 Republican presidential nomination and played a crucial role during the election crisis. Civil unrest was feared, and Curtis's advocacy for a legal solution as the American way did much to defuse more extreme stances and aided the formation of an electoral commission. The documentary record shows that Curtis took full advantage of his relationship with Hayes, particularly in asking that Hayes address the political spoils system in the New York Custom House from which Roscoe Conkling's political machine benefited and reappoint Oliver Fiske as US marshal (Fiske had lost his job purely due to the political spoils system). By the time Chester A. Arthur took office, even though Arthur had benefited significantly from Conkling patronage, he supported the work of the Civil Service Commission and Curtis was able to continue to advocate reform through the National Civil Service Reform League, which he helped establish at Newport on August 11, 1881, and continued to serve as president until his death in 1892.

Curtis could have added international diplomacy to his activities. Abraham Lincoln, Ulysses S. Grant, and Rutherford B. Hayes each offered him ambassadorships. However, to accept any of them would have meant living abroad, and Charles Eliot Norton said, "He loved his home and his friends too well to quit them for strange courts and brilliant company."[13] While Norton's comment further confirms Curtis's attachment to Elliottville, the words also reflect Curtis's understanding of public service. Of all American heroes, he most admired George Washington, who was celebrated for serving when his country needed him but remained primarily devoted to his family and Mount Vernon.

Renewed Fervor: Anna Leonowens

No matter how committed Elliottville residents may have been to Black education, women's rights, civil service reform, and improving conditions for the poor, none of these causes offered the same level of emotional engagement as abolitionism had. When a surprisingly exotic figure appeared in Elliottville in 1868, she inspired new fervor for antislavery work and presented a new focus for women's rights advocacy.

Anna Leonowens (1831–1915) arrived in Elliottville with a letter of introduction to Laura Johnson from Abby Hopper Gibbons (1802–1893) in July 1868. Gibbons presented Leonowens as a former governess in the court of the King of Siam, eager to open a school. After her arrival in the United States, Leonowens had sought out abolitionists. Gibbons, a friend of the Gays, was the daughter of Quaker abolitionist Isaac Hopper and the wife of abolitionist and philanthropist James Sloan Gibbons (1810–1892).[14]

Leonowens is best known today through the romanticized Broadway play and film loosely based on her accounts of Siam in the years 1862–1867. She had taken a leave from the Court of Siam to accompany her son Louis (1856–1919) to Ireland for school and to travel to the United States in search of opportunities for herself and her daughter Avis (1854–1902). In recent decades, several authors discovered Leonowens was mixed race and that after the death of her husband in 1859 she had created a new identity for herself to avoid racism and socioeconomic prejudice. Claiming to be a Welsh woman of genteel, but distressed, finances, she progressed from teaching officers' children in Singapore to employment as governess to the royal family of King Mongkut of Siam (Thailand). She was a woman adroit at self-promotion, and New York offered her opportunities for new identities as an antislavery campaigner in Siam and an expert on East Asian societies. Even as early as her first publications, people questioned the veracity of her accounts, but in Elliottville she won immediate support on which she built a career as a writer and lecturer.

From her first meeting with Leonowens, Johnson was entranced, and the two would maintain a close friendship even after Leonowens moved to Halifax years later. In her long description of Leonowens to Annie Fields, Johnson used the adjectives "modest," "capable," "agreeable," and "uncommon" and referred to Leonowens's claim to fluency in seven languages to illustrate her accomplishments.[15] The account of Leonowens's life Johnson retailed to Fields sounds like the well-rehearsed summary Leonowens would have presented upon first meeting someone, making clear that she had experienced hardships but overcame them through energy and hard work, while maintaining a good spirit. Johnson noted that Leonowens's "accounts of it all are very amusing. She makes you laugh and cry."[16]

Leonowens just happened to be carrying letters with her from the King and his "Heir apparent" to demonstrate how well she had taught them English (for she had also supposedly acted as the King's private secretary). One recent biographer of Leonowens has found that all the details she shared about herself were inaccurate or entirely false.[17] Leonowens informed Johnson that she had come to the United States to make a home for her children and out of preference for "the independence she should have in this country," reasons that would have more easily garnered support than forthright economic opportunism.[18] Johnson immediately pledged to help Leonowens, even offering space in the Johnson house as a first schoolroom. Although Leonowens did not start her school at the Johnsons, she and Avis did lodge there for a time. Later they moved to a cottage just outside Elliottville, near Richmond Terrace and Tompkins Court, from which they also operated the school.[19] Johnson's youngest child, Laura's five-year-old namesake, attended the school, as did the Gays' daughter, seven-year-old Mary. Sixteen-year-old Sarah Gay took drawing lessons with Leonowens. Johnson repeatedly wrote that people liked Leonowens and "seem[ed] inclined to help her and take an interest in her."[20] Although she praised

Leonowens's teaching, a published reminiscence by Mary (Gay) Willcox makes it clear that fourteen-year-old Avis was the one who primarily interacted with the children while Leonowens wrote.[21]

Initially, Johnson thought she was introducing Leonowens to Annie Fields, but Fields and her husband, publisher James Fields, had already met Leonowens, who was much more intent on publishing her account of Siam than on starting a primary school on Staten Island, especially once King Mongkut died in October 1868 and could no longer contradict her account.[22] James Fields, a friend of both Johnson and Curtis, printed a series of Leonowens's articles in *The Atlantic Monthly* in 1870.

The whole story of Leonowens becoming a published author and lecturer revolves around the influence of her friends in Elliottville. For instance, according to Johnson, it was Curtis who suggested Leonowens write magazine articles first.[23] Leonowens acknowledged Curtis's help and advice by prominently acknowledging him in the preface to *The English Governess at the Siamese Court* (Boston: Fields, Osgood, and Co., 1870). The very fact that she shaped her narrative as an episode in the universal war on slavery stemmed from her desire to appeal to abolitionists in general and her Elliottville friends in particular.[24] The fact that she incorporated Fourier themes in her next book, *Romance of the Harem* (Boston: James R. Osgood and Co., 1873) was due to her wish to strengthen her ties to Frank Shaw.[25] In the preface of that book she thanked Shaw "for valuable advice and aid in the preparation of this work for the press." Later, she also became a proponent of Henry George, whose ideas and writings were of such importance to Shaw. When Leonowens's first book was criticized, her Elliottville friends were incensed and they were most vocal in claiming that the editor and printer had introduced inaccuracies and Americanisms.

After the publication of *The English Governess*, Leonowens's Elliottville friends provided significant help as she embarked on a lecturer career. In 1871 they rented a hall for her on Staten Island and sold tickets for her benefit.[26] She repaid them later in the year (June 1871) by giving a benefit reading at the John C. Henderson mansion (some of Henderson's children were in her school). George Curtis used his connections to get Leonowens on the profitable Lyceum circuit; he even allowed her to use his written endorsement to advertise her Lyceum presentations. Her claims that she was a scholar of Malaysian and Siamese culture and had pursued missionary work among pagans attracted audiences, and her skilled delivery (she had taken elocution lessons) impressed them.[27] Abolitionists hearing of still-enslaved peoples could take satisfaction in the victories they had already won in the United States and be energized to support new struggles. Women's rights supporters appreciated hearing a well-spoken, cultured, self-confident, independent, eloquent, and learned woman. Few audience members ever realized that Leonowens knew very little about the societies of which she spoke, had never mastered the languages of which she claimed fluency, and had never been a missionary. Her publications and lecture earnings enabled her to move from her first Staten Island cottage in Factoryville, near the dye works drainage pond, to a house named Hawthorne in a much better area, near the intersection of Tysen and Fillmore Streets at 105 Tysen Street.[28] Although she was taken away from Staten Island by lecturing and summer travel (as a guest in the houses of affluent new friends in Newport and other resorts), Staten Island would still be her and Avis's primary residence up until 1874 when she moved into Manhattan to stay in the household of Dr. Frederick Barnard, president of Columbia College. By this time she had made other friends in Manhattan through Elliottville residents, including William Cullen Bryant (Sydney Gay was an editor at Bryant's *New York Evening Post*) and Anne Lynch Botta, at whose literary salon Curtis had been a regular for decades. Through Johnson, Leonowens had also become friends with Emily and Gordon Ford (business manager of the *New-York Tribune* and owner of the *Brooklyn Eagle*).

Even though Leonowens moved away from Staten Island, Elliottville residents continued to be important in her life and she visited them there and elsewhere. Johnson mentioned Leonowens's visits in letters in the 1870s,[29] and in 1881 Leonowens wrote to Emily Ford of Johnson, "I miss her, and long to see her."[30] Leonowens stayed with the Curtises at their summer house in Ashfield.[31] She became acquainted with Susie and Robert Minturn after they moved to Staten Island and sent some of their children to her school. In 1878, Minturn arranged a railroad job for Leonowens's son Louis.[32] Even after Avis married in 1878 to Thomas Fyshe, a Canadian bank manager, and Leonowens spent most of her time living in Canada, she corresponded with and visited her Elliottville friends through the 1880s and 1890s. In 1897, when Augustus Saint-Gaudens finished the sculpture for the Memorial to Robert Gould Shaw and the Fifty-Fourth Massachusetts Regiment, Leonowens was invited to the New York unveiling.[33]

Conclusion

The war and its aftermath brought mourning and disillusionment to Elliottville, but also children and grandchildren, providing consolation and renewal. Some of the children born during the war have already been introduced (Elizabeth Burrill Curtis, 1861, born just a few days after the firing on Ft. Sumter; Mary Otis Gay, 1861; Sarah Shaw Curtis, 1863; Laura Johnson, 1863; Robert Shaw Minturn, 1863; and Carlotta Russell Lowell, 1864). Another marriage and more births came after the war. Frank and Sarah's youngest daughter, Ellen (1845–1936), married Robert Gould's former tutor, Francis Channing Barlow (1834–1896), in 1867. Barlow had enlisted as a private in the Twelfth New York State Militia in April 1861 and played significant roles in major campaigns and battles. His wartime service earned him promotion to general and the distinction of being the only man during the war to have enlisted as a private and been promoted to that rank. His battlefield heroism and career after the war as a United States marshal, New York secretary of state, and New York State attorney general (he prosecuted the Boss Tweed ring) made him a fitting son-in-law for the Shaws. He and Ellen had two children: Robert Shaw Barlow (1869–1913) and Charles Lowell Barlow (1871–1965).

The Shaws also had the pleasure of seeing the house they had built in Elliottville fill with Susie and Robert Bowne Minturn's children after the Minturns purchased and moved into the house. In the years after the war, the Minturns had Sarah (1865–1914), Edith (1867–1937), Francis (1871–1878), Gertrude (1872–1939), Mildred (1875–1922), and Hugh (1882–1915).

Frank and Sarah Shaw had moved in December 1869 to a house at the corner of Richmond Terrace and Davis Street, no longer wanting a large house and thinking a waterfront location more desirable.[34] Shaw purchased the house James Parker had built sometime before 1848. Like him, Parker was one of the founders of the Unitarian Church on Staten Island.[35] Along with the house, Shaw purchased the large tract of land Parker had owned for many years that was adjacent to Elliottville and spanned the area between the streets that are now named Henderson Avenue and Richmond Terrace.

George William Curtis, who was given to announcing his feelings in correspondence with friends in florid prose, wrote James Russell Lowell about the Shaw's move when their old house was empty and still without a buyer:

Figure 4.1. Frank Shaw bought James Parker's house for its views over the Kill van Kull. However, there was soon a horsecar line running in front of the house, and in the following decades the house would be separated from the water by the B&O freight railroad line. *Source*: William Rhinelander Stewart, *The Philanthropic Work of Josephine Shaw Lowell* (New York: Macmillan, 1911), 50. Public domain.

> They have left the big house. They have laughingly cut the throat of one of the most beautiful homes, consecrated and endeared by all that makes home precious, where the girls were all married and their children all born, from which Rob and Charlie went to be killed—in which we have all been so happy and so sad—and all this to have a little smaller house and to look upon the water! I look over and pity the great, silent, gloomy, deserted house. Why should it be treated so?[36]

The depth of Curtis's emotional reaction to the Shaws' departure may seem exaggerated given the fact that their new location was only half a mile distant, but his words show how deeply he had valued the physical proximity of his parents-in-law and the great weight he gave to the association of memories with specific places.

As we will see in the next chapter, in the decades after the war Elliottville experienced more dramatic changes and the neighborhood began to lose its close-knit character. Newcomers, some of whom had sided with the South and others who actually fought as Confederates, settled in Elliottville. Their appearance was the first of a series of changes that would eventually destroy the community.

Chapter 5

The Gilded Age Yachtsman
The Disillusionments of Reconstruction

Introduction

The Civil War brought a new degree of affluence to Manhattan businessmen. With their new capital, they rapidly increased their wealth by investing in industrial capitalism, national corporations, and the national railroad network—all the elements rapidly transforming the country's economic and political life. Although the invested family wealth of long-settled Elliottville residents increased in the 1870s and 1880s, the wealth of newcomers was recent and had more direct origins in manufacturing or mercantilism. Furthermore, the relationship of the newcomers to their wealth was far different from the New England transcendentalists who were committed to using their wealth to help others and fund social reform. The newcomers devoted themselves to building ever-greater personal fortunes and to using their money for pleasure and social display. The introduction of showy architectural styles and the number of new owners who only used their properties as summerhouses, leaving large properties vacant for extended periods with only servants in residence, affected the feel of the neighborhood.

The newcomers had a number of characteristics in common with each other. First, they were overwhelmingly New Yorkers. Even if a few had New England ancestry, recent generations had lived in New York and their whole focus was on Manhattan. In addition, several newcomers were

Figure 5.1. Elliottville disappeared from maps in the 1870s to become part of New Brighton and the neighborhood was dominated by the properties of William K. Soutter and William Thorn Garner. *Source*: F. W. Beers, Atlas of Staten Island, Richmond County, New York, from official records and surveys (New York: J. B. Beers, 1874), section 3 1/2. Courtesy of College of Staten Island, Archives & Special Collections. Public domain.

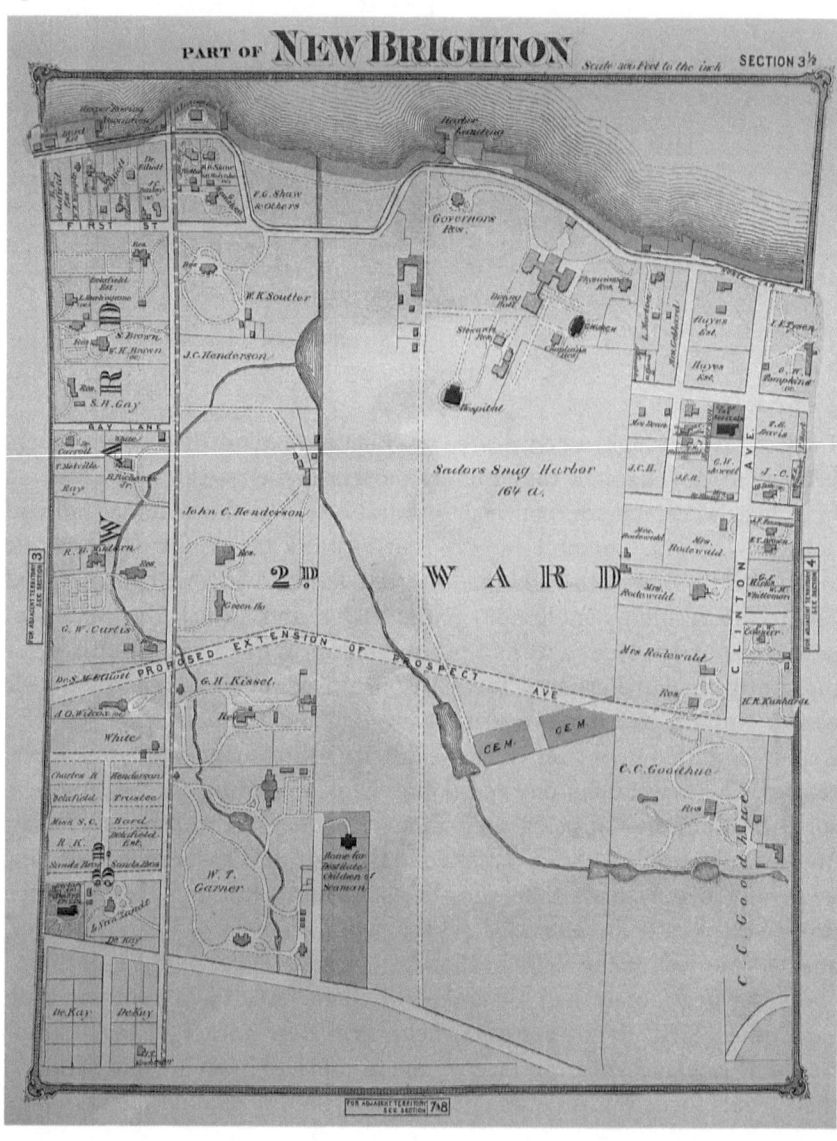

children of immigrants whose parents had made their fortunes in New York and had few family ties outside the metropolitan area.

Second, the newcomers were in "good" society. While people like the Minturns were active in Manhattan society, in general, long-settled Elliottville residents socialized with friends and family and valued cultural, not society, figures. They disdained people of fashion. In fact, as early as the 1850s, George Curtis had satirized the "new money" families who established themselves in society through social display. After the Civil War, the opulence of social display reached new extremes. Laura Johnson, in contrasting Boston with New York society, noted it is "far too expensive to keep down to the level of New York."[1] Sarah Gay described with incredulity society fashions (men wearing short coats to display their corset-confined abdomens and women obsessed with affecting "the Grecian bend").[2] In addition to attending and hosting social events and building ever grander residences in Manhattan, club activities and participation in sporting events had become important forms of social display for Gilded Age men. The newcomers attended and sponsored dinners at the Union Club and participated in high stakes horse racing and yachting competitions. While the nearby Staten Island neighborhood of Clifton became popular with members of the American Jockey Club (William Henry Vanderbilt kept some of his famous trotting horses on his farm there and the stables of Sir Roderick Cameron became internationally famous), Elliottville became home to leaders of the New York Yacht Club (NYYC).

Third, the newcomers had a much different understanding of Staten Island. Antebellum Elliottville settlers valued Staten Island for providing the opportunity to develop their health and spirituality by living close to nature. Most of the Gilded Age men regarded Staten Island as a venue for costly leisure activities and they were rarely interested in exchanging their Manhattan residences for Staten Island, instead treating their island houses as country places and summerhouses. Their attitude was far different from long-settled Elliottville residents who had established primary residences that became multigenerational homes.

Finally, almost all of the newcomers were linked to the South. In almost all cases, they were connected to the South economically, and in some cases they had actually fought for the Confederacy. Elliottville residents commented on the nauseating spectacle of "reconstructed" Southerners returning to political power. Nonetheless, when such people became neighbors, Elliottville could do little but exclude them socially and snipe at them, as Sydney Gay did about the troublesome Mrs. White, "I have hardly ever seen a Southerner who was not essentially vulgar, pretentious with their fondness of showy clothing, showy manners and without the slightest perception of that personal modesty."[3]

Perhaps surprisingly, neighborhood interlopers and the reidentification nationally of Elliottville as the "Fifth Avenue of Staten Island" did not weaken longtime residents' attachment to the neighborhood.[4] In fact, as neighborhood children matured, social life in Elliottville accelerated, and the Curtises, Gays, Shaws, Johnsons, and Minturns became even more involved in each other's lives.

William Thorn Garner

What had been known as Elliottville, and was now often referred to as the Bard Avenue neighborhood of West New Brighton, gained national exposure of a new sort in the 1870s through yachtsman William Thorn Garner (1840–July 20, 1876). Beyond newspaper articles, no documentary record exists for Garner. However, newspaper coverage of a yachting party he hosted in 1876 provides the opportunity to reconstruct his social circle and shows how their values and commitments differed from the "Boston people" in Elliottville. Whereas Boston people treasured family life and ties to a local community and to the history of the United States, Gilded Age people focused on conquering ever-larger social circles and were particularly interested in establishing themselves in European aristocratic circles. Nonetheless, no matter how far their lives took them from Elliottville, the people connected to the yachting party would continue to be identified with the event throughout their lives and even in their obituaries.

Garner bought his Bard Avenue mansion in 1870, at a time when the NYYC was based on Staten Island but before he was a member. However, his Bard Avenue property was near five NYYC members and he was a member within a year. Franklin Osgood (1826–1888), who lived in New Brighton in one of the waterfront Greek revival mansions built by Thomas E. Davis (Osgood later established an estate in Clifton), was one these. Osgood was one of the first members of the America's Cup Committee of the NYYC, formed in 1869. In 1870 he won the first defense of the America's Cup, sailing the schooner *Magic*, and he would become rear commodore of the NYYC in 1871. Anson Livingston (1807–1873), who lived on the shore at the foot of Bard Avenue, only blocks from the house

Figure 5.2. Garner, a Union Club member, had many ties to the South. *Source: Frank Leslie's Illustrated Newspaper*, August 5, 1876, 361. Courtesy of College of Staten Island Archives & Special Collections. Public domain.

that Garner purchased, had been NYYC rear commodore in 1866. Garner purchased his first yacht from Livingston in 1873.

From 1868 to 1871, the NYYC's clubhouse was near the Staten Island waterfront with a view of the mouth of New York Harbor. However, the NYYC underwent rapid change in the 1870s from a sportsman's club to a social club for men of great wealth whose yachts were captained by professionals and manned by paid, full-time crews. As the club's social aspect expanded, the club headquarters moved to a series of rented facilities in Manhattan before moving to a grand, specially commissioned building in 1898. Still, even after the 1871 move of its clubhouse, the NYYC had strong connections to Staten Island, in part because Garner donated and maintained a club facility on Staten Island from which to view the races held off Staten Island's shore.

Since NYYC Commodore Anson Livingston already lived in Elliottville when Garner arrived, it is useful to understand why Livingston fit in with the neighborhood's earlier residents in ways that Garner did not. Livingston moved to Elliottville in 1861, purchasing a house constructed by Dr. Elliott. Anson's brother Carroll Livingston (1805–1867), a Wall Street broker, already lived in Elliottville on a large property up the hill from the waterfront above Castleton Avenue. Anson Livingston was a trained lawyer and graduate of Columbia College (1822) and Union College (AM, 1825), but like Shaw, Livingston did not actively engage in business; he managed his investments and those of his siblings.[5] He was the great-grandson of the third and final Lord of Livingston Manor, Robert Livingston (1708–1790), who had inherited a 160,000-acre tract of land (in what is now New York and New Jersey) from his grandfather Robert Livingston the Elder (1654–1728), who had in turn obtained the tract as a grant from King George I. Anson Livingston had inherited significant wealth since his grandfather had broken with the family practice of primogeniture and divided Livingston Manor (Livingston reconsolidated some of the manor by marrying Anne Greenleaf Livingston, the daughter of Henry W. Livingston, another grandson of the third Lord of Livingston Manor). Livingston had many ancestors notable in the American Revolution and early days of the Republic and he was the son of Supreme Court Justice Henry Brockholst Livingston (1757–1823). In Elliottville, Livingston was regarded as "a gentleman of the old school."[6] Although his wife was teased for her social pretensions, the ladies of Elliottville socialized with her frequently since she hosted a conversational French group. Even Livingston's interest in the NYYC was more in keeping with Elliottville's values. Livingston was an enthusiastic sailor, capable of sailing his own yachts. He had been active with the NYYC from its earliest days when the club was still composed of men whose affluence was secondary to their enthusiasm for sailing.

Although Garner, like the Livingstons, had inherited wealth, his fortune was recent and acquired by his immigrant father, Thomas Garner (1806–1867). Thomas Garner had come to America with his brother James (1774–1860) in 1829 from Manchester, England. Of humble origins, the brothers learned the textile industry as laborers. Although they initially worked as sales agents for a small cotton factory in New York's Greenwich Village, they soon established their own commission business as dry goods merchants.[7] By 1831 they had leased a calico print works in New York's Rockland County.[8] A partner joined the firm in 1835, creating Garner & Co., and in 1838 the company purchased the leased property, laying the foundation for an enterprise that would control the textile industry for more than fifty years. After retirements and the addition of new partners in the 1850s (including Garner's maternal grandfather), a subsidiary was formed, Rockland Printing Works, to produce printed textiles, as well as dyed woolens and cotton and linen fabrics, that grew to include forty-two machines. The original textile factory in Rockland County also grew significantly and the surrounding factory town was named Garnerville.[9]

During the Civil War, Rockland Printing Works was a major producer of Union Army uniforms, which, as evidenced by the growth of the company in the period, was a lucrative undertaking.[10] By Thomas Sr.'s death in 1867, Garner and Co. and its subsidiaries owned textile operations employing thousands and had annual revenues in the millions of dollars, making it the largest cotton cloth fabricating establishment in the world.[11] Unlike many concerns, Garner and Co. fabricated cotton cloth, turned the cloth into printed fabrics, and then sold the fabrics directly at company-owned stores, rather than using commission merchants. The vastly expanded concern had salesrooms in Lower Manhattan at numbers 2, 4, 5, 8, 10 and 61 Worth Street, as well as a wholesale operation at 195 Franklin Street. Industry publications of the time noted the wide range of fabrics the company produced, claiming that they sold every style of printed cloth produced.[12]

Garner & Co.'s financial success resulted from control over not only production and distribution, but subsidiary operations like dye plants, brick works to supply building materials for factories and worker housing, and a transportation network that included docks on the Hudson River waterfront and a railroad line.[13] Such a level of integrated textile production put competitors at a disadvantage, as did the company-owned sales operation that won a large market share by uniform pricing for all buyers, while creating artificial demand by limiting the supply of the most popular items, prohibiting returns, and restricting sales to cash-only transactions.[14] While controlling such a significant percentage of the industry, the firm also kept labor costs down by making workers dependent upon the company (living in factory towns, workers relied on the company for housing and consumer goods, and they feared that if they left they would find no other job in the industry).

The kind of "wage slavery" Garner & Co. employees endured was an underlying social condition that Frank Shaw and other reformers hoped to eradicate by devising other modes of production that would give laborers greater control over their living conditions and a greater stake in the profits their labor generated. Furthermore, Elliottville residents' charities and Josephine Lowell's life work focused on the plight of single women and children in the textile industry and in factory towns.

William Garner and his brother-in-law Samuel W. Johnson (ca. 1838–1881) took over the management of Garner & Co. after the 1867 death of Thomas Garner Sr. and the 1868 retirement of Thomas Garner Jr. Garner was twenty-six years old at the time and had mostly lived in Manhattan from the time he was a young man, most recently in the Garner family house at 4 Washington Square North. Garner had not enrolled in college or fought in the Civil War (although he did register for the draft in 1863).[15]

Garner had married Mary Marcellite Thorn (1842–1876) in 1865, his first cousin once removed. She was the daughter of Garner's maternal grandfather's brother Frost Thorn (1793–1854).[16] While William Garner's family lived in the New York area, Mary Marcellite's family resided in New Orleans and Texas.[17] Frost Thorn and his future father-in-law, Haden Edwards (1771–1849), had obtained empresario contracts from the Mexican government on April 15, 1825.[18] Over time, Thorn came to control hundreds of thousands of acres of land in Texas and Louisiana and eventually established large agricultural enterprises, a salt mine, and a lumber company. He used slave labor and was an enthusiastic supporter of indentures to secure labor from Native Americans and immigrants.[19] As a major landholder, Thorn aided Stephen F. Austin in recruiting settlers to Texas and was an avid proponent of Texas independence. When he died in 1854, his son, Frost Jr. was only four years old, and Mary Marcellite was twelve years old. When his widow, Susan Wroe (Edwards) Thorn (1800–1891), remarried in 1856, she chose her deceased husband's nephew, James F. Thorn (1821–1876).[20] Although James had been living in Cincinnati, the new family unit moved to New York City after the marriage and lived there and in European cities while Mary Marcellite was growing up.[21] According to newspaper accounts she spoke French and Italian, had a debut at the Tuileries during the Second Empire, and was presented at the court of Italy's King Victor Emanuel.[22]

With the dependence of Garner & Co. on Southern cotton and the dependence of Mary Marcellite's family on agricultural land worked by slaves, it seems unlikely that the Garners supported abolitionism. Although Garner & Co. made uniforms for the Union Army once war broke out, this could easily have been a mere business decision (William's father's taxable income dropped from $350,000 in 1864 to $84,000 in 1865, the year the war ended). Concerns about cotton production and prices may well have had a big impact on the thinking of anyone connected with Garner & Co.[23] Mary Marcellite's sympathies seem relatively clear from her activities immediately after the war. She and Garner were married in April 1865 and soon afterward she hosted fundraisers in their residence to benefit Episcopal churches in the South.[24]

Most information about the Garners' life dates from the 1870s. Their city house was at 8 East Thirty-Third Street, around the corner from the mansions of the sons of Jacob Astor, one of whom, William Backhouse, had married Caroline Schermerhorn, who earned a reputation for being the gatekeeper of society in the post–Civil War period, when arrivistes were chivvying to be accepted.[25] During the time the Garners lived there, the neighborhood was the most prestigious residential area in the city. Although the report must have been speculative, the estimated expense of maintaining the Garners' standard of living was over $92,500 per year. In addition to the Manhattan residence, the one on Staten Island, a yacht (just the crew cost $1,200 per month), and a seasonal rental in Newport, there were the costs of servants, the stables, and entertaining up to two thousand guests per year (estimated at $20,000 per year) and at least one winter ball ($5,000).[26]

The estate Garner purchased in 1870 at 355 Bard Avenue included twenty-five acres of land and a house named Martinsdale constructed in 1859–1860 by Charles Corey Taber (1821–1892), a cotton broker and real estate developer who had made a great fortune during the Civil War and quite probably had had business dealings with Garner & Co.[27] The Second Empire style of Martinsdale (which survives) is far different from the picturesque, Romantic-style cottages favored by Elliott in the 1840s. To begin with, the structure is much larger than the typical suburban cottage of ten to fourteen rooms. Unquestionably a mansion, the exterior is brownstone chiseled into a meticulously smooth surface (when Dr. Elliott used stone it was not brownstone but locally quarried rock). The architecture recalls Chateau sur Mer (1852), the Oliver Kane residence in Newport. Taber, who owned land in Providence, Rhode Island, and had strong family and business ties to Rhode Island, was probably familiar with Chateau sur Mer. Like Chateau sur Mer's tower, Martinsdale's had water views (over New York Harbor), even though the structure is sited several miles inland, and a capacious porte cochere. The mansion cost Taber the extraordinary sum of $400,000 to build. When Martinsdale was last listed for sale as a private residence, in 1876, it was described as having "every convenience," including wide halls, parquet floors, terraces on three sides, a billiard room, a bowling alley, and extensive grounds. In addition to gardens, there were fountains and artificial streams, conservatories, and specialized greenhouses (one of which covered an acre and a half) for growing roses and grapes. The property also included the more typical carriage house, stable, cow house, and hen house.[28]

Unlike his neighbors in Elliottville, who were so committed to civic life, politics, community life, and charities, Garner only seems to have taken an interest in Staten Island ferry service. In 1872 he joined some of his Bard Avenue neighbors in signing a letter of protest concerning conditions on Dey Street in Manhattan, the East River landing site for the ferry originating from the foot of Bard Avenue.[29] Merchandise for sale directly on the street, as well as supplies in the process of being delivered to commercial establishments, impeded pedestrians and the publicly printed letter of complaint sought remediation. Garner signed, along with Curtis, Gay, Shaw, Livingston, and other Elliottville men. Although the

Figure 5.3. The Second Empire style, associated with the reign of Emperor Napoleon III (1852–1870), was nascent in the United States when Martinsdale was constructed. *Source*: Edwin S. Marsh, *Art Work of Staten Island* (Chicago: W. H. Parish, 1894), unpaginated. Public domain.

petition could be thought of as public-spirited, it was also self-interested since these men, at least on occasion, commuted to the city for business.

Garner also concerned himself with ferry service in a more direct way: as a businessman. His motivations are unclear, but there were certainly prominent examples of men making new fortunes in New York City transportation companies. Garner established a line of ferryboats, the principal of which was the *W. R. Martin*. In doing so he inserted himself into a contentious situation that featured rival ferry lines operating from different points on Staten Island, the most powerful of which was controlled by the Vanderbilts. Garner began ferry services after a boiler explosion on a Staten Island ferry on July 30, 1871, killed dozens of passengers, and Staten Islanders were enraged.[30] He faced hostile competition and had to deal with the political clout of rivals. In the fall of 1875, the New York Harbor Pilot Commissioners tried to stop his Garner Line (also known as the Opposition Line) completely and even destroy the NYYC clubhouse that Garner had constructed.[31] Whether these attacks were ever more than threats is unclear since Garner's ferries were still operating in 1876 and his clubhouse was still being used by the NYYC.

Much more is known about Garner's yachts than his Staten Island ferry service. He owned one famous yacht after another, was elected vice commodore of the NYYC, and in January 1876 was nominated to become the next commodore of the group.[32] The first yacht Garner purchased was the prize-winning *Vixen* from his neighbor Anson Livingston. After the purchase, Garner quickly became a known figure in the world of yachting. In 1874 he bought the schooner-yacht *Magic*. Although Franklin Osgood successfully defended the first America's Cup in 1870 with the vessel, by the time Garner purchased her, Rufus Hatch owned her (Hatch was one of the founders of the Chicago Board of Trade and in the 1870s was the managing director of Aspinwall's Pacific Mail Steamship Company).[33]

The year after buying the famed *Magic*, the *Aquatic Monthly and Nautical Review* announced Garner's plans for an NYYC facility on Staten Island, and later newspaper accounts say he completed the structure in 1875 for $25,000, but only charged the club a nominal rent.[34] Garner and James Gordon Bennett Jr. (1841–1918) were frequent rivals, and the fact that Bennett had provided the first clubhouse on Staten Island may have been a factor in Garner's actions. The club had sold the Bennett clubhouse in 1871 in favor of larger and more elegant quarters in Manhattan. By 1875 it may have become apparent that members still needed a base of some kind on Staten Island, and providing a structure was a way for Garner to further establish himself in the club. The Garner "clubhouse" had two stories and a cupola, a reception room with accompanying kitchen, wine storeroom, two dining rooms, and large verandas with expansive views over the harbor. Located in the center of the boat anchorage in Stapleton, the structure had a four-hundred-foot pier and was connected to the mainland with a private bridge.[35] Since a main yachting competition course was off Staten Island, the NYYC squadron often had occasion to be moored in front of the Garner clubhouse.

Garner's success in yacht races was, of course, even more important than the clubhouse for establishing him in the world of yachting. According to a firsthand account by Frederick Schiller Cozzens (1846–1928), on October 13, 1874, when Garner raced the *Magic* against the *Comet*, owned by William H. Langley (proprietor of the Langley Cotton Mills) in the Bennett Challenge Cup race off the shore of Staten Island, "as much as $100,000 changed hands" and Garner won enough money to fund the bulk of the construction costs for a new yacht.[36] Constructed in Greenpoint, Brooklyn, by J. B. Van Duesen and christened *Mohawk*, the centerboard schooner quickly became famous as the world's costliest and largest private yacht. Measuring 140 feet, the vessel had over 20,000 square feet of canvas and 32,000 square feet of sail area, as well as a thirty-foot beam and a draft of only six feet with her centerboard up.[37] For the yacht's launch, Garner hosted an elegant afternoon party on June 9, 1875, transporting guests to Brooklyn on a large, chartered steamboat.[38] However, when he raced the *Mohawk* over the next year he had mixed success and soon was mostly using the boat to host small parties.[39]

In preparing for the 1876 season, Garner enhanced the yacht's comforts with more furniture and added copper sheathing and an elaborate figurehead of a reclining Mohawk Indian to the exterior. His adaptation of the yacht as a pleasure craft was in keeping with the social aspect of the NYYC. From the earliest days club members would cruise in company up Long Island Sound to Newport, Rhode Island, with only occasional gentlemanly speed competitions. So the *Mohawk*'s shortcomings in races were largely outweighed by the social cachet of owning the yacht and being able to entertain in the graciously furnished, mirrored saloon that measured 784 square feet and contained a grand piano, upholstered chaises longues, a fireplace, and heavy velvet curtains. In addition to a long sideboard, kept well stocked with liquor, there was a library.[40] Hanging above the library was an "armory" of twenty-five Springfield breech-loading rifles.[41] The yacht had five staterooms, the largest of which, measuring

Figure 5.4. Claimed to be the largest private yacht in the world, the *Mohawk* won few races and Garner soon used the craft mostly for entertaining. *Source: Harper's Weekly*, November 13, 1875, 916. Collection of the author.

234 square feet, belonged to the Garners and included a silver vault[42] (sometimes used to store the racing cups, such as those Garner awarded at the Newport regatta in 1875).[43]

The Yachting Party

On July 20, 1876, the Garners hosted an afternoon cruise on their yacht. Although no contemporaneous sources claim there was a purpose for the cruise, later accounts say that the yachting party celebrated the engagement of Garner's brother-in-law Frost Thorn, twenty-six years old at the time. However, Frost was already married.[44] Even though his family never publicly acknowledged his marriage, he had two children with his legal wife, Lily Antoinette Davenport (1854–1878). Her parents were well-known English actors. Her mother was Fanny Elizabeth Vining Davenport (1829–1891) and her father was the Shakespearean actor Edward Loomis Davenport (1814–1877), who managed the Chestnut Street Theater in Philadelphia. At the time she and Frost met in 1872, Lily had been an actress for five years and was the leading actress at her father's theater. Frost, on the other hand, was still establishing a business career in Philadelphia, after leaving Yale College two years before in his junior year.[45] The couple eloped and married secretly, knowing that both their families would oppose the match (Lily's father eventually relented and accepted his son-in-law).[46]

The difference in values between Elliottville settlers, who held family relationships in such high regard, and people like the Thorns is stark. Not only did the Thorns refuse to acknowledge a marriage that had produced two children, but in New York society Frost presented himself as unwed, enjoying all the flirtations that the pretense afforded. In the extensive newspaper coverage of the yachting party, his wife and children were never mentioned.

The other members of the yachting party were not Garner family members. However, in addition to presumably being bound by any number of social ties that are, in retrospect, difficult to document, the male guests—Louis Brugiere Montant (1848–1877), Gardiner Greene Howland Jr. (1834–1903), and J. Schuyler Crosby (1839–1914)—were all New York society figures and had all been elected to the Union Club in 1871, the same year as Garner and James Gordon Bennett Jr. The club, founded in 1836, was established as a purely social organization to give American men the opportunity for the sort of club life available to English gentlemen;

George Curtis and his father were antebellum members.⁴⁷ As discussed in the previous chapter, Union Club members, many of whom were businessmen or investors, opposed the Civil War and the club refused to expel Southerners. A significant number of Union Club members left to support the Union cause by forming the Union League Club, among them Elliottville residents Curtis, Shaw, Robert Bowne Minturn Jr., and George Cabot Ward.

While the yachting party could not have been to celebrate Frost Thorn's engagement, it may have been organized for the men to enjoy the company of the beautiful Edith May; none of the men, except Garner, were accompanied by their wives. In addition to Edith May and Mrs. Garner, the young Adele Hunter (1845–1876), a friend of Edith's whose father and brother were both Union Club members, was on board.

Edith Sybil May (1854–1899) was the daughter of Dr. John Frederick May (1812–1891), who had continued his medical practice in Washington, DC, during the Civil War. He had both attended to the dying Abraham Lincoln and identified the body of John Wilkes Booth, a former patient. Dr. May's children and wife spent the war in Dresden, returning to the United States in 1875. They established themselves at 21 West Nineteenth Street and began launching Edith and her younger sister Caroline Kane (1856–1952) into "good" society. Edith was considered the most beautiful (and therefore successful) debutante of her year. Both Edith and Caroline had become acquainted with James Gordon Bennett Jr., and it was said that Bennett intended to marry Caroline.

May's life after the boating party involved affairs with several prominent yachtsmen, and, in reflecting upon Garner and his social circle, it seems relevant to make some brief reference to the rest of her life. The acquaintance between the May sisters and Bennett ended in a dual between their brother and Bennett over the latter's disrespect for the May sisters. Soon after the duel, Edith married a divorced Englishman, Arthur Randolph Randolph (1839–1885),⁴⁸ a man fifteen years older than she with troubled finances—the sort of match one might expect for a woman with a damaged reputation. Furthermore, after a modest wedding in Manhattan, the couple left Manhattan society and lived on the grounds of the Long Island estate of NYYC member William Proctor Douglas (1842–1919), with whose wife Adelaide (1853–1935) May was a great friend. J. P. Morgan Jr. (1837–1913) was also an intimate friend of the Douglases and Morgan and Edith engaged in an affair for more than a decade prior to Randolph's death. After his demise, the affair became so open that Morgan's wife finally insisted that the romance must end. Fortunately for the widowed Edith, she had already begun an affair with William C. Whitney (1841–1904). After his wife, Standard Oil heiress Flora Payne, died, Whitney wed Edith; both remained close friends of Morgan.[49]

The yachting party guests boarded the *Mohawk* from the Garner clubhouse around four o'clock, the focus of everyone due to the social prominence of the company and interest in the yacht. With a standing crew of twenty, plus two cooks and some cabin attendants, the vessel was under the command of Captain Oliver Rowland (1833–1903). The party was to be served an elaborate tea soon after setting sail. Because that year's Bennett Challenge Cup race was to be held on July 23, much of the NYYC squadron was moored within sight of the clubhouse.

Sailors in the area noticed the boarding party for reasons other than the guests. The sky had darkened, and in anticipation of a squall, all other sailing craft in the area had lowered their canvases. The *Mohawk* had all of her canvas out, prepared to sail. Shortly after the guests boarded, light rain began, and the Garner party went belowdecks after Garner commanded the yacht to set off. Then, sudden intense winds forced the *Mohawk* onto her beam-ends. The men in the party ran back onto deck and, finally realizing the danger, returned to the salon for the women. In less than five minutes, before any guests reemerged, another gust of wind turned the yacht onto her side so that her masts were lying flat in the water. A steamer yacht, *Ideal*, the vessel closest to the *Mohawk*, ineffectually attempted assistance.[50]

Exactly what happened in the brief time before the boat sank mostly happened belowdecks, out of sight of objective observers, and would never be accounted for in a way with which everyone agreed. Within days Crosby gave testimony at an inquest and his account became authoritative and was used in awarding him a lifesaving medal. Crosby said that after rushing belowdecks, the men tried to get the women on deck. Crosby rushed to May, who was standing in front of the fireplace in an area clear of furniture. Crosby got her up the companionway and Howland helped her out. Returning to the cabin, Crosby, Garner, and Montant focused on Mrs. Garner and Hunter, who had been thrown to the lee side and trapped by sliding furniture, pushing them against a sideboard. Crosby and Montant pulled off a chaise, but both women were still pinned down. Water began filling the salon and some furniture was blocking the companionway. Montant and Howland went onto the deck and began pulling furniture out. The rapidly filling boat covered Hunter in water,

Figure 5.5. Every aspect of the *Mohawk*'s sinking, including the recovery efforts and inquests, attracted newspaper coverage. *Source: Frank Leslie's Illustrated Newspaper*, August 5, 1876, 361. Courtesy of College of Staten Island, Archives & Special Collections. Public domain.

and Crosby focused on helping Garner rescue his wife. As water surged in, Crosby realized that only he and the sole *Mohawk* crew member to attempt aid, Carl Forsberg, were still able to free themselves. The glass of a side skylight had been broken out and they swam through.[51]

With all the craft and sailors in the area, the survivors were quickly retrieved. Staten Island yachtsmen Franklin Osgood and Beverly Robinson Jr. rescued Edith May, being supported by the exhausted Howland. The Garners, Hunter, Thorn, and a cabin attendant named Peter Sullivan all drowned. Hunter's body was found almost immediately, and the first inquest, on July 22, was held as soon as possible so that her remains could be released with a verdict of death by drowning before a formal inquest on July 23.

The inquest jury included Elliottville residents Robert Minturn, William K. Soutter (a stockbroker), and Benjamin Richards Jr. (a realtor), as well as Thomas Melville (Herman Melville's brother who was governor of Sailors' Snug Harbor) and was charged with ruling on the deaths of Hunter and Sullivan (the bodies of Frost and the Garners were still unrecovered) and reviewing the negligence complaint made against Captain Rowland. Newspaper accounts presented convincing testimony against Rowland, but the inquest took a surprising turn when Crosby defended him. Although the essence of Crosby's testimony stemmed from personal outrage that subordinates (Rowland's quartermasters) had criticized their superior, his testimony swayed the jury in clearing Rowland.

Newspapers and periodicals across the nation covered the *Mohawk* sinking in detail and the larger publications included illustrations. While only a few newspapers closely reported the inquest, New York papers gave the full verdict of the jury: that the vessel should never have set out given weather conditions and that Rowland should not have had the amount of sail out that he did. The jury also commented that had the furniture and ballast been properly secured, no one would have drowned. In the end, instead of criticizing Garner, the jury emphasized that he had died in a heroic attempt to save his wife.[52]

As the inquest was in session, the *Mohawk* was being raised. Mr. and Mrs. Garner were found in what appeared to be an embrace that was considered poignant (he could just as easily have been unable to free himself from her panic-stricken grip). The condition of the sails provided unassailable physical evidence that contradicted Rowland's inquest testimony.[53] The lack of concern with physical evidence, and the conflicting newspaper accounts that quoted witnesses, means that many crucial aspects of what happened on the *Mohawk* will never be known. Nonetheless, it is difficult not to conclude that Garner was culpable, at the very least.

Some newspapers editorialized on the verdict, seemingly along class lines. Conservative newspapers faulted only the crew and the captain's poor service to Garner for not supplying appropriate advice or managing the ship properly. Other newspapers roundly condemned Garner for being more concerned about catering arrangements than sailing conditions (he supposedly met with his steward before setting off, but not Rowland), even though he was risking the lives of his crew, guests, and people on surrounding yachts. As for the assertion that Garner died bravely, one editorialist observed, "No doubt the bravery of the owner, like that of Gen. Custer, will make amends for whatever else was wrong in omission or execution."[54] Of Crosby and Howland, the same editorialist observed, "Mr. Montant rescued Miss May . . . and Messrs. Crosby and Howland seem to have been so fortunate as to save Messrs. Howland and Crosby."[55] The statement regarding Montant echoes the earliest accounts; even though Crosby's testimony was widely circulated, for more than a year some reports still credited Montant with the rescue. In the end, Crosby and Forsberg, and not Montant, were awarded Congressional Gold Lifesaving Medals.

The funerals of the *Mohawk* victims, particularly the Garners', received wide press coverage that provides more insight into the social dynamic encompassing them and their friends. The first funerals were those of Adele Hunter and cabin boy Peter Sullivan. Hunter's, at the Church of the Transfiguration on Fifth Avenue (now known as the Little Church Around the Corner) was notably attended by Union Club and NYYC members. *Mohawk* cabin boy Peter Sullivan (1860–1876) received an impressive funeral, held in St. Peter's Catholic Church on Staten Island, just up the hill from the Pavilion Hotel. He was praised for dying bravely at his post and a procession of fifty carriages accompanied his body to St. Peter's Cemetery in Factoryville.

The funeral of the Garners and Frost Thorn on July 24, held at the Garner mansion on Staten Island, was covered nationally in newspaper and magazine articles, some of which included illustrations.[56] The principal mourners, the Garners' three young daughters, were spared from appearing at the funeral.[57] A Philadelphia newspaper pointed out the way that coverage glossed over the fact that Frost had been married with children. The

Figure 5.6. The extensive funeral reportage included descriptions and illustrations of the Garner mansion. *Source: Frank Leslie's Illustrated Newspaper*, August 12, 1876, 380. Courtesy of College of Staten Island Archives and Special Collections. Public domain.

service was simple, with no sermon or eulogies, only the reading of the Episcopalian Book of Common Prayer service. The ministers conducting the service were simply from the two nearest Episcopal churches, and no assertion was made that the deceased had ever attended either.[58]

Businesses were closed on Staten Island and the funeral had the quality of a public spectacle. Newspapers indicated the mixed nature of attendees by noting that women with babies were present.[59] The crowd, estimated at over four thousand, was problematic. While the affluent of the era were generally able to secure privacy, events like weddings and funerals were still difficult to control. The house was soon filled and many notable people who came from Manhattan could not get in.

A number of funeral attendees came in groups, representing the Union Club, NYYC, and employees of Garner & Co. One of the Garner ferries, the *Castleton*, swathed in mourning crepe, carried journalists, affluent Manhattanites, and Garner employees from Whitehall Street to Staten Island. The vessel also transported carriages and hearses for later use in Brooklyn for the trip to Greenwood Cemetery. Accounts mentioned only a few attendees from Elliottville: William K. Soutter (Union Club, 1871) and two sons of nearby neighbor Rufus King Delafield, Henry Parish Delafield (1842–1904) and his brother Edward Delafield (1837–1884), a stockbroker (Union Club, 1869).

After the funeral, an official procession accompanied the hearses to the *Castleton*. The crowd from outside the Garner mansion followed along. The hearses and family carriages drove directly onto the ferry; only family members and closest friends could accompany the cortege. In Brooklyn, an estimated crowd of three thousand people met the boat.[60] More crowds lined the route to Greenwood Cemetery and a "multitude" was waiting on the grounds.

Staten Island's Fifth Avenue

William Garner's dramatic death had a greater impact on Elliottville than his summer stays had. The national press coverage of the *Mohawk* established a new identity for the neighborhood: the "Fifth Avenue of Staten Island," the locale of great mansions, yachtsmen, and society life. While the neighborhood was mostly unchanged from the antebellum era, the 1870s did bring some new estates whose owners had more in common with Garner than with long-settled Elliottville residents.

The difference in value systems between people like the Garners (and their friends and family) and antebellum Elliottville residents is dramatic. While the affairs of women like Edith May were probably not retailed far beyond her elevated social circle, even the most cursory overview of Garner's wealth made his values clear. Mrs. Garner's family affluence was built on slavery and maintained after the war through the subjugation of "freedmen," immigrant laborers, Native Americans, and sharecroppers. The wealth that Mr. Garner displayed so shamelessly through his mansion and yacht came from textile mills notorious for employing women and children in conditions that had been the focus of philanthropists and reformers for generations. The textile industry was also intricately linked to the Southern economy, which before the war meant condoning the enslavement of people to produce cotton.

While we have no record of what Bard Avenue residents thought of the Garners, George Curtis, in an 1872 *Harper's* column that was widely reprinted, stated his alarm over the tendency to laud wealth while ignoring its sources.[61] He pointed out that even though it may be known that a man "buys judges, and steals vast properties, and procures laws to protect him[self]," instead of being condemned he is celebrated.[62] He decried the practice of putting "honor, truth, and respect" on the plane of ideals, with the aim of embracing power, pleasure, and luxury as the goals of the real life that everyday men live.[63] He despaired over the laudatory regard journalists accorded wealthy men for the luxuries they had acquired and the manner in which they honored such men for miserly charitable contributions that amounted to tiny percentages of their ill-gotten fortunes.[64] Garner's father had been celebrated for leaving $100,000 to charities, even though the amount represented less than 5 percent of his $20 million fortune. Garner's will was widely published, as his father's had been. Garner made no charitable bequests at all. Press coverage simply celebrated the size of his fortune.

None of the other Gilded Age newcomers to Bard Avenue could compare with the Garners in the rapacity with which their fortunes had been gained. Furthermore, the importers, mercantilists, real estate agents, and stockbrokers who became longer-lasting neighbors than the Garners could convincingly attribute their fortunes to their own efforts and business skills. However, all the newcomers had a much different understanding of wealth than Frank Shaw, for instance, who was committed to using his fortune to aid others.

Like Garner, other new Bard Avenue arrivals embraced values at odds with earlier Bard Avenue residents. Of course, with the exception of Curtis, who editorialized, it can be challenging to uncover the values of historical figures who left little or no archival record. Nevertheless, it is possible to find out enough about the lives of some Bard Avenue newcomers to get a sense of how they differed from earlier residents.

William Knox Soutter (1844–1891) was one such newcomer. He was elected to the Union Club in the same year as Garner, 1871. Although Soutter descended from a Southern family, like so many in Garner's circle he was a New Yorker. His mother Agnes (Knox) Soutter (1815–1899) was a lineal descendant of one of Virginia's first English settlers and her immediate family owned large plantations along the Rappahanock River.[65] Soutter was born in Norfolk, but the family soon moved to New York and his father James T. Soutter (1810–1873) became president of the Bank of the Republic, founded by his friend Gazaway Bugg Lamar (1798–1874) to meet the needs of Southern enterprises and the governments of Southern states. Even though the family lived in Astoria, they continued to have large landholdings in Virginia. As war approached, Lamar, under the bank's auspices, arranged financing for future Confederate states through loans and bond issues. He even purchased and stockpiled outdated weapons from federal arsenals in South Carolina and Georgia. When war broke out, Soutter's Virginia properties were confiscated, and a warrant was issued for his arrest. He fled to Paris and was reputed to continue to act as a financial agent for the Confederacy.[66] Lamar, who had left New York for Savannah, helped organize efforts to thwart the Union blockade.[67]

William and his brother Robert (1841–1873) were Confederate soldiers during the war. Robert served in the Confederate Army, mostly in Florida. William, who enlisted as a seventeen-year-old, served in the Signal Corps on ships running the Union blockade of Southern ports (he ran the blockade thirty-five times). During the war, Robert married Charlotte Antoinette Lamar (1840–1908), the daughter of Gazaway Bugg Lamar.

After the war, James T. Soutter was pardoned by President Johnson and his property was returned.[68] He established the banking firm of Soutter Brothers that later became Soutter & Co. By 1868, William Knox Soutter was a partner in Soutter & Co. and a member of the New York Stock Exchange. Soutter moved to Bard Avenue around 1870 and married Louisa A. Meyer (1850–1909) in 1871. His Elliottville estate featured a twenty-room house, bowling alley, five conservatories, a stable, cow house, and hennery, all maintained by six live-in servants.[69] When the house was robbed in 1874, the thieves got away with silverware and money valued at $9,000 that had been left lying about ($215,000 in today's money).[70]

Soutter's financial circumstances changed dramatically in 1885. His father and brothers had died by then.[71] Soutter & Co. had been celebrated in 1878 and 1879 for successfully taking bear positions against the much-disliked Jay Gould. When the country entered a serious economic recession, performance became indifferent. Then, during the credit shortage that caused the Panic of 1884, Robert Soutter's widow Charlotte (by then the Duchesse D'Auxy) sued Soutter and James T. Soutter's other executors over the handling of the estate. She demanded an accounting. The assets of Soutter & Co. were frozen and a lengthy, widely publicized lawsuit began, during which Charlotte briefly had Soutter imprisoned for grand larceny. In 1887, Soutter was found innocent; however, he never returned to business. He eventually tried to sell his Staten Island property. The house and grounds were listed as early as 1888. By 1889, the estate had been divided into lots, but it still took some years to sell.[72] When Soutter died six years later, his obituary presented him as a great clubman and his bank failure was attributed to liberality with his friends. Said to be one of the best dressed men in New York—the owner of eighty overcoats alone—his final residence was in one of his clubs.[73]

Although Soutter had owned his Bard Avenue estate for almost twenty years, Elliottville was sparsely represented at his funeral (mostly by Delafields, who, in addition to being his closest neighbors, were Union Club members). George Curtis did not attend. His absence may have many explanations, but his attitude toward men like Soutter had been known as early as the *Potiphar Papers* and was reasserted in his Easy Chair column, in which he poked fun at expensively attired clubmen who spent their days on display in the windows of their clubs.[74]

A few parallels between Garner and Soutter are obvious. Both Garner and Soutter had strong ties to the South and were sued by relatives for mishandling estates (Garner in the handling of his brother's). Whether the lawsuits were justified or not, the fact of family members suing each other was far different from the behavior of long-settled Elliottville residents in similar circumstances. When George Curtis's publishing ventures failed, his main creditor, Frank Shaw, did not sue, and Curtis and Frederick Law Olmstead worked for years to repay Shaw and other creditors as a moral, rather than legal, obligation. Soutter behaved quite differently. He never repaid his mother the losses she had suffered in the failure of Soutter & Co. and she cut William out of her will to punish him.[75]

Leopold Van Zandt (1837–1917) was another Gilded Age newcomer to Bard Avenue; he too had values at odds with residents of the 1840s and 1850s. Van Zandt descended from a New York colonial Dutch family and his grandfather, Wynant Van Zandt (1767–1831), was a New York City merchant and alderman associated with DeWitt Clinton and Nicholas Low.[76] On the other hand, Van Zandt's parents were expatriates. His father, Thomas Van Zandt (1794–1877), had married Louisa Underhill, the daughter of another Manhattan merchant, Townsend Underhill (1765–1799). The couple lived in Paris on income from inherited wealth. Their oldest son, William Thompson Van Zandt (1819–1898), lived in New York and managed the Van Zandt Estate, a trust consisting mostly of Wynant Van Zandt's real estate holdings, some of which were on Staten Island. William had strong ties to the South through his marriage in 1846 to Elizabeth Hazard Barker, the daughter of Jacob Barker (1779–1871), a New Orleans sugar planter and major slaveholder. When William's brother Leopold returned to the United States after the war, he married Marie Antoinette Austin in 1866, the daughter of an English immigrant civil engineer and coal dealer on Staten Island. In the 1870s, Leopold and his wife lived in the same household with William (sans wife) in a house on Bard Avenue, during which time Leopold was a steel importer.

Much of what we know about Leopold and William Van Zandt stems from a fire in 1878 at their Bard Avenue residence, located across the street from the Garner mansion. When a police detective, called in by William Van Zandt to investigate an office theft, found his clerk, William H. Howard, to be the culprit, the detective questioned why Van Zandt did not wish to prosecute the clerk. The detective intimidated the clerk into explaining that Van Zandt feared him since he knew that Van Zandt had set fire to his house on Staten Island. The detective investigated and collected damning evidence.[77] For instance, the Van Zandts removed valuables from the house immediately before the fire, upon which William Van Zandt had an inflated insurance policy, and Leopold Van Zandt had insured the house for an amount double its value. The clerk claimed that special, long-burning candles set alight in the attic to ignite kerosene-soaked sheet music accomplished the arson. The detective confirmed with a shop clerk that William Van Zandt had purchased such candles. When he was indicted, Van Zandt laughed off the accusations and was able to post the $5,000 bail. When William Van Zandt's relatives provided him with an alibi, the case was dismissed—even though witnesses at the trial had confirmed the detective's evidence.[78] In the end, Van Zandt's clerk was tried, found guilty of grand larceny for stealing $210 from his employer, and sentenced to eighteen months in prison.

Although the arson charges were dismissed, press coverage presented all the evidence that had been accumulated against the Van Zandts in meticulous detail and hinted at insurance fraud, as well as serious misrepresentation. At William Van Zandt's trial, the circumstances leading to Mrs. Leopold Van Zandt owning the property were presented in the *New York Herald*.[79] Before marrying Leopold, Mrs. Van Zandt had been the fiancée of a Mr. Kickhoever, a clerk who reportedly ruined his firm by absconding with $100,000. Before his departure, Kickhoever had deeded the Bard Avenue property to Miss Austin for a dollar. Some of the press animosity may have also stemmed from distaste for the Van Zandt trust, which was named in the articles and widely known for owning notorious tenement dwellings. Wynandt Van Zandt had accumulated real estate in Lower Manhattan, the heart of the city at the time that he was buying. He was a vestryman at Trinity Church and his house was at 71 Broadway (across the street from the church). By the 1830s, affluent people like the Van Zandts considered Lower Manhattan uninhabitable, due to overcrowding and the smells and disease associated with area industry. Fashionable Manhattanites moved uptown and the Van Zandts moved to Paris, financing their leisure through significant rental income from tenements. Not until the 1890s did the city act against such nineteenth-century slumlords. While it is not clear how many such properties comprised the Van Zandt Estate, in one day in 1896, the board of health condemned four Van Zandt rear tenements (structures constructed at the back of street-facing housing and notorious for lacking light and air). Located on Thompson Street, the four tenements alone housed more than one hundred people.[80]

In the previous chapter, we saw how Josephine Lowell dedicated all her energies to helping impoverished women and children. These were the very same people who men like the Van Zandts had as tenants, tenants whose rents supported their luxury-filled lives.

Continuity of Family Life in Elliottville

The interlopers who arrived in Elliottville after the war altered the public perception of Elliottville. Neighborhood residents, however, seem to have simply excluded the newcomers from their tight-knit social circle. Neither the sinking of the *Mohawk* nor the subsequent inquest and funeral nor the Soutter lawsuits nor the Van Zandt arson case got mentioned in letters. Instead, surviving letters are preoccupied with the Gays' move to Chicago. The letters share neighborhood news and include reflections by the Gays on how much they miss Elliottville and by neighborhood residents on how much they miss the Gays. Sarah Gay's correspondence is particularly detailed. She was still going to school in Philadelphia and her health was considered too fragile to endure Chicago. She was expected to write a letter each day to her mother, in which she recounted her activities.

Sydney Gay had been forced to leave his job at the *New-York Tribune*. Like his friends in the antislavery movement, he had begun to take issue with Horace Greeley after the war. As early as 1865, Curtis had written to Gay, "H. G. has made fearful mistakes and he cannot wriggle out of them."[81] Greeley began campaigning for political office, running for New York State offices and Congress before eventually running for president in the 1872 election. Lydia Maria Child described him as "woefully deficient in character."[82] Curtis said, "He is trusted as an editor, but nothing else."[83] Gay could not stay at the *New-York Tribune* when he did not support Greeley's political positions. Elizabeth Gay wrote her friend Sarah Pugh in August 1867 that Sydney was "very sad and overworked."[84]

Still, in 1868 no one in the Gay family seemed happy when Sydney Gay accepted the job of managing editor of the *Chicago Tribune*. Even though Elizabeth described the paper as the "leading liberal paper of the West"[85] and it seemed as though the position might be a cause for celebration, Elizabeth said they barely spoke of the new job and told no one in the neighborhood until the day before Sydney left for Chicago in July of 1868.[86] Martin, Sarah, and Elizabeth Gay all wrote letters to Sydney during their separation. Although Martin seemed excited about living in Chicago, which he seemed to associate with the Great Plains and American West, Sarah could not resist teasing Sydney about the deficiencies of Chicago. Elizabeth, based on his responses to her letters (that no longer survive), regarded the new job as evidence that Sydney was a poor provider and threat to Gay family life. The Chicago job did not pay well enough to enable Sydney to maintain two households and, for a long time, he was not confident about even being able to find a Chicago house to rent on his income. When Elizabeth wrote Sydney in March 1869 that she would have to sell Sarah's piano to make ends meet, he testily reminded her, "The only thing I live for, or care to live for is to work for thee and the children."[87] Apparently, the tone of Elizabeth's letters became shriller once the decision had been made to move the family to Chicago. In an April 1869 letter Sydney plaintively wrote, "I know that to leave S. I. must be painful exceedingly and then in every letter thou says something to remind me of all this, how is it possible for me to feel otherwise than that my failures in life and the hard necessity at my age to seek a living out here is a terrible blow to thee?"[88]

By May 1869 the Gay house had been rented out and most of the Gays were living in a leased Chicago house. Sarah's one visit made her ill, and she returned to stay on Staten Island, alternating among the Johnsons, Shaws, and George Cabot Wards (she also stayed at the Wards' Manhattan residence; at the Curtises' summerhouse in Ashfield, Massachusetts; and at Newport). She eventually traveled with the Wards in Europe, as a companion for Mrs. Ward, who was also ill.

The Gays' absence in Chicago was emotional for both the Gays and their friends. Only a few months after the move, Elizabeth Gay wrote that although she was determined to like Chicago, "I know that if I should find myself transported to my old household I should fall upon my knees and kiss it and grow wild with joy!"[89] George Curtis wrote letters over several years to tell Sydney how much he and all of Elliottville missed him: "We passed your old home last night. It was as dark as the old Shaw house, and a dog whining in the yard. We think of you and speak of you constantly."[90] Then on October 8, 1871, the Great Chicago Fire brought a panicked flurry of letters and telegrams from Elliottville before word came that the Gays and their dwelling were safe. Over the following months, Sydney worked with the Chicago Relief and Aid Society, Elizabeth worked as the recording secretary for the Ladies Relief Society, and Elliottville women gathered and shipped relief supplies to Chicago. By November, Sydney no longer had a job with the *Chicago Tribune* and Curtis offered help in finding a new position. Sydney continued his relief work and wrote the first annual report for the aid society.[91] However, in May 1872, Elizabeth announced the plan to return to Staten Island: "I am not glad that the fire burned this city, nor glad that misfortune overtook us, but I am glad to go home."[92]

The letters the Gays received from Elliottville during their absence informed them about neighborhood changes. Although the Garners, Soutters, and Van Zandts earned no mention, the residential development of Davis Avenue that began in the 1870s did. Running parallel to Bard Avenue, Davis Avenue's new houses had little in common conceptually with Ranlett-designed properties. The new houses were on much smaller lots and had few outbuildings. Frank Shaw, whose house purchase from James Parker included a long strip of land alongside Davis Avenue, built several such houses on his land as rentals. The new houses were built during a period of growth that also affected other areas of Staten Island and prompted infrastructure projects. Curbs and sidewalks were constructed, and streets macadamized. As more people moved into Elliottville, more fences were needed to define property lines. These improvements typically came at a cost to property owners, and Gay had to spend money he could ill afford.

Those long resident in Elliottville were selective about whom they welcomed into their social circle. Sarah Gay wrote her mother with amusement at the behavior of Anna Curtis. When Sarah called at the Curtises, the servant would not admit her. Then as Sarah was walking away Anna called her back and explained that she had initially thought Sarah was a lady of fashion come to call and only realized her mistake when she saw Sarah walking away.[93] Of the Gays' neighbors, the Whites, Sydney said that he supposed "in Virigina they were eligible to any society."[94] They were not welcomed in Elliottville, where they were ignored and ostracized. A neighboring family with whom the Gays did socialize wanted Sydney to close the lane he owned so that they would "be protected from any disagreeable consequences of the Whites owning" property so close to them.[95]

Unlike the Whites, the de Kay family was welcomed into the social circle of those long resident in Elliottville. The widowed Janet (Drake) de Kay moved to Bard Avenue in 1867 with three of her children, Julia, Helena, and Charles.[96] There were a number of reasons why Elliottville welcomed the de Kays. Firstly, Janet's husband had been Commodore George Coleman de Kay, a direct descendant of a director of the Dutch West India Company and one of the first merchants to arrive in New Amsterdam, settling there in 1640.[97] Secondly, the Commodore had achieved a certain measure of fame—initially as a skilled, self-taught navigator delivering ships for famed shipbuilder Henry Eckford (1775–1832) to such faraway places as South America, and then for the fortune and title of commodore he had won as a volunteer in the navy of the Argentine Republic capturing Brazilian ships. Thirdly, Janet, in addition to being Henry Eckford's granddaughter, was the orphaned only child of Manhattan poet and author Joseph Rodman Drake (1795–1820).[98] Laura Johnson, in sharing the news of the de Kays arrival with Annie Fields, excitedly identified Janet as Drake's daughter since Drake was a much-lionized poet during his brief life (and is still considered one of America's first poets).[99] Fourthly, the family had connections to the respected scholar and naturalist James de Kay.[100] Finally, the family had a tradition of sacrifice on behalf of others. The Commodore had orchestrated a famine relief mission to Ireland, three de Kay sons fought for the Union in the Civil War, and one of them died in the conflict.

Janet de Kay was fifteen years old when she married the worldly and affluent Commodore. The couple settled in a rural estate in New Jersey. Located in what is now Weehawken, across from Manhattan's Seventy-Ninth Street, the land came to be called de Kay's Point. Janet had her first child, Katherine (1834–1901), when she was still fifteen. She and de Kay went on to have five more children before Janet was twenty-eight: Joseph Rodman Drake (1836–1886), George Coleman (1843–1862), Juliana "Julia" (1841–1920), Sidney Brooks (1845–1890), and Helena (1847–1916).[101]

When Janet came of age in 1840, she became eligible to claim an inheritance from her grandfather, Henry Eckford, that consisted of his country estate, Love Lane, which encompassed the land that would later be described as lying between Twenty-Fourth and Twenty-Sixth Streets and Fifth and Seventh Avenues in Manhattan. Since the land had become quite valuable since Eckford made his will, and Janet's inheritance was now greater than the inheritances of his own children, Eckford's children contested the bequest. Although a protracted legal battle was required, the Commodore successfully defended his wife's claims in court and the family moved from New Jersey to the Manhattan estate.[102]

Instead of remaining settled, de Kay disrupted their life when he successfully petitioned Congress for use of the USS *Macedonian* on an Irish famine relief mission. Filling the vessel with donated food and clothing gathered from Bostonians and New Yorkers through the Middle States Relief Committee, de Kay underwrote the expenses of the trip out of his own funds, paying the costs of loading and unloading the ship and the wages for the crew and their provisions. His wife and oldest children sailed with him to Ireland in July 1847. The mission, which involved distribution of supplies in several ports, was a great success, but upon his return, de Kay's attempts to get his expenses reimbursed made no headway. He relocated his household to Washington, DC, to pursue the matter through social lobbying. His final child, Charles Augustus (1848–1935), was born there. Without recouping his losses (estimated at $30,000), de Kay died in Washington in 1849. His family accompanied his body back to Long Island for burial near his former patron, Henry Eckford, and moved into the household of his brother James de Kay. James, a physician and naturalist, had married Janet Eckford, Janet de Kay's aunt. In 1859, after the deaths of James in 1851 and Janet in 1854, Janet de Kay took her unmarried children to Dresden (Katherine had married in 1855), and they remained in Europe until 1861.[103] Although the exact financial arrangements from which Janet and her family benefited are unclear, sale of the land she had inherited from Henry Eckford must have cleared a sizable amount, and a financial device, the Eckford Trust, continued into the twentieth century.[104]

In some accounts, the family's return to the United States was prompted by the outbreak of the Civil War. Given de Kay's adventurous years as a sailor, it is no surprise that his sons, out of patriotism and/or a desire to prove themselves on the battlefield, joined the conflict. Since no one in the family seems to have been involved with abolitionist organizations, the de Kays' commitments on that front are less clear. All of George's sons enlisted, except for Charles, the youngest. Each de Kay served with distinction. Drake served on the staffs of Generals Mansfield, Pope, and Hooker and won the brevet of lieutenant colonel for gallantry.[105] George served as a lieutenant of artillery and afterward was on the staff of General Thomas Williams. In June 1862, the month after the capture of New Orleans, he was mortally wounded in a skirmish with bushwhackers near Grand Gulf, Mississippi.[106] Sidney joined the Seventy-First New York Infantry in 1862 and was afterward made lieutenant in the Eighth Connecticut Infantry. He served on the staffs of Generals B. F. Butler, Devens, and Terry, and received the brevet of major.[107]

Starting in 1861, the de Kays not in service lived in Newport, joining Katherine and her husband Arthur Bronson (1824–1885).[108] Bronson was the heir to a significant fortune built by his grandfather, who was a banker, land speculator, and promoter of westward expansion; although Bronson's income came from US real estate, he and Katherine lived most of their married life abroad.[109] In the early 1860s, the de Kays socialized a good deal in Newport with John LaFarge and members of the Henry James Sr. family. Henry Jr. became Katherine's lifelong friend and based at least one fictional character on her. His brother, William James, was smitten with Helena de Kay.[110] In 1864, Bronson built Ocean Cliff in Newport, a dramatically sited house designed by Peabody and Stearns (who would later design the original Breakers for the Vanderbilts) that was frequented by the de Kays over a number of years.

Before Janet, Julia, Helena, and Charles came to Staten Island, Drake was already settled in Tompkinsville on Staten Island, having located there immediately after his wartime service. Prior to the war, in 1860, he had also been the first of his family to return from Europe, when he had commenced a business career in New York soon becoming principal in the import house of Jonathan Thompson. His letters to his sisters reflected his enthusiasm for Manhattan, of which he said: "Surely there is no place more amusing—the crowds of people, the throng of carriages, cars, carts, and buses, the beautiful houses, magnificent stores—Everything to interest one is centered there."[111] His extensive family connections gave him entrée into society. His aunt, Juliana de Kay (1793–1874), had married Charles Augustus Davis (1795–1867), an iron merchant and author who was friends with Fitz-Greene Halleck and a member of James Fenimore Cooper's Bread and Cheese Club, along with James de Kay. Davis was also friends with businessmen, like William Henry Aspinwall. Davis introduced Drake to the August Belmonts, where he was invited to balls and teas, and secured his tickets to the grand ball held for the Prince of Wales in 1860. Even while still serving in the Union Army, Drake had anticipated his return to New York and advertised for property on Staten Island.

The de Kays had a long-standing connection to Staten Island. Commodore de Kay had purchased a large tract of land from Thomas E. Davis adjacent to New Brighton in 1846, which appears to have been an investment (he soon sold some of it).[112] In 1856, Janet purchased an even larger tract of land for $20,000 on Staten Island's Todt Hill.[113] Why Janet later bought more land on Staten Island, rather than locating on Todt Hill, is not clear. Perhaps the area seemed too remote. Conceivably, Janet made the decision based on a friendship with Dr. Elliott. Family correspondence refers to problems Sidney de Kay had with his eyes. In 1862, Janet referred to medical advice received from Dr. Elliott concerning Katherine.[114] Dr. Elliott also seems to have been a family friend, since Janet shared news of him with Helena in 1862, referring to Elliott's health problems and decision to go to Cuba to recruit soldiers for his regiment.[115] She delegated Drake de Kay to locate a suitable property, and on May 28, 1866 he purchased a tract of land in South Elliottville from Dr. Alexander B. Mott that included a house.[116]

In 1867, when Janet moved into the house located at the top of Bard Avenue, near today's southwest corner of Bard with Forest Avenue, the de Kays named the residence Kaywood. In the context of Bard Avenue, the house was relatively modest. Laura Johnson did not consider it entirely suitable for the family since it had no ballroom, so she made her own ballroom available.[117] Although family members moved to other

Figure 5.7. When the de Kays purchased most of South Elliottville from Dr. Alexander B. Mott in 1867, there was a house on this site that became their family home (photograph dated March 26, 1911). *Source:* William T. Davis, photographer. Courtesy of Staten Island Museum.

properties on Staten Island and Kaywood was periodically rented, the de Kays thought of the property as their family home, the house that Janet and the younger de Kays had lived in longest. Sidney lived there for several extended periods, including when he was recovering his health after military service. Even after they began using the house as a rental property, Kaywood was a physical repository of memories, as the family stored belongings and keepsakes in the attic.[118]

Elliottville immediately welcomed Janet and her children. They became great favorites in the neighborhood and were frequently mentioned in letters through the 1880s. Of all the de Kay children, Charles and Helena were most involved in neighborhood social events. Charles quickly became friends with Laura Johnson's son Oliver. Although Oliver was four years younger than Charles, both of them enjoyed rowing and occasionally circumnavigated Staten Island. Adults, like Elizabeth Gay, wrote about how much they enjoyed Charles's company, and he was often chosen to lead local dances (called "Germans"), a popular form of entertainment in Elliottville for adults and young people throughout the 1870s and 1880s. Laura remodeled the third floor of the Johnson house, in part to host Germans, improving the flooring and replacing the skylight let into the floor with ground glass to improve the experience of dancers.[119] The Germans were held during the social season, and George Curtis and Mrs. Staples often played piano for the dances.

Between Charles and Helena, Charles was the most appreciative of Staten Island. His love of Staten Island became a running joke for Helena. She disdained the suburban nature of Staten Island, which meant that "one is never *really* in the county. Everyone about you lives like city people, a great fault in a country place, I think."[120] Charles, on the other hand, wrote to Richard Watson Gilder of Staten Island, "I think it is an exquisite place, but of course I may be prejudiced. There are mosquitoes and fevers everywhere, methinks, but not everywhere such woods and glades, slopes and views inland and seaward vistas."[121] Until his marriage, Charles would return to Staten Island to live with Janet and Julia for extended periods of time, and Julia would write that even compared with Katherine (de Kay) Bronson's elegant palazzo in Venice "he likes nothing better than Staten Island."[122] Even though Helena was not as appreciative of Staten Island, for decades she visited her mother there for holidays and lived there for an extended period after the infant death of her first child.

Even as a young woman, Helena de Kay was admired for her beauty and made friends easily in Manhattan and Newport. However, she was inevitably drawn into social life in Elliottville. Surviving correspondence demonstrates that women of her mother's generation found her engaging. Elizabeth Gay maintained a correspondence with her through the rest of her life, as did Sarah Shaw. Shaw's surviving letters to Helena from decades later (1891–1898) show the strength of the friendship between the two women, which Shaw wrote grew out of her friendship with Janet de Kay.[123] Shaw repeatedly referred to Helena as her "dear adopted daughter."[124] From Helena's letters it is clear that she was also close to Mrs. Staples, and Anna Leonowens befriended her and even gave her the opportunity to create illustrations for her first book.

Helena de Kay also befriended the girls of Elliottville, including Sarah Gay, Bessie Johnson, and Caroline Cranch. Although surviving letters demonstrate lifelong friendships, Helena's correspondence with family members shows that she sometimes found socializing with the Elliottville girls challenging. One assumes this had much to do with age differences. Helena was between four and seven years older than the various girls. Helena was at her most waspish about Johnson. During the Philadelphia Centennial, she wrote Richard Gilder "what a bore" a visit with Bessie to the Centennial would be.[125] It is probable that her interest in art inspired the younger girls, since all of them began sketching and painting. Johnson eventually taught Caroline Cranch and Avis Leonowens and announced that Leonowens was a "promising" student and Cranch was progressing. In the end, Cranch seems to be the only one who developed facility as an artist, perhaps not surprisingly given the accomplishments of her father Christopher Pearse Cranch. She even executed a portrait of George Curtis that survives.[126] The other girls remained hobbyists, despite lessons from persons other than Johnson.

Helena de Kay's closest friend in the neighborhood, Maria Oakey (1845–1927), was only one year her junior. Maria was the daughter of William F. Oakey (1808–1888), whose family was living in Elliottville as early as 1854. Oakey was a Manhattan merchant with a store at 45 Barclay Street that imported Marshall & Co. linen thread. Maria's brother Daniel Oakey (1843–1888) served with the Second Massachusetts Infantry from 1861 through the end of the war (he trained at Camp Andrews on the grounds of what had been Brook Farm), surviving a serious wound. In addition to their families' shared commitment to the war, Helena and Maria were both artists and formed a lifelong friendship. During their years on Staten Island, they commuted together from 1866 to 1869 to study art at the Free School of Art for Women at the Cooper Union for the Advancement of Science and Art in New York City. Helena, a painter, and Maria, a sculptor, also shared studio space in Manhattan. Beginning in 1871, they were the first female members of a life drawing class at the National Academy of Design. Helena and Maria were frustrated over restrictions faced by women in the arts. In 1875, the two women, along with other art students disenchanted with the National Academy of Design, formed the Art Students League. In addition to embracing a European atelier model for instruction, a founding principle of the new organization was that men and women should be treated equally.[127]

Around this time, Helena de Kay began studying at the Tenth Street Studio Building with Winslow Homer, to whom Charles de Kay had introduced her. Homer depicted her in several paintings and fell in love with her.[128] Then, in 1872, Helena met Richard Watson Gilder (1844–1909) through Charles. During their two-year courtship, Gilder was a frequent visitor to Elliottville and participated in family life at Kaywood and social life in the neighborhood. Women in the neighborhood were entranced by the courtship. Although the couple quickly fell in love, Helena was less certain about marriage and how it would shape her life. Elliottville women intuited or were told by Janet de Kay about Helena's qualms. Once the engagement was finally announced, Bessie Johnson spread the word. When Mrs. Leonowens heard the news, she wrote Helena, "I have already placed [Richard's] name among the few I love as fully and wholly for his own sake as yours."[129] Laura Johnson, in particular, had been intrigued by the romance. After she learned of the engagement, she claimed that she had known for the previous year that Helena would eventually choose marriage, pointing to an evening on the ferryboat home when she saw Helena and Richard together as the sun set over the water and had written a poem, "Second Twilight," in their honor. When the couple married in 1874, the wedding party left from Kaywood, and in Helena's list of wedding gifts, every household in Elliottville was represented.

Helena de Kay's professional interest in art, her persistence in getting formal training, and her reluctance to marry usefully introduces the topic of the status of women in Elliottville. From the beginnings of the neighborhood, many residents embraced the concept that women were equal as one of the corollaries of their social reform commitments. After Elizabeth Gay was excluded from the World Anti-Slavery Convention in London in 1840, she remained friends with Elizabeth Cady Stanton and Lucretia Mott, who had also been excluded and Gay supported them in their advocacy for women's rights. Men in the neighborhood, like Frank

Figure 5.8. The courtship of Richard Gilder and Helena de Kay was a feature of Elliottville social life for more than a year. *Source*: Rosamond Gilder, *Letters of Richard Watson Gilder* (Boston: Houghton Mifflin, 1916), 60. Public domain.

Shaw and George Curtis, were convinced of women's equality and Curtis was active, along with his wife Anna, in New York State women's rights activities. He had first publicly supported women's rights in his 1858 speech "Fair Play for Women," which he was asked to present many times over the years. In 1867, he spoke on equal rights for women at the Constitutional Convention of New York, at Albany in 1867. In 1869, he helped found the American Woman's Suffrage Association and served for twenty years as one of its vice presidents. However, despite a broad acceptance of women's equality in Elliottville, the lived experience of women was quite different from the 1840s through the 1870s.

As the letters of Laura Johnson make clear, no matter how intelligent and well-read the women were, they had few opportunities for independence and limited outlets for their intellectual energies. For decades, Johnson was preoccupied with managing a large household that at times numbered over fifteen. She also had to deal with her husband and mother's long illnesses and deaths. William Templeton Johnson's death was particularly complicated since, in 1868, he had insisted against Laura's judgment that they travel to Europe for his health; he died soon after they landed in London. At the time of her husband's death, her youngest daughter and namesake was only five years old.

People commented on Anna Curtis's great energy and skill at organization, yet her only outlet for these qualities was in managing the family household. Sydney Gay, for one, admired her organizational prowess. He told his daughter Sarah Gay how much she would enjoy spending time in Vermont in 1864 with Anna Curtis, who "is such a cheerful person . . . I think she will stir up the country people, will make improvements in the mowing machines, introduce watering carts if the roads are dusty, or turn the springs upon them; improve the framing of houses, and put the calls into cards."[130] Other acquaintances contrasted her skills in practical matters with her husband's ineptitude "in the manual uses of our life."[131] Throughout their marriage, Anna oversaw all aspects of the couple's life together. For the first decades of their marriage, they were often separated for extended periods due to George's heavy lecture schedule, and Anna was left to manage the household, which eventually included three children, on her own. In addition to Anna's need to be vigilant about childhood illnesses (which could be deadly at the time), the Curtises' youngest daughter, Sarah "Sally" Curtis, was born with a developmental disability that caused much anxiety. After approximately eight years of caring for Sally at home, the Curtises placed her at the Syracuse State School around 1871, where she died three years later.[132] In addition to household and childcare responsibilities on Staten Island, Anna Curtis had to manage a second household. Starting in 1865, for several months each year, the Curtises resided in Ashfield, Massachusetts, and Anna was responsible for making all the arrangements for transferring children, servants, and animals back and forth.[133]

Elizabeth Gay's horizons were also limited to the family household; her only intellectual outlet was letter writing. Throughout their marriage, Sydney Gay had difficulties making a comfortable living and his papers show that he sometimes had to take sizable loans from Frank Shaw.[134] Just as her children were coming of age and she could more fully enjoy their company and that of their friends, she was forced to leave Staten Island for Chicago. Her oldest child, Sarah, was intermittently ill and often bedridden when she was not traveling for her health. After their return from Chicago, Sydney became increasingly remote. In 1872, he joined the editorial staff of the *New York Evening Post*, but he only worked there for

Figure 5.9. Lydia Maria Child described Anna Curtis as having "great innocent, honest eyes" and Sydney Gay, among others, admired her organizational skills. *Source*: Courtesy of Staten Island Museum.

two years before leaving to devote himself to ill-paid book projects that entirely preoccupied him, including the four-volume *Bryant's History of the United States*, which, even though solely authored by Gay, was credited to Bryant.[135] In addition to frustrations over her husband's abilities as a provider and his career choices, Elizabeth had to deal with his poor health. Starting as early as 1846, Elizabeth had written about Sydney's illnesses that often involved his eyes, digestion, and joints. In 1880, George Curtis wrote Christopher Pearse Cranch that Sydney would not go out in daylight.[136] Then, after a fall, Sydney became so incapacitated as to be bedridden. During another era, Elizabeth's intellect and convictions may have led her into a career, perhaps in social service organizations or political office. Instead, her days were occupied with caring for ill family members, managing a house so large as to be inefficient and tending a huge property, which could involve such tedious tasks as sewing and attaching cloth bags on the vineyard grapes to prevent bird raids. At one point, she became preoccupied with a new pest, the buffalo moth

(*Parapamea buffaloensis*), which attacked everything from clothing to the first generation of tennis balls.

Conclusion

Earlier we saw the ways in which the postwar period challenged Elliottville residents. In this chapter we have seen how Gilded Age figures intruded upon the cohesiveness of the neighborhood. How wrenching it must have been when men who had fought for the Confederacy or made fortunes from the war became neighbors, only a few years after the conflict in which loved ones had died. The earlier residents continued to expend their energies and fortunes to improve the lives of others. The newcomers devoted their fortunes to luxurious living and opulent display, rather than to the welfare of their fellows.

For long-settled Elliottville residents, family life became even more important as young people, born shortly before or during the Civil War, matured. Increasingly, social life in the neighborhood focused on the young. Their cultural preoccupations began to dominate conversation, and their activities, including amateur theatricals, dances, hayrides, sleigh rides, picnics, boating parties, hiking parties, and croquet games, began to dominate social life.

Chapter 6

The 1880s

The Ascendancy of the Middle Class

Introduction

Just as Elliottville came to be identified with William Thorn Garner in the 1870s, a man who epitomized Gilded Age wealth and was representative of other such men who earned the neighborhood the title "Fifth Avenue of Staten Island" for a time in the 1880s the neighborhood became widely known as the home of Maria "Midy" Morgan, a nationally known journalist celebrated for her expertise—livestock markets and racehorses—as well as her ability to make an upper-middle-class income, an unusual thing for a woman. Although she was dramatically unique in many ways, Morgan was also representative of other upper-middle-class Elliottville residents whose affluence stemmed from some of the same factors underlying Gilded Age fortunes: new national markets, improved transportation networks, and the rise of corporations. The expansion of the upper middle class was due, in part, to a growing respect for people adept at analyzing and mastering specialized bodies of knowledge; a class of experts and managers in and outside of business.

Livingston: A New Type of Suburb

The growth of the upper middle class in New York City accelerated suburban growth. From its earliest days, Elliottville appealed as a retreat from the city, easily reached from Lower Manhattan by a pleasant ferry ride. In the 1880s, as more people could afford houses outside Manhattan, the impact on Elliottville was inevitable. Improvements in street railway networks in Manhattan that reduced travel times within the city (the elevated train system had reached Battery Park by 1870) meant that commuting greater distances was possible. On Staten Island, entrepreneur Erastus Wiman (1834–1904) centralized transportation services in a neighborhood somewhat south of New Brighton that he called St. George. Centralization meant that Staten Island came to have one regularly scheduled ferry into Manhattan reached by railway and streetcar lines from all over the island.[1] The impact on Elliottville was almost immediate and was symbolized and advanced by the 1886 sale of the late Anson Livingston's house. His widow, the seventy-seven-year-old Ann (née Greenleaf) Livingston (1809–1887),[2] who turned out to be in the last year of her life, sold her mansion to be used as a railway station (after Anson Livingston's death he was found to be not as wealthy as previously thought).[3] The surrounding area, including Elliottville, was soon called "Livingston."

The designation "Elliottville" had begun to weaken as early as the 1860s as areas around the neighborhood became more populated and Elliottville blended into the larger precinct of West New Brighton. Once the Livingston railway station was established, the facility provided a landmark and name for an area that still felt distinct from West New Brighton, even though it was entirely residential.

Elliottville's intimate connection to the waterfront through a neighborhood ferry dock also changed when ferry services were centralized in St. George and a horsecar line separated Elliottville from the shore. The shore itself between Livingston and St. George also took on a new, industrial character with the advent of borax, plaster of Paris, and cement works. In the days of the Staples family, their boathouse had served as a neighborhood social magnet, with children swimming from the nearby beach and Mrs. Staples taking the children on excursions across the Kill van Kull to the salt marshes. By the late 1880s the Stapleses were gone, along with their house.

The changes in the 1880s were less dramatic than they might have been since a few families continued to reside on large tracts of land in Elliottville. One such family, that of John C. Henderson, had arrived in Elliottville in 1859 and shared some of the values of long-settled families. Other, more recently arrived families, also fit into the neighborhood more readily than had the Gilded Age yachtsmen and established family homes

Figure 6.1. The tracks of the horsecar railroad and the Staten Island Rapid Transit separated Elliottville from the open water of the Kill van Kull by 1887. *Source*: F. W. Beers, Atlas of Staten Island, Richmond County, New York (New York: J. B. Beers, 1887), section D. Courtesy of College of Staten Island, Archives & Special Collections. Public domain.

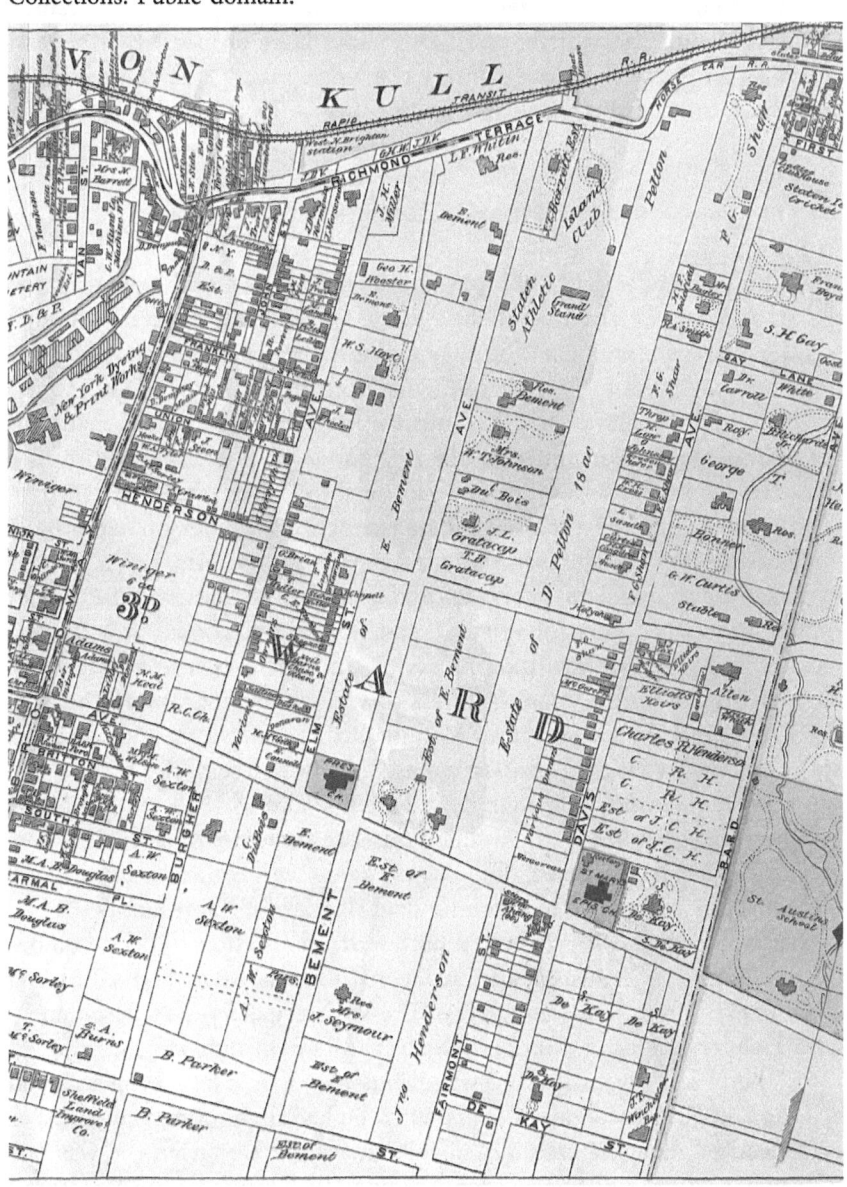

that they maintained over decades. Some of these were members of the Bonner family, who had made their fortunes in brokerage businesses in the 1860s and 1870s. Family members purchased several estates adjacent to each other in the early 1880s that became generational family homes. A somewhat later newcomer, Philip Rokeby, an English businessman involved in international ventures, also had a large property that he, and later his daughters, used as a primary residence. Finally, the de Kay family continued to keep their land mostly intact.

John C. Henderson

The John C. Henderson (1809–1884) property was on Bard Avenue across the street from the houses of the Shaws, Gays, and Curtises. Although Henderson was a merchant, he shared the social commitments and New England connections of earlier residents. Born in Cincinnati, Ohio, where his civil engineer father had laid out the city, Henderson had made his fortune in Manhattan. Entering the dry goods store of R. L. Smith as a clerk, he worked his way up to a partnership. When the firm failed in 1848, creditors agreed to partial compensation, but Henderson felt morally obligated to pay in full, even though repayment took him years. He was financially successful in later endeavors, including the manufacture of rubber products (shoes, shoe soles, and waterproof goods) at a factory, located in Paris, that was the first of its kind. He was also a partner in Henderson and Smyth, manufacturers of artificial flowers and feathers. In 1880, he founded the Matteawan Manufacturing Co., which imported furs and produced wool hats and straw-based fashion accessories.[4]

Henderson moved his family to Staten Island in 1859, staying at the Pavilion Hotel while a Bard Avenue house was being completed. The residence, called Linden Lawn, built of gray stone with brownstone cornices, was substantial, designed to accommodate Henderson's large family (he had twelve children who survived to adulthood). In addition to deep porches overlooking a generous expanse of lawns, Linden Lawn had a bowling alley, conservatory, and art gallery. The sizable gallery was designed to hold Henderson's art collection, which had its own published catalog.[5]

There were several reasons why Henderson would have been accepted by long-settled Elliottville residents. First, he had high moral standards, as evidenced by repaying creditors in full, and was a Unitarian (he was one of the first trustees of Staten Island's Unitarian Church of the Redeemer, along with George William Curtis). Second, while many mercantile businesses in New York had links to the slave economy, his did not; nor was he a war profiteer. Thirdly, he had strong ties to New England through his second wife, Jane Louisa Rapallo (1821–1880), whose aunts and uncles were important in Boston social life: one was the principal of the Boston Latin School, a Boston public official, and an East India merchant; another brother was the most distinguished astronomer of his generation; and one sister was a well-known poet.[6]

While the full range of Henderson's political and social commitments are not as obvious as those of some of his neighbors, his Manhattan real estate development, Henderson Place, is an indicator of his convictions. The tract had been part of John Jacob Astor's Hellgate estate when Henderson purchased it in 1869 and it was off the street grid. Even in 1879 after streets were established around the property at the intersection of Eighty-Sixth Street and Avenue B (now East End Avenue), it was still too remote to appeal to anyone but working-class people. Yet when Henderson constructed thirty-two houses between 1880 and 1882, he did not build tenements. He hired the architectural firm Lamb & Rich to design brick houses in the most fashionable styles of the day. The townhouses were somewhat narrower than others, but that meant Henderson could rent them for less than his rivals and still make a profit. In a very short period, they were appreciated for their charm, became sought after in the 1920s, and were among the first New York City structures to be landmarked by New York City in 1969.[7]

The care with which he constructed working-class housing, just as the way in which he had much earlier worked to repay creditors, along with his focus on building profitable businesses and raising a family (rather than club memberships and Manhattan society life), mark him as similar to long-settled Elliottville families. He was also notable for keeping intact his large property on Bard Avenue, even though, as a sometime real estate developer, he must have seen the potential for selling land or establishing rental properties.

After Henderson's death in 1882, maps show his property as owned by Henderson Real Estate. The tract was considerable, extending between Bard Avenue and the boundary of Snug Harbor (now Kissell Avenue) in one direction and from today's Castleton Avenue to today's Amelia Court on the other side (William Soutter's estate was on the other side of Amelia Court). As late as the first decade of the twentieth century, Linden Lawn's grounds and most of the Henderson Real Estate land was undeveloped, except for a small section along what had come to be called Henderson Avenue. The intact Henderson property, along with that of Anna Curtis, helped the heart of Elliottville retain much of its original character into the first decades of the twentieth century. Additional properties were preserved by members of the extended Bonner family.

The Bonner Family

In 1882, the year of Frank Shaw's death, the Minturns sold the Shaw family house on Bard Avenue to George T. Bonner (1837–1924), a wealthy man who had retired in 1877 at the age of forty.[8] Although his commitments differed from those that prompted Frank Shaw to retire, the men spent their retirements in broadly similar ways, devoting themselves to family life, past times, and philanthropy.[9]

George Bonner was born in Canada to an English immigrant family with a successful lumber business.[10] In 1851 his immediate family followed his oldest brother, newspaper man John Bonner (1828–1899),[11] to New York and later to Southfield, Staten Island. By this time, John was working as editor of *Harper's Weekly*, and the Bonners, like their neighbors—William K. Vanderbilt, Franklin B. Osgood, and Sir Roderick Cameron—were members of the American Jockey Club.[12]

When George Bonner began work in 1852, it was as a Manhattan shop clerk; however by 1856 he was working for the Wall Street brokerage firm de Coppet & Co.[13] Later, he established a brokerage business with his brother Edward Bonner (1838–1911).[14] In 1869, George Bonner married Isabel Grace Sewall (1842–1912) and established his own household.[15] Over the course of his life, he owned increasingly grander houses in Manhattan, culminating in 1910 with a Georgian Revival townhouse he commissioned from Grosvenor Atterbury at 18 East Seventy-Fifth Street.[16]

Although Bonner had impressive residences elsewhere, he kept his house on Bard Avenue until his death. Bonner renamed the house Frank Shaw had built Stadacona, after an area of Quebec where he spent his childhood.[17] Although he probably made alterations (we know, for instance, that he commissioned a pipe organ for the residence, constructed at the cost of $15,000, that was twenty-six feet high), the structure's footprint remained unchanged.[18] His brother, Edward Bonner, also purchased a large house on Bard Avenue, further to the east, from Benjamin Richards Jr., a real estate investor and New York Yacht Club (NYYC) member, and named his property Inchegeelagh.

Somewhat later, in 1886, Bonner's sister and her husband bought a house in the neighborhood. Mary Irene Bonner (1840–1921) had married Francis Ogle Boyd (1838–1900) in 1865 and the couple had lived in Chicago before returning to Staten Island. They purchased what had been the summer house of Stewart Brown, a Wall Street broker, on Livingston Court (a short street linking Bard and Davis Avenues), making the property their primary residence where each of them lived for the rest of their lives.[19]

Newspaper articles from the 1880s and 1890s reveal that the Bonners and Boyds were active in the social life of their neighborhood and Staten Island, generally. They were members of the Staten Island Country Club (the name of which changed over time) and the Richmond County Hunt Club, participating in dances as well as foxhunts. Nearer their house, they participated in clubs that met on the grounds of the Staten Island Athletic Club, including the North Shore Lawn Tennis Club. They also attended subscription balls at the German Clubrooms and the New Brighton (debutante) Assemblies at the Hotel Castleton and hosted related dinner parties. In 1893 George Bonner's wife was a leader of the Women's World's Fair Committee of Richmond County that put together an exhibition and related programming for the Chicago World's Fair.[20] They also attended many benefits for local institutions, like the S. R. Smith Infirmary, a publicly supported health care facility, which Frank Shaw and his family had helped found.[21] George Bonner was also an officer in the Staten Island Committee for the Prevention of Cruelty to Children founded by George Curtis.[22] The Bonner family was active in St. John's Episcopal Church on Staten Island, and when George Bonner's only child, Maud, married Francis Higginson Cabot (1859–1939) in 1893, the ceremony was held there, rather than in a Manhattan church popular with society.[23]

While George and Edward Bonner had made fortunes and lived on their investments, their brother-in-law Francis Ogle Boyd was an upper-middle-class manager. Boyd was born in Newry, County Down, Ireland. He arrived in New York City in 1851 as a thirteen-year-old with his two older brothers and a sister. He eventually worked as an alcohol distributor. He relied on producers in the major grain-producing areas of the Midwest, which may be why he and Mary lived in Chicago for as much as a decade after they married.

Boyd's firm, F. O. Boyd & Co., was one of the largest commission liquor houses in New York City. The firm had repeated legal difficulties in the 1870s over tax issues and was smeared in the press as party to "whiskey frauds."[24] Although the allegations did not lead to convictions, in 1878 F. O. Boyd & Co. declared bankruptcy due to the impact on the firm's reputation. The reorganized F. O. Boyd & Co. became a distributor of California wines and brandies. By 1890, Boyd chaired the Committee on Distilled Spirits of the New York Produce Exchange and was involved in other industry-wide organizations.[25] In 1890 and 1899 F. O. Boyd & Co. was repeatedly the assignee for wine and liquor merchants who had fallen into debt.[26]

Operating a successful business transporting and distributing alcohol is exactly the sort of occupation that one might think of as a post–Civil War phenomenon, dependent upon the development of corporate structures that supplied alcohol in quantity, as well as dramatically improved national transportation networks. As a manager, Boyd needed to know competing suppliers, distributors, and market conditions. To guarantee profit margins, Boyd would have to be current on legislation affecting his industry, particularly as it related to import duties and taxes. So it is no surprise that his name is associated with Staten Island political committees in newspapers of the time.

Ralph Rokeby

Ralph Thomas Rokeby (1863–1924) arrived on Bard Avenue considerably after Boyd and the Bonners. Nonetheless, he helped maintain the character of the Bard Avenue neighborhood far into the early twentieth century due to his attachment to his estate property, named Willowbrook. Like the Bonners and Boyd, Rokeby was an upper-middle-class businessman and an immigrant. He managed an international corporation and his family had been English landed gentry as far back as the thirteenth century. Rokeby's father, the Rev. Henry Rokeby (1831–1921), was the Archbishop of Leicestershire and Lord of the Manor of Arthingworth. Although Rokeby got a superior education at the Charterhouse School, he was a second son, and one gets the impression that he had to make his own way in the world.[27]

Rokeby did not arrive in the United States until 1882, after commencing a business career in Manitoba, Canada, holding executive positions in banks, corporate agriculture, railroads, and commercial breweries.[28] How he made the transition to New York is unclear. He may have had a connection to Boyd through the brewing industry, and several of his English friends were based in Manhattan. In 1898, Rokeby was one of the incorporators of the National Hudson Bridge Co., formed to construct a bridge across the Hudson to connect New York City with New

Jersey.²⁹ In 1898 he and some of the bridge company principals founded Uvalde Asphalt Co.³⁰ He continued as president of the company until his retirement in 1922. Uvalde received large city and state contracts to pave roads in and around New York City but was also international in scope. In Venezuela, Uvalde was responsible for building railroad track beds to a gold mine. The government of Cuba contracted with the firm to install a sewage system.

Through newspaper coverage of society weddings, we know that Rokeby was friends with Beverly W. Robinson Jr., the Bard Avenue resident from whom Edward Bonner purchased his house, and with Edward's son, Reginald E. Bonner (1873–1949), and Francis O. Boyd's son, Carlisle. Reginald and Carlisle were ushers for Rokeby's own marriage ceremony in 1900 to Maud Julia Eden (1877–1957).³¹ Prominent among the guests was former Staten Islander Anson Phelps Stokes (1838–1913).³² Eden was the daughter of Manhattan physician Dr. John Herman Eden, who had become wealthy as a real estate investor.³³

Another Staten Islander, Eberhard Faber (1859–1946), was also prominently mentioned in the coverage of Rokeby's wedding because the newlyweds stayed in his house during the first months of their marriage. Although Faber did not live directly on Bard Avenue, he did live nearby, and he was a great supporter of the Staten Island Athletic Club at the foot of Bard Avenue. Faber's father, John Eberhard Faber (1822–1879), of the Faber pencil manufacturing family, had settled on Staten Island on the edge of Elliottville in the late 1860s and raised his family there. Eberhard remained on the property.

Rokeby's friendship with Eberhard Faber no doubt had to do with cricket. In addition to being on his school's cricket eleven, Rokeby had been a member of the Winnipeg Cricket Club in 1891, and even though he died many years after his cricketing days on Staten Island and had retired to Ascot, England, his New York obituaries described him as a noted cricketer.³⁴

The Staten Island Cricket and Baseball Club had five hundred members at the time of Rokeby's wedding and hosted international cricket competitions on the grounds of the Staten Island Athletic Club on Bard Avenue. Originally located in St. George, the club had moved in 1886 to the property originally owned by William Bard and then by Rufus King Delafield (he had married Bard's daughter Eliza).³⁵ Faber was a president of the club and repeatedly provided financial support until he inadvertently owned the property. The attractive grounds insulated Bard Avenue residents from shore industries. The athletic clubs (rowing and tennis among others) also functioned as social organizations, hosting balls and elaborate social events. Rokeby was on the first eleven of the Staten Island Cricket Club (SICC) for many years and was an organizer of tournaments, especially when play was against visiting British teams.

Another source of neighborhood enthusiasm for cricket was St. Austin's School, housed in the former Garner mansion. The property had been on the market for a decade when, in 1886, the St. Austin Episcopal School for Boys acquired the estate and added a gymnasium.[36] Rev. Alfred Garnett Mortimer, rector of nearby St. Mary's Episcopal Church, had founded the school prior to 1883 (the school's name soon changed to St. Austin's Military School). St. Austin's was modeled on English boys' schools and the resident masters came from such institutions as Cambridge and Oxford. The boys played cricket and competed in SICC matches.

The blocks near St. Austin's were the first to be intensively developed in a tract called St. Austin's Place. The development was less than a block from the Curtis house and George Bonner's Stadacona. More than twenty-five house lots were laid out in an area smaller than George Bonner's property.

The Enterprising Drake de Kay

While two of Commodore de Kay's children, Charles de Kay and Helena (de Kay) Gilder, were prominent in the cultural life of their era, Drake and Sidney de Kay engaged in business and politics, more closely matching the upper-middle-class managers discussed so far in this chapter. Drake de Kay's postwar business career focused on brokering deals. In 1871 he took part in a filibuster expedition to arm Cubans. Whether he was politically committed, or saw an opportunity to profit from arms sales, is unclear. In 1874 he promoted railroad tunnels underneath the Kill van Kull to link Staten Island docks and cotton warehouses in Tompkinsville to national markets.

De Kay's endeavors, in retrospect, seem more daring than practical, although he supposedly made a fortune. He established a Manhattan residence at 85 Clinton Place (today the address is on West Eighth Street) and was joined by Janet and Julia de Kay. At the time, Dewitt Clinton's widow lived nearby on University Place (the two block Clinton Place had been named in her husband's honor) and the address was highly fashionable.

In the late 1870s, De Kay began promoting mines through a firm called the American Bureau of Mines, of which he was the secretary. In 1878 he was involved with Horace Tabor's Chrysolite Silver Mining Co. (with properties in Leadville, Colorado). Based on reports of rich silver veins, the stock value increased rapidly, enabling high dividends. The mining required very expensive, deep shafts. Dividends were calculated to attract investment and had no basis in actual silver production. In 1879, Charles de Kay wrote Helena and Richard Gilder about his earnings on Chrysolite stock and later made them a substantial cash gift with some of the money.[37] As soon as 1880, though, there was no way to keep Chrysolite going. By August 1880, Helena wrote Drake de Kay was looking "very badly," has been "anxious and harassed about the mine," and is the subject of the "lion's share of abuse and vilification."[38] When the scheme collapsed later in the year, de Kay lost everything he had and much more. He then began working to pay back his debts. By 1885, de Kay was in the Bloomingdale Asylum.[39] When he died the following year from exhaustion, he supposedly was within a few thousand dollars of full debt repayment.[40] Drake de Kay's experiences are a good reminder that while emerging markets and new corporate structures in the decades after the Civil War helped create a new upper middle class, individual participants could experience devastating losses. Drake de Kay's brother, Sidney de Kay, also encountered financial challenges.

Of all the de Kays, with the exception of Janet and Julia, Sidney de Kay lived longest on Staten Island. During the Civil War, de Kay had been on General Benjamin Butler's staff and after the war the association continued, an association that he felt a need to defend to his family, probably due to the accusations against Butler of abuse of power and corruption before, during, and after the war.[41] In 1867, de Kay briefly absented himself from Butler's sphere of influence when he fought in the Cretan Revolt. Severely wounded, de Kay returned to Kaywood on Staten Island in 1868 to recuperate.[42] After his recovery, he was reunited with Butler, assisting him with the National Asylum for Wounded Veterans and later becoming Butler's private secretary. However, de Kay eventually returned to New York, again living periodically at Kaywood. He graduated from Columbia University Law School in 1870 and married Minna Craven (1843–1927) in 1871. She was the daughter of Alfred W. Craven (1810–1879), chief engineer of the Croton Aqueduct, and Maria Schermerhorn Craven (1813–1864), a relative of Caroline Schermerhorn Astor. Minna was well connected politically and socially. Perhaps it was merely a coincidence, but in the year following the wedding, de Kay was appointed United States district attorney for New York and he also obtained a staff appointment from New York governor John A. Dix. Members of the de Kay family had contentious relations with Minna for years. Although the dynamic is challenging to understand based simply on correspondence, it seems that Minna was considered pretentious and controlling.

Given the family tensions, it is surprising that when Minna came into her inheritance in 1879 from her father's estate, she and Sidney decided to locate near Janet de Kay, purchasing the burned-out Van Zandt house.[43] They rebuilt the house, renaming the property Haywood, and constructed two rental houses on the land, furnishing them with inherited Craven family furniture.[44] However, by the time Sidney de Kay died, Minna discovered she was living in a mortgaged property and was left to wrangle with her in-laws since the mortgage was taken from the Eckford Trust. Whether de Kay had directly invested in Chrysolite or not, family correspondence makes it clear that he aided Drake de Kay financially, perhaps out of a concern for his own public reputation.

Artists and Writers

Men like Henderson, Bonner, Boyd, and Rokeby made their fortunes by understanding post–Civil War changes that brought new national markets, robust transportation networks, and the rise of corporations. Another new element of upper-middle-class society was composed of artists and writers. After the Civil War, American literature and art gained international respect.

One longtime resident of Elliottville, Laura Johnson, transformed her identity in the 1870s and 1880s, becoming a published author. During the Civil War and afterward, she had been instrumental in establishing a posthumous literary reputation for her brother Theodore Winthrop. After the death of her husband, Johnson began to embrace her independence and satisfy her intellectual curiosity. For instance, she and her daughter Bessie traveled to Europe and met significant artists and writers through letters of introduction from her friend Annie Fields. Back in the United States she took singing lessons and began to perform in oratorio societies. She had written poetry privately for years, and now she edited it into a volume and published her work as *Poems of Twenty Years* (New York: De Witt C. Lent, 1874). Among her poems were several dedicated to her neighbors (openly to George Curtis and Sarah Shaw; privately to

Helena Gilder). Then, inspired perhaps by the Western travel accounts of her brother that she had edited for publication, she published an account of her 1874 travels in the Wyoming Territory with Bessie in *Lippincott's Magazine* in June and July 1875. Her sister, Elizabeth Winthrop, had the account posthumously published to honor Johnson (*Eight Hundred Miles in an Ambulance* [Philadelphia: J. P. Lippincott, 1889]). George Curtis contributed an introduction to the work, noting Johnson's contributions to Elliottville and concluding with a poem by him in honor of his "sprightly neighbor."[45]

Bessie Johnson, as "Elizabeth Winthrop Johnson," also became an author. In addition to publishing magazine fiction, she published novels and a book of short stories. Her first book, *Studio Arts* (New York: Henry Holt, 1878) was a guidebook to art that included definitions, an overview of nineteenth-century art, and a bibliography. *Yesterday: An American Novel* (New York: Henry Holt, 1882) traced the stories of young people and their activities around New York harbor on boats and beaches, with Staten Island viewed in the distance. *Two Loyal Lovers* (New York: Frederick A Stokes, 1890) was set during the Civil War. After her mother's death, she moved to California, living the rest of her life in Pasadena, and that state became the setting for her later works, including *Orchard Folk: Two California Stories* (New York: Continental, 1898).

Other Elliottville residents also became figures in literary and artistic circles in the 1870s and 1880s, including Dr. Samuel R. Elliott (1836–1909), Dr. Elliott's son. As a boy, the younger Elliott composed poetry and music that impressed his father's famous patients. Louis Gottschalk, for one, foretold a musical career. In the end, Henry Wadsworth Longfellow's offer to train him as a poet while living in his household held sway, and as an eight-year-old, Elliott went to school at Boston Latin School while residing with the Longfellows. Nonetheless, he prepared for a medical career, completing his coursework at his father's alma mater, New York Medical College, before he was of age. He received his diploma when he was nineteen. The following years he spent in further medical study in Heidelberg and Paris. In Paris, he was also admitted to study music at the prestigious Paris Conservatory, where he completed a diploma. After Paris, he spent time in Elizabeth and Robert Browning's circle in Florence (no doubt initially gaining entrée through the de Kay's since the Brownings were friends of Katherine (de Kay) Bronson and frequented her salon). In Florence he was appreciated for his piano recitals and musical improvisations.

After returning to the United States and fighting with his father's Seventy-Ninth Highlanders (he was later a surgeon in other Union units), he joined his father's medical practice, which by this time was located on the ground floor of the University Building on Waverly Place, a convenient location for the focus of his social life, Pfaff's. In fact, the medical office was informally characterized as an adjunct to that establishment, one where the writers who frequented the rathskeller were as likely to be fed and entertained as receive medical treatment. Elliott, who had lived in the Latin Quarter of Paris in the 1850s, seems to have found some semblance of his bohemian life there in the company of Pfaffians. His medical office was untraditional in other ways, as well as serving as an open bar and kitchen. It was claimed that he was one of the first physicians to use music as a therapy. Also, like his father, he sometimes "prescribed" a several weeks' stay at his country residence on Staten Island or at the Elliott family summer residence in New London, Connecticut.

Elliott published essays and sketches on the Civil War and accomplished women in *The Atlantic Monthly*, *The Delineator*, and *Harper's Weekly* and poems in the *Churchman* and *Congregationalist*. However, his greater output was in the form of spontaneous verse, musical composition, and plays performed in the circle of his friends. While Manhattan was a major focus of his life, he and his wife, Amy née Dinsmore, lived on Richmond Terrace near the foot of Bard Avenue.[46]

Without slighting Curtis and Gay, members of an earlier generation, one can say that de Kay family members were the most culturally influential figures in Elliottville in the last decades of the nineteenth century, becoming recognized arbiters of taste and friends and promoters of well-known American artists and writers. Helena's husband, Richard Watson Gilder, had grown up in New Jersey and defended the Union as a Civil War soldier. He found early success as a magazine editor, first at *Scribner's Monthly* beginning in 1870 and then as editor of *The Century Magazine* for twenty-eight years.[47] Much admired as a poet in his own day, he published nine books of poetry over his life. While courting Helena, Gilder spent time visiting on Staten Island and his son Rodman Gilder stated that the bulk of his first book of poetry was written while a guest at Kaywood.[48]

As the publisher of works by William Dean Howells, Henry James, Mark Twain, and Walt Whitman, Gilder helped shape literary taste. He also had a lifelong commitment to Progressive reform, focusing on good government, civil service reform, and improved living conditions and education for the poor, and he sometimes worked with George Curtis and Josephine Lowell.[49] His political influence was at its height during the presidential administrations of Grover Cleveland. He and Helena were close personal friends of Cleveland and his wife. Early in their marriage, the Gilders established a salon at The Studio, an old stable near Washington Square, at 103 West Fifteenth Street, repurposed for them by their friend Stanford White in 1881.[50] The Studio became an American version of Katherine Bronson's salon at Ca' Alvisi in Venice frequented by Bronson's great friends John Singer Sargeant, Robert Browning, and Henry James.[51] The Gilders' "Friday Nights" at The Studio also became legendary: "To the hospitable welcome of that modest dwelling everyone who came to New York in those days, bearing a passport of intellectual worth, appeared to find his way . . . [it was a place where] artists, and actors, musicians and writers . . . mingled with a varied collection of philanthropists, millionaires, and penniless philosophers."[52] The Gilders' social set included John Borroughs, Samuel Clemens, John La Farge, Emma Lazarus, Helena Modjeska, Thomas Moran, Augustus St.-Gaudens, Charles Dudley Warner, and Walt Whitman.

In addition to their salon and Gilder's role at *The Century Magazine*, artists were attracted to the Gilders due to their efforts to open the art world to women and artists working in the decorative arts. Helena Gilder was one of the founders of the Art Students League and of the Society of American Artists, a reaction to the staid National Academy of Design.

Charles de Kay, the sibling closest in age to Helena Gilder, was also deeply involved in literary and artistic culture.[53] After graduating from Yale in 1868, he traveled for a year in Europe, frequenting his sister Katherine Bronson's households in Paris and Italy and making friends within her social circle. Upon his return to the United States, de Kay quickly earned the nickname "charmer of New York." As in Europe, he continued to build friendships with artists and writers, including Helena Gilder's mentor, John La Farge, as well as Albert Pinkham Ryder, Augustus St.-Gaudens, John Quincy Adams Ward, and Daniel Chester French. Emma Lazarus, who was attracted to him, encouraged his writing and sent some of his poetry to one of her mentors, Ralph Waldo Emerson.[54] Nonetheless, de Kay's first book was a novel, *The Bohemian: A Tragedy of Modern Life* (New York: Scribner, 1878). The romance attempted to capture the excitement of social life in Manhattan in the 1870s. The main character, an impoverished Southern man, moves to New York to remake himself. Working as a shop clerk, he meets a wealthy heiress, and the rest of the novel traces the romance to a surprising denouement. Laura Johnson wrote of trying to avoid de Kay on Staten Island out of a fear that she would have to comment favorably on his novel.[55] Even beyond Staten Island, the work does not seem to have found much of an audience. De Kay also drew on Staten Island as inspiration for a short story and several poems that were published in his *Hesperus and Other Poems* (New York: Scribner, 1880).

The main focus of de Kay's writing, perhaps due to his social connections with writers and artists, was literary and art criticism. Starting in 1876 and continuing until 1894 he was the literary and art editor for *The New York Times*. After a stint as US consul general to Berlin (1894–1897), he returned to New York and wrote for *The New York Times Book Review* until 1923. He took a particular interest in the American Arts and Crafts Movement and wrote the authorized biography of Louis Comfort Tiffany.[56] Although his inclusive perspective on art would become customary, the

Figure 6.2. Charles de Kay traveled in Europe repeatedly and lived in Berlin as US consul general for three years. However, he said he preferred Staten Island to any other place. *Source*: Henry P. Wright, *History of the Class of 1868, Yale College: 1864–1914* (New Haven, CT: Tuttle Morehouse and Taylor, 1914), 118. Public domain.

fact that he considered photography and jewelry artistic endeavors was innovative at the time. In addition to contemporary criticism, de Kay published on Irish culture and Asian art and religion.

For many years of his bachelor life (he did not marry until 1888), Charles de Kay rented in the University Building on Washington Square East, the building in which the Drs. Elliott had their office.[57] The turreted Gothic building constructed for New York University in 1836 had a section of bachelor apartments as early as 1840 and Theodore Winthrop had partly set his novel *Cecil Dreeme* in the building.[58] The accommodations were spartan with no running water and heat haphazardly generated from open-fire grates or stoves. However, the central location and low cost made it popular with journalists, writers, and artists who found the structure and views across Washington Square Park inspiring.[59] The building was particularly convenient for de Kay since the Gilders were less than a block away at 103 East Fifteenth Street. He also lived for extended periods with Janet and Julia de Kay on Staten Island, and after 1883, summered at the Gilders' house in Marion, Massachusetts.[60]

Maria "Midy" Morgan (1828–1892)

Midy (sometimes also "Middy") Morgan, of all the new generation of writers in the 1870s and 1880s, became most widely associated with the Bard Avenue neighborhood. Given the fact that she was a journalist whose personal life was often the subject of newspaper articles, this fact is not surprising.

As we have noted, Janet de Kay kept most of her land in South Elliottville in the 1870s and 1880s, with few exceptions. One exception was her land sales to Margaret Stackpole Winchester (b. 1835) in the 1870s. Winchester and her second husband, banker and broker James Thorndike Winchester (b. 1845) built a mansion on the land near the intersection of Bard Avenue and de Kay Street.[61] Janet also used some of her land to build a house for herself and Julia after the failure of the Chrysolite mine meant that they were no longer residing in Manhattan with Drake de Kay. The frame house she constructed near the intersection of today's Davis Avenue and Dekay Street eventually had the address 435 Davis Avenue. Janet, Charles, and Julia all lived there in the 1880s. Janet may have built the house out of concern for Julia's future; Julia had never married, and relatives described her as eccentric. Janet was over sixty years old when

Figure 6.3. This house at the corner of Davis and DeKay Streets was the primary residence of Janet and Julia de Kay in the 1880s and the occasional home of Charles de Kay before his marriage. *Source*: William T. Davis, photographer, 1938. Courtesy of Staten Island Museum.

she built the house and may have been feeling aged or ill; she would only live for another six years.

The other plot of land Janet sold was to Midy Morgan in 1882. However, because Morgan was a British citizen, she could not take possession until 1883, through an action of the New York State Legislature, and the transaction was not completed until 1884.[62] The property was less than a block from Janet's new house.

The connection between Morgan and Janet de Kay is unclear, but Morgan was not just an anonymous single woman; she was nationally known. As one of the first female journalists in the United States, employed beginning in 1869 as a livestock reporter for *The New York Times*, she had been a work colleague of Charles de Kay for seven years by the time of the property purchase. Furthermore, Helena Gilder's sister-in-law, Jeannette Leonard Gilder (1849–1916), was a close friend of Morgan.[63]

Jeannette Gilder, like Morgan, was a journalist, and in the late nineteenth and early twentieth century people would debate about whether Gilder or Morgan was the first female reporter.[64] Gilder had also begun working in 1869, but for the *Register* (Newark, New Jersey). After Richard Gilder became editor of *Scribner's Monthly*, Jeannette became literary editor for the publication. She went on to become a drama and music critic for the *New York Herald*. In 1881, she and her brother Joseph Benson Gilder (1858–1936) founded the literary magazine *The Critic*, of which they served as co-editors until 1906, when it was purchased by G. P. Putnam's and Sons, who changed the name to present a third incarnation of *Putnam's Monthly Magazine* (it was with the first incarnation that George Curtis had been so disastrously involved). The reorganized publication, officially titled *Putnam's Magazine and the Critic: A Magazine of Literature, Art, and Life* continued to feature Gilder's popular column that she had developed for *The Critic* and called Lounger, a take on Curtis's well-known Easy Chair column for *Harper's Weekly*.

Gilder and Morgan's ability to earn a comfortable living as journalists was due to changes in the newspaper industry triggered by the Civil War. The accelerated development of telegraphy and railroads during the war led to national newspapers that could quickly receive news from around the world and distribute newspapers through the mail due to the expansion of the Railway Mail Service. The demand for war news also fostered the development of bigger and faster printing presses and methods of illustration that led to higher and higher circulation numbers. The modern mass-circulation daily newspaper and the national illustrated weekly newspaper became enduring legacies of the Civil War. Once war news no longer filled newspaper columns, the public's heightened news appetite created opportunities for greater numbers of journalists writing about a wider range of topics. Although getting a job as a female journalist was challenging, the possibility existed. The fact that Morgan was both a reporter and the subject of human-interest stories increased her marketability and, therefore, her ability to earn a living.

By the time Midy Morgan bought land on Bard Avenue in 1883, she had been a national figure for more than a decade due to the newsworthy fact that she was an independent woman who was able to support herself as a writer because of her expert knowledge about livestock—a topic pertinent to many people. Some earned their living raising poultry and cattle. Many more raised their own food and depended upon their own horses for transportation. While Morgan's columns conveyed useful information, her readers never seemed to get over their incredulity that a woman was considered an expert, with knowledge superior to her male colleagues. Other women in the United States supported themselves as writers, but mostly by writing serialized fiction or women's columns. Although Morgan's friend Jeannette Gilder was breaking new ground for women, as a literary editor and columnist, Gilder was working in a field in which women were active. Men were the experts in animal husbandry and no other woman claimed expertise.

Looking back at Morgan's career, it is obvious that she attracted readers by creating an appealing public persona to which a large cross section of newspaper readers could relate. Creating such a persona was necessary since so much about her may have troubled a nineteenth-century US public. To begin with, she was both unmarried and lived independently at a time when that was considered odd. Furthermore, she publicly frequented all-male environments when there was harsh social censure against women appearing outside the domestic sphere. Finally, she had been born in Ireland, never became a US citizen, and was in the public eye when there was still virulent anti-immigrant sentiment, particularly against the Irish.

The main elements of the popular narrative about Morgan, which appeared regularly across the decades of her career, are fairly consistent. Since most of the accounts were unsigned, it seems legitimate to question how much of the content she authored, in order to establish a public image that would help her professionally. The necessity for this made her different from Jeannette Gilder, whose career had been eased by her brothers and the fact that Gilder co-owned the publication for which she wrote.

The Midy Morgan narrative that appealed to nineteenth-century newspaper readers transformed the troubling aspects of her identity into assets. For instance, although she was the daughter of a member of the Irish landed gentry, she learned about horses through working in her father's stables. Furthermore, she did not inherit wealth and position. Instead, she was forced to leave home when her brother inherited the estate and she, her mother, and her unmarried sister Jane (1833–1899) were left with "a slender portion."[65] They left for Italy in 1865, not for pleasure but so that Jane could work as a sculptor. In Italy, Morgan got work as well; her knowledge of horses attracted the attention of King Victor Emmanuel II, who commissioned her to purchase Irish mares on his behalf. Her work in Italy also led to work in the United States when Americans she met there—Charlotte Cushman, among them—encouraged her to search for a job in New York City. When she arrived in New York, although she had letters of reference from well-known people, she had difficulties and had to support herself as a chambermaid. In August 1869, she finally got a job as livestock reporter for *The New York Times*. However, she faced hostility. She overcame the challenges to her career with knowledge, a direct manner, a lack of pretense, and hard work. It was only after she earned respect for these qualities that she became a well-paid writer, rewarded for her skills and able to live independently by pursuing her genuine love of livestock and horses. Then, after earning a fortune and anticipating retirement, she was able to build a house on the "Fifth Avenue of Staten Island" to finally establish a domestic life.

Although this popular narrative gave the general outline of her life, the actual facts had been reshaped to emphasize some aspects and downplay others. She was the daughter of Anthony Morgan (1785–1865) of Prospect Hill in Carrighrohane, County Cork, who owned a significant estate that included over 2,300 acres of land in Ireland and who had been a captain in the Ninety-Fifth (Derbyshire) Regiment of Foot.[66] Her father's principal heir was his only son, Anthony Morgan [II] (1858–1924).[67] Even though the popular narrative claimed that her father insisted she conform to traditional expectations for a lady, both Morgan, who was said to be fluent in several languages, and her sister Jane, who had received years of instruction as a sculptor, were educated at a time when that was not customary. Furthermore, even though Anthony Morgan [II] was the primary beneficiary of his father's estate, Morgan, Jane, and their mother were not exactly left impoverished by the death of Anthony Morgan [I].

They had the funds to live abroad for two years in Rome. Although the city may have been inexpensive, there were costs to living there and paying for Jane's activities as a sculptor. Furthermore, Morgan socialized with important people and needed the right clothing and the funds to engage in reciprocal entertaining.

Additionally, it was unlikely that sheer knowledge of horses would have earned Morgan a commission from King Victor Emmanuel II. At the very least, she would have needed an introduction. The introduction probably came from one of the nineteenth century's most enduring female celebrities, Charlotte Cushman, one of Morgan's most important contacts in Rome. Cushman was at the center of a circle of female sculptors, much written about at the time and in subsequent years, that included Harriet Hosmer, Edmonia Lewis, and Emma Stebbins; Jane Morgan was discussed alongside them in an 1866 article in *The Art Journal*.[68] The article recounted Jane's prior career, extending over the previous decade, which included private study with prominent Irish teachers and sculptors and creating prize-winning sculptures. The degree to which Jane was connected to the artistic household of "bachelor" women that Cushman maintained, at 38 Via Gregoriana, is unclear. However, Cushman hosted salons at her residence, where she entertained a wide circle of friends and acquaintances.[69]

Many newspaper articles said that Cushman, Stebbins, and Midy Morgan were friends, and given Morgan's horsemanship, the connection is plausible. Morgan was an unusually tall woman—over six feet, when the average height for a woman was five feet two inches.[70] She must have presented a striking vision riding on the Corso, a popular pastime of the era that Cushman and Stebbins also favored. Many of Cushman's friends were avid horsewomen. Among the known horsewomen in her circle in Rome were Welsh sculptor Mary Lloyd (1819–1896) and Lloyd's lover, Irish journalist Frances Power Cobbe (1822–1904).[71] Although there is no proof that Cobbe and Morgan were acquainted, it would have been extraordinary that they would not have been drawn together by Cushman, their shared Irish origins, and their love for riding.

Jane Morgan, on the other hand, was unlikely to have become part of the Cushman circle. Jane had the reputation of being a very religious woman. Indeed, all her surviving paintings are of biblical subjects. We cannot say for certain, but we can imagine that Jane might have had some distaste for the women in Cushman's circle, some of whom adopted male attire. At any rate, after about fifteen months Jane left Rome due to illness and returned with her mother to Ireland.[72]

At that point, Morgan followed Cushman and Stebbins to Florence, and it was there that she gained entrée to the stables of King Victor Emmanuel II.[73] Cushman made a point of befriending influential politicians and diplomats who could aid her friends. For instance, she had befriended Secretary of State William Seward and then influenced him into appointing her nephew Edward "Ned" Charles Cushman (1838–1909) as US consul in Rome (1865–1869).[74] Years later, Morgan named Italian noblemen as her acquaintances in Florence. Cushman is likely to have made the introductions and any of those noblemen may have presented Morgan to the King she acclaimed as "the most sporting of crowned heads in Europe."[75] From Morgan's perspective, one of her lifetime's proudest achievements was purchasing Irish horses for the King's stables. Not only was she entrusted with such an important task, she successfully undertook the responsibility of transporting the horses, over a trek that involved changing modes of transportation thirty-two times, mostly switching back and forth from railroad cars to steam ships.[76] In partial recompense for her services the King gave her a watch "from his breast," with his initials set into the case in diamonds, which she treasured and bequeathed to the Metropolitan Museum of Art. Morgan prized her connection to the King throughout her life and went into mourning for a year when the monarch died.[77]

Even though the popular narrative about Morgan claimed that she arrived in New York with little besides some letters of introduction, her experiences and the contacts she had made in Italy gave her advantages far exceeding those of the average Irish immigrant. Morgan left Italy in 1869, around the same time that Cushman relocated to London to begin breast cancer treatments. Morgan arrived in New York with letters of introduction to Horace Greeley of the *New-York Tribune* and Henry Jarvis Raymond (1820–1869), co-founder of *The New York Times*, as well as to Leonard Jerome (1817–1891). Jerome, "The King of Wall Street," was a great horseman who, along with August Belmont Sr. and other investors, had built Jerome Park Racetrack in 1866 in Fordham (now the Bronx) and had founded the American Jockey Club there.[78]

While popular narratives emphasized that the letters did not lead to a job (Raymond had died shortly before her arrival in New York and Greeley dismissed her out of hand), Jerome did provide entrée to the world of thoroughbred racing. Supposedly, Jerome had heard of Morgan in Paris due to her royal commission.[79] Jerome provided a letter of introduction to American Jockey Club member Manton Marble (1834–1917), proprietor and editor of the *New York World*, who tried Morgan out by sending her to report on the 1869 Saratoga race meeting.[80] Jerome, August Belmont Sr., and Sir Roderick Cameron all had horses in the various races, and all of them would become Morgan's friends.

While Marble did not give her a continuing position, he did give her articles front-page placement.[81] Furthermore, in November 1869, *The Sun* published a front-page notice that Morgan was seen riding in Central Park on the horse of Mrs. August Belmont[82] and referred to Morgan as the "distinguished agricultural writer," even though she had only published a few articles. Without Jerome, it seems incredible that so shortly after arriving in the United States Morgan would have been riding a Belmont horse. Furthermore, Jerome was probably the person who introduced her to William Kissam Vanderbilt (1849–1920). Vanderbilt had been born on Staten Island and was the eldest son of William Henry Vanderbilt (1821–1885), who was the eldest son of Commodore Vanderbilt. Although much younger than Jerome, like him Vanderbilt was a sportsman. Both of them were NYYC members and both were founders of the Coney Island Jockey Club and of the Sheepshead Bay Racetrack. Vanderbilt seems to have introduced Morgan to his father. Several articles published during her lifetime claimed that Morgan and William Henry Vanderbilt became friends and that he helped her invest in the New York Central Railroad.[83]

While Morgan descended from a significant Irish family, had impressive social connections in Italy, and frequented the most elevated circles in US horsemanship, to have broad public appeal she needed to appear self-made. So articles about her claimed that she had given her last coins to a beggar on her first day in New York and supported herself as a chambermaid at the Stevens House (a Lower Manhattan hotel) when she first arrived in New York.[84]

Another matter that her public persona needed to navigate was the fact that she was a woman in a man's profession. This was done by establishing her as a larger-than-life figure who exploded traditional gender roles. She was said to be admirably unwomanly. Admittedly, this was an odd emphasis given the fact that attention was being called to her because she was a woman. Nonetheless, she was celebrated as a "very masculine looking woman."[85] In part, this was attributed to her height, which was reported variously to be up to six feet four inches. She was also said to have broad shoulders and not to "mince" when she walked. Without dainty, ladylike steps, people claimed she appeared to be a man dressed in women's clothing, not knowing that one of her legs had been crushed in a horse-riding mishap.[86] Furthermore, instead of wearing the fashionable clothing of a lady, she wore practical clothing and shoes to the stockyards. She also had none of the politesse or affected gentility of a lady. Instead, she had a direct, no-nonsense manner that helped her in dealing with rough men. Also, unlike a lady, she did not rely on men to defend her, rather she was able to physically intimidate men by carrying her own gun for self-defense against those males who assumed they could easily take advantage of a woman. In summing up her qualities, one article asserted, "Soundly practical is she and determinedly prosaic . . . she has a penchant for pigs."[87]

Of course, the danger in placing too much emphasis on Morgan's manly virtues in the era of the cult of true womanhood was that she might appear aberrant since ladies were assessed with reference to domesticity, piety, purity, and submissiveness.[88] One article said Morgan's tastes were "gentlemanly."[89] In the stockyards of Communipaw, she was supposedly nicknamed "The Last Rose of Summer"[90] due to her unwed status. Furthermore, she was outspoken in denying any interest in marrying. In this context, to forestall claims of deviance, articles emphasized that she was the refined daughter of an aristocrat and spent time in the court of a king. Others pointed out that despite her dress, she was always a lady, with immaculately white skin and the ability to remain "self-possessed, dignified and lady like," even in the roughest settings.[91] Her exterior "concealed a heart that was all genuine and womanly."[92]

The careful management of her public persona was clearly successful. By 1871, in addition to *The New York Times* she was writing for *Turf, Field, and Farm* and was listed in *Livestock Journal* advertisements as one of their "eminent and able writers."[93] Over the course of her decades-long career, she used the credibility she had earned to advocate for some of her causes. She encouraged horsemanship as a means of improving the health of women and she disdained opulent riding attire and equipage as being in poor taste.[94] She wrote passionately in defense of animals, with rhetoric calculated to win over an audience convinced that animals had no purpose beyond the uses to which humans put them. She encouraged owners to understand horse behavior and use fairness and kindness to make them more productive and valuable.[95] She tried to ameliorate the suffering of cattle on stock cars and in stockyards, using the argument that healthy, uninjured cattle brought more money.[96] She also suggested improvements in the design of stock cars and stockyards. Her efforts led to testimony in Washington and a special meeting with President Chester Arthur.[97] Furthermore, she advocated for more humane treatment in raising

Figure 6.4. While news stories described Midy Morgan as manly, images of her show a middle-aged woman in practical attire. Sizer, the phrenologist, said, "Being six feet high, and endowed with an ample amount of bone and muscle, she was a good representative of the Motive Temperament." *Source*: Nelson Sizer, *How to Study a Stranger by Temperament, Face and Head* (New York: Fowler and Wells, 1894), 63. Courtesy of Amherst College Archives and Special Collections. Public domain.

FIG. 67.—MISS MIDY MORGAN.

poultry, again emphasizing the financial benefits to owners of healthy birds.[98] Finally, she turned her attention beyond agricultural production to condemn the killing of animals for reasons other than food production.[99] In particular, she encouraged milliners to rely on artificial flowers and fruits, rather than feathers. She expressed horror over the massacre of wild birds that was pushing some species into extinction and pointed out that many economically distressed girls and women would be able to support themselves by producing ersatz millinery items if the use of bird feathers was banned.[100]

Midy Morgan's House

We have seen how Elliottville's built environment expressed residents' understanding of their relationship nature and to each other. Morgan's house, as the most distinctive house to be constructed in Elliottville, and one about whose interior we know most, is worthy of in-depth consideration. Unlike other Elliottville houses at which we have looked, it was not architect designed. Morgan planned the residence to address her priorities. The house was also unlike others in Elliottville intended to house a family unit with husband, wife, children, and servants. Instead, the building was for Morgan and her sister. Finally, while Ranlett-designed houses were meant to refine the taste (and thus morals) of passersby and houses like Garner's were meant to impress, the focus of Morgan's house was internal, on the residents. The only consideration given to nonresidents focused on securing the property from their intrusion. In the end, no matter Morgan's intentions, the house was transformed by the interior her sister created, which, as a perfect expression of the emerging English Arts and Crafts Movement, was a complete rejection of the burgeoning industrial, modern age that Morgan had successfully navigated to acquire the fortune that paid for the house.

Many articles were written about Morgan's house between 1888 and 1902, and all of them identified the place as her future retirement home. While that may, in fact, have been her plan, a house on Bard Avenue was inconsistent with her public persona. Living in a house on Bard Avenue would have identified her in the public mind with the "Fifth Avenue of Staten Island," a locale of mansions. Furthermore, one could only imagine Morgan living in such a place if she had in fact retired. How could such a dwelling, on a suburban plot, with no space to graze cows or horses or have pigs or even flocks of poultry, be the house of the famous livestock reporter with such an interest in animal husbandry.

The other structure identified with Midy's domestic life, a train flag station, was much more in keeping with her public persona. At some point prior to 1885, the Pennsylvania Railroad hired Morgan to manage Robinvale flag station near Metuchen, New Jersey.[101] As part of her compensation, she could live in the station and take free train rides for her commute to the stockyards in Jersey City and her office on Park Row. This station agent position earned her the distinction of being one of the first women to be employed in this manner. The station seems to have been rudimentary, with just one room downstairs and a sleeping loft reached by a ladder that could be pulled up for security.[102] Even though Morgan seems to have delegated most of her modest responsibilities to another woman (whose identity and circumstances are unknown), the thought of Morgan living in the flag station must have perfectly fit her public image as admirably practical and caring nothing for appearances.

Morgan's house on Bard Avenue was presented in the press in a manner just as calculated as her background, appearance, and personality had been presented. Accounts described her dwelling as unusual, practical, and yet refined.[103]

Some of the house's unusual character derived from the site. Still extant and located at an address that is now 16 Dekay Street, the house feels like it is atop a hill.[104] Bard Avenue between Livingston Station and Sidney de Kay's Haywood is relatively flat. A slope begins on the other side of Castleton Avenue that continues until leveling out around the plot where Morgan built her house. From the prospect of her house, the land fell away all the way down to Livingston Station and the Kill van Kull beyond. Morgan's three-story house was constructed with a central bank of bay windows on each level to take advantage of water views in the distance. From street level the continuity of the windows gives them the appearance of a tower.

Despite the elevation, the land was adjacent to a spring-fed pond and the house's immediate surrounding was marshy. Morgan had tried unsuccessfully to get publicly funded drainage.[105] So the approach to the property was through the marsh. She left intact the mature trees on her lot, giving the structure a woodland setting. This was out of keeping with the landscape gardening integral to Ranlett's philosophy. The wildness was also widely divergent from common middle-class property management in the time period. Houses were expected to be surrounded by meticulously maintained lawns, with symmetrical flower beds laid out in geometric patterns imitating oriental carpets, and exotic specimen plants, not native trees and shrubs.

The other unusual features of the house had to do with the architecture and decoration. The house had a mansard roof with coin-shaped tiles; such a roof was not unusual stylistically. Mansard roofs came into fashion after much of Paris was rebuilt during the reign of Napoleon III. Between 1853 and 1870 Georges-Eugene Haussmann designed street after street of apartment buildings that utilized mansard roofs to house concierges and servants. In the United States, the style evoked the most

Figure 6.5. Although Morgan's house had an austere exterior and puzzled people by not having a front door, the interior created by her sister Jane Morgan, incorporating animal hooves, horseshoes, and seashells, made the house truly unique. *Source:* William T. Davis, photographer, 1938. Courtesy of Staten Island Museum.

up-to-date contemporary design, becoming popular in the late 1850s and then peaking in residential architecture by 1885.[106] In the Bard Avenue context, the Garner mansion in the mid-distance, down the hill from Morgan, also had a mansard roof, but Morgan, who had a reputation for resisting fashion, likely chose the mansard for the practical reason of creating a studio space for Jane, echoing the use to which all of those mansards in Paris had, even by the late nineteenth century, begun to be employed.

In addition to the roof, the first thing one noticed about the house was that there was no porch and no central door. The entrance was on the side, near the back of the house. There was a shed roof, projecting from the tower-like body of the three-story house, supported by decorative cast iron pillars, but no porch floor, and the roof only functioned to protect residents and visitors from the elements. Today, the missing front door and floor-less porch make the house look odd, but contemporaries were scandalized by the design.[107] Almost every account of the house emphasized that Morgan designed the structure to accord with her own fixed ideas about construction and aesthetics.[108]

Another unusual aspect of the house was that it was overbuilt for domestic use. Instead of the typical frame construction of the period, the facade was brick, with two narrow bands of colored bricks as a decorative element, as well as bricks with impressed geometric designs and bricks set at an angle. An inner masonry wall behind the brick facade provided space for insulation. The innermost face of the second masonry wall was surfaced with Georgia pine. Finally, the floors and roof were supported by iron, instead of wood. These construction techniques made for unusually thick walls.[109]

The entrance, in addition to being to the side instead of the front, was also unusual for the security precautions—visitors felt like they were entering a prison. The exterior door, made of heavy, quartered oak and crossed and recrossed with iron bars, looked medieval and had no visible lock or latchstring, but a barred peephole. From inside, the owner could use an inner lock to secure the door and use the peephole to converse with a visitor or open the top half of the door without letting the visitor inside. Beyond the exterior door was a door of barred iron with a keyhole and lock. A third and final door of wood concealed the forbidding iron surface from being viewed from the interior.[110]

In an era when houses had many dedicated, closed off spaces (i.e., breakfast room, drawing room, parlor, butler's pantry, day room, morning room), Morgan, who supposedly hated interior doors, created open spaces. Each floor primarily consisted of one room, twenty-five by thirty-five feet, around a central chimney with two large fireplaces.[111] In the end, this arrangement proved too austere even for Morgan, and the original design was slightly modified to include a few rooms.

While security clearly dictated some design elements, a fear of fire dictated many others. The use of doubled masonry walls and iron beams was one fireproofing technique. Another was the use of iron for the only staircase. In addition to the ornamental ironwork steps and railings, the spacious, square landings were made of iron instead of wood. This type of staircase was becoming common in commercial buildings and would have been much costlier than a standard domestic staircase, as well as having an austere, institutional effect.[112] To further fireproof the house, the floors were tiled or fabricated out of poured concrete with added colorant.

Just as descriptions of Morgan contrasted her nonconforming gender presentation with her inner refinement and womanly heart, descriptions of her house contrasted the unusual exterior and architecture with the refined interiors designed by Jane Morgan, who claimed that every aspect of the interior matched Morgan's tastes. The furniture and interiors were a masterful early expression of what would come to be identified as English Arts and Crafts design. Furniture, household objects, and wall decorations were created through employing historic decorative artisanry (embroidery, wood carving, calligraphy, stained glass) and integrating the products into a harmonious whole. Despite Jane's importance to the design, journalists provided scant information about her sophistication as an artist, merely mentioning her study at the Royal College of Art in London and in Copenhagen, Dusseldorf, Paris, Rome, and Munich, preferring to emphasize the interior as a reflection of Jane Morgan's devotion to her sister.[113]

In fact Jane Morgan's creation expressed a sophisticated aesthetic that stressed the inherent beauty of materials, the importance of nature as inspiration, and the value of simplicity. For instance, while the floors were fireproof poured concrete, the concrete was red tinted and contrasted with cerulean stuccoed walls. The decorative elements of the dining room drew upon nature. Seashells from all over the world covered the ceiling; most left natural, but a few highly polished, gilded, or painted. The window frames had conch shells mounted over them with their rose-colored apertures facing out. Instead of a wallpaper border, Jane Morgan created a decorative cornice by pressing lobster claws, crab shells, and clamshells into wet plaster. In the drawing room, she skillfully carved rosewood and ash, using the contrasting colored woods to create patterned wood panels that covered the ceilings, lined the walls, and framed the oversized mantel mirror. She fashioned openings in the wood panels to frame and integrate her own biblically themed canvases into the overall design. As a tour de force of wood carving, she created an exact replica of the coronation chair at Westminster Abbey, copying the chair's elaborate lion sculptures and intricate gilding, to dominate the first floor room (presumably, the chair was meant as a conversation piece rather than a throne for Morgan).

The stairway leading to the second floor featured Jane Morgan's gilding and Gothic calligraphy. The gilding accented the portions of the iron openwork on the railings of the stairs and undersides of the landings. As a decorative motto on the first floor landing, she chose the biblical text, "Unless the Lord Keep the City, the Watchman Waketh but in Vain." The text is from the Songs of Solomon (Psalm 127:1). Perhaps she chose the verse to remind Morgan that despite all the precautions against fire and break-in, only the Lord could offer true safety.

Midy Morgan's quarters took up the entire second floor (Jane Morgan's third-floor studio and bedroom received no description in published accounts). The large bay window that dominated Midy Morgan's bedroom featured panes of colored glass. A calligraphy wall motto stated, "I laid me down in peace and waked for God sustained me" (a version of Psalm 3:5). For the wooden mantelpiece Jane Morgan carved the Morgan family heraldic device, a flying griffin wearing a helmet in turn surmounted by the head of a griffin with the reported motto "Fides et Aubax," although the journalist probably confused the actual phrase, "Fides et Audax," faith and courage.[114] As in the drawing room, Jane Morgan carved a piece of furniture to dominate the room; in this case, a settle. She fashioned the high-backed bench out of carved and painted wood to look like an open bookcase filled with the lettered spines of many books.

In the rest of Morgan's second-floor suite, Jane Morgan again introduced natural elements for decoration, employing animal bones and horns. In the bedroom, she attached white-polished oxtail bones to the walnut window surrounds. In the study she created a frieze of cow's horns mounted in an intertwining pattern, setting off the room corners with Rocky Mountain sheep horns. As a crown molding, she used pig's hooves mounted on circular wooden plaques. She ornamented the fireplace with horseshoes presented to Midy Morgan from racetracks throughout the country.

While contemporary articles described the interior of Morgan's house in great detail, the tone was not exactly admiring. Clearly, while the practical aspects of the construction were consistent with Morgan's public persona, the artistic interiors were more difficult to reconcile with the journalist. Furthermore, while contemporary readers, in the aftermath of widespread admiration for the Arts and Crafts Movement extending over several generations, might find the interiors appealing, in Morgan's time such interiors may have seemed eccentric.

There were other peculiar aspects of the residence. To begin with, although Midy Morgan paid for the house and planned the construction, she never really seems to have been a full-time resident. The place is listed as her residence in city directories starting in 1886, but her 1892 death certificate lists Robinvale, New Jersey, as her home address.[115] At the time, the residence would also have been considered odd for being an exclusively female household and one that had no servants. Jane supposedly performed many heavy and laborious tasks, like carrying wood and coal, keeping the furnace and fireplaces lit, removing ashes, spading the garden, pruning, and dealing with refuse.

No matter how intimately Morgan was associated with Bard Avenue in the national press during the last years of her life, no written comments of Elliottville residents regarding her or her sister survive. Of course, this may merely be due to a lacuna in the documentary record. Nevertheless, the Morgans may simply not have had much social impact on the neighborhood. Midy Morgan was obdurately single in a neighborhood that valued family life. Furthermore, she single-mindedly focused on professional activities and socialized mostly with other female journalists and leaders in the world of horse breeding and racing. Her sister, in addition to being focused on art-making, seems to have been a prickly character, prone to extended disagreements. She shows up in accounts of local board of supervisor meetings since she repeatedly complained about the lack of drainage around Midy Morgan's property. When streetlights were installed, she complained about inadequate illumination. She also got into an extended legal wrangle over the terms of her sister's will. Although Jane Morgan received a life interest in the Dekay Street property and her sister's substantial investments, she could only make testamentary disposition of 50 percent of whatever assets were left at the time of her own death. If she made no arrangements, the 50 percent would go to the Morgans' nephew John Thomas Hodder. In order to get some assets directly from her sister's estate, she initiated a lawsuit for compensation for her work on the interior of the Dekay Street house. More acrimoniously, she contested her sister's bequest of 50 percent of her estate to Margaret Selena

Eren Cameron (1867–1919). Cameron was the daughter of Sir Roderick Cameron, the world-famous horseman whose estate, Clifton-Berley, was located on Staten Island. The exact nature of Midy Morgan's connection to the woman, who was almost forty years younger than she was, is unclear, but Jane Morgan was incensed that her sister should settle so much of her estate to Cameron.

Although the social impact of the Morgans on Elliottville is unclear, their house had significance within the built environment, and the structure illustrates how the neighborhood was becoming less socially cohesive. Earlier properties expressed their owners' social commitments. Midy Morgan's house, both architecturally and in terms of landscape design, expressed an extreme form of individualism. On the one hand, the elements designed by Midy Morgan focused on personal safety. On the other hand, Jane Morgan's interior looked backward to England's Middle Ages, when Church and Crown controlled society. Focusing exclusively on the evidence of the house, even the attitudes of the Morgans toward nature seems very different from their transcendentalist neighbors. The Morgans seem to have thought nature should be controlled, rather than contemplated. In Midy Morgan's case nature was controlled through animal husbandry to select, through breeding, ever more desirable characteristics. Even though Jane may have found inspiration in natural forms, her art actively transformed natural elements into complex designs through time-consuming manipulation.

Conclusion

In 1880, Elliottville remained a distinctive neighborhood. The houses Dr. Elliott had constructed decades earlier were prevalent and many of the same families from the 1840s still lived in them. While the influx of wealthy men in the 1870s had not disrupted neighborhood life for longtime residents, as the 1880s progressed, social life in Elliottville did begin to change. Newcomers came to Bard Avenue, upper-middle-class men and the journalist Midy Morgan. While most of these newcomers embraced Progressive reform movements, many of them had little connection to New England and or to American transcendentalism. The newcomers did not move to Staten Island to settle near like-minded people. While some of them were accepted in Elliottville and participated in social life, their friendships in the neighborhood had a different quality. They associated with each other on the basis of living in the same suburb, which came to be called Livingston. As transportation networks continued to develop, new streets were laid out adjacent to Bard Avenue, new houses were constructed, and, as the population of the area increased, the old boundaries of Elliottville became less distinct. Nonetheless, the people who lived along Bard Avenue in singular houses, on large properties, still set Bard Avenue apart from the rest of the area.

In the 1870s a new generation began to dominate social life in Elliottville as children born shortly before or during the Civil War came of age. Their social activities were enhanced by the development of the Staten Island Ladies Club, the Staten Island Cricket and Baseball Club, and various boating clubs that grew dramatically on the grounds of the Staten Island Athletic Club on the old Delafield property along Bard Avenue. The clubs drew members from all over Staten Island and the region, attracted visitors from a broad area encompassing New York and New Jersey, and even attracted cricket teams from abroad. Nonetheless, the property was still a neighborhood resource for Bard Avenue residents, many of whom even took up tennis (the first court in the United States was set up at the Staten Island Cricket and Baseball Club in 1874).[116] The club property had so much impact locally that Laura Johnson remarked that she had nicknamed her neighborhood the "three of clubs," for the Athletic Club, the Cricket Club, and the North Shore Tennis Club.[117]

Nevertheless, from the letters of Sarah Gay and the journal kept by Louis Pope Gratacap (1851[?]–1917), it is clear that the households of Bard Avenue remained the bedrock of young Elliottville residents' social life.[118] Bessie Johnson, Sarah Gay, Rosamond (1848–1928) and Helen (1851–1920) Weston, and for a time Caroline "Carrie" Amelia Cranch (1853–1931) frequented each other's households and devoted a significant amount of their leisure to sketching, painting, and other artistic pursuits.

While Christopher Pearse Cranch and his wife were long-standing friends of George Curtis, the sometime Unitarian minister, transcendentalist, artist, and poet was also a friend of many in Elliottville. During the period from 1871 to 1873 the Cranches lived on Staten Island, renting a cottage from Louis Hoyt (which the family inevitably nicknamed Hoity-Toity Cottage). The rental, in addition to putting them close to Curtis, brought them near Christopher Pearse Cranch's sister, Margaret, who had married Staten Islander Erastus Brooks.

While Oliver Johnson and Charles de Kay spent a good deal of their free time in rowing and athletic pursuits at the Staten Island Athletic Club and elsewhere, they also socialized with the young women in Elliottville in organized and casual ways. Throughout the year, people hosted dances and dinners in their houses. At his house, Frank Shaw also organized lectures and musical performances attended by the young people. In the summer there would be long croquet games and tennis afternoons, accompanied by picnics. Young people would visit for tea and bring the instruments they played, leading to impromptu concerts and sing-alongs. Adults would organize masquerades, *tableaux vivants*, and amateur theatricals, as would the young people themselves. Such events involved weeks of rehearsals, the sewing of costumes, printing of programs, and decoration of home theaters. For a few years Richard Delafield (1853–1930) organized ambitious classical music concerts, heavily attended by young people in addition to adults.

At all times of year, the young people would go on long walks through the countryside to admire favorite views. An aspect of land ownership, unchanged since the Colonial era, was the concept of public rights of way. Walking paths crisscrossed the island with individual property ownership posing no impediments. From the earliest days of Elliottville, such paths extended from the neighborhood, intersected with others, and afforded the opportunity to walk for many miles. Such walks were an important form of recreation for George Curtis and Sydney Gay, and in the 1870s young people socialized on group hikes over the paths. One September 1873 excursion described by Louis Gratacap included Carrie Cranch, Bessie Johnson, Sarah Gay, Martin Gay, and Avis Leonowens. Gratacap captured the frivolity of the outing. At one point, some of the boys carried girls. The company urged Johnson on (she was prone to heaviness, easily fell behind, and was often teased for her general self-presentation).[119] Later, boys cut tree branches and pretended to be the "wood of Dunsinane" and dressed Leonowens in colorful leaves until she "looked like the Genius of Autumn."[120]

Smaller groups of young people also made excursions to Manhattan for art exhibits, concerts, and theater or to Philadelphia during the Centennial Exposition. Gratacap recounted orchestra and opera outings in his diaries. Most of Elliottville attended the exhibitions of the National Academy of Design and the American Watercolor Society, since they knew members (e.g., Christopher Pearse Cranch was an Academician) and the artists included in exhibitions, like Winslow Homer, Elihu Vedder, and their own Helena Gilder and Maria Oakey. Louis Gratacap was also a friend of Oliver Ingraham Lay (1845–1890) and Fidelia Bridges (1834–1923).

Concomitantly with the rising dominance of a new generation in neighborhood social life, an older generation was ebbing away. For instance, after Sydney Gay returned from Chicago, he devoted himself to writing history, becoming reclusive. He eventually became paralyzed after a fall. Frank Shaw died in 1882 and a few years later Sarah Shaw moved to New York City to live side by side with her daughter Josephine Lowell and granddaughter Carlotta at 118 and 120 Thirtieth Street. As the 1880s came to a close, changes in ownership and the transformation of properties were triggered by deaths: John Bethune Staples (1884), John C. Henderson (1884), Anson Livingston (1886), George Cabot Ward (1887), Sydney Howard Gay (1888), and Laura Johnson (1889).

Eventually, after Jane Morgan's death in 1899, Midy Morgan's house was dramatically altered as well, subsequent to the division of her residual estate between Margaret Selena Eren Cameron and John Thomas Hodder.[121] The house was put up for sale, but fortunately Hodder had arranged for his wealthy cousin Lt. Col. Anthony Hickman Morgan (1858–1924) to buy the interiors and the furnishings.[122] Once stripped out and transported across the sea, Morgan's architects incorporated these elements into a new, fifteen-bedroom house in Skibereen, Ireland.[123] The interiors of Morgan's house contributed to the success of the residence as one of the rare Irish examples of an Edwardian mansion to be constructed in the English Arts and Crafts style. However, Morgan's house and property—one of the most distinctive in the neighborhood—upon the removal of its distinctive interior was brought into line with the other suburban dwellings with which it was increasingly surrounded.

Chapter 7

Erastus Wiman and the Death of Elliottville

Introduction

Although the period 1880 to 1900 saw the departure or death of many members of the original Elliottville families and industrial and residential development in the vicinity, the heart of the community, the properties along Bard Avenue, remained physically intact. Some members of the Curtis, Gay, Henderson, and Shaw families remained, along with a few affluent newcomers with social commitments consistent with those of earlier Elliottville residents. The neighborhood remained distinctive for its residents, some of whom were national figures and most of whom had social significance that extended far beyond their local, or even regional, community. What finally drove away the distinctive people who had characterized Elliottville was the physical transformation brought by the development of the waterfront.

Early in this book a description of the waterfront drive that became Richmond Terrace conveyed some of the physical appeal of Elliottville, with its direct access to a shoreline whose only development consisted of rowing club and private boathouses. Directly across the Kill van Kull were the wild salt marshes of New Jersey. The busy docks and warehouses of Manhattan were six miles away, so that only the picturesque aspects of the harbor—the sailing ships from all over the world—dominated the view. Starting in the 1870s, the view over the Kill van Kull became increasingly industrial as oil refineries began to dominate the New Jersey landscape. The refineries polluted the air and water. Furthermore, the Staten Island shoreline was soon obscured by railroad tracks that were brought by Erastus Wiman's efforts to tie Staten Island into the national railroad network.

Social changes accompanied the physical changes. To promote his railway line, Wiman organized large-scale entertainments to bring people to Staten Island, increase transportation revenues, and eventually sell newcomers land. Some of these entertainments were adjacent to the ferry, where the New York Metropolitans baseball team played games. Major performers of the time appeared there as well, including the Seventh Regiment New York State Militia Band directed by Carlo Antonio Cappa, which gave concerts and provided accompaniment for the nighttime display of Wiman's grand illuminated fountain. Ringling Brothers's rival, Adam Forepaugh, also offered an elaborate show there, "The Fall of Babylon" in 1887, featuring chariot races and mock sea battles.[1] Further north, in the Port Richmond neighborhood, on the other side of Elliottville, Wiman established a kind of fairground, naming the park Erastina, in a play on his first name. For several seasons that venue was the New York City home for Buffalo Bill's Wild West Show. Wiman was aided in his efforts to attract people to Staten Island by the island's breweries, which opened beer halls to which working-class German immigrants flocked from throughout the city on weekends.[2]

With the consolidation of transportation to Manhattan beginning in the 1880s, Elliottville residents needed to travel to St. George to take the ferry. For Bard Avenue residents, who had been accustomed to taking the ferry from near the foot of Bard Avenue to commute to Manhattan in the company of their neighbors, the change was dramatic. Being outnumbered by a wide range of people was a new experience for them. Even if they took private carriages to the ferry, on the ferry ride there were people of all sorts, instead of neighbors. The change prompted many settled families to move away, including the Minturns.[3]

While on one level the change in ferry service and the increasing population in areas adjacent to Elliottville had a trivial impact on daily life in the neighborhood, on another level the changes were so consequential that they would bring an end to Elliottville. The neighborhood was being drawn into ever-larger social and political networks that would destroy the ability of Elliottville residents to maintain their romanticized images of themselves as Jeffersonian yeoman farmers.

An End to Living Cottagely

The built environment along Bard Avenue had remained remarkably cohesive from 1840 to 1880. The street's large houses were set within grounds and had outbuildings that enabled a degree of self-sufficiency. While their owner's philosophical perspectives may have varied slightly, householders in the neighborhood had some shared convictions that shaped antebellum Elliottville. William Ranlett had articulated a way of life he referred to as living cottagely that celebrated the freedom of independent households as expressive of Republican values, in tune with nature, and as the basis for the improvement of the community in which they were sited. Dr. Elliott's choice of Ranlett designs for so many of the first houses in Elliottville shaped the built environment in sympathy with Ranlett's philosophy for decades. While Elliottville residents may have articulated their perspectives in different ways, they were more similar than different in their convictions as to the importance of their lives as householders. Sydney Gay bought a property designed by Ranlett, implicitly endorsing the architect's views. In the course of his family's life on the property, the Gays embraced the concept of living cottagely through their landscape gardening and the energy they put into raising fruit and vegetables. George Curtis, as an admirer of Alexander Jackson Downing, was perhaps most in sympathy with Ranlett philosophically and frequently wrote to his friends about the inspiration he drew from the way in which his house was sited in the midst of nature. Since Ranlett openly critiqued the phalanstery life of Fourierists, one might think Frank Shaw was most at odds with the architect. However, even though Shaw may have built a house with aspects similar to Fourierist structures, he did so to create a space for perfected family life, not the communal life of the phalanx. He also hosted events that uplifted the community, like lecture series and orchestra concerts. While little is known about the architecture of the Johnson's house, Laura Johnson was known for her extensive gardens and she altered the third floor of her house into a ballroom to improve community life in the neighborhood by hosting social events.

Those who settled in Elliottville after Ranlett's influence had diminished were still heavily invested in the concept of the independent householder.[4] The Garner estate was grandiose but was not just showy. The property functioned like a small farm to provide food to the Garner family and their guests. The Henderson mansion, another house that was grand in scale, was large, not to be merely impressive but to accommodate the large Henderson family. The Hendersons were also known for their landscape garden, which was sometimes the setting for fêtes champêtres of a semipublic nature. Furthermore the Hendersons demonstrated a commitment to improving public taste by hosting lectures in their ballroom and opening their art gallery to visitors.

Elliottville residents in the 1840s through 1870s also had in common their alienation from urban life. Dr. Elliott believed that the air of Elliottville, close to the waterfront and scented by woodland, restored his patients' health, which had been impaired by working in offices and living in cities. Manufacturing facilities placed side by side with city residences, a proximity that contaminated households, had disturbed the Gays while living in a Manhattan boarding house. Other early residents like the Shaws and Curtises had become alienated from city life intellectually, through reflections prompted by Ralph Waldo Emerson, whose concept of self-reliance was connected to an agrarian ideal of providing for the material needs of oneself and family by engaging directly with nature to raise food. City dwellers were disconnected from nature and were dependent upon complex systems and captives to societal pressures that ultimately corrupted the individual.

Nonetheless, in the decades leading up to the Civil War, Manhattan had rapidly established itself as the most influential center of political, economic, and intellectual life in the United States, and New England intellectuals engaged in writing, publishing, and finance were inevitably drawn to the burgeoning city. Yet living in Manhattan was antithetical to the constellation of values held dear by men like Curtis, Gay, and Shaw—including intimacy with nature and a social life centered on family and neighbors. Staten Island made possible a life consistent with their values, while a short ferry ride provided access to their offices and the intellectual, social, and political opportunities of the city. They found the natural setting of Staten Island remarkable for the open land that afforded rambles through woodland, an undeveloped shoreline for swimming and boating, and the high hills that afforded remarkable views of the landscape and harbor.

The members of the New York Yacht Club who had moved to Elliottville in the 1870s were not alienated from the city in the ways Gay, Shaw, and Curtis were. However, even they chafed against the physical constraints of urban life. No matter how much money they had, they could only insulate themselves from the city's disease, odors, and lack of privacy up to a point. Furthermore, although their wealth could buy them substantial city residences, for open countryside in which to hunt and unhindered moorings for their yachts they needed types of space the city could not provide.

Living side by side with Gilded Age men may have presented personal challenges for Elliottville residents, but they were accustomed to living among men whose values they opposed. In the decades leading up to the Civil War, as Curtis, Gay, and Shaw devoted their energies to abolitionism, they were far outnumbered in their professional and social lives by men who considered their views radical and destructive. Part of being a light of truth in the world meant shining in the darkness. In fact, Curtis, while traveling around the country on the lecture circuit, welcomed encounters with people who opposed him; he could hone his persuasive powers by better understanding his opponents.[5] Even ordinary Elliottville residents, like Laura Johnson, whose life was circumscribed by the boundaries of the domestic sphere, went out of her way to be the "missionary, social" of the neighborhood.[6] She interacted with people from vastly different socioeconomic backgrounds whose personal habits and political and social commitments she found distasteful in order to provide them access to her own social and intellectual refinement. So no matter what complicated feelings settled Elliottville residents might have toward neighbors like Garner, they did not move away, but remained, committed to their family circle, neighborhood book club, local drama club, French conversation groups, front-porch socializing, "Germans," and united charitable efforts.

The 1880s newcomers to the neighborhoods surrounding Elliottville, attracted by expanding transportation networks, were categorically different from Elliottville residents of the 1840s because they were drawn primarily by the opportunity to affordably own or rent property. They were not alienated from urban life, but were simply a whole new class of commuters who could live on Staten Island and still get to their jobs in banking, insurance, and retail. These newcomers would challenge life in Elliottville in ways that the Gilded Age men had not.

As transportation networks on Staten Island developed, residential development took off in areas adjacent to Elliottville. The letters the Gay family received while they were in Chicago in 1870 and 1871 recorded dramatic change around the neighborhood, as houses were built on speculation and to serve as rentals. By November of 1871, seven new houses had been constructed across Davis Avenue from the Gays' property. Gay was advised to subdivide his own land to participate in the boom. Frank Shaw, the Curtises, and Laura Johnson all eventually owned rental properties in the area, even though they bemoaned the changes. Frank Shaw was most directly exposed to change due to the location of his new house. Although he granted that the horse cars were convenient, they passed by three times per hour, "very full and mak[ing] a horrible squeaking."[7] In dry seasons the dust from the horse cars went everywhere, upsetting Elizabeth Gay.

With population increases in areas adjacent to Elliottville, the neighborhood was impacted in an unexpected way. Elliottville became a locale within larger administrative designations, particularly since the neighborhood was entirely residential and nearby areas began to have commercial districts that became identifying foci. Due to this and other factors, Elliottville residents gradually lost the degree of independence they had in the 1840s through 1870s.

Their loss of independence was symbolized by a change in postal delivery. Elliottville residents were so engrossed in their neighborhood that they may have been oblivious to the fact that they had become part of West New Brighton from the standpoint of postal delivery. Bard Avenue residents were surprised when they could no longer simply use their street addresses without including the designation West New Brighton, since their mail would go astray. Their courteous letters of complaint did not alter the situation. The situation worsened once letters mailed on Staten Island went first to New York City to be sorted. In the end, Bard Avenue residents could only submit to being incorporated into a new neighborhood designation by the post office and grudgingly remind correspondents of their new addresses.

Their fight over postal delivery was just a small indication of the ways in which their properties were increasingly enmeshed in ever-larger webs of infrastructure that diminished their sense of living cottagely in independent households. Even though Ranlett had said his designs meant the poor man as well as the rich man could live cottagely, by the 1870s it was less likely that people of modest means could live in Ranlett style, even in the extended New York City region. Rapid increases in population continued to inflate land prices, and the typical plots of land purchased near Elliottville by people of modest means were not large enough to support the agricultural endeavors required to support even a small family. The houses built on them, unlike Ranlett's cottages, were of necessity orientated toward the street, with little space for landscape gardening. Increasingly, such houses needed to be supported by complex infrastructure.

Ranlett-type properties could accommodate wells, sewage pits, holding areas for barnyard waste, and rubbish pits. As the area population increased, and more people lived on smaller properties, disposing of waste and maintaining fresh water supplies needed to be managed. In the absence of knowledgeable municipal oversight, private companies formed to provide water and sewer systems, like the Staten Island Water Supply Co., incorporated in 1879, and the Crystal Water Co., which began operation in 1883. Sometimes several companies competed to offer the same services, disrupting or even sabotaging each other's lines.[8] At other times, individual companies simply did not have the technical expertise to provide promised services, even if they had successfully obtained a franchise from the local board of supervisors. After paying to connect to water services, people who lived on hills, for instance, found that only a trickle of water came from their taps and there was not enough water to flush toilets. Systems of authority and mechanisms for oversight were in development over a period of decades, making it difficult to prevent or even effectively censure individuals who diverted their wastewater into the streets or used their property borders for refuse and the decaying corpses of dead cattle.[9]

Managing water supplies is a complex matter, but even something as simple as providing street access to properties was challenging due to the lack of mutually agreed upon practices and divided opinions on responsibilities. With increased use, customary plank roads, graveled streets, and dirt carriage drives became unusable, and hard surfaces for sidewalks and paved roads, which had previously been exceptions, became the norm. The expenses often had to be borne by property owners. Sydney Gay got into an extended wrangle when his Davis Avenue neighbors decided that they wanted curbs and paving. Most of them owned modest properties, but the extent of Gay's property meant he had to pay a sizable amount of money. A similar controversy put Bard Avenue neighbors at odds when a street-widening project entailed much greater expense for owners on one side of the street than the other.[10] Often, after property owners paid assessments, the laying of sewer and water lines destroyed the streets or forced repaving because of the heights of manhole covers.

As properties were bought and sold and there was increasing focus on ownership and boundaries, property descriptions and addresses needed to be regularized. In the early days of Elliottville, when properties were not usually orientated toward a street, houses simply had names, like Linden Lawn or Ailanthus Cottage, and a local awareness of who lived where and the extent of their properties was adequate. With many people getting about on foot, there was also a shared comfort with the concept of a common right of way, with little concern for actual property boundaries. In fact, it was this concept that made rambles on Staten Island so pleasant, as people need have no qualms about crossing other peoples' land to admire views. All of this changed fairly rapidly in the 1870s and 1880s, and systems of property description with street names and house numbers needed to be established.[11]

In part, the need for systems of property identification stemmed from an increasing population with less direct knowledge of their neighbors and their properties, as well as the needs of companies, like suppliers of utilities or property insurance, who might rarely have direct contact with property owners. A rising sense of insecurity was another reason closer attention was paid to property ownership. Part of this feeling of insecurity came from alms seekers, sometimes in small groups, going from door to door. In earlier periods, most homeowners acted on a moral imperative to help anyone who asked, usually by providing food or small amounts of money. This practice was based in part on tradition, in part on biblical precepts, and in part on the assumption that the indigent were neighbors. As the population increased and transportation from New York City became easier, the beggars became more anonymous, and householders felt less convinced about how they should respond. One outcome was the founding of the Charity Organization of Castleton, with Elizabeth Curtis as secretary. The organization had the effect of deterring door-to-door begging by creating an application process for assistance supplied by centrally collected donations from householders, during which the actual need of applicants could be assessed.

Ruffianism was a more unsettling source of feelings of insecurity. While as early as the 1850s people had complained about the "rowdyism" of packs of boys and Elizabeth Gay had written to Sydney about their front gate being stolen and their orchard raided, the scale of rowdyism increased dramatically after the Civil War. In part, this was due to the greater numbers of young men and boys with free time on their hands and the increasing anonymity of individuals. The factories and infrastructure projects on Staten Island employed increasing numbers of young men and boys who had moved from elsewhere and lived in rooming houses. They lived outside the context of family life, where they would have had little free time due to household demands and constant supervision. Although they sometimes gathered in saloons (the brewery industry on Staten Island had grown rapidly and most breweries operated bars), they also formed gangs that would occupy street corners and harass passersby, particularly young women. People identified the rowdies with crimes against property, the arson of outbuildings and fences, and the increasing number of burglaries, although direct evidence was often difficult to accumulate. Several Elliottville residents wrote to friends about robberies. Lydia Maria Child responded: "I feel uneasy about accounts of thieves ravaging Staten Island. The feeling of insecurity occasioned by such a state of things is worse than the loss of property."[12] People found it difficult to rely on police enforcement. At first, county supervisors paid New York City to provide officers, but the arrangement meant limited hours worked by patrolmen unfamiliar with localities. Later, when a resident police force developed, there simply were not enough officers to provide coverage. Usually, enforcement efforts consisted of ineffective shows of force. For instance, when packs of feral dogs roaming at large became a major problem, police simply organized dog shoots, meaning that many families unobservant of the law lost their pets. These shows of force exacerbated class divisions. For instance, young men were punished for engaging in active recreation on Sundays (their only day off), and nude swimmers along the shore (a customary practice among males in most working-class communities) were fined. For decades, starting in 1860, public-spirited citizens had established and supported reading rooms to give working men an alternative to spending their free time in bars, but were periodically outraged to realize that reading room users spent their time playing cards, instead of engaging in reading and other self-improving activities.[13]

If living cottagely became challenging in the 1870s and 1880s due to the impact of population increases in the vicinity of Elliottville, residents were also challenged by new technologies that made their households less independent. Perhaps it is surprising that the earliest of these was the telephone. In 1882, the Staten Island Telephone Exchange Co., with Erastus Wiman as president, was established on Richmond Terrace in New Brighton. George Curtis wrote with pleasure when he and the Shaws were "on the telephone."[14] Lydia Maria Child was soon entranced by the idea of telephones connecting friends in this world, but more intrigued by the idea of spiritual telephones enabling communication through the ether with deceased friends.[15] While telephone use afforded new convenience in communicating with neighbors, it also introduced a new immediacy, which required adjustment. Much as Child was attracted to the idea, she did not think she would like to be constantly available to callers.[16] Surviving bodies of correspondence show that neighbors had typically sent notes to each other, even when issuing informal invitations or expressing gratitude for garden fruits or flowers. These notes, though casual, validated friendships and conveyed respect. Telephoning was devoid of the ceremonious quality of a written note, sent by hand, often through a servant. Over time, telephoning also had an impact on the tradition of making calls, in which women might visit a neighbor to socialize, often with a basket of sewing or other handiwork to avoid idleness. Men might call on male neighbors in the evening after dinner. These activities had a social dimension that telephoning did not, since a telephone conversation was between two individuals and in calling on neighbors one would inevitably engage with multiple members of a family, as well as other neighbors making calls.

Even technologies like gas lines altered social interactions. When lanterns and candles supplied light, a good bit of time was spent cleaning and readying lighting devices for the evening. Although this was sometimes a servant's task, it was also often an opportunity for the women of the house to engage in a shared activity. This opportunity for social interaction disappeared once gas wall sconces supplied lighting.

There were other issues with employing new technologies: the pollution created by large-scale manufacturing and the loss of local control to national corporations. Many longtime residents of Elliottville believed in an intimate connection between health and environment in thinking that is common today, but was less common at the time. Petroleum refineries began developing in Bayonne across the Kill van Kull from Elliottville in 1877, after the Standard Oil Co. took over a small refinery. The industry developed rapidly, and Bayonne became the world's largest center of oil refining. Even at the start, in 1877, Elizabeth Gay was writing, "Several people hereabouts have had both [headaches and nausea] from the petroleum smells. I hear people being sick from it more and more."[17] In addition to the air pollution, the water in the Kill van Kull was occasionally covered with oil slicks from the refineries and increasingly polluted by effluents from New Jersey factories. When one of the Minturn's children died from diphtheria in 1878, older people died of respiratory ailments, and the Gay's daughter Sarah Gay became disabled by headaches and attacks of rheumatism, many in the neighborhood despaired that their environment was becoming unhealthy. By 1887, local newspapers were calling incidents of "acid sludge" in the Kill van Kull an epidemic.[18] When Staten Island residents tried to get individual companies to take responsibility and modify their practices, each company claimed another was the culprit. Laura Johnson's grandson said that by the early twentieth century, when he was living in the Johnson house as a boy, soot-laden smoke had made the neighborhood uninhabitable.[19]

Living cottagely had celebrated the independent household as epitomizing individual freedom in the context of the Republic. By the 1880s, Curtis and other men in Elliottville were fighting the stifling control of political parties, epitomized by Tammany Hall, and corporate monopolies like Standard Oil. Their ability to live as independent householders had seriously diminished as their properties became enmeshed in larger and larger systems of external control and their households became dependent upon services like, gas, water and sewer lines, and electricity and telephones. The previously health-giving air and harbor water had surreptitiously fallen under the control of corporations, unresponsive to their calls for fair play. In the midst of all of these changes that had eroded their ability to live cottagely, Erastus Wiman, in the name of progress and prosperity, brought corporate control to their shoreline.

The Duke of Staten Island

In some ways, Erastus Wiman, the man often referred to by his contemporaries as "the Duke of Staten Island," exemplifies the rise of the post–Civil War management class. He got his start in Canada in the 1850s as a commercial editor and publisher. His success got the attention of Robert Graham Dun, president of a new type of business, a mercantile reporting agency through which subscribers could acquire objective credit information about companies. After a few years of proving himself in the firm's Canadian operations, in 1866 Wiman was made a partner in Dun, Barlow, and Co.'s Manhattan office. When Barlow died in 1880, Wiman purchased the deceased man's share of the company and became general manager, paying himself the considerable salary of $90,000.[20]

Figure 7.1. In the 1880s Wiman promoted so many Staten Island projects that the island was starting to become associated with him as much as it had been with George Curtis. Source: *Illustrated Sketch Book of Staten Island, New York: Its Industries and Commerce* (New York: S. C. Judson, 1886), 40. Public domain.

Through Dun, Wiman, and Co., Wiman was well positioned to see the opportunities that national markets and corporate structures presented. In one of his first ventures, he partnered with Jay Gould to organize the Great Northwestern Telegraph Co. of Canada, becoming the firm's president in 1881. However, the dream of linking Staten Island into the national railroad network and creating a profitable freight and passenger depot on the island soon preoccupied him.

Wiman had started living on Staten Island in 1865, in a house on Hamilton Place in Tompkinsville in an area later part of St. George. At that point, a very limited steam railroad passenger service operated between Tottenville and Vanderbilt Landing in Clifton, where passengers could transfer to a ferry that served South Ferry in Manhattan. Horse-drawn streetcars running from the Narrows around the shoreline to Mariner's Harbor provided additional passenger service on the Staten Island's North Shore (sections were in operation in the 1860s, but regular service did not come until the 1880s).[21]

By 1880, railroad development linking other areas around New York Harbor into the national railroad network was already underway or had been completed. At its closest points, Staten Island was within rowing distance of New Jersey, where both passenger and freight railroad service was rapidly increasing, but no bridges connected the two. In addition, from the shore near New Brighton, the island was only six miles across the harbor from Manhattan's freight docks and railway lines.

On the strength of a secret deal with his friend Robert Garrett, president of the Baltimore & Ohio (B&O) Railroad, that the B&O would be the railroad to benefit from Staten Island docks, Wiman began acquiring waterfront land for the railroad project and other land for investment since the railroad link would inflate property values. Garrett and Wiman were also in league with Reon Barnes, who could buy up land for wharves and depots from unsuspecting property owners through a dummy corporation set up by the B&O in the 1870s, long before any railroad plans had been announced.[22] While getting the land for his project was relatively easy, for Wiman to carry out the rest of his vision of consolidating railroad and ferry services on land he controlled, he needed to engage in complex negotiations.

First of all, the Vanderbilt family controlled the most important rail lines on Staten Island. Secondly, even if Wiman were able to get control of the Vanderbilt rail lines, to reach his waterfront land he would need to extend the rail lines through federally controlled land. Thirdly, although he controlled the land he wanted to use for docks and warehouses, he did not own the waterfront rights. When New Brighton was taking shape, savvy investor George Law acquired the rights to the land underwater off the shore. Finally, he would have to get legislators to agree to a railroad bridge linking Staten Island and New Jersey.

Although these were significant challenges, Wiman had another powerful friend in addition to Robert Garrett: Roscoe Conkling, lawyer, politician, and friend to railroad corporations. Like Wiman, he was an enemy of William Henry Vanderbilt. They shared their enmity with George Law. Previously, Law had mounted a rancorous fight with Cornelius Vanderbilt over ferry franchises. By helping Wiman succeed, in addition to their under-the-table financial gains, Garrett, Conkling, and Law all knew they would also irritate Vanderbilt.

Elliottville presented Wiman with a different sort of challenge from the others he faced. The most efficient way of connecting his land for the railroad depot with Erastina and New Jersey was by running the B&O freight lines along the waterfront, passing by the foot of Bard Avenue. To do so would separate Elliottville from the shore. One of the key features of Elliottville's pastoral appeal, access to the shoreline, would be forever destroyed.

Wiman anticipated Elliottville's opposition and took preemptive steps. In the public announcement of his proposal, which took the form of a lengthy letter to the *Richmond Sentinel* published February 11, 1881 (reprinted by Wiman as a pamphlet), he called out "some who would like to keep this suburb a rural arcadia," sneering at their concerns that "a railway across the waterfront may make some difficulties in the approach [to their] villas."[23] The audience for Wiman's pamphlet, of course, was the vast majority of Staten Islanders, who did not live in Ranlett-designed villas. Wiman asserted that while the "tastes" and "individual interests" of some might be offended, and their property values diminished, the public good lay in progress, of which he was the agent.[24] In his account, preservation was a hindrance and drag upon progress. Wiman's skill at such demagoguery was crucial to his plan's success because of the broad political support he needed to get the railroad bridge linking Staten Island and New Jersey constructed, and he consistently used newspapers to promote his views. To aid his efforts, he purchased the *Richmond County Sentinel* in 1881 and, in 1882, consolidated that newspaper with the *Richmond County Gazette*.

Not surprisingly, Curtis employed his skills as an essayist and orator to thwart Wiman. While his rhetorical stances had been effectual with New

England antebellum audiences, by the 1880s mass audiences included a large percentage of recent immigrants on whom his subtle and sophisticated rhetoric was lost. Take for example his closing oration at the 1883 Staten Island Bicentennial celebration, during which he reframed the definition of progress, the force that Wiman claimed to represent.

After reviewing the history of the island, presenting picturesque and romantic images, he compared Staten Island to an awakening Rip van Winkle revitalized for the future, not by Wiman's railways or industrial growth but by the bicentennial observance itself. Hundreds of Staten Islanders had planned and funded the daylong event, and over the course of the day most of the island's population participated. Curtis claimed, "Whatever in a community fosters local pride, and stimulates local interest develops that local spirit, which is the main spring of prosperity and progress in every state."[25] In Curtis's vision, the improved emotional connections among neighbors, evidenced by the bicentennial celebration, represented the most valuable form of progress, not Wiman's blueprint for transportation infrastructure connecting Staten Island to national markets. Curtis's message was unlikely to sway his audience in an era when railroads were dominant and Staten Island's population included many Irish immigrants who worked on railroad construction.

In addition to speeches, Curtis engaged in social lobbying by directly interacting with Wiman and another railroad supporter, William Butler Duncan (1830–1912). Earlier in the bicentennial year of 1883, Curtis had joined with ministers of various Staten Island churches to establish a charitable institution, the Staten Island Eye and Ear Hospital for the treatment of the poor.[26] As founding president, Curtis recruited Wiman and Duncan, a railroad president and board member of several national corporations who resided on Fifth Avenue but summered on Staten Island.[27] One can picture Curtis's gratification in being able to help the poor and tacitly instruct Wiman and Duncan on the value of charity and the true nature of progress.

Of course, Wiman simply continued to lay the groundwork for his vision of progress. He maneuvered himself into leadership positions in relevant organizations, continued to shape public opinion, acquired land, and developed a formal agreement with the B&O and an informal one with George Law. Wiman later claimed that Law's decision to cede his waterfront rights to Wiman grew out of Law's amusement over Wiman's pledge that the neighborhood around the ferry terminal would be renamed "St. George" in Law's honor.[28]

The most important roadblock for Wiman had been the recalcitrance of the Vanderbilt-controlled Staten Island Railroad Co. to cooperate with his plan or sell. The company's rail line ran from Vanderbilt Landing to Tottenville on the South Shore, and the company controlled the four ferries that operated between Manhattan and Staten Island's East Shore. Although the Staten Island Railroad Co. might have little financial importance in the Vanderbilt empire, the origins of the family fortune lay in "Commodore" Cornelius Vanderbilt's Staten Island–based ferry service, and the current head of the family, William Henry Vanderbilt, had held his first significant business position as president of the company. The family's direct connection to the company was through the Commodore's brother, "Captain" Jacob Hand Vanderbilt (1807–1893), who had represented Vanderbilt family interests in the company for thirty years as president of the board of directors.

Wiman's open attempts to first influence and then gain control of the railroad repeatedly failed. Then, at the company's 1883 annual meeting Wiman dramatically announced that he controlled the board. He, and other members of his Staten Island Rapid Transit (SIRT) Co., had purchased or obtained proxies for a majority of Staten Island Railroad Co. shares. According to Wiman, William Henry Vanderbilt was so enraged that that very night he sent Wiman a note by messenger submitting a water bill. The steam engines of the Staten Island Railroad Co. had drawn their water from Vanderbilt's Staten Island land at no charge, and now Vanderbilt wanted reimbursement. In addition, Wiman claimed, Vanderbilt reneged on a substantial pledge to the Staten Island Eye and Ear Hospital because of Wiman's prominent involvement with the charity.[29]

In addition to the challenges Vanderbilt had posed, Wiman needed legislative approval for construction of the Staten Island railroad bridge. His oppositions' last-ditch effort to derail his plans in 1885 took the form of several lengthy, well-reasoned essays in Staten Island Republican newspapers that attacked the bridge plans and Wiman's vision of a transportation network on Staten Island that included freight service, a freight depot with docks, and passenger lines. Curtis probably wrote the unsigned essays (they were clipped and saved in a Curtis family scrapbook that included his articles and mentions of his speeches and activities).[30] Although the essays made many points, the main thrust was that what was special about Staten Island, "often compared to the Isle of Wight," was that it was a place for homes and that the very finest homes would be made worthless through having "the never ceasing rattling and hubbub of a coal road beneath the windows."[31] Furthermore, "The great attraction [of the island for visitors and residents alike] has always been the possibility of proximity to water, with the accompanying enjoyment of beautiful marine views, boating, bathing and ease of access to the vessels which constantly communicate with the city."[32] With the rail lines on the waterfront, an essential aspect of what was special about Staten Island would be lost. Finally, the essays dismissed the claim that the project was for the public good; the promoters were primarily motivated by enriching themselves. When the venture failed (as it would, since there were so many far more convenient freight warehouses than those on Staten Island would be), the public money would have been spent and the beauty of the shoreline destroyed. The promoters would keep their fortunes, but the environmental destruction would be irreversible.

In addition to the rail lines, Wiman had decided in 1884 that the foot of Bard Avenue was the most desirable location for a coal-fueled electric power plant. This facility, across the street from the Shaw house at 4 Davis Avenue, was under construction until the 1890s. An earlier plant in St. George, near the corner of Richmond Terrace and South Street, burned down. That plant, first in operation in 1886, had mostly supplied power for the entertainments presented by Staten Island Amusement Co. at St. George, and later at Erastina. The complex history of centralized electrical power service on Staten Island has much to do with the various companies Wiman created and restructured and his periodic sales of franchises, equipment, and facilities to Edison Electric Illuminating Co., of which he was a member of the board of directors. When the facility at the foot of Bard Avenue was finally completed, it became a more immediate source for soot and ash than the oil refineries across the Kill van Kull. Later, Consolidated Edison created a dramatically enlarged facility on the site that went into operation in 1929.

Although much was left to be accomplished, Wiman organized a grand celebration for December 1885 to celebrate the agreement between his SIRT Co. and the B&O. The B&O would compensate the SIRT for use of its rights of way and Staten Island land for its freight terminal. In return the B&O would undertake the cost of completing connections to New Jersey, which involved a tunnel on Staten Island and a bridge across the Kill van Kull. In retrospect, the celebratory banquet was the high point of the relationship since the operations on Staten Island would prove costly to the railroad. Not only was the necessary tunnel through 610 feet of solid rock under the US Lighthouse Service facility at Tompkinsville, but

Figure 7.2. James and Maria Lowell lived in this house with Dr. and Mrs. Elliott while Maria was Elliott's patient around 1844. In 1884, Erastus Wiman began constructing a coal-fueled electric plant whose smokestacks eventually towered over this and other nearby houses (the smokestacks here are from a similar power plant constructed in the 1920s). *Source*: William T. Davis, photographer, 1938. Courtesy Staten Island Museum.

tunneling under federal land required a special act of Congress. Another act of Congress and agreement from the secretary of war and New Jersey was needed for the bridge project. Finally, the contract with the SIRT stipulated that the through freight traffic, for which the B&O compensated the SIRT at a set rate per ton, had to at least equal the local passenger traffic (on both ferries and trains) averaged during the first two years of the contract. So Wiman devised huge public entertainments on Staten Island to increase the local passenger traffic and establish much higher payments than the B&O might otherwise have expected.[33]

In his book *Chances of Success*, in part a celebration of the opportunities offered by business combines (that we would today refer to as corporations), national and international markets, and advertising, Wiman used the December 16, 1885, banquet announcing the B&O/SIRT agreement as a perfect example of how he had been able to get free national publicity for his projects.[34] Although some attendees thought the event was a celebration of completed work, like new docks in St. George and a new North Shore rail line, in fact the docks at which guests arrived from Manhattan and their short rail journey to the Pavilion Hotel were all on temporary facilities. The event only anticipated the success of Wiman's venture. The guest list included Manhattan politicians, the governors of all the states through which the B&O passed, the mayors of cities served by the B&O, and many journalists.

Wiman had selected George Curtis to give a toast of welcome to Robert Garrett and the executives of the B&O on behalf of Staten Island at the event. Curtis's fame as an orator meant he was frequently an invited keynote speaker for public events, like the dedication of statues and institutions and the funerals of well-known literary and political figures. For instance, the following week he spoke at the dedication of the Pilgrim monument in Central Park, commemorating the anniversary of their Plymouth landing. Curtis may have agreed to participate because representing Staten Island at an event featuring so many dignitaries from off the island was a natural role for him, given his public reputation. While some men might have used the opportunity to cast doubt on the project or embarrass Wiman in some other way, Curtis presented a lengthy, florid toast of welcome to Robert Garrett with literary allusions and witty conceits. Major East Coast newspapers printed his remarks alongside those of Wiman and Garrett.

Not surprisingly, Curtis's toast was too subtle to be appreciated by a crowd of three hundred in a hotel banquet room with a good many

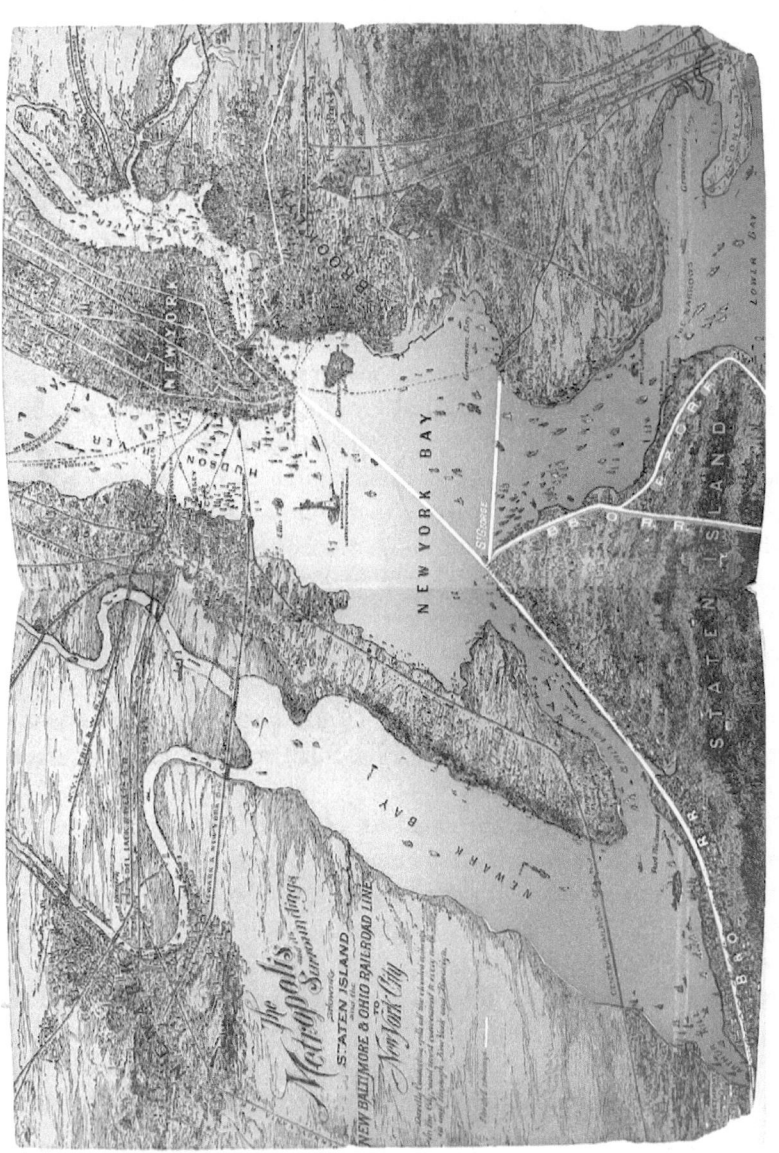

Figure 7.3. This map represents connections to Manhattan and Brooklyn as though the mode of transportation is continuous, even though, when completed, the connections would be by horsecar, train, trolley, and ferry. Source: *Toasts and Reponses: Dinner to the Presidents and Executives, Baltimore & Ohio Railroad* (New York: American Bank Note, 1885), endpaper. Public domain.

distractions. The printed program makes it clear that Wiman only intended Curtis to give a toast. Curtis did toast Garrett and the B&O executives, but very briefly and oddly. Curtis compared Garrett to Antonio in Shakespeare's *Merchant of Venice*, depicting him as "peering in maps for ports and piers and roads," recalling the image of the businessman made miserable by worry over his fortune, invested in merchandise he needed to ship overseas.[35] Later in his remarks Curtis reminded his audience that rail service for Staten Island was a business venture and not a philanthropic undertaking. Curtis devoted most of his oration to his views about the coming of rail service to Staten Island.[36]

Curtis's main theme was that Staten Island, located across the harbor from Manhattan, had no choice over being caught up in the era's march of progress. However, he called for Staten Islanders to make certain that they would benefit from the venture. He acknowledged that not every Staten Islander favored the loss of their rural arcadia, and he made a parallel with the anticipated losses on Staten Island caused by a "hanging belt of fire and smoke" and those on the upstate shores of the Hudson River, where railroads had forever destroyed the shoreline beauty and serenity.[37] While he ostensibly celebrated the integration of Staten Island into the national railroad network as the "dawn of development and the great prosperity of Staten Island," his vision of prosperity was an enrichment of the spirit, and he regarded the actual promise of the railroad to lie in its role of "moral agent."[38] Surrounded by politicians and businessmen, he instead celebrated invisible guests bringing with them invisible treasures: "A better intelligence, a wider sympathy, a fuller knowledge, a stronger patriotism, a noble Americanism."[39]

As a young man Curtis had rejected the life of a businessman, but other men of his generation who had gone into business in the 1830s and 1840s also felt out of touch with the new, postwar economy represented by the men at the banquet. George Cabot Ward's brother Samuel Gray Ward wrote at some length about the moral shift underlying the economic changes. Ward claimed that antebellum New England wealth, the source of Francis George Shaw's prosperity and that of other of Elliottville's "Boston people," flowed from "the commercial marine," a system of shipbuilding and trade that had a moral dimension and was the foundation of the New England civilization that Ward praised highly. This form of commerce required heavy investment (ship, crew, traveling expenses) for long-deferred returns: "Such a business too, called for the highest qualities of courage, foresight, patience, and varied information."[40] Bills of exchange were at

Figure 7.4. Curtis in his home study, the place he preferred to his office for all his writing, including correspondence. As Elliottville transformed, he wrote his threnody for the lost neighborhood here. *Source:* Courtesy of Staten Island Museum.

the heart of the system, for the United States had no manufactured goods worth exporting; furthermore, the currency of the country was of no interest to Asian trading partners. However, New England merchants and ship owners could obtain bills of exchange issued by London banks that were respected universally (particularly those bills issued by Barings). Ward asserted that New England merchants and ship owners were able to get bills of exchange because they were "so trustworthy that 'their word was as good as their bond,' literally."[41] Although Barings required merchants to obtain credit solely from Barings, the bank made large amounts available, and the system of mutual confidence was so complete that business was conducted on a handshake, and instead of holding bills of lading as securities, Barings allowed merchants to retain possession of their trade goods, as though they were purchased with their own money.

The system of mutual trust that Ward described required the highest moral standards, and, from his perspective, the corollaries to these qualities of character created New England civilization. One corollary was interest in and knowledge of the world. As a result, cultivated New England merchants, who had time and affluence, also had the far-reaching interests that inspired them to build library collections, endow museums, establish institutions of higher learning, collect art, engage in philanthropy, and advocate for political and social reforms that would benefit their fellow citizens.

While Ward's account of the antebellum economy of New England focused narrowly on the China trade and the activities of Barings, it is probably characteristic of the views of Elliottville residents, like Sydney Gay (who represented his relatives' trading house in the Far East), Frank Shaw (whose family fortune was built upon the China trade), George Cabot Ward (who, along with his brother Samuel, represented Barings in New York), and even George Curtis (whose exposure to business was through his banker father in the 1830s). One must note that nowhere in Ward's account did he acknowledge the larger antebellum economic forces in the United States based on the so-called Triangle Trade (sugar, rum, and slaves), or the cultivation and export of cotton (dependent upon slave labor).

Nonetheless, from Ward's perspective, by the late 1870s, steamships, telegraphs, and a vast increase in capital had brought about an absolute "revolution in the modes of doing business."[42] Business was no longer based upon a handshake between men of great character and personal integrity but had become the province of corporations with teams of bankers and lawyers. The commercial maritime sector had collapsed because British-made iron steamers had replaced New England clipper ships and, in Ward's view, narrowly ignorant US politicians had insisted upon maintaining antiquated protective systems that meant that only ships built in the United States were granted US registries. The collapse of the commercial maritime sector resulted in the "vast overbuilding of railroads yet to be paid for."[43]

For men like Ward, and the residents of Elliottville, who accorded so much value to individual freedoms, rights, and responsibilities in the American Republic, newly emerging corporate structures and the terms in which Wiman celebrated them were foreign. This fact needs pointing out in our own day, when corporations have been granted rights and abilities similar to, and in some ways exceeding, those of a natural person, including duration, limited liability, and easy transferability of interests.

So, then, while Curtis's speech at the B&O banquet might seem idiosyncratic to readers today, his remarks would have struck a chord with men of his generation who had been inspired by Emerson and shared the perspective of Elliottville residents. For them, business, like all their activities, had a moral and spiritual dimension and should foster "a better intelligence, a wider sympathy, a fuller knowledge, a stronger patriotism, a noble Americanism."[44]

In the year following the banquet, journalists interviewed Curtis for articles discussing Staten Islanders' widespread dissatisfaction with the implementation of Wiman's plan. Curtis said that after the elevated rail lines in Manhattan had reached the Battery in the 1870s, people had moved to Staten Island for a convenient commute to rural residences. These same people were now moving away from Staten Island as the island was being transformed into "the freight terminus of the Baltimore and Ohio Railroad."[45]

In the autumn of 1888, their cause lost, Elliottville residents formed the New Brighton Village Improvement Association. Josephine Lowell spearheaded the initiative. The stated purpose was to address "the conditions of neglect and dilapidation which are securing a constantly increasing foothold in the Village of New Brighton and depriving us of our best class of residents."[46] Although the name implied a New Brighton focus, conditions in St. George and along the entire length of Richmond Terrace were also concerns and Bard Avenue was specifically mentioned. In fact, Bard

Avenue families—the Shaws, Gays, Curtises, and Johnsons—dominated the membership. Francis O. Boyd was association president. Following Elliottville practice, the association provided the money for public improvements. The financial aspect was the work of the men, and Boyd pointed out that the ladies, with their refined sensibilities, would identify the projects to be carried out (Laura Johnson, locally celebrated for her gardens, was the association secretary). Also, in true Elliottville fashion, Wiman, the agent of the destruction they were trying to ameliorate, was recruited as a sponsor.

In 1889, Curtis used his *Harper's* column to lament the disappearance of suburbia in general and of Elliottville in particular. The suburbia he mourned was the one described by Andrew Jackson Downing and realized in several Northern communities in the antebellum era (in addition to Elliottville, the Tulpehocken Station District outside Philadelphia and Llewellyn Park in New Jersey). For Downing (and Curtis), the suburb was a rural retreat near the city, and not the sort of place the name "suburb" denotes today. Drawing upon what was happening around him in Elliottville, Curtis mournfully described a defiled community: the gracious country villa partitioned into a multifamily dwelling; attractive grounds denuded and overlaid with paving; residences overshadowed by new, cheaply constructed buildings and factory smokestacks; meadows replaced by street railways; the nighttime sky obscured by electric lamps and telephone wire; the air and water polluted by factories. The suburban refuge characterized by "fields and trees and pastures, and the singing of birds, and silent green shades, and the scent of fresh earth in spring and the breath of new-mown hay is forever gone."[47] At the same time Curtis wrenchingly expressed his sorrow over his island home's losses, he acknowledged that anger and scorn was as pointless as Dame Partington trying to keep rising storm waters from flooding her home by wielding a mop. The battle was ended, although it would take a few more decades for the remnants of Elliottville on Bard Avenue to be obliterated.

Wiman's bridge to New Jersey was constructed and named the Arthur Kill Bridge. A swing-span railroad bridge with a center pier, it was complicated and costly to build. Although the US Congress authorized construction in 1886, a delay ensued while awaiting approval from the secretary of war and the resolution of an injunction brought by the State of New Jersey. The authorizing legislation had imposed a two-year deadline for completion, but the delays meant construction mostly occurred in 1888 with much higher costs ($450,000) for round-the-clock labor. The bridge

Figure 7.5. Railroad tracks along the waterfront forever destroyed Elliottsville's direct access to the water. *Source*: Edwin S. Marsh, *Art Work of Staten Island* (Chicago: W. H. Parish, 1894). Public domain.

would not open for two years after completion since the approaches needed to be engineered and finished. Upon dedication on January 1, 1890, it was the longest such bridge in the world. Although touted as a public benefit, the bridge impeded shipping since it was built so low to the water that it had to be constantly swung open to accommodate barge traffic. With the help of Curtis's political foe, Roscoe Conkling, Wiman and his associates had defeated a plan to build a high bridge at a different location that would not have negatively impacted shipping but also would not have made sense for the location of the B&O freight terminal in St. George.[48]

Although Wiman had defeated Curtis and Elliottville, he could not resist a final jab at the man and the genteel, do-gooding spirit of the community that Curtis had come to epitomize. In 1892, just as it was becoming clear that his railroad enterprise would not bring him the increased wealth on which he had counted, Wiman published letters in newspapers claiming serious mismanagement at the S. R. Smith Infirmary, of which Curtis was president of the board of trustees. For many years, Staten Island women's auxiliaries had raised money for public health care. Their efforts culminated in the infirmary, whose impressive new building was dedicated in 1890. As evidence for his claim of mismanagement, Wiman broadcast the accusation of a newly hired nurse that surgical instruments were not being properly sterilized. He also pointed to disagreements between long-serving physicians and the new nurse over medical procedures that had led to the resignation of physicians and ladies' auxiliary members who thought their leadership was being ignored. In retrospect, the nurse seems to have been "planted" by Wiman to cause trouble, which he took glee in publicizing.[49]

Curtis and a board member responded to Wiman's newspaper letters with letters of their own. Unlike his letters, theirs were written in the politest of tones, thanking Wiman for his observations and his interest in the well-being of the infirmary.[50] Nonetheless, it was clear that Wiman had wanted to embarrass Curtis, and the very fact that Curtis had to respond at all made him look defensive. Wiman then resigned from the board only to orchestrate a takeover. Infirmary bylaws stated that anyone who contributed five dollars to the institution could vote for board members, and Wiman made certain that he would control the election (through SIRT contributions alone, he controlled one hundred votes). In addition, Wiman hired all the horse cabs on the island on election day so that he could send supporters to the voting site and impede his opposition.[51]

Wiman got control of the infirmary board through the same sly pettiness he had utilized in his business affairs and described pridefully in the self-congratulatory book *Chances of Success*.

Conclusion

Wiman's great fall did not come until after Curtis's 1892 death. Wiman's troubles commenced even before the railroad line began operation. In 1887 Robert Garrett's ill health forced his retirement and new powers at the B&O were not as committed to Wiman, weighing his demands for investment against infrastructure concerns on other parts of the line.

In anticipation of rising property values, Wiman had energetically acquired Staten Island real estate with borrowed money for years, thinking that the island's population would increase dramatically due to the convenience of integrated passenger service. However, he had not considered the reluctance of passengers to use multiple forms of transportation, the number of competing trolley lines that would emerge, or rivalry for the Staten Island rail and ferry business. When the fiscal crisis of 1893 came, he had no liquidity and could not profitably sell his land.[52]

Around this time, Wiman was discovered to have taken advantage of his position at Dun to finance his enterprises and there was at least the appearance of embezzlement, leading to his ouster from the company and a demand for repayment. Although Dun was his principal creditor, he was also indebted to over sixty more. Wiman's Staten Island properties fell into receivership. The following year, Dun charged Wiman with forgery for attempting to cash a check for $5,000 from R. G. Dunn made out to a false name. Wiman was convicted in 1895 (although the conviction was overturned on appeal). All Wiman's remaining property, business interests, and financial instruments went to repay creditors, but they only recovered one half of one cent on the dollar.[53] In 1901 Wiman had a stroke; never fully recovering, he died in 1904 in the mansion he had built for himself on a hillside overlooking the St. George docks and warehouses that he had expected to be his crowning achievement. In the weeks before his death, even his household furniture was sold off to cover living expenses.[54]

Curtis had not foretold Wiman's financial crash, but his prediction that the physical beauty of Staten Island's North Shore would be irrecoverably destroyed proved accurate. Elliottville had thrived due to an

Figure 7.6. Wiman's many proposals in the 1880s for Staten Island included tunnels under New York Harbor and siting the 1892 World's Fair there. The fair proposal called for even more transportation infrastructure that would have cut off much more of the island from the waterfront. *Source*: Erastus Wiman, *An Argument for Staten Island as the Most Desirable Site for the World's Fair 1892* (New York: The author, 1889), endpaper. Public domain.

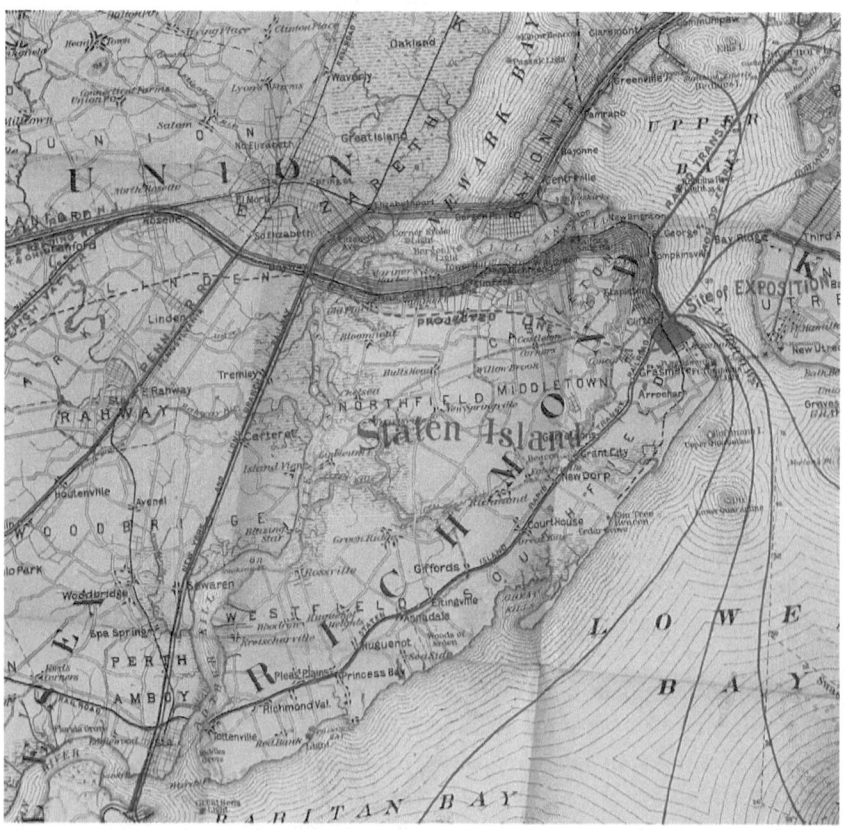

intimate connection to nature, and especially to the waterfront. Once that was gone, the place continued to exist only as a memory of what had been. Some residents with pre-1883 connections to the neighborhood continued to live in their villas from another age, enlivened by memories of people now dead and a place that no longer existed. No new people of their sort would come after 1890. The following decades would bring only diminishing change. The history of the place as a neighborhood of remarkable people rapidly became a vague reminiscence.[55]

Conclusion

Grant me, O Lord, the power to stem
That madness which lays low the wood
... And throttle in its lair the greed.

—Charles de Kay, "Woodland Creed"[1]

The quality of life experienced by Elliottville residents deteriorated rapidly in the 1880s as air and water pollution worsened and the noise, dirt, and inconvenience of the transportation lines running along the waterfront obtruded in their lives. Once ferry service was consolidated in St. George, getting into Manhattan had become much more complicated. As early as 1880, Elizabeth Gay complained about the wait for the ferry and the "little car" to transport her home.[2] It was that year that Erastus Wiman organized the SIRT Co., and soon locomotives were delivering ever greater numbers of people to the old Livingston mansion, the station closest to the Staten Island Athletic Club, and by 1886 steaming on along the shore to Erastina on the Buffalo Bill Express. The stands at Erastina could accommodate ten thousand, but for special events, as many as twenty thousand people were traveling to Erastina by the rapid transit.[3] Elizabeth Gay began to long for a quiet place, "far from Rail Roads and Erastus Wyman [sic]."[4]

Nevertheless, a few women, a remnant of Elliottville residents from the 1840s and 1850s, were so attached to the neighborhood that they continued to live there into the twentieth century. In 1887, George Curtis, corresponded with Frederick Law Olmsted about the destruction of the neighborhood and wrote, "My wife and daughter are too much attached to the old home to permit anticipation of any speedy change upon our part."[5] Curtis lived in his Bard Avenue house until his 1892 death. His daughter and wife continued to live there until their deaths, as well as Elizabeth Curtis until 1914 and Anna Curtis until 1923.

Two of the Gays also lived in the neighborhood until their deaths: Sarah Gay until 1901 and Mary Willcox until 1933. Mary had first socialized with her future husband, William Willcox, while playing tennis at the Staten Island Athletic Club. The couple lived their entire married life in a house they constructed on part of the Gay family's original property and raised their family there (four children survived to adulthood). Their young son Daniel Goodenow Willcox (b. 1896) was killed by a locomotive while crossing the tracks in 1907, a death weighted with symbolism given the deleterious effect that the freight rail line had on the neighborhood.[6]

The female remnants of Elliottville continued to act on their social commitments. Anna Curtis, Elizabeth Curtis, Sarah Gay, and Mary Willcox were all active in local and state women's organizations. Elizabeth was the founder of the Political Equality Club of Staten Island, vice president at large for the New York State Woman Suffrage Association, delegate to state and local suffrage conventions, and a speaker for women's rights at the New York State Constitutional Convention in 1894.[7] The Political Equality Club, founded in 1895, fostered discussions of the political equality of men and women through shared readings and member-authored essays. The club met at the Gays' house. Sarah Gay gave speeches at club meetings and elsewhere that focused on the economic issues women faced, drawing upon the writings of Henry George. Mary Willcox led state women's rights organizations, including the City Party, and was particularly active in presenting lectures in support of a New York State suffrage amendment in 1915. By 1919 Willcox became active in the League of Women Voters, the independent, nonpartisan group aimed at enhancing women's political power, educating voters, and constraining partisan corruption. She chaired the league's Richmond County chapter.

Even though she had moved out of the neighborhood, Sarah Shaw maintained her social ties to Elliottville from her new home in New York City. We know from an account by her friend Henry Dwight Sedgwick (1867–1951) that her years on Staten Island were far more vivid to her than her life in Manhattan. She shared memories with Sedgwick of Robert Gould Shaw's boyhood, her pride in his command of the Fifty-Fourth Massachusetts, and her sorrow over his death. She also reminisced about daughter Josephine Lowell's emotional turmoil after the death of her husband and her conviction that she would die in childbirth and be reunited with her spouse. Shaw was proud of the fact that when Lowell did not die, she transformed her life into "a monument to her husband's memory . . . devoting herself to the poor, to orphans, outcasts, to all who are desolate and oppressed."[8] Shaw shared loving reminiscences of her sons-in-law George Curtis, Charles Lowell, and Francis Barlow, "men who thought that there were things worth fighting for, who had accepted traditions of right, wrong, duty, self-sacrifice."[9] For Sedgwick, Shaw made real the spirit of Elliottville through her stories, but also through her presence: "To me she was like an emblem of dignity, come down from George Washington's time, part of the great character that he left to the nation, an emblem of simplicity, of Roman matronhood, of self-respect and self-restraint."[10] However, for Sedgwick himself, in the 1890s the spirit of Elliottville was as distant as the days of the early Republic.

Today, with no living link, the spirit of Elliottville seems even more remote, and even a physical impression of the place is irrecoverable. Land sales accelerated as the nineteenth century came to a close. Within a few years of Janet de Kay's death in 1890, the undeveloped de Kay land that had helped preserve the Bard Avenue neighborhood was being sold. The de Kay land along Bard Avenue was platted into house lots, generally 100 feet wide and 144 feet deep. However, nearby the land was divided into much smaller lots. In just two blocks, between Castleton and Dekay Streets and Bard Avenue and Shawmut (now Davis) Street, sixty-two lots were laid out. The developer W. F. Lynch, who had purchased de Kay land further away from Bard, between Davis and Fairmount, laid out his lots with a one-hundred-foot depth and only a twenty-five-foot width, platting 120 lots. Although some purchasers bought more than one of the de Kay lots for their houses, investors also bought lots to further subdivide, following the lot sizes on neighboring streets (which were twenty-five by fifty feet). Closer to the waterfront, as the Henderson estate subdivision began, blocks and cross streets were laid out with more than 180 house lots (six house lots took the place of Henderson's Linden Lawn alone). Although selling the land and building all the houses took decades, the future of the neighborhood was clear. The houses from earlier periods, impediments to the platting of the small house lots, were gradually torn down as remaining family members died off.

While the spirit of Elliottville may live on in the descendants of neighborhood residents, or even in later arrivals to the neighborhood, the built environment and the natural setting that was so important to Elliottville residents is irrecoverable, the environment polluted, the woodlands and meadows gone for more than a century. Although a few remnants

Figure C.1. On Labor Day, Monday, September 2, 1907, 214 lots from the de Kay estate were auctioned. *Source*: "Auction Labor Day, Monday, September 2, 1907," New York Public Library Digital Collections, https://digitalcollections.nypl.org/items/5f79c940-1d60-0131-3c26-58d385a7b928.

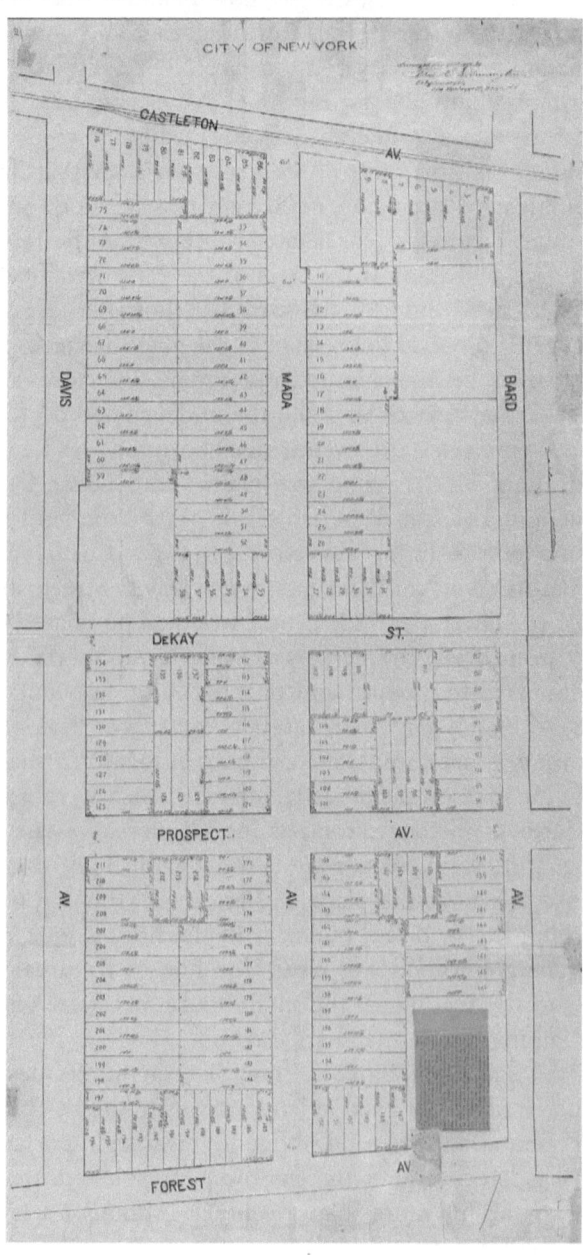

of structures survive, without their grounds and neighborhood context, their meaning is sadly diminished.[11]

In 1929 when Mabel Abbott, a curator at what is now the Staten Island Museum, was trying to document Staten Island writers, she visited the only surviving house in which Frank Shaw had lived, the house on Richmond Terrace. Her description of its fate captures the fate of most of the other houses in the neighborhood. Used as a boardinghouse during the previous decade, the dwelling still contained Shaw furnishings. The boarding house proprietor said that Dr. Frank Curtis (Shaw's grandson) had tried to sell them to antique dealers but found no buyers. During her visit, Abbott noted everything was "set in dirt and confusion—like a junk shop."[12] Still there was a grandfather clock in the hall, a floor-to-ceiling mirror in the drawing room with a heavy gilt frame, and elaborate cornices over the windows. Abbott wrote that there had been a fire in the basement some time before and a resulting sizable hole on the first floor was merely covered with rickety boards. The boarding house proprietor was in the midst of packing and the house's demolition was imminent. The Consolidated Edison power plant that had replaced Wiman's, was across the street. The land underneath the Shaw house had been sold in several individual parcels. The front porch had already been torn down, since the land underneath it went with a parcel on which small shops were to be built. After the planned demolition of the remaining structure, modest houses were to be constructed.

Source Abbreviations

CPC	Christopher Pearse Cranch Papers (MS N-1047), Massachusetts Historical Society, Boston
CEN	Charles Eliot Norton Papers, ca. 1845–1908 (MS Am 1088), Houghton Library, Harvard University
GM	Gilder MSS, 1781–1984 (LMC 2345), Lilly Library, Indiana University, Bloomington
GWC	George William Curtis Papers (25.GWC), Staten Island Museum, Staten Island
JRL	James Russell Lowell Papers, 1842–1924 (MS N-1604), Massachusetts Historical Society, Boston
JRL & SHG	James Russell Lowell and Sydney Howard Gay Papers (MS Am 1246), Harvard University, Houghton Library
LWJ	Laura (Winthrop) Johnson Papers, 1862–1889 (MSS Col 1573), Manuscript and Archives Division, New York Public Library
MA	Mabel Abbott Papers (1.mA), Staten Island Museum, Staten Island
SHG	Sydney Howard Gay Papers, 1748–1931 (MS no. 0475), Rare Book and Manuscript Library, Columbia University
SBSS	Letters to Sarah Blake (Sturgis) Shaw from Various Correspondents (MS Am 1417), Houghton Library, Harvard University
TW	Theodore Winthrop Papers (MSS Col 3363), Manuscripts and Archives Division, New York Public Library

Notes

Introduction

1. The year of Elliott's birth varies on census records, but the record for his arrival in New York in 1834 stated he was twenty-seven years old. So he would have been born around 1807.

2. The neighborhood sometimes appears as Elliottsville, but Dr. Elliott clearly intended the name to be "Elliottville," as demonstrated by his use of this name in his publication about the wartime service of the Seventy-Ninth Regiment.

3. Charles G. Hine and William T. Davis, *Legends, Stories, and Folklore of Old Staten Island*, part 1, *The North Shore* (Staten Island, NY: Staten Island Historical Society, 1925), 31.

4. The most effective way of conveying the hatred of the era is by quoting directly from sources that use racial epithets, as has been done throughout this book.

5. Marian Holyoke and Mabel Abbott, interview, May 6, 1949, 1.mA, box 1, folder 7, MA.

6. Hine and Davis, *Legends, Stories, and Folklore*, 1:66.

7. Hine and Davis, 77.

8. Eric Foner, *Gateway to Freedom: The Hidden History of the Underground Railroad* (New York: Columbia, 2015), 229.

Chapter 1

1. Milton Melzer, *Henry David Thoreau: A Biography* (Minneapolis: Twenty-First Century Books, 2007), 55–56.

2. Lydia Maria Child to Francis George Shaw, May 9, 1843, MS Am 1417, box 1, SBSS.

3. Margaret Fuller to Sarah Blake (Sturgis) Shaw, July 1, 1835, MS Am 1417, box 1, SBSS.

4. Lydia Maria Child to Francis George Shaw and Sarah Blake (Sturgis) Shaw, August 17, 1838, MS Am 1417, box 1, SBSS. For the most complete biography of Shaw, see Lorien Foote, *Seeking the One Great Remedy: Francis George Shaw and Nineteenth-Century Reform* (Athens: Ohio University Press, 2003).

5. For the most complete account of his thought, see Foote, *Seeking the One Great Remedy*.

6. For more information about Brook Farm, see Sterling F. Delano, *Brook Farm: The Dark Side of Utopia* (Cambridge, MA: Belknap Press of Harvard University, 2004).

7. Foote, *Seeking the One Great Remedy*, 71.

8. Foote, 60–61.

9. See SBSS and *Letters of Lydia Maria Child* (New York: Houghton Mifflin, 1883).

10. Patricia G. Holland, "Lydia Maria Child as a Nineteenth-Century Professional Author," *Studies in the American Renaissance*, 1981, 160, www.jstor.org/stable/30227480.

11. Foote, *Seeking the One Great Remedy*, 60–61.

12. Sarah Blake (Sturgis) Shaw to Elizabeth (Neall) Gay, June [?], 1850, series 1, box 61, SHG.

13. Frank Shaw to Sydney Howard Gay, June 21, 1850, series 1, box 19, SHG.

14. Richmond County, NY, Deed Book 33:427, Samuel and Letitia Elliott and Francis G. Shaw, April 4, 1854, Clerk of Courts, Staten Island.

15. For a full account of Warner Mifflin's antislavery activities, see Gary B. Nash, *Warner Mifflin: Unflinching Quaker Abolitionist* (Philadelphia: University of Pennsylvania Press, 2017).

16. Gay maintained a detailed notebook of his activities that has been analyzed in Eric Foner, *Gateway to Freedom: The Hidden History of the Underground Railroad* (New York: W. W. Norton, 2015); and Don Papson and Tom Calarco, *Secret Lives of the Underground Railroad in New York City: Sydney Howard Gay, Louis Napoleon, and the Record of Fugitives* (Jefferson, NC: McFarland, 2015).

17. For more information about Neall and her parents, see Nash, *Warner Mifflin*, 240–44.

18. Irma and Paul Milstein, Division of United States History, Local History and Genealogy, New York Public Library, "New York City Directory," *New York Public Library Digital Collections*, 1846. http://digitalcollections.nypl.org/items/e1081b90-8225-0136-88d6-376951526e42.

19. Sydney Howard Gay to Elizabeth (Neall) Gay, undated, series 1, box 64, SHG.

20. Sydney Howard Gay to Edmund Quincy, February 2, 1847, series 1, box 29, SHG.

21. Sydney Howard Gay to Elizabeth (Neall) Gay, undated, series 1, box 64, SHG.

22. Sydney Howard Gay to Edmund Quincy, March 19, 1847, series 1, box 29, SHG.

23. Gay to Quincy, March 19, 1847, series 1, box 29, SHG.

24. Sydney Howard Gay to Anne Weston, August 2, 1847, series 1, box 29, SHG.

25. For a more detailed presentation of real estate development on Staten Island, see Adam Zalma, "Staten Island in the Harbor Metropolis: The Making of a Region and the Disappearance of an Island, 1790–1858" (PhD diss., Rutgers University, 2014).

26. The Rothschild Archive, accessed February 24, 2020, https:/forum.rothschildarchive.org.

27. Marjorie Pearson and Elisa Urbanelli, eds., "St. George/New Brighton Historic District Designation Report," New York City Landmarks Designation Commission, unpublished, 7.

28. George A. Ward, "Description of New Brighton on Staten Island, Opposite the City of York," s.n., 1836.

29. John Archer, "Country and City in the American Romantic Suburb," *Journal of the Society of Architectural Historians* 42 (May 1983): 152.

30. "The Heyday of The Pavilion Hotel," *Staten Island Historian*, April–June 1951, 9.

31. For a discussion of residential development in nineteenth-century Manhattan, see Edwin G. Burrows and Mike Wallace, *Gotham: A History of New York City to 1898* (New York: Oxford University Press, 1998), 715–20.

32. See Archer, "Country and City," 139–56.

33. David Tatham, "The Pendleton-Moore Shop: Lithographic Artists in Boston, 1825–1840," *Old-Time New England* 62 (Fall 1971): 226.

34. In 1860, William S. Pendleton became a chief investor in the North Shore Staten Island Ferry Company. In the 1880s, his son, William H. Pendleton, was the director of the ferry company. See Charles W. Leng and William T. Davis, *Staten Island and Its People: A History, 1609–1929*, vol. 2 (New York: Lewis Historical Publishing, 1930), 701–2.

35. The People's Ferry Service operated from the 1850s to the 1880s, carrying passengers on scheduled trips to and from Manhattan and Brooklyn. The ferry service only really made sense for the people who lived in the immediate neighborhood and was referred to as the "private" or "social ferry" as opposed to the public service close to New Brighton. Elliottville residents would reminiscence about what it was like to take a ferry most of whose riders were neighbors. For more information see Charles G. Hine and William T. Davis, *Legends, Stories, and Folklore of Old Staten Island*, part 1, *The North Shore* (Staten Island, NY: Staten Island Historical Society, 1925), 29.

36. Hine and Davis, 32–33.

37. Charles G. Hine, *History and Legend of Howard Avenue and the Serpentine Road, Grymes Hill, Staten Island* (New York: Charles Gilbert Hine, 1914), 27.

38. Some published sources claim that Elliott arrived in 1833 on the *Teresa Anderson*. However, local historian Kristin Choo was unable to find a ship of that name or a Samuel Elliott arriving in 1833. Elliott's descendant, Stephen Livingston, found a record for a Samuel Elliott arriving as the ship's surgeon for the packet ship *Clarissa Andrews* on August 26, 1834. See New York, Passengers Lists 1820–1957. Year: 1834; Arrival: New York, New York; Microfilm Serial: M237, 1820–1897; Microfilm Roll: Roll 024; Line: 26; List Number: 703.

39. Charles August Murray, *Travels in North America During the Years 1834, 1835, & 1836* (New York: Harper and Brothers, 1839), 52.

40. *Appleton's Cyclopaedia of American Biography (1887–1889)*, under "Samuel Mackenzie Elliott."

41. "Samuel Mackenzie Elliott," *New York Times*, May 1, 1875.

42. Borough of Richmond County Clerk's Office, Deeds, vol. 6, 326.

43. See designs and site plans in William H. Ranlett, *The Architect: A Series of Original Designs*, vols. 1 and 2 (New York: Dewitt & Davenport, 1847–1849).

44. For more information about Ranlett's life and architecture, see Richard C. Muhlberger, "William Ranlett 19th Century Architect and Publisher," *Historic Preservation: Quarterly of the National Council of Historic Sites Buildings* 22 (January–March 1970): 10–15.

45. Louise Wigglesworth to Jane Norton Wigglesworth, May 15, 1843, MS Am 1136, box 5, Papers of the Grew, Andrews, Norton, and Wigglesworth Families, Houghton Library, Harvard University.

46. Louise Wigglesworth to Jane Norton Wigglesworth, December 4, 1843, MS Am 1136, box 5, Papers of the Grew, Andrews, Norton, and Wigglesworth Families, Houghton Library, Harvard University.

47. Louisa Wigglesworth to Thomas Wigglesworth, June 7, 1843, MS Am 1136, box 5, Papers of the Grew, Andrews, Norton, and Wigglesworth Families, Houghton Library, Harvard University.

48. "Live High: A Knife in My Eye," *The Sun* (New York), Sep. 14, 1874; "Obituary: Dr. Samuel Mackenzie Elliott," *The Sun* (New York), May 2, 1875; "Obituary: Dr. Samuel Mackenzie Elliott," *New York Times*, May 1, 1875.

49. *Appleton's*, under "Samuel Mackenzie Elliott."

50. Sydney Howard Gay to Edmund Quincy, September 23, 1847, series 1, box 29, SHG.

51. Gay to Quincy.

52. Gay to Quincy.

53. Gay to Quincy.

54. Gay to Quincy.

55. Born Alban Gilpin Smith, he legally changed his surname to Goldsmith in 1839 (due to a decades-long professional controversy with Dr. Daniel Drake). Otto Juettner, *Daniel Drake and His Followers: Historical and Biographical Sketches* (Cincinnati: Harvey, 1909), 148–49.

56. Juettner, 149.

57. Juettner, 149.

58. His name is given as Alban Goldsmith in the *New York State Naturalization Index*.

59. Given the abbreviated format of an obituary, it is surprising that space is given to listing the examining physicians: Robert Ogden Doremus (1824–1906) and Benjamin Fordyce Barker (1818–1891), and for a specialist examination: Valentine Mott (1785–1865), John William Draper (1811–1882), Samuel Henry Dickson (1798–1872), and Granville Sharp Pattison (1791–1851). Doremus and Barker were among the founders of the Bellevue Hospital Medical College, an institution that did not incorporate until 1861. The other men listed were faculty members at the University of New York (later the University Medical College and then New York University). Dickson was only there from 1847 to 1850 and Pattison died in 1851.

60. Elliott's *Appleton's* biography claims that he was a visiting professor, but he was not. For lists of visiting professors, see Frederick Clayton Waite, *The First Medical College in Vermont, Castleton, 1818–1862* (Montpelier: Vermont Historical Society, 1949).

61. "Obituary: Dr. Samuel Mackenzie Elliott," *The Sun* (New York), May 2, 1875.

62. *Catalogue of the Officers of the College of [New York Medical] College, Session, 1851–52* (New York: Baker, Godwin, 1851), [2].

63. New York Academy of Medicine, Minutes of Meetings, December 12, 1846–October 29, 1862. Stated meeting November 6, 1851, at the university. For an account of the meeting, see Philip Van Ingen, *The New York Academy of Medicine: Its First Hundred Years* (New York: Columbia University, 1949), 54–55.

64. *New York Medical Gazette and Journal of Health*, January 15, 1852, 22–23, https://archive.org/details/newyorkmedicalga3185unse/page/n31.

65. The account of the meeting drawn upon and quoted from in this paragraph is from "New York State Medical Society," *Albany Evening Journal*, February 6, 1852, 2, https://newspapers.com/image/82639016.

66. For an account of Lowell that discusses his life challenges, see Martin B. Duberman, *James Russell Lowell* (Boston: Houghton Mifflin, 1966).

67. Edward Everett Hale, *James Russell Lowell and His Friends* (Boston: Houghton Mifflin, 1899), 89.

68. Hale, *James Russell Lowell*, 89.

69. Hale, 89.

70. Hale, 89.

71. Ferris Greenslet, *James Russell Lowell* (Boston: Houghton Mifflin / Riverside Press, 1905), 61.

72. Luther Samuel Livingston, *A Bibliography of the First Editions in Book Form of the Writings of James Russell Lowell* (New York: Privately printed, 1914), 18.

73. According to Hine and Davis, *Legends, Stories, and Folklore*, Lowell returned to live in Elliottville so that Dr. Elliott could treat his wife, Maria White Lowell (1821–1853). Since she was ill for an extended period before her early death, the exact dates are unclear, although treatment began after their 1844 marriage.

74. C. Harvey Gardiner, ed., *The Papers of William Hickling Prescott* (Urbana: University of Illinois Press, 1964), 187.

75. Gardiner, 188.

76. Gardiner, 188.

77. Although he did not undergo a lengthy treatment program, he does seem to have received some treatment, possibly of a one-time nature. See Peter O. Koch, *William Hickling Prescott: The Life and Letters of America's First Scientific Historian* (Jefferson, NC: McFarland, 2016), 167.

78. Information about Norton's life during this time period is drawn from James C. Turner, *The Liberal Education of Charles Eliot Norton* (Baltimore: Johns Hopkins University Press, 1999).

79. Turner, 44–45.

80. Edward M. Cifelli, *Longfellow in Love: Passion and Tragedy in the Life of the Poet* (Jefferson, NC: McFarland, 2018), 212.

81. Fanny Longfellow to Zilpah Longfellow, postmarked October 25, 1843, qtd. in Edward Wagenknecht, *Mrs. Longfellow: Selected Letters and Journals of Fanny Appleton Longfellow, 1817–1861* (New York: Longmans, Green, 1956), 97.

82. Fanny Longfellow to Anne Longfellow Pierce, postmarked January 17, 1844, qtd. in Wagenknecht, *Mrs. Longfellow*, 103.

83. Fanny Longfellow to Anne Longfellow Pierce, postmarked November 10, 1843, qtd. in Wagenknecht, *Mrs. Longfellow*, 98.

84. Cifelli, *Longfellow in Love*, 213.

85. Cifelli, 213.

86. Henry Dwight Sedgwick, *Francis Parkman* (Boston: Houghton Mifflin / Riverside Press, 1904), 193.

87. Howard Doughty, *Francis Parkman* (New York: Macmillan, 1962), 142–43.

88. Sedgwick, *Francis Parkman*, 196.

89. Doughty, *Francis Parkman*, 143.

90. Doughty, 141–45.

91. Cifelli, *Longfellow in Love*, 212.

92. Koch, *William Hickling Prescott*, 167.

93. "Live High: A Knife in My Eye," *The Sun* (New York), September 14, 1874.

94. John Fiske, *Edward Livingston Youmans, Interpreter of Science for the People: A Sketch of His Life* (New York: D. Appleton, 1894), 44.

95. Horace Greeley, who was also being treated by Elliott at this time, was staying in the same boarding house.

96. Fiske, *Edward Livingston Youmans*, 44–46.

97. Fiske, 72–73.

98. Eliza Ann Youmans, "Sketch of Edward L. Youmans," *Popular Science Monthly* 30 (1887): 691.

99. Youmans, 697.

100. "Live High: A Knife in My Eye," *The Sun* (New York), September 14, 1874.

101. "Live High." No matter what assessment is currently given oatmeal, we must remember that Elliott was from Scotland, where the food has historically been held in very high regard.

102. Anna (Shaw) Curtis to Charles Eliot Norton, August 17, 1892, MS Am 1088, box 9, Charles Eliot Norton Papers, ca. 1845–1908, Houghton Library, Harvard University.

103. Anna (Shaw) Curtis was interviewed by Charles Gilbert Hine. See Hine Collection, box 2, 93, Staten Island Museum.

104. Although since this was not an official visit, he had to be referred to by one of his other titles, Baron Renfrew.

105. Samuel Mackenzie Elliott, *The Highland Brigade* (Elliottville, Staten Island: s.n., 1861).

106. The Civil War service of the Seventy-Ninth is documented in William Todd, *History of the 79th New York Highlanders* (Albany, NY: Brandon, Barton & Co., 1886).

107. James Cameron, who had served in the Mexican-American War, was sixty-one years old when he arrived in Washington, DC. One source that claims influence in his selection is William L. Burton, *Melting Pot Soldiers: The Union's Ethnic Regiments* (New York: Fordham University Press, 1998), 162.

108. Hine and Davis, *Legends, Stories, and Folklore*, 36.

109. For more information on the structure, known as Tower House, see Hine, *History and Legend*, 26–28.

110. Richmond County, NY, Deed Book 6:326, William and Catherine Bard and Thomas E. and Anne Davis & Samuel and Letitia Elliott. Property transactions show that Elliott made a series of purchases from William and Catherine Bard between 1839 and 1853.

111. Valleau was the granddaughter of Peter Fauconnier (1659–1745) and, through her mother, inherited approximately 3,600 acres of land in Putnam County, New York.

112. Catherine was the daughter of slave trader Nicholas Cruger (1742–1800), the son of a Manhattan merchant who had built a fortune in the Atlantic trade based upon the sale of slaves, sugar, and rum. Nicholas married the wealthy Ann de Nully (1747–1784), from whose fortune Catherine also benefited. For more information, see Douglas Wright Cruger, *A Genealogical and Biographical History of the Cruger Families in America* (Portland, ME: D. W. Cruger), 1989.

113. William Bard, New York Life Insurance and Trust Company, *Report of the New-York Life Insurance and Trust Company; made to the Chancellor of the State of New York, March 29, 1831* (Albany, NY: Croswell and Van Benthuysen, 1831).

114. William Bard and Dr. Elliott were often involved in cooperative projects, although they continued to sometimes be at odds with each other. For instance, both of them were involved in founding St. Mary's Episcopal Church (for which Dr. Elliott constructed and furnished the first small chapel on his land). However, a later controversy over the church led the congregation to divide.

115. Hine and Davis, *Legends, Stories, and Folklore*, 36.

116. Delafield had married William Bard's daughter, Eliza, in 1836, and they made the Bard Avenue property their primary residence and a much-admired country seat, raising seven children there. Rufus was the son of Anne (née Hallett) Delafield (1766–1839) and John Delafield (1748–1824), a founder and director of the Mutual Insurance Company, who was one of the wealthiest men in the country. Rufus was an officer of the Phenix Bank from 1823 to 1835 and actuary and secretary of the Farmers Loan and Trust Company (which later became Citibank) from 1835 to 1852. He was also the founder and president of the Delafield & Baxter Hydraulic Cement Company. See George Norbury Mackenzie, *Colonial Families of the United States* (New York: Grafton, 1907), under "Delafield, Rufus King."

117. Hine and Davis, *Legends, Stories, and Folklore*, 32.

Chapter 2

1. Mary Otis (Gay) Willcox, "A Gay Life," typed manuscript, series 4, box 78, SHG.

2. Ranlett lived in a house at what is now 508 Clove Road, Staten Island. Richard C. Muhlberger, "William H. Ranlett: 19th Century Architect and Publisher," *Historic Preservation: Quarterly of the National Council for Historic Sites and Buildings* 22 (Jan.–Mar. 1970): 11.

3. William H. Ranlett, *The Architect: A Series of Original Designs, for Domestic and Ornamental Cottages and Villas* [. . .], vol. 1 (New York: William H. Graham, 1847), 19.

4. Qtd. in Albert Fein, *Landscape into Cityscape: Frederick Law Olmsted's Plans for a Greater New York City* (Ithaca, NY: Cornell University Press, 1967), 63–88.

5. Qtd. in David Schuyler, *Apostle of Taste: Andrew Jackson Downing, 1815–1852* (Baltimore: Johns Hopkins University Press, 1996), 204.

6. William H. Ranlett, *The Architect: A Series of Original Designs*, vol. 2 (New York: Dewitt & Davenport, 1849), 3.

7. Ranlett, *The Architect*, 2:3.

8. Sydney Howard Gay to Edmund Quincy, March 19, 1847, series 1, box, 29, SHG.

9. For a complete biography of Gay, see Raimund E. Goerler, *Family, Self, and Anti-Slavery: Sydney Howard Gay and the Abolitionist Commitment* (PhD diss., Case Western Reserve University, 1975), 117–18.

10. Goerler presents a detailed chronology for this period in Gay's life, referencing the Gay correspondence, *Family, Self, and Anti-Slavery*, 121–55.

11. See Goerler for a detailed account of the abolitionism debate in Hingham and Gay's development into an abolitionist, *Family, Self, and Anti-Slavery*, 188–219.

12. Sydney Howard Gay to Thomas W. Higginson, October 12, 1882; qtd. in Goerler, *Family, Self, and Anti-Slavery*, 3.

13. The Gays purchased the property from Dr. Elliott in 1850. Receipts for the transaction are in SHG.

14. Sydney Howard Gay to Edmund Quincy, August 10, 1847, series 1, box 29, SHG.

15. The Gays consistently referred to the porches on their house and those of their neighbors as piazzas.

16. Gay to Quincy, August 10, 1847.

17. Elizabeth (Neall) Gay to Sydney Howard Gay, April 12, 1847, series 1, box 19, SHG.

18. Elizabeth (Neall) Gay to Sydney Howard Gay, August 4, 1847, series 1, box 19, SHG.

19. Richmond County, NY, Deed Book, 2:157, Samuel and Letitia Elliott & Sydney H. and Elizabeth Gay, July 17, 1850, Office of the Clerk. The Gays may have justified the large purchase price by regarding the large plot of land as an investment. They subsequently sold some of their land to Augustus Depeyster. See 30:382, July 2, 1853, and 40:442, September 29, 1857. They supposedly sold some land to Frank Shaw as well, but there is no record of the transaction in the official record of deeds.

20. Charles Haight Farnham, *A Life of Francis Parkman* (Boston: Little, Brown, 1923), 25.

21. Dwight was born and grew upon in Roxbury, Massachusetts, and is on the 1850 census for that town. Given the fact that he did not establish his own practice until 1862, the Shaws may have chosen him based on a friendship formed while they lived in West Roxbury; although, given their broad family relationships, he may also have been a relative.

22. Duncan Russell, ed., *Blue Eyed Child of Fortune: The Civil War Letters of Robert Gould Shaw* (Athens: University of Georgia Press, 1992), 11.

23. Ranlett, *The Architect*, 1:iii.

24. Description based on the floor plan in the collection of the New York Historical Society, Architects and Engineers Collection, PR 3, box PR, 3–19.

25. Joan Waugh, *Unsentimental Reformer: The Life of Josephine (Shaw) Lowell* (Cambridge, MA: Harvard University Press, 1998), 21.

26. Elizabeth (Neall) Gay to Sarah Pugh, June 10, 1855, series 1, box 19, SHG.

27. James Russell Lowell to Sarah Shaw, November 30, 1855, series 1, box 1, JRL.

28. Russell, *Blue Eyed Child of Fortune*, 11.

29. See, for example, Lydia Maria Child to Sarah Blake (Sturgis) Shaw, December 20, 1856, box 1, SBSS.

30. In a particularly evocative letter to Charles Eliot Norton, Curtis described standing at the open window in his study on an early spring morning "looking out over the bright meadows and hearing the birds and the merry brook." George William Curtis to Charles Eliot Norton, March 26, 1862, CEN.

31. The first night that the Curtises spent in the house was the last week of March 1860; see George William Curtis to Charles Eliot Norton, March 21, 1860, CEN.

32. For more information about Downing and his friendship with Curtis, see Schuyler, *Apostle of Taste*, 87–89.

33. For a discussion of the influence of Downing's writings on Ralph Waldo Emerson, see Robert D. Richardson Jr., *Emerson: The Mind on Fire* (Berkeley: University of California Press, 1995), 433–34.

34. Downing was killed in a steamboat explosion on July 28, 1852.

35. Alexander Jackson Downing, *Cottage Residences: Or a Series of Designs for Rural Cottages and Adapted to North America* (New York: Wiley and Putnam, 1842), 88.

36. For more information about Olmsted as a farmer and his life on Staten Island, see Laura Wood Roper, *FLO: A Biography of Frederick Law Olmsted* (Baltimore: Johns Hopkins University Press, 1973).

37. For more about Putnam's Staten Island house and social life, see George H. Putnam, *George Palmer Putnam: A Memoir* (New York: G. P. Putnam's Sons, 1912) 108–9.

38. George William Curtis, "Oration," 16–33, in New England Society of New York, *Unveiling of the Pilgrim Statue by the New England Society in the City of New York: At Central Park, June 6, 1885* (New York: The Society, 1885), 24.

39. Curtis, 19.

40. Curtis, 28.

41. George William Curtis, "James Russell Lowell," 1–54, in *Memorials of Two Friends: James Russell Lowell; George William Curtis* (New York: NY: Privately printed, 1902), 23.

42. The archival record for George Cabot Ward consists primarily of letters to his father, Thomas Wren Ward, written between 1842 and 1850. The information here is drawn from that correspondence. Obviously, Ward's thoughts on abolitionism developed over time and were likely influenced by his friendship with the Shaws after he moved to Staten Island. George C. Ward Correspondence, Thomas Wren Ward Papers (MS N-1726), Massachusetts Historical Society, Boston, MA.

43. Samuel Gray Ward and Frank had much in common. Like Frank, Samuel left his father's firm in 1845 to live an agricultural life on a farm near Lenox, Massachusetts, to pursue a transcendentalist life of self-culture. Unlike Frank, he was called back into business when his father died. For more information, see Ward-Perkins Family Papers, MSS 129, Department of Special Collections, Davidson Library, University of California, Santa Barbara and Samuel Gray Ward and Anna Hazard Barker Ward Papers, MS Am 1465, Houghton Library, Harvard University.

44. Elizabeth was the daughter of William Young, president of the Ulster Iron Works, Saugerties, New York.

45. In Thomas Day and James Murdock, *Brief Memoirs of the Class of 1797* (New Haven, CT: B. L. Hamlen, 1848), under "Staples, Seth Perkins."

46. For more information about *The Amistad*, see Marcus Rediker, *The Amistad Rebellion: An Atlantic Odyssey of Slavery and Freedom* (New York: Viking, 2012).

47. This description of activities based at the Stapleses' house is drawn from Charles G. Hine and William T. Davis, *Legends, Stories, and Folklore of Old Staten Island*, part 1, *The North Shore* (Staten Island, NY: Staten Island Historical Society, 1925), 44.

48. Information about Johnson is drawn from Benjamin W. Dwight, *The History of the descendants of Elder John Strong* (Albany, NY: Munsell, 1871), 636–37.

49. For more information about her ancestry, see Benjamin Woodbridge Dwight, *The History of the Descendants of John Dwight, of Dedham, Mass.* (New York: J. F. Trow & Son, 1874), 252–53.

50. Theodore Winthrop, writing Laura soon after her wedding (partial date [1847], series 1, box 1, MSS Col 3363), notes how sorry he is to hear William Templeton Johnson is still ill. Hearing news of their impending move, Theodore asserts, "It appears to me just the thing." Theodore Winthrop to Laura (Winthrop) Johnson, June 20, 1850, series 1, box 1, TW.

51. Laura (Winthrop) Johnson to Annie Fields, January 22, 1869, box 1, LWJ.

52. Laura (Winthrop) Johnson to Annie Fields, February 23, 1868, box 1, LWJ.

53. Samuel Gray Ward, *Ward Family Papers* (s.n., 1900), 85.

54. Ward, *Ward Papers*, 85.

55. Ward, 109.

56. Ward, 164.

57. Since Emerson visited his brother and lectured in New York City, it is tempting to think that he visited friends in Elliottville. If he did, such visits are not documented, but they would most likely have occurred in the 1850s. William Emerson purchased his first Staten Island land in 1837 and over several years continued to make real estate investments. From letters, we know that Ralph Waldo visited William on Staten Island, particularly in 1840, 1842, and 1843 when William was living in a modest farmhouse nicknamed the "Snuggery." By the time Emerson returned to lecture in New York City in 1850, William had constructed a pillared mansion named "Helvellyn" above the Snuggery. In the years 1852 and

1854, Ralph Waldo also visited William at Helvellyn. By 1860, William had leased his Staten Island property for three years and finally sold it in 1864. Afterward he lived in New York City until his death in 1868.

58. Sarah Blake (Sturgis) Shaw to Charles Eliot Norton, September 27, 1898, box 35, CEN.

59. Letter, James B. Curtis to Charles Eliot Norton, November 28, 1892; George William Curtis, "Emerson" in *Homes of American Authors* (G. P. Putnam's Sons, 1896).

60. Qtd. in Charles W. Leng and William T. Davis, *Staten Island and Its People: A History, 1609–1929*, vol. 2 (New York: Lewis Historical Publishing, 1930), 815.

Chapter 3

1. See Edward Clark Bridgman (1849–1931) interview with Mabel Abbott, July 14, 1929, MA.

2. Biographical information about Curtis draws upon Gordon Milne, *George William Curtis and the Genteel Tradition* (Bloomington: Indiana University Press, 1961); and Linda Dowling, *Galahad in the Gilded Age: A Life of George William Curtis* (Bloomington, IN: Xlibris, 2021).

3. George Curtis senior remained a banker for the rest of his life and in his final years was president of the Continental Bank. The Curtis house at 27 Washington Place was only a few doors away from 21 Washington Place, the residence of the Henry James Sr. family, where the writer Henry James would be born in 1843.

4. Earlier, Quincy had accompanied his cousin Francis Parkman on the journey in the American West that Parkman wrote about in *The Oregon Trail*.

5. George William Curtis, *The Howadji in Syria* (New York: Dix, Edwards, 1857), 348.

6. Appleton published several books but is best known today for his epigrams and spent most of his life traveling for pleasure.

7. Joshua E. Kastenberg, *The Blackstone of Military Law: Colonel William Winthrop* (Latham, MD: Scarecrow, 2009), 12.

8. This is clear from the letters James Russell Lowell sent Gay. See, for instance, James Russell Lowell to Sydney Howard Gay, April 15, 1848, series 1, box 1, JRL & SHG.

9. The baby's illness is mentioned in letters, and he is also referred to as Sydney Jr. See James Russell Lowell to Sydney Howard Gay, March 17, 1850, series 1, box 1, JRL & SHG; and Frank Shaw to Sydney Howard Gay, June 20, 1850, series 1, box 19, SHG. In writing to Frank Webb, Sydney also refers to "our little boy," Sydney Howard Gay to R. D. Webb, June 9, 1850, MS A. 1.2 v. 19, 14, Boston Public Library Rare Books and Manuscripts Department.

10. James Russell Lowell to Sydney Howard Gay, April 20, 1851, series 1, box 1, JRL & SHG.

11. James Russell Lowell to Sydney Howard Gay, January 3, 1851, series 1, box 1, JRL & SHG.

12. Edward Cary, *George William Curtis* (Cambridge, MA: Riverside Press / Harvard University Press, 1900), 102.

13. Milne, *George William Curtis*, 80.

14. Ezra Greenspan, *George Palmer Putnam: Representative American Publisher* (University Park: Pennsylvania State University Press, 2000), 85.

15. For more information on Olmsted and *Putnam's Monthly Magazine*, see Laura Wood Roper, "'Mr. Law' and *Putnam's Monthly Magazine*: A Note on a Phase in the Career of Frederick Law Olmsted," *American Literature* 26, no. 1 (March 1954): 88–93.

16. Gay kept his Record of Fugitives in 1856 and 1857. Foner estimates that during those years, mostly with the help of Louis Napoleon and William H. Leonard, Black men he employed in the offices of the *National Anti-Slavery Standard*, two hundred fugitives received aid in passing through New York City. See Eric Foner, *Gateway to Freedom: The Hidden History of the Underground Railroad* (New York: W. W. Norton, 2015), esp. 160.

17. Foner, 96.

18. The most effective way of conveying the racial hatred of the era is by quoting directly from sources that use racial epithets, as is done in this paragraph and elsewhere in the book.

19. See, for example, articles in the *Semi-Weekly Staten Islander*, July 9, 1856, 2, and July 25, 1857, 2.

20. Information about the Union Safety Committee and Aspinwall and Law's activities is drawn from Eric Foner, *Business and Slavery: The New York Merchants and the Irrepressible Conflict* (Chapel Hill: University of North Carolina Press), 1941.

21. Among these men were Samuel Ward (1786–1839), Gabriel Poillon Disosway (1799–1868), and William Alexander Duer (1780–1858). Both Disosway (a co-founder of Randolph Macon College in Ashland, Virginia) and Duer (who worked in Edward Livingston's law office in New Orleans) had direct experience of life in slave states.

22. This information is taken from Foner, *Gateway*, 188.

23. The notebook was first analyzed by Don Papson and Tom Calarco in *Secret Lives of the Underground Railroad in New York City: Sydney Howard Gay, Louis Napoleon, and the Record of Fugitives* (Jefferson, NC: McFarland, 2015).

24. Foner, *Gateway*, 177.

25. Louis Napoleon House Application, National Park Service, National Underground Railroad Network to Freedom, 2011.

26. Foner, *Gateway*, 99.

27. Foner, 177.

28. Foner, 230.

29. There are a number of websites and newspaper articles that make this claim. As early as 1980, the claim was made about one of Dr. Elliott's houses. See Dr. Samuel MacKenzie Elliott House: National Register of Historic Places Inventory, Nomination Form, 1980.

30. Foner, *Gateway*, 175.

31. For more information about Hamlet's arrest and public reaction, see Albert M. Rosenblatt, *The Eight: The Lemmon Slave Case and the Fight for Freedom* (Albany: State University of New York Press, 2023) 80–81.

32. Law and Vanderbilt engaged in lengthy and hostile rivalries. Law had purchased the New York and Harlem Railroad and the Mohawk Railroad, an impediment to Vanderbilt's railroad interests in and around the city. On Staten Island, Law had cleverly purchased the submerged land off the shore around what is now St. George, seeing the potential for ferry service from there into the city since it was the shortest distance (the ferry Vanderbilt had previously established was further to the south and a greater distance from Manhattan). By the time Vanderbilt sold his ferry to Law, Vanderbilt had lost a legal battle over a ferry service franchise and had begun to focus on large railroad projects.

33. David B. Danbom, "The Young America Movement," *Journal of the Illinois State Historical Society* 67, no. 3 (1974): 299, https://www.jstor.org/stable/40191117.

34. Danbom, 298.

35. Elizabeth (Neall) Gay to Sarah Pugh, December 11, 1859, series 1, box 19, SHG.

36. Gay to Pugh, December 11, 1859.

37. "Fanaticism-Sympathy-John Brownism," *Richmond County Gazette*, February 7, 1859, 2.

38. For more on this issue, see Foner, *Gateway*, 229.

39. Milne, *George William Curtis*, 91.

40. Lorien Foote, *Seeking the One Great Remedy: Francis George Shaw and Nineteenth-Century Reform* (Columbus: Ohio State University Press), 79.

41. *The Staaten Islander*, July 19, 1857, 2.

42. Elizabeth (Neall) Gay to Sarah Pugh, undated, series 1, box 20, SHG.

43. Elizabeth (Neall) Gay to Sydney Howard Gay, undated, series 1, box 20, SHG.

44. George William Curtis to Christopher Pearse Cranch, June 3, 1856, series 2, box 2, CPC.

45. George William Curtis, *The Duty of the American Scholar to Politics and the Times: An Oration Delivered on Tuesday, August 5, 1856, before the Literary Societies of Wesleyan University, Middleton, Conn.* (New York: Dix, Edwards, 1856), 42.

46. Lydia Maria Child to Sarah Blake (Sturgis) Shaw, October 27, 1856, box 1, SBSS.

47. *The Staaten Islander*, August 12, 1856, 2.
48. *The Staaten Islander*, November 29, 1856, 2.
49. *The Staaten Islander*, November 12, 1856, 2.
50. Dowling, *Galahad in the Gilded Age*, 195.
51. Charles E. Beveridge and Charles Capen McLaughlin, eds. *The Papers of Frederick Law Olmsted*, vol. 2 (Balitmore, MD: Johns Hopkins University Press, 1981), 21–23.
52. Dowling, *Galahad in the Gilded Age*, 196.
53. George William Curtis to Charles Eliot Norton, January 3, 1860, box 9, CEN.
54. George William Curtis to Christopher Pearse Cranch, May 2, 1856, series 2, box 3, CPC.
55. Josephine (Shaw) Lowell Papers, RA.A/L915, Radcliffe College.
56. Hobart Clark, *A Retrospect of Fifty Years: A Discourse* (Boston: George H. Ellis Printers, 1903), 5–7.
57. Elizabeth W. Winthrop, "Letter 2, no Title," *The Literary World: A Monthly Review of Current Literature (1870–1904)*, June 1, 1873, 10, American Periodicals Series (Proquest).
58. L. P. Gratacap Diary, 1873, MSS Col 1199, New York Public Library, Manuscripts and Archives Division.
59. Mrs. Emily Hare, pseud. Laura (Winthrop) Johnson, *Little Blossom's Reward: A Christmas Book for Children* (Boston: Phillips, Sampson, 1854).
60. For effect, Johnson may have conflated Bergen Point Lighthouse (established 1849), which did have grounds around it, and Robbin's Reef Lighthouse (established by the federal government in 1838 as the first offshore lighthouse in New York harbor), which would have been more visible from the Johnsons' but did not have grounds. Each lighthouse had modest living quarters, but the Bergen Point Lighthouse had a structure similar to what Johnson describes. In her account, an elderly couple lived there and sold apples, cakes, and beer to visitors.
61. Hare, *Little Blossom's Reward*, 21.
62. Kastenberg, *Blackstone of Military Law*, 70.
63. Theodore Winthrop to Laura (Winthrop) Johnson, partial date 1847, series 1, box 1, TW.
64. Theodore Winthrop to Laura (Winthrop) Johnson, October 2, 1847, series 1, box 1, TW.
65. George William Curtis, "Theodore Winthrop," *Atlantic Monthly*, August 1, 1861, 242–52.
66. Theodore Winthrop to Elizabeth Woolsey Winthrop, July 3, 1851, series 1, box 1, TW.
67. Theodore Winthrop to Elizabeth Woolsey Winthrop, July 3, 1851.
68. Theodore Winthrop to Elizabeth Woolsey Winthrop, August 24, 1851, series 1, box 1, TW.

69. Theodore Winthrop to Elizabeth Woolsey Winthrop, July 25, 1852, and, June 16, 1851, series 1, box 1, TW.

70. Anne Mazlish, ed., *The Tracy Log Book, 1855: The Diary of Charles Tracy on Mount Desert Island* (Bar Harbor, ME: Acadia / Mount Desert Historical Society, 1997), 153.

71. This trip is detailed in Mazlish, *Tracy Log Book*.

72. Biographical information about Shaw is drawn from Russell Duncan, ed., *Blue-Eyed Child of Fortune: The Civil War Letters of Colonel Robert Gould Shaw* (Athens: University of Georgia, 1992).

73. Theodore Winthrop to William Templeton Johnson, March 17, 1857, series 1, box 1, TW.

74. Theodore Winthrop to William Templeton Johnson, March 17, 1857.

75. Theodore Winthrop to Laura (Winthrop) Johnson, May 15, 1857, series 1, box 1, TW.

76. Annette Blaugrund, *The Tenth Street Studio Building: Artistic Entrepreneurs from the Hudson River School to the American Impressionists* (Washington, DC: Parrish Art Museum, 1997).

77. After his death, Winthrop's family asserted that he had written his novels at the Johnson house on Staten Island. We learn from her letters that Laura (Winthrop) Johnson maintained Theodore's room in his memory and showed it to visiting admirers of his novels as the place where he had written them. Her son, Oliver T. Johnson, in writing to his relative F. Winthrop White April 18, 1932, also stated: "All Theodore's books were written in the old house."

78. Winthrop wrote a forty-page booklet about the painting that was available when the work was first exhibited at Lyric Hall and Tenth Street Studio in New York in 1859. For more on Winthrop at the Tenth Street Studios, see David Peters Corbett, "Art, Morality, and the National Interest: Theodore Winthrop, Frederick Church, and Martin Johnson Heade at the Tenth Street Studios in 1859," *European Journal of American Studies* 30, no. 2 (June 2011): 57–72.

79. George William Curtis, "Theodore Winthrop," *Atlantic Monthly* 8, no. 46 (August 1861), 248.

80. Corbett, "Art, Morality, and the National Interest," 57–72.

81. "Obituary: Charles Pfaff," *New York Times*, April 26, 1890, 2.

82. Annie Fields considered William Templeton Johnson "cumbrous." Journal entry qtd. in Rita K. Gollin, *Annie Adams Fields: Woman of Letters* (Amherst: University of Massachusetts Press, 2002), 54.

83. Kastenberg, *Blackstone of Military Law*, 26.

84. The analysis of the Winthrops' abolitionism is from Kastenberg, 70.

85. Starting in the 1850s new lines of ready-made clothing of a higher quality clothed other social classes, including '49ers during the gold rush.

86. "Response to the Election," *Richmond County Gazette*, 2.

87. *Richmond County Gazette*, January 16, 1861, 2.

88. *Richmond County Gazette*, January 23, 1861, 2.

89. Mike Wallace and Edwin G. Burrows, *Gotham: A History of New York City to 1898* (New York: Oxford University Press, 1999), 866.

90. For a detailed account of the meeting based upon contemporary newspaper accounts, see Richard M. Bayles, *History of Richmond County, New York: From Its Discovery to the Present Time* (New York: L. E. Preston, 1887), 277.

91. Qtd. from a letter by Robert Gould Shaw to Sarah Blake (Sturgis) Shaw, April 20, 1861; Duncan, *Blue-Eyed Child of Fortune*, 76.

92. Duncan, 70.

93. Joan Waugh, *Unsentimental Reformer: The Life of Josephine (Shaw) Lowell* (Cambridge, MA: Harvard University Press, 1997), 52.

94. Duncan, *Blue-Eyed Child of Fortune*, 83.

95. Kastenberg, *Blackstone of Military Law*, 77.

96. Benjamin F. Butler and Jessie Ames Marshall, *Private and Official Correspondence of General Benjamin F. Butler*, vol. 1 (Norwood, MA: Pimpton, 1917), 136.

97. Butler and Marshall, 78.

98. Warren Lee Goss, "Recollections of a Private: Up the Peninsula with McClellan," *Century Illustrated Magazine*, March 1, 1885, 767–68.

99. The burden of Elizabeth Woolsey Winthrop's bereavement was deepened by anxiety over her surviving son William Winthrop who served out the war with the Seventh New York Regiment. He received a commission as sharpshooter October 1, 1861; became a captain September 22, 1862; and was promoted to major and judge advocate on September 19, 1864. He went on to serve in the regular army after 1867, eventually being promoted to lieutenant colonel and deputy judge advocate in 1887. A professor for many years at the US Military Academy, he is known for his writings on military law. For more information, see Kastenberg, *Blackstone of Military Law*.

100. Elizabeth (Neall) Gay to Laura (Winthrop) Johnson, undated, series 1, box 22, SHG.

101. See, for instance, his letter to his mother, June 16, 1861; Duncan, *Blue-Eyed Child of Fortune*, 109.

102. The tribute was published in *The Atlantic Monthly* (citation above). He later prefixed this material to Winthrop's first posthumously published novel. George William Curtis, "Biographical Sketch of the Author," in *Cecil Dreeme* (Boston: Ticknor and Fields, 1862), 5–19.

103. Strong discusses Winthrop in his journal, George Templeton Strong, *The Diary of George Templeton Strong*, vol. 2, *1850–1859*, eds. Allan Nevis and Milton Halsey Thomas (New York: Macmillan, 1952), 110.

104. Strong, *Diary of George Templeton Strong*, 110.

105. Curtis, *Cecil Dreeme*, 6, 8.

106. Curtis, 17.

107. Curtis, 19.
108. Curtis, 14.
109. Typewritten copy of Sarah Blake (Sturgis) Shaw to Robert Gould Shaw, February 6, 1863, box 14, GM.
110. Lydia Maria Child to Sarah Blake (Sturgis) Shaw, January 17, 1869, box 1, MS. S–709, John Parkman Papers, Massachusetts Historical Society.
111. Duncan Russell, *Where Death and Glory Met: Colonel Robert G. Shaw and the 54th Massachusetts Infantry* (Athens: University of Georgia, 1999), 92–99.
112. Duncan, *Blue-Eyed Child of Fortune*, 52–53.
113. *American National Biography*, under "Shaw, Robert Gould."
114. George W. Frederickson, "The Martyr and His Friends," in *The Inner Civil War: Northern Intellectuals and the Crisis of the Union* (Urbana: University of Illinois Press, 1965), 151–65.
115. Annie left the United States before the war's end and spent much of her life living in France and Switzerland, accompanying her mother, Elizabeth Sedgwick Kneeland Haggerty (1813–1888), and her sister, Clemence Haggerty Crafts (1841–1912), who in 1868 had married James Mason Crafts (1839–1917). Crafts, who spent much of his career as a professor of chemistry at MIT, divided his time between MIT and the Sorbonne. Annie maintained some contact with the Shaw family through a correspondence with Josephine (Shaw) Lowell but was never part of the Staten Island community.
116. *Richmond County Gazette*, "Fourth of July," June 11, 1862, 2.
117. Bayles, *History of Richmond County*, 287.
118. Charles G. Hine and William T. Davis, *Legends, Stories, and Folklore of Old Staten Island*, part 1, *The North Shore* (Staten Island, NY: Staten Island Historical Society, 1925), 69–79.
119. Hine and Davis, 72.
120. The account of the efforts to raise money to avoid conscription is adapted from Bayles, *History of Richmond County*, 287ff. He points out that as new quota demands were made in October 1863, March 1864, and July 1864, more and more money was raised to buy recruits. By the last year of the war, the Richmond County debt had risen to $700,000.
121. "The Riots on Staten Island," *Richmond County Gazette*, July 22, 1863.
122. "The Riots on Staten Island."
123. Laura (Winthrop) Johnson to Annie Fields, September 24, 1863, box 1, LWJ.
124. Lydia Maria Child to Francis George Shaw, December 26, 1852, box 1, SBSS.
125. Laura (Winthrop) Johnson to Annie Fields, January 12, 1863, box 1, LWJ.
126. Lydia Maria Child to Sarah Blake (Sturgis) Shaw, January 17, 1869, box 1, MS S–709, John Parkman Papers, Massachusetts Historical Society.

127. Sarah Blake (Sturgis) Shaw to Elizabeth (Neall) Gay, June 25, 1864, series 1, box 61, SHG.

128. Robert Bowne Minturn Jr., *Memoir of Robert Bowne Minturn* (New York: Published by the author, 1871), 183.

129. Robert Bowne Minturn Jr. presents an extensive account of his father's life; see Minturn, *Memoir of Robert Bowne Minturn*.

130. Information about Charles Russell Lowell and his courtship and marriage to Josephine Shaw is drawn from Edward W. Emerson, *Life and Letters of Charles Russell Lowell* (Boston: Houghton Mifflin, 1907); and Waugh, *Unsentimental Reformer*.

131. Josephine (Shaw) Lowell Papers, RA.A/L915, Radcliffe College.

132. Albert Bigelow Paine, *Thomas Nast: His Period and His Pictures* (New York: Macmillan, 1904), 218.

133. Milne, *George William Curtis*, 118.

134. Milne, 132.

135. Milne, 126.

136. Milne, 128.

137. Laura (Winthrop) Johnson to Annie Fields, September 20, 1862, box 1, LWJ.

138. George William Curtis to Anna (Shaw) Curtis, August 17, 1862, box 2, folder 8, GWC.

Chapter 4

1. Joan Waugh, *Unsentimental Reformer: The Life of Josephine Shaw Lowell* (Cambridge, MA: Harvard University Press, 1998), 90–91.

2. Laura (Winthrop) Johnson to Annie Fields, September 24, 1878, box 1, LWJ.

3. Johnson to Fields, June 14, 1880, box 1, LWJ.

4. Johnson to Fields, June 14, 1880, box 1, LWJ.

5. Josephine (Shaw) Lowell was an active board member on the New York State Board of Charities until 1889. She also founded the New York Charity Organization, 1882; the House of Refuge for Women, 1886 (later known as the New York Training School for Girls); the New York Consumer League, 1890; the Woman's Municipal League, 1894; and the Civil Service Reform Association of New York State, 1895. At the time of her death in 1905 she was widely acknowledged for her good works. A memorial dedicated in 1912 and known as the Josephine Lowell Memorial Fountain is located in Bryant Park at 41 West Fortieth Street in New York City. Waugh, *Unsentimental*.

6. Lorien Foote, *Seeking the One Great Remedy: Francis George Shaw and Nineteenth-Century Reform* (Athens: Ohio University 2003), 168–73.

7. Foote, 176.

8. Remarks of Hon. George William Curtis of Richmond Co. on the Report of the Committee on the Right of Suffrage, Delivered in Convention, July 19, 1867 (S.I., 1867), 372.

9. Gordon Milne, *George William Curtis and the Genteel Tradition* (Bloomington: Indiana University Press, 1961), 99–102.

10. Sarah Blake (Sturgis) Shaw to Helena (de Kay) Gilder, August 23, 1894, series 1, box 14, GM. Shaw and Gilder were at odds over women's suffrage. Gilder publicly opposed the vote for women, claiming that political responsibilities would weaken women's role in the household as moral compass, educator, and nurse of children. Even Shaw's scare tactic in this letter—introducing the image of immigrant hordes of men whose vote could be nullified if intelligent White women had the vote—was of no avail.

11. For more on Elizabeth Curtis's activities, see Maggi Smith Dalton, "Biographical Sketch of Elizabeth Burrill Curtis," https://documents.alexanderstreet.com/d/1010113893; for more on Mary Willcox's activities, see Ashley Tatum, "Biographical Sketch of Mary Otis Gay Willcox," https://documents.alexanderstreet.com/d/1009860164.

12. For more on Curtis and civil service reform, see Linda Dowling, *Galahad in the Gilded Age: A Life of George William Curtis* (Bloomington, IN: Xlibris, 2021), 262ff.

13. Charles Eliot Norton, *Memorials of Two Friends, James Russell Lowell: 1819–1891, George William Curtis: 1824–1892* (New York: Gilliss Press, 1902), 88.

14. The Gibbons family had housed escaped slaves at their residence at 339 West Twenty-Ninth Street, and a mob burned down their house during the draft riots of 1863. James Gibbons, a cousin of Horace Greeley, had also written the inspirational Civil War song "We Are Coming, Father Abraham."

15. Laura (Winthrop) Johnson to Annie Fields, August 16, 1868, box 1, LWJ.

16. Laura (Winthrop) Johnson to Annie Fields, August 16, 1868.

17. See Alfred Habegger, *Masked: The Life of Anna Leonowens, Schoolmistress at the Court of Siam* (Madison: University of Wisconsin Press, 2014), 317.

18. Laura (Winthrop) Johnson to Annie Fields, August 16, 1868, box 1, LWJ.

19. This location was relatively close to the Barrett family's New York Dyeing and Printing Establishment. This large-scale textile operation was expanding during the time Leonowens was in the neighborhood. In addition to the factory buildings and worker housing, there was a large factory pond filled with wastewater. After a year, Leonowens rented another cottage on the other side of Elliottville, close to Sailors' Snug Harbor. Neither of Leonowens's rental cottages are extant.

20. Laura (Winthrop) Johnson to Annie Fields, undated [September 1868?], box 1, LWJ.

21. Charles G. Hine and William T. Davis, *Legends, Stories, and Folklore of Old Staten Island. Part 1, The North Shore* (Staten Island, NY: Staten Island Historical Society, 1925), 93.

22. According to Habegger, the king monitored the foreign press and issued rebuttals to inaccuracies. See Habegger, *Masked*, 309.

23. Laura (Winthrop) Johnson to Annie Fields, undated [August 1868?], box 1, LWJ.

24. Habegger, *Masked*, 315–16.

25. William Radler Hunt, *Suffragettes and the Romance of the Harem: The Evolution of Sympathy and the Afterlives of Sentimentality in American Feminist Orientalism, 1865–1920* (PhD diss., Duke University, 2016), 45ff.

26. *Richmond County Gazette*, June 28, 1871.

27. Susan Morgan, *Bombay Anna: The Real Story and Remarkable Adventures of the King and I Governess* (Berkeley: University of California Press, 2008), 180.

28. The location is documented in Mrs. F. Theodore White to Mabel Abbott, December 17, 1948, box 1, folder 21, MA. Leonowens's rental cottage no longer exists.

29. For instance, Laura (Winthrop) Johnson to Annie Fields, April 5, 1877, box 1, LWJ.

30. Anna Leonowens to Emily Ford, April 4, 1881, box 1, folder 1, Anna Harriette Leonowens Papers, 1872–1888, MSS Col. 3453, New York Public Library.

31. Habegger, *Masked*, 339.

32. Laura (Winthrop) Johnson to Annie Fields, September 24, 1878, box 1, LWJ.

33. Habegger, *Masked*, 342.

34. William Rhinelander Stewart, *The Philanthropic Work of Josephine (Shaw) Lowell* (New York: Macmillan, 1911), 49

35. Parker's daughter married Charles Goodhue and she donated their Staten Island house to the Children's Aid Society.

36. George William Curtis to James Russell Lowell, December 29, 1869, series 1, box 1, JRL.

Chapter 5

1. Laura (Winthrop) Johnson to Annie Fields, undated [Spring 1878?], box 1, LWJ.

2. Sarah Mifflin Gay to Sydney Howard Gay, undated [October 1868?], series 1, box 23, SHG.

3. Sydney Howard Gay to Sarah Mifflin Gay, undated [1871?], series 1, box 32, SHG.

4. The phrase "Fifth Avenue of Staten Island" first appears in Manhattan newspapers, but Staten Island newspapers soon picked up the phrase, and week after week in the 1880s and 1890s the phrase was used in real estate advertisements for property on Bard Avenue.

5. Henry Hall, ed., *America's Successful Men of Affairs: The City of New York* (New York: New-York Tribune, 1895), under "Anson Livingston," 398–99.

6. For more on the regard Elliottville residents had for Livingston and his wife, see Charles G. Hine and William T. Davis, *Legends, Stories, and Folklore of Old Staten Island*, part 1, *The North Shore* (Staten Island, NY: Staten Island Historical Society, 1925), 34.

7. Information about the history of Garner & Co. is from William R. Bagnall, *Sketches of Manufacturing Establishments in New York City, and of Textile Establishments in the United States* (North Andover, MA: Merrimack Valley Textile Museum, 1908; repr. 1977), 1620ff.

8. The founder of the works, John Glass, had been killed in a steamboat explosion.

9. "The Harmony Mills Company," in George Rogers Howell and Jonathan Tenney, *History of the County of Albany, N.Y. from 1609–1886* (New York: W. W. Munsell, 1886), 952–56.

10. US Department of the Interior/National Park Service, *National Register of Historic Places Registration Form, Rockland Print Works*, 16.

11. Bagnall, *Sketches*, 1647.

12. US, *Register*, 17.

13. US, *Register*, 17.

14. US, *Register*, 17.

15. Howell and Tenney, *History*, 952–56.

16. William's mother, Frances Mathilda Thorne (1809–1862), had been born in Glen Cove, Long Island and grew up in New York City. Her parents were William Thorne (1777–1861) and Anne Knapp (1782–1856). William Thorne was the brother of Frost Thorn (1793–1854), Mary Marcellite's father. William and Frost's parents were Charles Thorne (1753–1818) and Anne Kirby (1752–1845). Most of Charles' children simplified the family name to Thorn, only Frances's father seems to have kept the final "*e*." Although Frances Mathilda had the final "*e*" in her surname, either she or her son dropped the final "*e*" in his middle name, William "Thorn" Garner. Based on multiple genealogy entries, Family Search, accessed, October 9, 2023, https://www.familysearch.org.

17. According to his grave marker in Greenwood Cemetery, Brooklyn, Garner was also born in New Orleans.

18. The Mexican government granted land through empresario contracts in exchange for recruiting new settlers. See Mary Virginia Henderson, "Minor Empresario Contracts for the Colonization of Texas, 1825–1834," *The Southwestern Historical Quarterly* 31, no. 4 (1928): 295–324, http://www.jstor.org/stable/30242530.

19. For instance Frost Thorn to Stephen Austin, July 22, 1828, Digital Austin Papers, https://digitalaustinpapers.org/document?id=APB1569.

20. James was the son of Frost Sr.'s brother Hallet Thorn, 1790–1872.

21. Texas State Historical Association. Handbook of Texas History Online, accessed June 14, 2018, http://tsha.utexas.edu/handbook/online, under "Thorn, Frost (1793–1854)."

22. "Lady Gordon-Cumming and Her Mother," *Once a Week: An Illustrated Newspaper*, Aug 4, 1891; 7, 16, American Periodicals Series (Proquest).

23. In general, opposition to the war in the New York City area was strong due in great part the city's economic dependence on the South as a source of cotton for the textile industry and Southern markets for the sale of goods. The city's mayor, Fernando Wood, was a "Peace Democrat" who led opposition to the war.

24. T. P. O., "Reminiscence of a Texas Lady," *Galveston Daily News*, July 23, 1876, Readex: America's Historical Newspapers (Newsbank).

25. Garner's maternal uncle, William Knapp Thorn (1807–1887), had married Emily Almira Vanderbilt (1823–1896), a daughter of Cornelius Vanderbilt, but it would not be until after 1882 that the Vanderbilt connection would have provided entrée into the best society.

26. "Sea Side Notes," *Portsmouth Journal of Literature and Politics* 86, no. 35 (August 26, 1876): [2], Readex: America's Historical Newspapers (Newsbank).

27. "William T. and Marcellite Garner Mansion," New York City Landmarks Preservation Commission Research File.

28. "William T. and Marcellite Garner Mansion," New York City Landmarks Preservation Commission Research File.

29. "The Dey Street Nuisance," *New York Times*, November 3, 1872, 4.

30. "Appalling Disaster," *New York Times*, July 31, 1871, 1.

31. "Another Indignation Meeting," *New York Times*, October 10, 1875, 7.

32. "The New-York Yacht Club," *New York Times*, January 22, 1876, 5.

33. "The Queen of Yachts," *Aquatic Monthly and Nautical Review: Devoted to the Interests of the Yachting and Rowing Communities* 5, no. 1 (January 1, 1875): 45, American Antiquarian Society Historical Periodicals (Gale).

34. "New-York Yacht Club," *Aquatic Monthly and Nautical Review: Devoted to the Interests of the Yachting and Rowing Communities* 5, no. 3 (March 1, 1875): 177, American Antiquarian Society Historical Periodicals (Gale).

35. Description from, "A Sad Yachting Calamity," *New-York Tribune*, July 21, 1876, 1. The Garner clubhouse was much more elaborate than the NYYC club stations the organization had in the 1890s, at Bay Ridge, NY; Whitestone, NY; New London, CT; and Glen Cove, NY. See John Parkinson, *The History of the New York Yacht Club from Its Founding through 1973* (New York: New York Yacht Club, 1975).

36. Parkinson, *History of the New York Yacht Club*, 66.

37. "The Yacht *Mohawk*: Launch of the Largest Sailing Yacht in the World, Her Build and Dimensions," *New York Times*, June 10, 1875, 10.

38. Fred S. Cozzens, et al., *Yachts and Yachting*, rev. ed. (New York: Cassell, 1888), 67.

39. "Sketches of Mr. and Mrs. Garner," *New York Times*, July 21, 1876, 1

40. "The Wreck of the *Mohawk*," *New York Times*, July 24, 1876, 8.

41. The rifles were, in some ways, an odd choice. Springfield first introduced the breech-loading firearm in 1873 and the same year the rifle became the first standard-issue breech-loading rifle to be adopted by the US Army and was used extensively in the Indian Wars. These were not the type of rifles that a sportsman would choose for hunting; they might be used to arm a militia.

42. "The Wreck of the *Mohawk*," *New York Times*, July 24, 1876, 8.

43. "Yacht Racing in a Calm: The Race for the Garner Cups at Newport," *New York Times*, September 17, 1875, 5.

44. "William T. and Marcellite Garner Mansion," New York City Landmarks Preservation Commission Research File.

45. "The Davenports and Thornes," *St. Louis Globe-Democrat*, January 29, 1878, 2, American Periodicals Series (Proquest).

46. "Death of Mrs. Davenport Thorne," *New York Times*, January 15, 1878, 1.

47. Reginald T. Townsend, *Mother of Clubs: Being the History of the First Hundred Years of the Union Club of the City of New York* (New York: W. E. Rudge, 1936).

48. Born Arthur Randolph Mullings, Mullings legally changed his name to Arthur Randolph Randolph to meet stipulations required to inherit from a Randolph relative.

49. For more information about Morgan's affair with May, see Jean Strouse, *Morgan: American Financier* (New York: Random House, 2014), 285–99. The romance between May and Whitney is presented in W. A. Swanberg, *Whitney Father: Whitney Heiress* (New York: Charles Scribner's Sons, 1980).

50. Accounts varied and no investigation was conducted. The *Ideal* was criticized later for not immediately going alongside the *Mohawk*, but first steering around her. An eyewitness claimed that the *Ideal* made fast to the *Mohawk*'s stern, rather than to the bow, which was still out of the water, and was perceived to have pulled the *Mohawk* further under water.

51. "The *Mohawk* Calamity: End of the Coroner's Inquest," *New York Times*, July 23, 1876, 12.

52. "*Mohawk* Calamity," 12.

53. "The Wreck of the *Mohawk*," *New York Times*, July 24, 1876, 8.

54. "The *Mohawk* Squall," *Sunday Mercury* (New York), July 23, 1876, 4, Readex: America's Historical Newspapers (Newsbank).

55. "*Mohawk* Squall," 4.

56. "The *Mohawk* Catastrophe: Funeral Obsequies of Mr. and Mrs. Garner and Mr. Frost Thorne," *Frank Leslie's Illustrated Newspaper*, August 12, 1876, 380

57. First among these was Frances "Fanny" Adelaide (Garner) Lawrance (1841–1908) and her husband Francis Cooper Lawrance (1834–1912), who became

wards of the Garner daughters. The other principal mourners were Harriet Amory Garner (b. 1837), widow of William's brother Thomas (1838–1869). Garner's other sisters in attendance were Josephine Garner (1837–1892), Caroline Garner (b. 1842) and Anna Garner James (b. 1851).

58. Rev. Mr. Johnson, Pastor of Christ Church, New Brighton, and the Rev. Horace E. Pratt, the former rector of St. Mary's Church.

59. "The *Mohawk* Victims: Funeral Rites at New Brighton," *New York Times*, July 25, 1876, 8.

60. "The *Mohawk* Catastrophe: Funeral Obsequies of Mr. and Mrs. Garner and Mr. Frost Thorne," *Frank Leslie's Illustrated Newspaper*, August 12, 1876, 380.

61. George William Curtis, "Shall Bad Men be Praised because They are Dead?," *Universalist (Boston)*, March 30, 1872, 1, American Antiquarian Society Historical Periodicals (Gale).

62. Curtis, 89.

63. Curtis, 89.

64. Curtis, 89.

65. The account of the Soutter family is from Emily Soutter Dix, *Reminiscences of the Knox and Soutter Families of Virginia* (Charlottesville, VA: De Vinne Press, 1895). Even though Dix had married a New York clergyman and was writing thirty years after the war and had lived in New York during most of that time, she still referred to the war as the Northern invasion of the South.

66. James T. Soutter's daughter, Emily Woolsey Dix, described the family life in Paris. The Soutters lived at 16 Rue de Marignan and neighboring houses were occupied by James Mason and John Slidell, who, according to Dix, were in constant telegraphic contact with men on the other side of the Atlantic and "nearly every Southern man in Paris was either at our house or opposite" (Dix, *Reminiscences of the Knox and Soutter Families*, 48). One of the Southrons waiting for a ship to command, Captain Charles Fauntleroy, married Dix's sister Sallie while the family was in Europe. According to Dix, it was James T. Soutter who carried a letter from Jefferson Davis to the Pope. Although she does not recount the outcome, in a letter back to Davis the Pope addressed him as "Illustrious and Hon. Jefferson Davis, President of the Confederate States of America," which some used to claim that the Vatican had officially recognized the Confederacy (49). According to Dix, after the war her father devoted himself and a substantial part of his income to relief efforts in Virginia and was a close friend of Robert E. Lee. On a trip to the South, most of the family visited Jefferson Davis in prison.

67. For more on Lamar, see Thomas Robson Hay, "Gazaway Bugg Lamar, Confederate Banker and Business Man," *Georgia Historical Quarterly* 37, no. 2 (June 1953): 89–128; and Stephen Wise, *Lifeline of the Confederacy* (Columbia: University of South Carolina Press, 1988).

68. Since James T. Soutter's wealth was in land, he had an easier time than his former business associate, Gazaway Bugg Lamar. Lamar had taken the so-called

Lincoln loyalty oath as General Sherman's forces approached Savannah and capture was certain. His efforts to reclaim his cotton from warehouses in Georgia and Florida and get compensation for vast quantities of cotton destroyed by Union troops took years, but he was finally compensated in 1874 with $580,000, the largest government settlement made. His heirs pursued additional claims that were settled in 1919 for $75,000. See Robert Neil Mathis, "The Ordeal of Confiscation: The Post-Civil War Trials of Gazaway Bugg Lamar," *Georgia Historical Quarterly* 63, no. 3 (Fall 1979): 339–52.

69. The house and grounds were described in sales materials in 1888; see, for instance, an advertisement in the *New-York Tribune*, July 20, 1888, 7. The 1880 federal census enumerates the household.

70. "Modern Bandits," *New York Times*, January 6, 1874, 5.

71. James Taylor left Rugby School in 1868 and was graduated from Corpus Christi College, Oxford, in 1872. In New York, he was a member of the University Club and was a cricket player and president of the St. Georges Cricket Club based on Staten Island, that competed internationally.

72. "Staten Island," *New York Times*, June 25, 1889, 2.

73. "William Knox Soutter," *New-York Tribune*, March 14, 1891, 7, Readex: America's Historical Newspapers (Newsbank); "William K. Soutter Buried," *New York Times*, March 17, 1891, 8.

74. George William Curtis, "Public Benefactors," in *From the Easy Chair* (New York: Harper and Brothers, 1894), 160.

75. "Mrs. Soutter's Will Filed," *New-York Tribune*, March 11, 1899, 9, Readex: America's Historical Newspapers (Newsbank).

76. Wynant was also involved in shipping and had a property in Little Neck (now Douglaston), New York. When he died, his property was sold to George Douglas of Douglaston, the father of William Proctor Douglas (the yachtsman mentioned above).

77. "Alleged Incendiarism: William T. Vanzant Indicted and Arrested for Arson," *New York Herald* 43, no. 233 (August 21, 1878): 9, Readex: America's Historical Newspapers (Newsbank).

78. *New York Herald* 43, no. 240 (August 28, 1878): 10, Readex: America's Historical Newspapers (Newsbank).

79. "Vanzandt Acquitted: The Charge of Arson Against Him Dismissed—Pretty Tall Swearing Somewhere," *New York Herald* 43, no. 240 (August 28, 1878): 10, Readex: America's Historical Newspapers (Newsbank).

80. "Condemnations," *NY Journal*, July 15, 1896, 18, Readex: America's Historical Newspapers (Newsbank).

81. George William Curtis to Sydney Howard Gay, August 23, 1865, series 1, box 10, SHG.

82. Lydia Maria Child to Sarah Shaw, May 20, 1872, box 1, SBSS.

83. George William Curtis to Sydney Howard Gay, August 23, 1865, series 1, box 10, SHG.

84. Elizabeth (Neall) Gay to Sarah Pugh, August 24, 1867, series 1, box 19A, SHG.

85. Elizabeth (Neall) Gay to Sarah Pugh, [partial date] 1868, series 1, box 19A, SHG.

86. Gay to Pugh, [partial date] 1868.

87. Sydney Howard Gay to Elizabeth (Neall) Gay, March 15,1869, series 1, box 31, SGH.

88. Sydney Howard Gay to Elizabeth (Neall) Gay, April 24, 1869, series 1, box 31, SHG.

89. Elizabeth (Neall) Gay to William Winthrop, August 18, 1869, series 1, box 19A, SHG.

90. George William Curtis to Sydney Howard Gay, February 7, 1869, series 1, box 10, SHG.

91. Although the work is unsigned, Gay takes credit as author, see Sydney Howard Gay to Thomas Wentworth Higginson, October 28, 1882, series 1, box 37, SHG.

92. Elizabeth (Neall) Gay to Sarah Mifflin Gay, May 6, 1872, series 1, box 19b, SHG.

93. Sarah Mifflin Gay to Elizabeth (Neall) Gay, December 24, 1870, series 1, box 23, SHG.

94. Sydney Howard Gay to Sarah Mifflin Gay, undated [1872?], series 1, box 32, SHG.

95. Sydney Howard Gay to Sarah Mifflin Gay, undated [1872?], series 1, box 24, SHG.

96. By 1868 Johnson is already writing about letting Julia plan parties at the Johnson house, see Laura (Winthrop) Johnson to Annie Fields, February 23, 1868, box 1, LWJ.

97. For more about the Commodore and the de Kay family, see Leona Mae DeKay Fisher, *The DeKay Family in America* (Downy, CA: n.p., 1973).

98. De Kay's brother James Ellsworth de Kay (a well-known physician and naturalist) had married Eckford's daughter Janet (1802–1854) in 1831. Information about de Kay is presented in the article on his brother in *Appletons' Cyclopædia of American Biography* (1900), under "de Kay, James Ellsworth."

99. Laura (Winthrop) Johnson to Annie Fields, March 7, 1867, box 1, LWJ.

100. *Appletons' Cyclopædia of American Biography* (1900), under "de Kay, James Ellsworth."

101. Katherine de Kay Bronson, "Recollections of My First Decade," series 2, box 15, GM.

102. Bronson, "Recollections."

103. Robert L. Harrison, "The de Kay Family," accessed October 9, 2023, https://www.oysterbayhistorical.org/submissions-summer-2011.html.

104. The Eckford Estate, a trust, was still active long after Julia's death. At that point, Richard Watson Gilder and Charles de Kay were trustees. Some information about the trust can be found in Gilder MSS, 1781–1984 (LMC 2345), Lilly Library, Indiana University, Bloomington.

105. *New York Times*, June 12, 1886, 5.

106. *New York Times*, July 28, 1862, 3.

107. *New York Times*, August 31, 1890, 5.

108. For more information about the de Kays's time in Newport, see Lyndall Gordon, *A Private Life of Henry James* (New York: Norton, 1999). Katherine's pregnancy and the birth of her first child was one reason the de Kays were in Newport. Janet's first grandchild, Edith, was born in 1861. Edith eventually married Count Cosimo Rucellai in 1895 and lived in Italy at the Villa Rucellai. She died in 1956. *New York Times*, December 6, 1956, 37.

109. For information about the Bronson family wealth, see John D. Haeger, *The Investment Frontier: New York Businessmen and the Economic Development of the Old Northwest* (Albany: State University of New York Press, 1981).

110. Gordon, *Private Life of Henry James*.

111. Drake de Kay to Helena (de Kay) Gilder, January 6, 1863, series 1, box 3, GM.

112. Richmond County, NY, Deed Book 14:422, Thomas E. and Anne Davis and George C. de Kay, September 18, 1846, Clerk of Courts, Staten Island. He sold the land to Jane S. Ward, et al., 18:118, October 19, 1848.

113. Richmond County, NY, Deed Book 41:500, Sidney and Frances Brooks and Janet H. de Kay, December 13, 1856, Clerk of Courts, Staten Island.

114. Janet (Drake) de Kay to Helena (de Kay) Gilder, April 23, 1862, series 1, box 3, GM.

115. Janet (Drake) de Kay to Helena (de Kay) Gilder, February 12, 1863, series 1, box 3, GM.

116. For more information about the purchase, see Richmond County, NY, Deed Book 65:381, Alexander and Arabella Mott and Drake de Kay, May 30, 1866, Clerk of Courts, Staten Island. Dr. Elliott had a long association with Dr. Alexander Mott and his father Dr. Valentine Mott.

117. Laura (Winthrop) Johnson to Annie Fields, February 23, 1868, box 1, LWJ.

118. Rosamond de Kay Gilder, unpublished manuscript, series 2, box 17, GM.

119. Sarah Mifflin Gay to Elizabeth (Neall) Gay, September 27, 1868, series 1, box 23.

120. Helena (de Kay) Gilder to Charles de Kay, July 23, 1880, series 1, box 4, GM.

121. Charles de Kay to Richard Watson Gilder, August 24, 1880, series 1, box 3, GM.

122. Janet (Drake) de Kay to Helena (de Kay) Gilder, August 23, 1885?, series 1, box 3, GM.

123. Sarah Blake (Sturgis) Shaw to Helena (de Kay) Gilder, August 23, 1894, series 1, box 14, GM.

124. See, for instance, Sarah Blake (Sturgis) Shaw to Helena (de Kay) Gilder, partial date [8/29], series 1, box 14, GM.

125. Helena (de Kay) Gilder to Richard Watson Gilder, September 14, 1876, series 1, box 5, GM.

126. In the collection of her father's papers (CPC) at the Massachusetts Historical Society.

127. In 1877, frustrated with the exhibition policies of the National Academy of Design, Helena (de Kay) Gilder and Richard Watson Gilder were among the founders of the Society of American Artists. Maria Oakey wed Thomas Wilmer Dewing (1851–1938), a fellow painter, in 1880.

128. Some scholars have contended that Helena's rejection prompted Winslow Homer to spend most of his time living in social isolation on Prout's Neck near Scarborough, Maine.

129. Anna Leonowens to Helena (de Kay) Gilder, undated letter from Sea Verge Cottage, Newport, Rhode Island, series 1, box 12, GM.

130. Sydney Howard Gay to Sarah Mifflin Gay, June 23, 1864, series 1, box 31, SHG.

131. John W. Chadwick, "Recollections of George William Curtis," *Harper's New Monthly Magazine*, February 1893, 472. American Antiquarian Society Historical Periodicals (Gale).

132. Linda Dowling, *Galahad in the Gilded Age: A Life of George William Curtis* (Bloomington, IN: Xlibris, 2021), 302–3.

133. The date 1865 is the one Charles Eliot Norton used in talking of Curtis's summer stays at Ashfield, although Curtis did not have his own summer home, at 14 South Street in Ashfield, until 1873. See Charles Eliot Norton, James Russell Lowell, and George William Curtis, *Memorials of Two Friends, James Russell Lowell: 1819–1891, George William Curtis: 1824–1892* (New York: Privately printed [Gilliss Press], 1902), 73.

134. Frank Shaw to Sydney Howard Gay, April 16, 1874, enclosing a check for $5,400, series 1, box 61, SHG. At the time of Frank Shaw's death, Gay still owed him money; see Francis George Shaw Will, *Richmond County Sentinel*, January 10, 1883.

135. Bryant wrote the preface for the multivolume work but was dead before the first volume was published. Gay took great satisfaction in the historical survey, claiming that his work had become the model for popular histories with

documented sources. He was later recognized as an accomplished historian for his biography, *James Madison* (Boston: Houghton Mifflin, 1884).

136. George William Curtis to Christopher Pearse Cranch, January 7, 1880, series 2, box 4, CPC.

Chapter 6

1. Robert Craig Brown, "Wiman, Erastus," in *Dictionary of Canadian Biography*, vol. 13 (University of Toronto/Université Laval, 2003), accessed October 29, 2024, http://www.biographi.ca/en/bio/wiman_erastus_13E.html.

2. Ann and her two daughters (one single and one widowed) moved to a new city residence at 351 West Eighty-Seventh Street. Ann's daughters were Mary Allen Livingston Harrison (1830–1921) and Ann Ludlow Livingston (1832–1913). Mary Allen's husband, Massilon Harrison (b. 1818), a lieutenant in the US Army, had died at Fort Schuyler in 1854.

3. Elizabeth (Neall) Gay to Sarah Mifflin Gay, undated [1873?], series I, box 19b, SHG.

4. *New York Times*, March 12, 1884, 5.

5. The description of the house is drawn from Charles W. Leng and William T. Davis, *Staten Island and Its People: A History, 1609–1929*, vol. 5 (New York: Lewis Historical Publishing, 1929), 70. For information about the art, see *A Catalogue of Paintings in the Gallery of John C. Henderson, Linden Lawn, Staten Island* (New York: W. C. Bryant, 1860).

6. She was the daughter of Benjamin A. Gould (1751–1814), who had a distinguished career in the Revolutionary War. Mrs. Henderson's uncles and aunts included Benjamin A. Gould (1787–1859), principal of the Boston Latin School, an East India merchant, an author, and a Boston public official; poet Hannah Flagg Gould (1789–1865); and Benjamin Apthorpe Gould (1824–1896), the most distinguished astronomer of his generation. See Lyman Horace Weeks, *Prominent Families of New York* [. . .] (New York: Historical Company, 1898), under "Rapallo."

7. NYC Landmarks Preservation Commission, "Henderson Place Historic District LP-0454," February 11, 1969, no. 4.

8. The partnership with his brother did not end until 1886; see "Advertisement," *New York Tribune*, June 3, 1886, 6, Readex: America's Historical Newspapers (Newsbank). He kept his seat on the New York Stock Exchange until 1901 when he sold for $65,000. He had only paid $50,000 for the seignury; see "Condensed Telegraphic News," *St. Albans Daily Messenger*, April 25, 1901, 1, Readex: America's Historical Newspapers (Newsbank).

9. Francis H. Cabot, *The Greater Perfection: The Story of the Gardens at Les Quatres Vents* (New York: Hortus / Norton, 2001), 24. Bonner may have had many connections to the Minturns, but one of the most enduring stemmed from

the fact that he and Susie (Shaw) Minturn summered in Murray Bay, Quebec, Canada (later renamed La Malbaie). Bonner was following a family tradition begun in 1842 and he was enthusiastic about outdoor life and salmon fishing in La Malbaie. In 1898 he built a riverbank house in Point au Pic (once a separate municipality and later a neighborhood of La Malbaie). After the death of Robert Minturn, Susie had constructed a house near Bonner's that became the focus of a summer colony and included relatives and friends from such prestigious families as the Bowditches, Harlans, Oliverses, Sedgwickses, and Stokeses, and, eventually, William Howard Taft, who summered there from 1901 through 1929 in a family house on the same grounds as that of his brother Charles Taft. Bonner was so attached to the area that he purchased the seigneury of Cap-a-l'Aigle, a tract of land eighteen miles long and six miles wide extending from Murray Bay to some distance below Quebec that included a Canadian title, and shortly after his oldest daughter Maud (1877–1955) married Francis Higginson Cabot (1859–1939) in 1893, he gave five hundred acres and the title to her. For more on the summer colony, see Philippe Dube, *Charlevoix: Two Centuries at Murray Bay*, trans. Tony Martin-Sperry (Kingston: McGill–Queen's University Press, 1989).

10. George T. Bonner was the son of John Bonner (1792–1869) and Sarah Noyes Bonner (1800–1842), who resettled in Quebec from England in 1813. John established a lumber business.

11. George supplied the date of his immigration from Quebec to New York on his passport application. He became a naturalized citizen of the United States in 1864. "New York Naturalization Index (Soundex), 1792–1906," FamilySearch, under George T. Bonner, 1864, https://www.familysearch.org/ark:/61903/1:1:QVT7-49 QZ.

12. George was also a founder of the Travelers' Club (1865) and a member of the New York Yacht Club. See Francis Fairfield, *The Clubs of New York* (New York: H. L. Hinton, 1873), 101, 194, 257.

13. "Legislative Acts/Legal Proceedings," *New York Herald*, December 6, 1856, [1], Readex: America's Historical Newspapers (Newsbank).

14. Edward and George each had a seat on the New York Stock Exchange prior to 1869. See Francis L. Eames, *The New York Stock Exchange* (New York: T. G. Hall, 1894), 53.

15. *New York Times*, November 30, 1869, 5.

16. Peter Pennoyer and Ann Walker, *The Architecture of Grosvenor Atterbury* (New York: W. W. Norton, 2009), 272.

17. The few details available about George's life are from Cabot, *Greater Perfection*, 22ff.

18. "For Sale," *New York Observer and Chronicle*, September 8, 1898, 320, American Periodicals Series (Proquest).

19. The Boyds purchased the house from the estate of Stewart Brown, a Wall Street broker whose primary residence was at 21 West Thirty-Fourth Street.

See Richmond County, NY, Deed Book 165:356, Stewart Brown, dec'd. & Mary and Frances O. Boyd, May 10, 1886, Clerk of Courts, Staten Island.

20. *New York Times*, January 22, 1893, 17.

21. *New York Times*, March 30, 1894, 3.

22. *New York Times*, January 9, 1896, 8.

23. *New York Times*, April 6, 1893, 4.

24. "Crooked Whiskey: Arrest of F. O. Boyd and Others," *Commercial Advertiser*, May 10, 1876, 4, Readex: America's Historical Newspapers (Newsbank).

25. *New York Times*, September 1, 1895, 24.

26. See, for instance, *New York Times*, May 28, 1899, 22.

27. Information about the Rokeby family is taken from Bernard Burke, *A Genealogical and Heraldic History of the Landed Gentry of Great Britain and Ireland*, 7th edition, vol. 2 (London: Harrison), 1886, under "Rokeby of Arthingworth."

28. "Business Troubles," *New York Herald*, February 2, 1893, 11, Readex: America's Historical Newspapers (Newsbank).

29. "National Hudson Bridge Company," *New York Tribune*, January 24, 1898, 7, Readex: America's Historical Newspapers (Newsbank).

30. He was the president of the firm until his retirement in 1922; *New York Times*, May 24, 1924, 15.

31. She was the daughter of Dr. John Herman Eden, a New York City physician who made a fortune in real estate; see obituary record of Yale College, 1915.

32. By this point a former Staten Islander whose son Isaac Newton Phelps Stokes (1867–1944) had married Robert and Susie Minturn's daughter, Edith (1867–1937), in 1895 at La Malbaie, Quebec, Canada.

33. Rokeby's best man, Charles Warren Bowring (1871–1940), and one of his ushers, Cecil Baring (1863–1934), evidence his high status in English society. Bowring was a member of the Bowring family of London that owned the C. T. Bowring Shipping Co. and subsidiary enterprises. Baring was in New York working at Kidder, Peabody, but would later head Baring Brothers (and late in life receive the title Third Baron Revelstoke). Baring's sojourn in the United States ended around the time Grace Wilson broke their engagement (she subsequently married Cornelius Vanderbilt III). He began a decade-long break from business in 1901. After marrying Maude Louise (née Lorillard) Tailer of New York, the youngest daughter of the tobacco millionaire Pierre Lorillard IV (she had divorced one of Baring's business partners), he devoted himself to natural history, agriculture, and restoring an Irish castle.

34. *Brooklyn Daily Eagle*, May 25, 1924, 51.

35. The club paid $40,000 for the five-and-one-quarter-acre property that included the main house, stable, and out buildings. *Richmond County Gazette*, January 23, 1886, 12–13.

36. The Garner property, consisting of fifteen acres, a stable, and outbuildings, in addition to the main house, sold for $50,000. *Richmond County Gazette*, January 23, 1886, 12–13.

37. Charles de Kay to Richard Watson Gilder, March 22, 1880, series 1, box 3, GM.

38. Helena de Kay to Charles de Kay, August 2, 1880, series 1, box 4, GM.

39. Francis F. Nicholls to Helena (de Kay) Gilder, January 9, 1885, series 1, box 13, GM.

40. "Obituary of Col Drake de Kay," *New York Times*, June 12, 1886, 5.

41. Sydney de Kay to Helena (de Kay) Gilder, October 1, 1868, series 1, box 3, GM.

42. "New York Passenger Lists, 1820–1921," FamilySearch, under Sidney De Kay, 1868 (https://www.familysearch.org/ark:/61903/1:1:QVPJ-T5TN.

43. Julia de Kay to Helena de Kay Gilder, May 18, 1879, series 1, box 3, GM. Julia wrote that the Craven furniture Minna inherited would be used to furnish the rental properties.

44. It may seem surprising that the couple bought a house, rather than built one, on de Kay land. In fact, the de Kay Estate remained remarkably intact until the late 1890s.

45. In the latter half of the nineteenth century in the United States, the term "ambulance," in the context of Western travel, denoted a prairie schooner. A trip of this sort had become possible due to the completion of railroad lines through the Rockies and the series of military forts that had developed into self-contained settlements to which officers brought their families. Johnson's party of twelve included only three men, six women, and three children, one of whom was Johnson's daughter Laura. One of the number was related to a paymaster at Fort Laramie and the fort served as a base and provider of troop escorts. Although the party camped on the plains, visited Indian villages, and experienced some of the hardships of trail life, the actual threats were largely controlled. The group did interact with Sioux tribes and met famous chiefs, like Sitting Bull. At one point, a Native American guide warned that some tribes had been incensed by Custer's activities in the Black Hills, particularly the massacre of a whole village, and urged the group to turn back, but the officers escorting the party laughed off the threat. Less than a year later, of course, such a trip would have been impossible in the aftermath of the battle at Little Big Horn.

46. Details about Dr. Samuel R. Elliott's life are drawn from a biographical essay: E. D. Doster, *Sun*, December 1, 1909, 8, image 8, *Chronicling America: Historic American Newspapers*, Library of Congress, https://chroniclingamerica.loc.gov/lccn/sn83030272/1909-12-01/ed-1/seq-8/.

47. *Cyclopædia of American Biography* (1918), under "Gilder, Richard Watson."

48. The book was Richard Watson Gilder, *The New Day* (New York: Scribner, 1876). Rodman Gilder to Mabel Abbott, December 7, 1937, box 1, folder 6, MA.

49. See the GM and the Richard Watson Gilder Papers, Rare Books and Manuscripts Division, New York Public Library.

50. As an illustration of the interconnectedness of Elliotville social circles, while the Gilders were abroad in 1879, Christopher Pearse Cranch and his family

stayed in The Studio. See Leonora Cranch Scott, ed., *The Life and Letters of Christopher Pearse Cranch* (Boston: Houghton Mifflin, 1917), 301. The building survived until the mid-twentieth century. Although efforts were made to preserve the structure, The Studio was torn down in 1955.

51. After 1875, when her husband's mental illness became incapacitating and required institutional care, Katherine Bronson made her primary home in Venice at Ca'Alvisi, situated near the mouth of the Grand Canal, opposite Santa Maria della Salute and featuring a balcony with a dramatic view, much admired (and painted) by Whistler. The house had a separate wing in which Whistler, Browning, James, and others stayed for extended periods. Seasonally, Bronson also spent time at a country residence in Asolo, usually in the company of members of her social circle of artists and writers.

52. Artist Will Low, who frequented The Studio, quoted in Bette Roth Young, *Emma Lazarus in Her World: Life and Letters* (Philadelphia: Jewish Publication Society, 1995), 67.

53. Henry Parks Wright, *History of the Class of 1868: Yale College, 1864–1914* (New Haven: Tuggle, Morehouse & Taylor, 1914), under "Charles August DeKay."

54. To learn more about Lazarus and her friendship with Helena Gilder and Charles de Kay, see Esther Schor, *Emma Lararus* (Nextbook / Schocken, 2017).

55. Laura (Winthrop) Johnson to Emily Ford, undated, box 1, LWJ.

56. *The Art Work of Louis C. Tiffany* (New York: Country Life Press, 1914). Charles de Kay was friends with several generations of Tiffanys, and his nephew, Rodman de Kay, married Louis's daughter Louise C. Tiffany in 1911.

57. He wed Lucy Edwalyn Coffey (1869–1949).

58. Charles set a short story there as well.

59. Winslow Homer had also rented in the building.

60. Charles also frequented his clubs. He founded the Fencer's Club in 1880 and the Author's Club in 1882. He was later among the founders of the National Sculpture Society in 1892 and the National Arts Club in 1899.

61. Richmond County, NY, Deed Book 89:122, Janet H. de Kay & Margaret S. Winchester, October 31, 1870, Clerk of Courts, Staten Island. Property records show that de Kay sold additional land to Winchester in 1870 and 1875. See 89:416, November 31, 1870; 113:129, November 30, 1875.

62. Richmond County, NY, Deed Book 145:29, Janet H. de Kay & Maria Midy Morgan, September 29, 1882, Clerk of Courts, Staten Island. Also, 153:1, March 29, 1884.

63. "The Founder of the Critic," *Frank Leslie's Weekly*, March 25, 1897, 198.

64. F. N. Sommer, *Sommer's Newspaper Manual* (Newark, NJ: Author, 1903), 25.

65. *New York Times*, June 2, 1892, 5.

66. "Landed Estates: Ireland's Landed Estates and Historic Houses, ca. 1700–1914," accessed October 29, 2024, https://landedestates.ie/estate/2279.

67. Hugh Montgomery-Massingberd, *Burke's Irish Family Records* (London: Burke's Peerage, 1976), under "Anthony Morgan." Like his father, Morgan was a captain in the Ninety-Fifth (Derbyshire) Regiment of Foot. In the period 1854 to 1856, he served with his regiment in the Crimean War. In 1857, he married Elizabeth Tymons of Riverstown, County Clare, and afterward made his home at Bunalun, Skibbereen, County Cork, Ireland. He also owned 1,216 acres in County Clare that he may have obtained through his marriage.

68. "Lady Artists in Rome," *The Art-Journal*, vol. 28, 1866, 177ff.

69. Lisa Merrill, *When Romeo Was a Woman: Charlotte Cushman and Her Circle of Female Spectators* (Ann Arbor: University of Michigan Press, 1999), 190.

70. Scott Alan Carson, "Height of Female Americans in the 19th Century and the Antebellum Puzzle," *Economics and Human Biology* 9, no. 2 (March 2011): 157–64.

71. Merrill, *When Romeo Was a Woman*, 195. For more information about Cobbe and Lloyd, see Sally Mitchell, *Frances Power Cobbe: Victorian Feminist, Journalist, Reformer* (Charlottesville: University of Virginia Press, 2004).

72. "Obituary: Miss Midy Morgan," *New York Times*, June 2, 1892, 5.

73. "Obituary."

74. Merrill, *When Romeo Was a Woman*, 234.

75. Ishbel Ross, *Ladies of the Press: The Story of Women in Journalism by an Insider* (New York: Harper and Brothers), 146.

76. Ross, 146.

77. Meyer Berger, *The Story of The New York Times, 1851–1951* (New York: Simon and Schuster, 1951), 85.

78. See Francis Fairfield, *The Clubs of New York* (New York: H. L. Hinton, 1873), 167ff.

79. Berger, 85.

80. "Saratoga Springs," *New York World*, August 11, 1869: 2, Readex: America's Historical Newspapers (Newsbank).

81. "European Blooded Stock," *New York World* (New York), August 9, 1869: 1, Readex: America's Historical Newspapers (Newsbank).

82. "Middy Morgan on Horseback," *Sun*, November 15, 1869, 1, Readex: America's Historical Newspapers (Newsbank).

83. Ross, *Ladies of the Press*, 148.

84. "Middy Morgan, A New York Market Reporter," New York Letter to *Cincinnati Commercial, Massachusetts Ploughman and New England Journal of Agriculture* 39, no. 36 (Jun 5, 1880): 4, American Periodicals Series (Proquest); Walker Fuller, "The Career of a Successful Woman," *Lakeside Monthly*, December 1, 1872, 424, American Periodicals Series (Proquest).

85. "A Woman's Success: How Miss Midy Morgan Made Herself Famous," *Boston Daily Advertiser*, June 3, 1892, 2, Readex: America's Historical Newspapers (Newsbank).

86. Ross, *Ladies of the Press*, 145.

87. "Middy Morgan," Correspondence of the *Cincinnati Gazette, Daily Central City Register*, January 19, 1870, 3, Readex: America's Historical Newspapers (Newsbank).

88. Merrill discusses the cult of true womanhood at some length, summarizing the work of Barbara Welter, Merrill, *When Romeo Was a Woman*, 22.

89. "Middy Morgan," *The Weekly Arizona (Prescott) Miner*, March 19, 1870, 5, Readex: America's Historical Newspapers (Newsbank).

90. "Middy Morgan," *Miner*.

91. "Middy Morgan," *The News and Observer (Raleigh)*, October 3, 1882, 15, Readex: America's Historical Newspapers (Newsbank).

92. "Death of Midy Morgan," *Turf, Field, and Farm* 54, no. 23 (June 3, 1892): 644, American Periodicals Series (Proquest).

93. See for instance, *The Cultivator & Country Gentleman* 36 (February 23, 1871): 944, American Periodicals Series (Proquest).

94. Midy Morgan, "Hints About Horses, Etc.," *Hearth and Home* 2, no. 49 (November 26, 1870): 71, American Periodicals Series (Proquest).

95. "Stock: Vicious Horses," *Ohio Farmer* 22, no. 17 (April 26, 1873): 262, American Periodicals Series (Proquest).

96. Midy Morgan, "Why Is Live Stock Trade Unprofitable?," *Ohio Farmer* 19, no. 42 (October 13, 1870); 659, American Periodicals Series (Proquest).

97. Morgan, "Why Is Live Stock Trade Unprofitable?"

98. "Warren Leland's Poultry," *The Independent* 23, no. 115 (February 16, 1871): 7, American Periodicals Series (Proquest).

99. Midy Morgan, "Letter," *Forest and Stream* 26, no. 6 (March 4, 1886): 104, American Periodicals Series (Proquest).

100. Morgan, "Letter."

101. "Jersey's Female Ticket Agents," *Bismarck Daily Tribune*, December 10, 1891, 23, Readex: America's Historical Newspapers (Newsbank).

102. Ross, *Ladies of the Press*, 148.

103. Although there were a number of articles published across the country about the house, most of them were excerpting (sometimes incorrectly) the two main articles: "An Original Dwelling," *Woman's Cycle* 2, no. 20 (July 10, 1890): 15, American Periodicals Series (Proquest); and "Odd Home of Two Sisters," *New-York Tribune*, June 30, 1895, 21, Readex: America's Historical Newspapers (Newsbank). Jenny June's article was published before the house interiors were finished. The *New-York Tribune* article described the finished house. Unless otherwise noted, the descriptions of the house here are drawn from these two articles.

104. The much-altered house is still standing and the author visited and photographed aspects of the exterior and interior in October 2016.

105. June, "An Original Dwelling," 15.

106. Although in New York City, the style would see a recrudescence after zoning laws requiring setbacks on tall buildings created new reasons for utilizing the mansard. Leland M. Roth, *A Concise History of American Architecture* (New York: Harper and Row, 1980), 128–32.

107. "Odd Home of Two Sisters," 21.

108. Ross, *Ladies of the Press*, 148.

109. Ross, 148.

110. Ross, 148.

111. June, "An Original Dwelling," 15.

112. Some accounts claimed only a ladder proved access to the upper floors so that it could be pulled up for security. However, even some of the earliest articles describe the substantial iron staircase. The articles that mention a ladder are confusing Morgan's Staten Island house with her train station abode and its ladder-accessed loft.

113. The Royal College of Art, founded in 1837 as the Government School of Design, in 1853 became the National Art Training School with a Female School of Art in a separate building. It was renamed the Royal College of Art in 1896. However, for most of the nineteenth century the institution was referred to as the South Kensington Schools. Christopher Frayling, *The Royal College of Art: 150 Years of Art and Design* (Newton Abbott, UK: David and Charles, 1987).

114. June, "An Original Dwelling," 15.

115. Although starting in 1886 city directories listed Midy's home address as on Dekay Avenue near Bard, her death certificate lists Robinvale, New Jersey. Calendar of Wills and Administrations, 1858–1922, https://www.willcalendars.nationalarchives.ie/reels/cwa/005014907/005014907_00279.pdf.

116. Elizabeth (Neall) Gay to Mary Otis Willcox, June 2, 1893, series 1, box 19b, SHG.

117. Laura (Winthrop) Johnson to Annie Fields, June 12, 1887, box 1, LWJ.

118. Louis Gratacap lived almost all of his adult life in his family's house at 163 Bement Avenue. His father, John L. Gratacap (1810–1892), had an upholstery business that received lucrative contracts from the American Packet Co. and other firms to upholster ship cabins. After retiring from business in 1853, he relocated his family to Staten Island in 1857. Six-year-old Louis grew up in Elliottville. A graduate of City College (1869) and the Columbia College School of Mines (1876), he had a long career as curator of mineralogy at the American Museum of Natural History. An avid naturalist, Gratacap also had an appreciation of art and music, and though of a much younger generation he had much in common with early Elliottville residents, particularly with Laura Johnson, with whom he had a close friendship. His journal entries show that he was deeply affected by her death.

119. Annie Fields was at her harshest in describing Bessie, although she admired her friend Laura Johnson's "devotion to her queer nervous daughter

Bessie." Annie Field's journal entry quoted in Rita K. Gollin, *Annie Fields: Woman of Letters* (Amherst: University of Massachusetts Press, 2002), 154.

120. L.P. Gratacap Diary, 1873, MSS Col 1199, New York Public Library, Manuscripts and Archives Division.

121. Although Jane could have made a testamentary bequest by the terms of Midy's will, she did not in any meaningful way. Bizarrely, she bequeathed her nephew, Rev. Edward Morgan, the son of Anthony Morgan (II), who was a resident of San Francisco, the right to collect on a loan that Jane claimed she had made to his father decades before.

122. Anthony Hickman Morgan was a wealthy man. His principal residence was at 14 Grosvenor Place. Since he was a justice of peace and deputy lieutenant for County Cork, he also maintained a residence in Ireland at Skibereen. See https://www.AngloBoerWar.com, under "Morgan, Anthony Hickman."

123. For more about the house see *The Builder* 84, no. 3147 (April 25, 1903): 436; and Cork County Council, *Heritage Houses of County Cork* (Cork, Ire: Heritage Unit of Cork County Council), 2014.

Chapter 7

1. The production was soon taken over by Imre Kiralfy. Known for incorporating ballet into his spectacles and his innovative use of electric lighting, Kiralry subsequently presented *Nero, or The Fall of Rome* on Staten Island with two thousand performers in 1888.

2. Staten Island newspapers of the era covered all of these public entertainments in great detail.

3. Although none of the Minturns' written observations on the changes survive, another affluent Staten Islander, Anson Phelps Stokes, who had owned the Pendleton house on Pendleton Place for decades, left a record. He noted in his autobiography: "I found my wife had been disgusted with some conditions at Staten Island, where the opening of the Fall of Babylon show and cheap excursion places had caused the ferry-boats to be overcrowded and had brought a rough element . . . we never returned to live at Staten Island." *Stokes Records*, vol. 1, part 2 (New York: Author, 1910), 240.

4. Ranlett went to San Francisco in 1849 to work as an architect, but returned to New York City in 1858 and worked out of offices at 52 John Street. See Richard C. Muhlberger, "William H. Ranlett, 19th-Century Architect and Publisher," *Historic Preservation: Quarterly of the National Council for Historic Sites and Buildings* 22 (Jan.–Mar. 1970), 14.

5. For his presentation of this viewpoint, see George William Curtis to Anna (Shaw) Curtis, January 14, 1863, 25.GWC, box 2, folder 10, GWC.

6. Johnson describes herself in this way. See Laura (Winthrop) Johnson to Annie Fields, February 23, 1868, LWJ.

7. Frank Shaw to Sydney Howard Gay, May 17, 1870, series 1, box 61, SHG.

8. *Richmond County Advance*, October 31, 1891.

9. As late as 1891, the New Brighton Board of Health publicly acknowledged that cesspools drained into the water company's supply. "Board of Health," *Richmond County Gazette*, September 26, 1891.

10. *Richmond County Gazette*, June 7, 1890.

11. As late as 1886, when the Boyds were purchasing their house, the Gays needed to sign an agreement with them regarding property boundaries that referenced the lack of clarity of 1840s property descriptions. See Richmond County, NY, Deed Book 165:394, Elizabeth and Sydney Howard Gay & Mary and Frances O. Boyd, May 12, 1886 Clerk of Courts, Staten Island. Also 153:1, March 29, 1884.

12. Lydia Maria Child to Sarah Blake (Sturgis) Shaw, January 15, 1874, box 1, SBSS.

13. "Stapleton Free Reading Room," *Richmond County Gazette*, April 4, 1860, [2].

14. George William Curtis to Christopher Pearse Cranch, February 18, 1882, series 2, box 4, CPC.

15. Lydia Maria Child to Sarah Blake (Sturgis) Shaw, June 20, 1877, box 1, SBSS.

16. Lydia Maria Child to Sarah Blake (Sturgis) Shaw, June 20, 1877.

17. Elizabeth (Neall) Gay to Mary Otis (Gay) Willcox, June 5, 1877, series 1, box 19b, SHG.

18. *Richmond County Advance*, July 10, 1886.

19. Oral History Interview with Winslow Ames, 1987, April 29–June 2, Smithsonian Museum of American Art, [4], https://www.aaa.si.edu/collections/interviews/oral-history-interview-winslow-ames-12047.

20. *Dictionary of Canadian Biography*, vol. 13 (University of Toronto/Université Laval, 2003), under "Wiman, Erastus," http://www.biographi.ca/en/bio/wiman_erastus_13E.html.

21. The Narrows to Mariner's Harbor line was called the Staten Island Belt Line Railroad Co. by 1887. In 1885, another horsecar line had begun running from the West New Brighton dock to Eckstein's Brewery at Four Corners.

22. Although Barnes (1845–1920) is celebrated on Staten Island today (see https://www.realestatesiny.com/reon-barnes.php), in addition to cheating landowners on behalf of the B&O, he helped cheat the B&O. The dummy company the B&O organized had been capitalized with $100,000. When all the land had been purchased and the B&O wanted the company assets transferred back, it found that the dummy company's officers had issued themselves stock in the amount of $700,000. However, they said they would make the transfer back to the company

if they were collectively paid $50,000 in cash. The B&O brought a lawsuit, but the final negotiations were kept secret.

23. Erastus Wiman, *Rapid Transit for Staten Island* ([Staten Island, NY]: The author, 1881), 4.

24. Wiman, 4.

25. Local newspapers provided complete coverage of the event including the text of Curtis's lengthy speech. See "The Bi-Centennial: How It Was Observed," *Richmond County Standard*, November 24, 1883, [1].

26. See the account in "A Much Needed Charity," *Staten Island Gazette & Sentinel*, March 7, 1883.

27. Duncan, a Scottish immigrant, nonetheless had strong ties to the South. In 1853 he married Jane Percy Sargent (1833–1905) in New Orleans. She was the granddaughter of Winthrop Sargent, the governor of the Mississippi Territory and secretary of the Northwest Territory. Although his political allegiances cannot be known with finality, unlike other Scotsmen, like Dr. Elliott and Sir Roderick Cameron, Duncan did not support the Seventy-Ninth New York during the War. He lived at 1 Fifth Avenue, but between 1858 and 1896 the Duncan family (including three children and one adopted nephew) summered in the Staten Island house, Capo di Monte, that Duncan had purchased from Suzette Grymes and from which she had presided over a social set of Southerners. Duncan had significant landholdings in the South, including plantations in Natchez, Mississippi. At the New York Yacht Club, Duncan was known as "No. 1," since he was considered the first member. For more information about Duncan, see "Wm. Butler Duncan Dies in 82nd Year," *New York Times*, June 21, 1912.

28. Erastus Wiman, *Chances of Success: Episodes and Observations in the Life of a Busy Man* (New York: American News, 1893), 225.

29. Wiman, 228.

30. The clippings do not include the title of the newspaper but do have the date of February 28, 1885. Scrapbooks 25.GWC, box 20, GWC.

31. Scrapbooks.

32. Scrapbooks.

33. Wiman sponsored baseball, cricket, and two New York seasons of Buffalo Bill's Wild West Show.

34. The banquet was to have been on December 10, 1885, but had been postponed due to the death of William H. Vanderbilt. Vanderbilt had been in his home study, meeting with Garrett, when he died of an apoplectic stroke. Vanderbilt and Garrett's father had had some rancorous interactions in the context of railroad competition. Although it was unlikely that Garrett triggered any anger, the meeting appears to have been kept secret from Vanderbilt's family and staff. See "Dead Amid Great Riches," *New York Times*, December 9, 1885, 1.

35. "The New Trunk Line: Celebrating the Baltimore and Ohio's Expected Entrance to New York," *New York Herald*, December 17, 1885, 1, Readex: America's Historical Newspapers (Newsbank).

36. Curtis left no record of his opinion of Garrett, who had run away at sixteen to fight with Robert E. Lee, although his father had retrieved him and forced him to sit out the war as a Princeton student. Garrett still followed Lee, in a way. In his first job he succeeded Robert E. Lee as the president of a Virginia railroad that would become a branch of the B&O.

37. "The New Trunk Line: Celebrating the Baltimore and Ohio's Expected Entrance to New York," *New York Herald*, December 17, 1885, 1, Readex: America's Historical Newspapers (Newsbank).

38. "The New Trunk Line."

39. "The New Trunk Line."

40. Samuel Gray Ward, *Ward Family Papers: Collected and Written* (Boston: Merrymount Press, 1900), 151.

41. Ward, 151.

42. Ward, 198.

43. Ward, 199.

44. "The New Trunk Line: Celebrating the Baltimore and Ohio's Expected Entrance to New York," *New York Herald*, December 17, 1885, 1.

45. "Staten Island: The Transit Scheme Not Wholly Beneficial," *Evening Post*, December 1, 1886.

46. "A Well-Backed Movement: The New Brighton Association and Its Sponsors," *The Sentinel*, May 17, 1888, 3.

47. "Well-Backed Movement."

48. Curtis had been at loggerheads with Conkling many times over Republican Party issues. Conkling had made his first fortune while serving as a congressman and having the political access and information that enabled him to benefit from wartime cotton profiteering. The most crucial difference between Curtis and Conkling lay in the fact that Conkling was the king of the spoils system to which Curtis was so deeply opposed. Wiman prided himself on his friendship with Conkling and credited Conkling with getting him the political support he needed (Wiman, *Chances of Success*, 236). As a demonstration of their closeness he described entertaining Conkling and Conkling's mistress (although unnamed, given the context, the woman in Wiman's account was most likely Kate Chase Sprague).

49. Scrapbook 25 GWC, box 24, GWC.

50. Scrapbook 25 GWC.

51. Scrapbook 25 GWC.

52. The B&O did not own access to a Manhattan tunnel. In one of his schemes that never got very far, Wiman began planning for a tunnel to Brooklyn. Without tunnel access, B&O passengers had to make a transfer in Jersey City to board another company's service through a tunnel into Manhattan.

53. "Death of Erastus Wiman: Staten Island Financier and Promoter Succumbs to Paralysis," *New York Times*, February 10, 1904, 7.

54. "Death of Erastus Wiman," 7.

55. By 1925, even the reminiscences seemed in danger of being lost, and Staten Islanders Charles G. Hine and William T. Davis published *Legends, Stories, and Folklore of Old Staten Island*, part 1, *The North Shore* under the auspices of the Staten Island Historical Society. A book of firsthand accounts, rather than documented history, Hine and Davis were able to interview Anna Curtis, Martin Gay, and Mary Willcox to tell the story of "Literary West New Brighton," as the Bard Avenue neighborhood had come to be remembered.

Conclusion

1. Charles de Kay, "Woodland Creed," *New Continental Magazine* 1, no. 1 (1912): 88–89.

2. Elizabeth (Neall) Gay to Mary Otis (Gay) Willcox, March 30, 1880, series 1, box 19b, SHG.

3. Andrew Wilson, "Found Staten Island Stories: 3," New York Public Library, September 23, 2016, https://www.nypl.org/blog/2016/09/23/clone-found-staten-island-stories-3-buffalo-bills-wild-west-mariners-harbor-1886-and.

4. Elizabeth (Neall) Gay to Mary Otis (Gay) Willcox, December 16, 1887, series 1, box 19b, SHG.

5. George William Curtis to Frederick Law Olmsted, April 17, 1887, box 22, reel 21, MSS 35121, Frederick Law Olmsted Papers, Library of Congress.

6. Rail lines on Staten Island caused many deaths, mostly at poorly designed railroad crossings. However, there were a disproportionate number of deaths along Richmond Terrace where fences and elevated pedestrian crossings were inadequate.

7. Maggi Smith-Dalton, "Biographical Sketch of Elizabeth Burrill Curtis," in *Part III: Mainstream Suffragists: National American Woman Suffrage Association*, accessed October 9, 2023, https://documents.alexanderstreet.com/d/1010113893.

8. Henry Dwight Sedgwick, *Memoirs of an Epicurean* (Indianapolis: Bobbs-Merrill, 1940), 129.

9. Sedgwick, 128.

10. Sedgwick, 128.

11. The George William Curtis house (234 Bard Avenue) and the house landmarked as Dr. Samuel Mackenzie Elliott's (69 Delafield Place) have intact facades. The house where the Lowells stayed with Dr. and Mrs. Elliott at 30 Bard Avenue survives, minus the front porch. The William Thorn Garner mansion (355 Bard Avenue) survives, mostly intact, as hospital administrative offices. The exterior of Midy Morgan's house (16 Dekay Street) is also mostly intact. The remnants of a house constructed out of locally quarried gray stone with an astronomical observation tower is now part of the property of the Freedom in God Ministries Church at 555 Bard Avenue.

12. "Shaw House, Richmond Terrace at Davis Avenue, West Brighton," series 7, box 7, MA.

Index

abolitionism, 10–11, 85, 123; Civil War and, 119–20; Garrisonian position, 16, 81, 85, 124; Gay, Elizabeth (Neall) and, 80, 81; Gay, Sydney Howard and, 11, 54–55, 85, 120; Leonowens, Anna and, 128, 130; Minturn, Robert Bowne and, 116; popular attitudes toward, 71; Shaw, Frank and, 14, 16–17, 126; Shaw, Robert Gould and, 113; Shaw, Sarah and, 16, 17; Staten Islanders and, 71, 79–81, 115; Ward, George C. and, 66, 258n42; Winthrop, Theodore and, 99–100, 102, 110
Ailanthus Cottage, 56
American Anti-Slavery Society, 14, 16, 54, 79
American Colonization Society, 81
American Freedmen's and Union Commission, xxiv, 116, 120
Amistad, The, 66, 102
Anti-Slavery Fair Association (1857), 81
Arthur Kill Bridge, 236–38
Aspinwall, William H., 83–84, 97–98, 105, 107, 166

Baltimore & Ohio Railroad (B&O), 224, 228–32, 239

Bard Avenue (Staten Island), 209, 213, 214–16; de Kay land sales, 243; ferry service, 3, 90, 144, 214; name, 1, 49–50, 138, 201, 269n4, 290n55; New Brighton Village Improvement Association and, 235–36; postal delivery and, 218
Bard, Catherine (Cruger), 50, 93, 114, 255n112
Bard, Eliza. *See* Delafield, Eliza (Bard)
Bard, John (grandfather of WB), 50
Bard, Samuel (father of WB), 30, 49–50
Bard, William (WB), 30, 49–50, 183, 256n114, 256n116
Barlow, Ellen (Shaw), 132
Barlow, Francis Channing, 99, 132, 243
beggars, 125, 220
Bement, Edward, 33, 98
Bennett, James Gordon, Jr., 145, 148, 149
Black education, 123–24
Bonner, Edward H., xv, 181, 183
Bonner, George T., xv, 180–81, 184, 278n9, 279n10, 279n12
Bonner, Mary Irene, 181
book club, 90–91, 217
Boston People, 68, 138, 232
Boyd, Francis (FB), 181–82, 183, 236

Boyd, Mary Irene (Bonner) (wife of FB), 181
Bronson, Katherine (de Kay), 165, 168, 187, 189, 282n51
Brook Farm, 3, 15–16, 58, 117; Curtis, George and, 61, 74; Shaw, Frank and, 16, 19, 126; transcendentalism and, 15–16
Brown, John, 84–85
Bryant's History of the United States (Gay), 173, 277n135
Butler, Benjamin, 108, 165, 185

Cameron, Margaret Selena Eren (daughter of RC), 207–208, 211
Cameron, Roderick (RC), 48, 137, 180, 198, 208
Castleton, 1, 32, 86
Cecil Dreeme (Winthrop), 100–101, 109–10, 191
Charity Organization Society, 125, 220
Child, Lydia Maria, 13, 20, 161, 220, 221; homeopathy and, 47; Shaws and, 7, 14, 18, 59, 87, 112, 115–16; Spiritualism and, 115–16, 221
children, 53, 67, 91, 92–96, 125
Church, Frederic, 100–101
Civil War, 93, 106–108, 113–15; Curtis, George and, 106, 110, 116–17, 119; Elliott, Samuel Mackenzie and, 48–49, 106; Gay, Sydney and, 119–20; Lowell, Charles Russell and, 117–18; Shaw, Robert Gould and, 106–107, 109, 111–13; Winthrop, Theodore and, 108–11
Compromise of 1850, 79–86 passim
Conkling, Roscoe, 127–28, 225, 238, 289n48
conversion disorder, 40, 44–45
corporations, 222–23, 230, 234–35

Cranch, Caroline (daughter of CPC), 169, 209, 210
Cranch, Christopher Pearse (CPC), 61, 74, 75, 209, 210, 281n50
Craven Minna, 185–86
cricket, 183–84, 209, 274n71, 288n33
criminality, 220–21
Crosby, J. Schuyler, 148, 150–52, 153
cult of domesticity, 2, 199
Curtis, Anna (Shaw) (AC), 90; courtship and marriage, 61, 77, 88; homeopathy and, 47; personality, 163, 172; women's rights and, 171, 242
Curtis, Elizabeth (daughter of AC and GWC), 132; charity work of, 125, 127, 220; women's rights and, 127, 242
Curtis, Frank (son of AC and GWC), 47, 91, 245
Curtis, George, 7, 186–87, 221, 243; ambassadorship offers, 128; Ashfield, MA, and, 172, 277n133; Brook Farm and, 61, 73–74; charity work of, 125, 226, 238–39; civil service reform and, 127–28; Civil War and, 106, 110, 113, 116–17, 119; courtship and marriage, 61, 77, 88; death of, 47; "The Duty of the American Scholar to Politics and the Times," 87–88; Easy Chair column, 73, 158; education and early career, 73–75; "Fair Play for Women," 126; family of origin, 73; *Harper's Magazine* and, 73, 78, 110; *Harper's Weekly* and, 73, 110, 113; high society, attitudes toward, 76, 137, 158; Howadji sobriquet, 75; Leonowens, Anna and, 130–31; Lounger column, 73; orator, 77, 85, 87, 88–89, 91, 106, 217, 225–26, 230; political engagement, 86,

87, 102–103, 121; *The Potiphar Papers*, 76; Puritan heritage and, 64; *Putnam's Monthly Magazine* and, 77–78, 88–89; residence of, Bard Avenue, 61–63, 258n30–n31, 290n11; Shaw family and, 73, 74, 132–34; Staten Island and, 69, 73, 89, 90, 91, 226, 227, 232, 235, 241; suburbia, on destruction of, 236; transcendentalism and, 73; travel writing, 75; wealth, attitude toward, 156; women's rights and, 126–27, 171

Curtis, Sally (daughter of AC and GWC), xxiv, 172

Cushman, Charlotte, 196–97

Dana, Charles, 46, 74, 75, 78, 119

Davis Avenue (Staten Island), 49, 56, 67, 162–63, 191, 219

Davis, Thomas E., 22–24, 25–26, 30, 49, 138, 166

De Hart, Nicholas "Old Claus," 11, 53

de Kay, Charles (son JDK and GDK), 168, 170, 189–91, 193, 209, 241, 282n56

de Kay, Drake (son of JDK and GDK), 165, 165–66, 184–85

de Kay, George (GDK), 163–65, 166

de Kay, Helena (daughter of JDK and GDK). *See* Gilder, Helena (de Kay)

de Kay, James (naturalist), 164–65

de Kay, Janet (Drake) (JDK), 163–65, 166–68, 191–93, 243

de Kay, Katherine (daughter of JDK and GDK). *See* Bronson, Katherine (de Kay)

de Kay, Minna (Craven), 185–86

de Kay, Sidney (son of JDK and GDK), 165, 185–86

Delafield, Eliza (Bard) (ED), 50, 93, 256n116

Delafield, Richard (son of ED and RD), 91, 93, 210

Delafield, Rufus King (RD), 50, 91, 116, 155, 183, 256n116

DePeyster, Fred, 33

Dewing, Maria (Oakey), xvi, 3, 169, 210, 277n127

distinctiveness of, 1–2, 32, 33, 51, 63–64, 68; loss of, 208–209, 239–40, 243–44

Douglass, Frederick, 55, 85, 126

Downing, Alexander Jackson, 51, 52, 61–63, 77, 236

Draft Riots (1863), 114–15

"Duty of the American Scholar to Politics and the Times, The" (Curtis), 87–88

Dwight, Benjamin Franklin, 58, 257n21

Eckford Trust, 165, 186, 276n104

Eckford, Henry, 163, 164

Eight Hundred Miles in an Ambulance (Johnson), 187, 281n45

Election of 1860, 102–103

electric power plant, 228

Elliott, Dianah Taylor (common law wife of SME), 48

Elliott, Letitia (Irvine) (LE), 36–37, 48

Elliott, Samuel Mackenzie (SME), 166, 249n1, 252n38, 256n114; Castleton Medical College, attendance at, 38; Civil War and, 48–49, 106; eccentricities of, 47–48; Glasgow Royal College of Surgeons and, 37; holistic practice, 44–45, 46, 47, 216; homeopathic practice, 39; medical training of, 37–38; New York Medical College, graduation from, 38–39; real estate transactions, 19, 22, 30–32, 51, 58, 140; reputation of, 38–39, 40; surgical practice, 38, 45, 46–47

Elliott, Samuel R. (son of LE and SME), 48, 49, 101, 187–88
Emerson, Ralph Waldo (RWE), 22, 66, 68–69, 189, 259n57
Emerson, William (brother of RWE), 13, 259n57
Erastina, 214, 225, 228, 241

Faber, Eberhard, 183
"Fair Play for Women" (Curtis), 126
ferries, 3–4, 286n3; Bard Avenue, 22, 90, 251n35; Garner, William and, 144, 145; Gratacap, Louis Pope and, 92; St. George, 176, 214, 224–25, 226, 241
Fields, Annie (Adams), 8, 264n82, 285n119. *See also under*, Johnson, Laura (Winthrop); Fields, Annie (Adams) and
"Fifth Avenue of Staten Island," 138, 155, 195, 201, 269n4
Fifty-fourth Massachusetts Volunteer Infantry, 111–13, 131, 242
Foner, Eric, 10, 79, 81, 82, 261n16
freedmen, advocacy for, 120, 123–24
Frémont, John, 73, 87, 88
Fugitive Slave Law. *See* Compromise of 1850
Fuller, Margaret, 13, 17, 18, 66, 119
Fyshe, Avis (Leonowens), 128, 130, 131, 169, 210

Garner & Co., 140–42
Garner, Mary (Thorn), 142, 150–52
Garner, William, 138–55; death of, 150–52; funeral of, 153–55; Garner Line, 145; *Magic* and, 145; *Mohawk* and, 146–48; *Mohawk*, sinking of, 150–52; NYYC clubhouse of, 145–46; residence of, 143–44; *Vixen* and, 145

Garrett, Robert, 224, 225, 230, 232, 239, 288n34
Garrison, William Lloyd, 16, 47, 126
gaslight utility, 222
Gay, Elizabeth (Neall) (EG), 19–20, 161, 162, 170, 241; abolitionism and, 80, 81; Chicago Fire and, 162; correspondence and, 5–7, 59, 169; courtship and marriage, 20–21; domestic life, 172–74, 217–18, 220, 222; Frémont, John and, 87; gardening and, 53; Shaw, Robert Gould and, 109; World Anti-Slavery Convention (1840) and, 19–20
Gay, Martin, (son of EG and SHG), 93, 114
Gay, Mary Otis (daughter of EG and SHG). *See* Willcox, Mary Otis Gay
Gay, Sarah, (daughter of EG and SHG), 126, 129, 137, 163; illnesses, 162, 172, 222; women's rights and, 242
Gay, Sydney Howard (SHG), 55–58, 131, 138, 172; abolitionism and, 11, 54–55, 120; abolitionists and, 55, 85; *Bryant's History of the United States*, 173, 277n135; Chicago Fire and, 162; *Chicago Tribune* and, 161; Civil War and, 114, 119–20, 121; correspondence of, 7–8; courtship and marriage, 20–21; Curtis, Anna (Shaw) and, 172; Elliott, Samuel Mackenzie, assessment of, 34–37; illnesses, 22, 54, 173, 211; *National Anti-Slavery Standard* and, 20, 81, 91; *New-York Tribune* and, 91, 114, 119–20, 161; residence of, Elliottville, 21, 56, 58, 219; residence of, Manhattan, 21; social life of, 90; Underground Railroad and, 10, 20, 81–82; urban life, attitude towards, 22, 54, 58

Gay, Walter Otis (son of EG and SHG), 76–77
George, Henry, 126, 130, 242
Gilder, Helena (de Kay), xvi, 3, 168–70, 189, 210; artistic endeavors of, 169–70; 277n127; correspondence of, 8, 169; courtship and marriage, 170; Homer, Winslow and, 170, 277n128; James, Henry Sr. family and, 165; women's rights and, 268n10
Gilder, Jeannette Leonard, 193, 194–95
Gilder, Richard, 170, 188–89, 194–95, 277n127
Goldsmith, Alban, 30, 37–38, 253n55
Gratacap, Louis Pope, 9, 92–95, 210, 285n118
Greeley, Horace, 114, 119, 120, 161, 197, 255n95
Grymes, Madam Suzette, 104, 288n27

Hamilton Park, 27
Hamlet, James, 82–83
Hare, Emily, pseud. *See* Johnson, Laura (Winthrop)
Haywood, xvi, 186
Henderson Real Estate, 179–80, 243
Henderson, Jane (Rapallo), 179, 278n6
Henderson, John C., 130, 178–80, 211, 215
homeopathy: Child, Lydia Maria and, 47; Curtis, Anna (Shaw) and, 47; Elliott, Samuel Mackenzie, 39; Gays and, 47
horse cars, 217, 224
householding. *See under* Ranlett, William; householding, philosophy of
Howland, Gardiner Greene, 148, 150, 152

Hunter, Adele, 149, 150, 152, 153
hysterical blindness, 40, 44–45

Inchegeelagh, 180
Industrial School for Girls, West New Brighton, 124

Jeffersonian democracy, 52, 214
Jerome, Leonard, 197–98
Johnson, Bessie (daughter of LJ and WTJ), 67, 209, 210, 285n119; literary endeavors of, 169, 187
Johnson, Laura (Winthrop) (LWJ), 209, 211, 217, 285n118; Boston people, usage of term, 68; charity work of, 124–25; correspondence of, 8, 102, 108–109, 115–16, 120, 163; cultural activities of, 186–87; domestic life, 96, 166, 168, 171–72, 217; *Eight Hundred Miles in an Ambulance*, 187, 281n45; Emerson, Ralph Waldo and, 69; Fields, Annie (Adams) and, 68; gardening and, 53, 236; Gilder, Helena (de Kay) and, 170; Leonowens, Anna and, 128, 129–30, 131; *Little Blossom's Reward: A Christmas Book for Children*, 95–96; New York society and, 137; *Poems of Twenty Years*, 186–87; Winthrop, Theodore, literary reputation of, and, 109, 110–11, 186, 264n77
Johnson, Laura W. (daughter of LJ and WTJ), 67
Johnson, Oliver (son of LJ and WTJ), 67, 168, 209
Johnson, William Templeton (WTJ), 67, 90, 98, 264n82; illnesses, 102, 171–72, 259n50

Kaywood, xii, 166–68, 170, 185, 188

law enforcement, 220–21
Law, George, 83–84, 92, 225, 226, 262n32
Leonard, William, 11, 81, 261n16
Leonowens, Anna 128–31, 169, 170, 268n19
Leonowens, Avis. *See* Fyshe, Avis (Leonowens)
Lincoln, Abraham, 73, 103, 104, 105–106, 108, 120
Linden Lawn, 178, 243
Little Blossom's Reward: A Christmas Book for Children (Johnson), 95–96
Livingston (Staten Island), 1, 50, 175–76
Livingston, Anson Livingston, xxv, 139–40, 145
Livingston, Ann (Greenleaf), 140, 176, 278n2
Longfellow, Fanny, 42–43, 44
Longfellow, Henry Wadsworth, 42–43, 75, 76, 86, 187
Lowell, Carlotta (daughter of JSL and CRL), 118, 132, 211
Lowell, Charles Russell (CRL), 117–18, 243
Lowell, James Russell (uncle of CRL), 7, 40–41, 65, 77, 254n73
Lowell, Josephine (Shaw) (JSL), 117–18, 125, 211, 235, 242–43, 267n5

Martinsdale, 143–44
May, Edith Sybil, 149–50, 152
McKeon Street (Staten Island), 85, 114–15
Minturn, Robert Bowne, 116
Minturn, Robert Bowne, Jr., 116–17, 131, 132, 149, 152
Minturn, Susie, 114, 116–17, 131, 132, 278n9
Mohawk, 146–48; *Mohawk*, sinking of, 150–52

Montant, Louis Brugière, 148, 150, 153
Morgan, Lt. Col. Anthony Hickman, 211, 286n122
Morgan, Jane, 195–96, 205–208, 211, 286n121
Morgan, Maria "Midy," 175, 191–208; animal rights advocacy, 199–200; Cushman, Charlotte and, 196–97; employment by railroad, 201–202; employment by Stevens Hotel, 198; family of origin, 195; horsemanship, 197, 198; residence of, Elliottville, 201, 202–207; residence of, New Jersey, 201–202; Victor Emmanuel II (king of Spain) and, 197

names used for, 1, 49–50, 290n55; Bard Avenue, 1, 49–50, 138, 201; "Fifth Avenue of Staten Island," 138, 155, 175, 195, 201, 269n4; "intellectual part of Staten Island," 2; Livingston, Staten Island, 1, 50, 175–76
National Anti-Slavery Standard, 7, 13, 18, 79; Gay, Sydney Howard and, 10, 20, 81, 91, 261n16
National Civil Service Reform League, xxv, 128
National Freedmen's Relief Association of New York, 123, 124
New Brighton Association, 26
New Brighton (Staten Island), 22–26, 176, 181, 221, 225
New Brighton Village Improvement Association, 235–36
New-York Tribune, 74, 75, 87, 91, 99, 131. *See also under* Gay, Sydney Howard; *New-York Tribune* and
New York Yacht Club (NYYC), 137, 138–39, 140, 146. *See also under* Garner, William; NYYC clubhouse

Norton, Charles Eliot, 18, 42, 69, 89; Curtis, George and, 7, 47, 74, 75, 128, 258n30

Oakey, Maria. *See* Dewing, Maria (Oakey) (1845–1927)
Olmsted, Frederick Law, 52, 63, 84, 116, 241; *Putnam's Monthly Magazine* and, 78, 88–89
Osgood, Franklin, 138, 145, 152, 180

Parkman, Francis, 18, 43–44
Pattison, Granville Sharp, 30, 39, 253n59
Pavilion Hotel, 26, 29, 178, 230
Pelton, Daniel, 32
Pendleton Place, 27, 286n3
Pfaff's, 101, 188
physical setting of, 29, 95–96, 176, 213, 216, 225
Pine, Charles M. (father), 33
Pine, Charles T. (son), 33
pollution and, 222, 241
Potiphar Papers, The (Curtis), 76
Prescott, William Hickling, 41–42, 254n77
property boundaries and, 219, 287n11
Pugh, Sarah, 6, 59, 80, 161
Putnam, George Palmer, 63, 77–78

Quarantine facility, 30, 86–87
Quincy, Edmund, 8, 22, 34, 56, 58

Ranlett, William, 51–53, 56, 218, 256n2, 286n4; architecture, philosophy of, 30, 32, 59; householding, philosophy of, 53, 63, 215; landscape design, philosophy of, 53, 202; living cottagely, concept of, 53, 214–15
residents, shared characteristics of, 68, 138, 232

Richmond County Society for the Prevention of Cruelty to Children, 125, 181
Richmond County Visiting Committee, 125
Richmond Dramatic Club, 67, 93
Richmond Terrace (Staten Island), 29, 213, 235, 290n6
rights of way, 210
Rokeby, Ralph Thomas, 182–84
Rowland, Oliver, 150, 152–53
rowdyism, 220–21

S. R. Smith Infirmary, 124, 181, 238–39
Sailors' Snug Harbor, 24–25, 29, 30, 33, 152
Sandy Ground, 10, 85
Schuyler, Louisa, 89, 107, 118, 125
Seventh Regiment, New York National Guard, 106–108, 110, 111, 265n99
Seventy-Ninth New York Militia, 48–49, 106, 188
Shaw, Anna (daughter of SS and FS). *See* Curtis, Anna (Shaw)
Shaw, Ellen (daughter of SS and FS, 132
Shaw, Frank (FS), 10, 14–19, 115, 163, 172; abolitionism and, 14, 16–17, 126; Brook Farm and, 15–16, 19; civic engagement, 86; Fourierism and, 15, 19, 59, 126, 130; freedmen and, 120, 123–24; political engagement, 86; publications of, 16; residence of, Bard Avenue, 58–59, 180, 210; residence of, Richmond Terrace, 132–33, 217, 228, 245; retirement from business, 15; social reform and, 14–15, 125–26, 170–71; transcendentalism and, 14; Unitarianism and, 14, 58, 132
Shaw, Josephine (daughter of SS and FS). *See* Lowell, Josephine (Shaw)

Shaw, Quincy Adams, 74, 260n4
Shaw, Robert Gould (son of SS and FS), 59, 99; Civil War and, 106–107, 109, 111–13, 115–16, 131
Shaw, Sarah (SS), 14, 84, 115–16, 242–43; abolitionism and, 14, 16; charity work of, 124–25 correspondence of, 7, 9, 59, 169; illnesses, 17–19, 76, 77; transcendentalism and, 14; women's rights and, 127, 268n10
Shaw, Susie (daughter of SS and FS). *See* Minturn, Susie (Shaw)
Smith Infirmary, 124, 181, 238–39
social life in, 2–3, 68, 89–91, 251n35, 281n50
Southerners on Staten Island, 26, 71, 103–104
Soutter, William Knox, 152, 155, 157–59
Spiritualism, 47, 115–16, 221
St. Austin's Military School, 184
St. George (Staten Island), 224, 228, 235, 239; naming of, 226; transportation, centralized in, 176, 214, 238, 241
Stadacona, 180
Staples, Elizabeth Douglass (Young), 67, 90, 169
Staples, John Bethune, 66–67, 93, 211
Staten Island Athletic Club, 181, 183, 209, 241, 242
Staten Island Baseball and Cricket Club, 183, 209
Staten Island Committee for the Prevention of Cruelty to Children, 125, 181
Staten Island Railroad Co., 227
Staten Island Rapid Transit Co. (SIRT), 227, 228, 230, 238, 241
Staten Island residents: abolitionism, attitudes toward, 71, 79–80, 81, 115; Blacks, 85; Blacks, White attitudes towards, 79–80, 115; Civil War, attitudes toward, 104–105, 113–14, 115; Republicans, attitudes toward, 80, 86–87; South, attitudes toward, 103–104; Southerners as, 26, 71, 103–104
suburban character, 52, 63–64, 175–76; Gilder, Helena (de Kay) and, 168; Wiman, Erastus and, 225
suburbia, 3–4, 22–24, 25–27; abolitionists and, 62–63; Curtis, George, on death of, 236; Downing, Andrew Jackson on, 52; Olmsted, Frederick Law on, 52; Ranlett, William on, 52
Sullivan, Peter, 152, 153
Sumner, Charles, 45, 75, 84

telephone service, 221
tennis, 181, 184, 209, 210, 242
Tenth Street Studio Building, 100, 170
therapeutic community, as, 18, 30, 32, 33
Thoreau, Henry David, 13, 74, 119
Thorn, Frost, 142
Thorn, Frost (younger), 142, 148, 153–55
Thorn, Lily Antoinette (Davenport), 148
Thorn, Mary Marcellite, 142, 152, 153–55
Tompkins, Daniel, 24
Tracy, Charles, 99
transcendentalism, 3, 62, 64, 66, 69, 74, 135; Brook Farm and, 15–16; Cranch, Christopher Pearse and, 209; Curtis, George and, 73; Morgans and, 208; Shaws and, 14; Ward, Samuel Gray and, 259n43; Winthrop, Theodore and, 98
Tuckerman, Lucius, 33
Tyler, Julia, 104

Underground Railroad, 9–10, 20, 80–82

Union Club, 76, 117, 137, 148–49, 153, 155, 157, 158
Union League Club, 116–17, 149
Union Safety Committee, 71, 80, 82–83, 84, 105
Unitarian Universalist Church of the Redeemer, xxii, 88, 89, 117, 178
Unitarians, 14, 51, 58, 66, 68, 89–90, 99, 132, 178, 209
University Building, 188, 191
urban life, alienation from, 3, 22, 27, 54, 58, 98, 216
US Marine Hospital, 29–30, 86–87, 107

Van Zandt, Leopold, 159–60
Van Zandt, Marie (Barker), 159
Van Zandt, William, 159–60
Vanderbilt, Cornelius (CV), 83, 84, 225, 227, 262n32, 271n25
Vanderbilt, William Henry (son of CV), 137, 198, 225, 227, 288n34
Vanderbilt, William Kissam (grandson of CV), 180, 198
Vault at Pfaff's, 101, 109, 188

Ward, George C., xxii, 65–66, 69, 91, 120, 149, 162, 211; abolitionism and, 66, 258n42; Civil War and, 114
Ward, Samuel Gray, 66, 68–69, 232–35; transcendentalism and, 259n43
waste management, 218–19
water services, 218–19
West New Brighton (Staten Island), 138, 176, 218, 290n55
Weston, Richard Warren, 21, 91
Weston, Sarah Maria (Grant), 21
Wigglesworth, Edward, 58
Wigglesworth, Louise, 34
Willcox, Mary Otis (Gay), xxvi, 9, 10, 51, 80, 130, 242; social activism of, 124, 125, 127

Willcox, William Goodenow, xxvi, 124, 242
Willowbrook, 182
Wiman, Erastus, 176, 213, 223–30, 234–39
Winthrop family, 67, 75–76, 102
Winthrop, Elizabeth, xxvi, 75–76, 90–91, 92–93, 187
Winthrop, Elizabeth (Woolsey), 96
Winthrop, Theodore, 96–101, 259n50, 264n77; abolitionism and, 99–100, 102, 110; *Cecil Dreeme*, 100–101; 109–10, 191; Civil War and, 106–109, 113; cultural estimation of, 109–11, 121, 186; death of, 108; Pfaff's and, 101; St. Louis and, 100; Staten Island and, 98; transcendentalism and, 98; travels of, 98–99; urban life, attitudes toward, 98
Winthrop, William, 96, 102–103, 106, 265n99
women, 2–3, 170–74, 241–42; charity work of, 124–25, 238; Civil War and, 107; domestic life of, 53, 93; social activities of, 67, 90
women's rights, xvii, 2, 14, 131; Curtis, Anna (Shaw) and, 126–27, 170–71; Curtis, Elizabeth and, 127, 242; Curtis, George and, 126–27, 170–71; Gay, Elizabeth and, 20, 170; Gay, Sarah and, 242; Gilder, Helena (de Kay) and, 268n10; Shaw, Frank and, 16; Shaw, Sarah and, 127, 268n10
women's suffrage. *See* women's rights
Wood, John B., 46–47
Woolsey, Theodore Dwight, 97
Youmans, Edward Livingston, 45–46
young adults, 91–92, 168, 174, 209–10
Young America movement, 83–84

About the Author

James A. Kaser is a professor and archivist at the College of Staten Island/ City University of New York. Previous works include three book-length annotated bibliographies on works of fiction set in Chicago, New Orleans, and Washington, DC, and a book dealing with the contested memories of the Twenty-First Ohio Volunteer Infantry, entitled *At the Bivouac of Memory: History, Politics, and the Battle of Chickamauga*.

www.ingramcontent.com/pod-product-compliance
Lightning Source LLC
Chambersburg PA
CBHW020121240426
43673CB00038B/551